THE PARNELL SPLIT
1890-91

Frontispiece 'Deposed' (*The Graphic,* 13 Dec. 1890)

THE PARNELL
SPLIT
1890-91

FRANK CALLANAN

CORK UNIVERSITY PRESS

First Published in 1992 by
Cork University Press
University College
Cork
Ireland

Copyright © Frank Callanan 1992

British Library Cataloguing in Publication Data

A CIP catalogue record for this book is available from
the British Library.

ISBN 0 902561 63 4 Hardback
0 902561 64 2 Paperback

Typeset by Tower Books of Ballincollig, Co. Cork
Printed in Ireland by Colour Books of Baldoyle, Dublin

For Fionnbar and Margaret

CONTENTS

List of illustrations   *page* ix
Foreword by Conor Cruise O'Brien   xi
Preface   xv
Acknowledgements   xviii
Abbreviations   xx

INTRODUCTION   1

I   THE SPLIT   7

    1   Divorce   9
    2   Committee Room 15   37
    3   The Split in Ireland   60
    4   Boulogne   80
    5   Healy Ascendant   110
    6   The Final Phase   139
    7   The Death of Parnell   160
    8   'A Proved British Prostitute'   187

II   PARNELL'S LAST CAMPAIGN   193

    9   Parnell's Defence   195
   10 Independence   201
       Independent Opposition   204
       Gladstone and the Liberal Party   218
       The Anti-Parnellites   227
       The 'Appeal to the Hillsides': Parnell and the
         Fenians   238
       Clerical Dictation: Parnell and the Catholic
         Church   260
   11 The Political Economy of Parnellism   276

APPENDIX: A Note on the Correspondence of
           T.M. Healy and the Composition of
           Letters and Leaders of My Day   308

Bibliography   311
Index   319

ILLLUSTRATIONS

Frontispiece: 'Deposed' (*The Graphic*, 13 Dec. 1890). The menacing, faintly demoniacal Parnell of Committee Room 15, as imagined by Sydney P. Hall, reflects contemporary perceptions of the Irish leader.

Figure 1:
page 8

Parnell's re-election as chairman of the Irish party on 25 November 1890 (*Illustrated London News,* 6 Dec. 1890). In Walter Wilson's vivid reconstruction, Parnell is seated, with arms folded. The party whip, Richard Power, standing on his right, declares him elected on the proposal of Thomas Sexton, who stands beyond Power. Justin McCarthy is immediately to Power's left. Henry Campbell sits with outstretched arm on Parnell's left.

Figure 2:
page 40

The Split (*St. Stephen's Review*, 13 Dec. 1890). The reconvened meeting of the Irish party dissolves into a faction fight conducted beneath busts of Pigott and Gladstone, an uproarious rehearsal of the proceedings of an Irish parliament. On the back left, Healy quails before the blows of Edward Harrington. On the extreme right, Parnell (with crown) catches an adversary by the throat. Phil May's fluid line brings caricature to the brink of animation.

Figure 3:
page 134

'A Startling Contrast' (*Weekly National Press*, 18 July 1891). The recently married, and enriched, Parnell of Healy's rhetoric cocks a snook at the evicted tenants of the Plan of Campaign.

Figure 4:
page 163

'The Wrecker Wrecked' (*Weekly National Press*, 8 Aug. 1891). Parnell contemplates the watery abyss, while Dillon and O'Brien sail sternly on, navigating towards the 'sunburst' of an Irish Parliament: representatively provocative Healyite cartoon.

Figure 5:   'Under which King, the Desperado or the Driveller?' (*St.*
page 194   *Stephen's Review*, 31 Jan. 1891). Anti-home rule caricature:
a maniacal Parnell towers above the hapless anti-Parnellite
leader, Justin McCarthy, in the House of Commons.

Figure 6:   'Scuttled!' (*St. Stephen's Review*, 21 Mar. 1891). Revisiting
page 217   the glimpses of the moon: Parnell hacks the bottom of the
Liberal boat.

Figure 7:   'The National Disgrace' (*Weekly Freeman's Journal*, 23 May
page 232   1891). Parnellite cartoon of the brothers Healy in suggestive
pose.

FOREWORD

The Parnell Split, 1890-91 is a major contribution to Irish historical studies. That split is the most traumatic episode in that span of modern Irish history that lies between the Great Famine and the Easter Rising of 1916. Mr Callanan's book is the most far-reaching and thoroughgoing investigation of the split that has ever been undertaken. It covers the political events in detail and with great lucidity and it also sensitively explores the social and psychological implications of these events and of the strong emotions which they aroused.

This book is solidly based on years of research, and brings massive amounts of important new material to light. A notable example is the account in Chapter 2 of a meeting between Edward Byrne (representing Parnell) and Archbishop Walsh on 16 December, 1890. This account is based on a memorandum which was extracted from the main body of the Walsh papers and was not formerly available to historians. It embodies Walsh's suggested basis for a resolution of the split. As Mr Callanan comments 'Walsh's initiative revealed an extraordinary degree of goodwill towards Parnell'. Mr Callanan has also made extensive and effective use of the newspaper material — particularly important for this period of intense political agitation, both local and national — as well as of contemporary articles, works and memoirs, and the general secondary sources.

In firm control of his sources, Mr Callanan uses them with fine discrimination and the full panoply of the historian's skills. He has a dramatic story to tell, and he tells it vividly and powerfully. He has a number of riddles to enquire into and he applies to them a formidable range of analytic skills. Above all, he possesses a quality which most historians lack, and many disdain what Giambattista Vico called *fantasia*, meaning imaginative insight. Of *fantasia*, Sir Isaiah Berlin writes:

> We call great historians only those who not only are in full control of the factual evidence obtained by the use of the best critical methods available to them, but also possess the depth of imaginative insight that characterises gifted novelists.[1]

xi

In this book, Mr Callanan meets these criteria. It would not be helpful to hail a young historian as 'great' on the strength of his first book, but he already possesses the two basic qualities for becoming one, by the Berlin criteria.

In *The Parnell Split*, there are just two protagonist–antagonists: Charles Stewart Parnell and Timothy Michael Healy. In some of the retrospects, Healy is made to appear a somewhat marginal figure, shocking respectable anti-Parnellites with his scurrilous excesses. Mr Callanan shows that Healy was in reality the general in charge of the campaign against Parnell, and that his scurrilous excesses were calculated, and central to its success. Respectable anti-Parnellites, like John Dillon and William O'Brien moaned privately against Healy's brutality, but in practice they left him to get on with it. Never can brutality and brilliance have been so combined as in Healy's copious and incandescent diatribes against Parnell in 1891. This book, quoting many of Healy's articles, gives a far better idea of the nature of his campaign than has been available before.

The towering figure, even in the split period, is not the victorious Healy, but always Parnell himself, now doomed. Mr Callanan challenges a prevailing orthodoxy among historians in relation to the split period. It is an orthodoxy to which I have myself subscribed. In his introductory section Mr Callanan quotes an interpretation of mine of the Parnell of the split (in the Epilogue to *Parnell and his Party*, 1957) and comments: 'The suggestion that Parnell succumbed to a kind of mythic self-infatuation underestimates both the trenchancy of Parnell's campaign in the split and the rationality of the Parnell myth'. Mr Callanan addresses similar criticisms to somewhat similar observations by the late F.S.L. Lyons. In both cases I believe, that by his copious quotations from Parnell speeches, and his placing of these in context, and by showing an unexpected degree of continuity with past statements, Mr Callanan does show that Parnell's position during the split, though marred by 'a measure of reckless cynicism' and by 'intermittent vehemence', had a lot more sense to it than had been hitherto supposed. For example he shows that Parnell's dealings with Fenians in 1891 — which have been much criticized — were of the same type as he had made use of much earlier, in 1879-82. In both cases he tried to have the Fenians on his side without in either case, making substantial political concessions to them.

Basic to Mr Callanan's interpretation of the Parnell of the split are the related concepts of 'professionalism' and 'independence'. Parnell felt that he had the political skills and strength of personality to negotiate with the Liberal and Tory leaders, while being himself accepted as the leader of an independent party in Parliament. He also felt that none of his Irish challengers — McCarthy, Dillon, O'Brien, Healy — possessed that combination of characteristics and capacity. Parnell was absolutely right on both points. No English politician had any doubt about that, and the only Irish politician who had was Healy.

Mr Callanan, I believe rightly, sees much of Parnell's rage during the split as coming from 'affronted professionalism'. He was furious with those who were trying to take away from him a job which he could do and they could not. And this was not just, or mainly, *amour propre*. He saw that the incompetence of his rivals and successors-to-be would make them incapable of defending the core of his policy: the independence of the Parliamentary Party. Even before the first of those terrible by-elections in 1891, the Parliamentary Party had demonstrated its capacity to defend its own independence, without Parnell. The chronology of the early part of the split is conclusive on that point:

15-17 November 1890:	Divorce Court verdict against Mrs O'Shea and Parnell.
25 November:	Sessional meeting of Irish Party; Parnell re-elected Chairman.
26 November:	Gladstone's letter published. Special meeting of Irish Party asks Parnell to reconsider his position. The split begins.

When Parnell accused his Party of abandoning him 'at the bidding of an Englishman', that at least was one charge that he could document.

Some differences of interpretation and emphasis are inevitable. It seems to me that, in some passages, Mr Callanan, in his admiration for what he calls Parnell's 'subtle statecraft', may lose sight, momentarily, of the terrible constraints continuously imposed, on any efforts at statecraft, by the divorce court factors relentlessly exploited by Healy (in forms recorded as never before by Mr Callanan) from the beginning of the split up to, and a little beyond, Parnell's death.

This, however, is not a place to linger on differences of interpretation (which are in any case few). What I want to do, essentially, in this foreword, is to recommend, to all who are interested in Irish history, a work which is both a major pioneering work of scholarship and compelling reading by reason of its dramatic and narrative power.

Cork University Press is to be commended for publishing *The Parnell Split, 1890-91*.

Conor Cruise O'Brien
September 1992

References

1 'Giambattista Vico and Cultural History' in *The Cooked Timber of Humanity: chapters in the history of Ideas*, ed. Henry Hardy (London and New York, 1990). The Vico essay was first published in the United States in 1983.

PREFACE

As if we had ever forgotten. As if he was not always there, haunting
the pages of *A Portrait*, in the hearts of the Irish people, in odd ballads
still sung at country fairs, in the imagination of young dramatists seated
at battered typewriters in shabby attic rooms — a haughty aristocratic
presence at the mere breath of whose name it was still, fifty years on,
as if somebody had exploded a battery of depth-charges deep down
amid the black sea caves and sunken wreckage of the Irish mind.

Denis Ireland [1]

The Parnell split of 1890-91 has proved as rich in divergencies of historical
interpretation as in contemporary differences of opinion. I have tried to
maintain a dialogue between contemporary sources, conflicting historical
interpretations, and the texts and images of the Parnell of 1890-91. The
elucidation of the split itself, of Parnell's political purpose, and of the
abiding resonance of his name in Irish politics and literature, requires a
consideration of the complex dialectic of the Parnell myth. I have sought
to convey something of the play of rhetoric and reason, of sentiment and
ideology, in the conflicting posthumous myths and remembrances of the
Irish leader.

F.S.L. Lyons wrote in 1980 of 'the almost impossible task of writing
an important new book about Parnellite Ireland'.[2] The part of Parnell's
career which remains least scoured, and richest in interpretative sug-
gestiveness, is its last phase, rather than its historiographically more
fashionable beginning and middle. I have endeavoured to re-argue the
Parnellism of the split, and to sketch the lineaments of populistic anti-
Parnellism (more visceral, and politically formative, than the comparatively
civil anti-Parnellism of the Committee Room).

Inevitably, Parnell has been perceived in nationalist tradition through
the constricting vista of the years 1891-1922. His image has been alternately
overcast by the failure of the home rule project under his successors, and
starkly illumined by the inauguration in flames of the Irish state. In the
hundred years which have elapsed since the death of Parnell, the six decades

of independent statehood now counterweigh the four of the prelude to independence. The experience of independence, as much as the struggle to
achieve it, informs the contemporary retrospect. There is now perhaps a
deepened intimation of the dilemmas of statehood, with which Parnell's
political thinking was instinct: of the conflict of state and nation, of the
dangers of morbid Catholic nationalist excess, of the difficulties of achieving a secular framework of state, of Irish economic deficiencies. The unfolding history of the Irish state has cast into high relief the subtlety and
the audacity of Parnell's political endeavour, and the fragility of what was,
in its least understood aspect, a liberal craft of state.

I have not here treated of the political career of T.M. Healy prior to
the split, his early relations with Parnell, and his political formation as
a conservative nationalist. The antagonism between Parnell and Healy has,
then and since, been interpreted in terms of biographical predestination,
with the split as an ineluctable revenger's tragedy. T. P. O'Connor wrote
representatively that there could not have been two personalities 'more
destined by their inner psychology' for their collision in the split.[3] Yet
their conflict in the split was not reducible to mutual antagonism, and had
deep political roots. Parnell and Healy propounded conflicting conceptions
of the Irish 'nation', and to them rallied adherents of those opposed
nations.

I have tried to avoid duplicating existing published material on Parnell.
While this is not a biography, I have wherever possible added to the corpus of available information concerning Parnell.

Rhetoric is the living tissue of nationalist history, and the split was a
rhetorical engagement of exceptional importance. R. D. Edwards, review-
ing F. S. L. Lyons's *Fall of Parnell* argued that there was 'too little of the
voice of the chief'.[4] In relation to the speeches of both Parnell and Healy,
I have frequently chosen to quote passages *in extenso*, rather than to
paraphrase them. In extended quotations, I have retained the interpella-
tions of 'cheers', 'groans', and 'laughter' in the reports, in the hope of conveying something of the crowd response. It might be added that it was
frequently asserted by Healy and the *National Press* that references to 'great
cheering' and suchlike through the reports of Parnell's speeches in the
Freeman's Journal reflected the zeal of Parnellite sub-editors rather than
the enthusiasm or number of the crowd. In the references, I have inserted
the place of delivery of the speeches quoted; unless otherwise stated, the
date of delivery is the day preceding the date of the newspaper.

I have used the term 'the split' to designate the period from the first
day of the divorce proceedings, 15 November 1890, to the death of Parnell
on 6 October 1891. It designates, in this slightly anomalous but compelling usage, the final phase of Parnell's career. The term has been more commonly used to designate the actual schism of the Irish party on 6 December
1890, or in a rarer sense to refer to the decade which spanned the

break-up of the party and its reunification under the leadership of John
Redmond on 30 January 1890.

References

1 Denis Ireland, 'October Afternoon at Glasnevin', *Threshold*, 3.5 (Winter
   1959-60).
2 *Times Literary Supplement*, 15 Feb. 1890.
3 T. P. O'Connor, *Memoirs*, i, p. 107.
4 R. D. Edwards, 'The Fall of Parnell: 1890-1: Seventy Years After', *Studia Hiber-nica*, vol. 1 (1961), p. 210.

ACKNOWLEDGEMENTS

This book originated as a doctoral thesis for University College Dublin, and I must first acknowledge the unfailing encouragement and instruction of my supervisor, Professor Donal McCartney.

I cannot adequately convey my gratitude to Dr Conor Cruise O'Brien, who is both Parnell's most exacting scholarly critic and the embodiment of a Parnellite tradition in Irish politics and letters. His and Máire's hospitality, and the vivacity of their learning, have much alleviated the solitariness of writing history. Their friendship has meant much to me.

Dr Margaret O'Callaghan, the finest young historian of modern Ireland and herself a distinguished authority on Parnell, has been an unflagging critic. Her encouragement and intellectual generosity has sustained me throughout. She has read and commented on several drafts, and her suggestions and criticisms have leavened this text.

Patrick Healy, has provided constant stimulus, erudition and wit. He has read and criticised this work, and over more than a decade we have discussed its subject. He has kept me apprised of scholarship beyond the historian's domain. I thank him for the inspiration of his friendship.

Kyran FitzGerald and Eugene Gleeson have stoically borne, and responded to my interest in Parnell with sympathetic intelligence, tempered by a benign mordancy, for which I am grateful. My friend of many years, Maurice Biggar, has been a shrewd commentator, as well as a good Parnellite round whom I have frequently gathered. Laurence Browne, Gerry Harrison, Diarmuid McGuinness, and Peter Flood have provided much encouragement. The republican civilities of Patrick McCarthy have gone some way to mitigate the asperity of my own political formation. Patrick McEntee SC skilfully goaded me towards completion. Vaughan Kinghan tempered the vulgarity of my prose.

Professor Patrick Lynch urged me on from an early stage. David Sheehy gave valuable assistance. I would like to thank Robert Kee for the benefit and pleasure of discussing Parnell with him. I am grateful to Eileen Battersby and Michael Holroyd. I thank the Parnell Society for the opportunity to canvass some of the arguments of this book.

Eileen Francis word-processed the drafts with exactitude and endurance. Anna Farmar patiently reviewed the text.

My parents, brothers, and sisters responded with forbearance and charity to what must have seemed an ominously open-ended absorption in my subject.

The late James Dillon very helpfully told me what he knew of Parnell and Healy from his father, and his own related recollections. I should also record my thanks to the late Sean MacBride SC, who alerted me in the Law Library to his suspicions of T.M. Healy.

For permission to make use of and to quote from various collections of papers I am grateful to the following: the Director and Trustees of the National Library, Dublin; the Director of the National Archive, Dublin; University College Dublin; the Board of Trinity College Dublin; the Historical Library of the Religious Society of Friends in Ireland; His Grace the Archbishop of Dublin; the British Library; the Record Office of the House of Lords, and the trustees of the Beaverbrook Foundation; Dr T.M. Healy; Mrs Nuala Jordan; Sir William Gladstone, and Sir John Moberley.

Frank Callanan
Dublin, August 1992

ABBREVIATIONS

I Writings by T. M. Healy

Healy, 'Rise and Fall'	T. M. Healy, 'The Rise and Fall of Mr. Parnell', *New Review*, vol. IV (Mar. 1891), pp. 194-203.
Healy, 'A Great Man's Fancies'	T. M. Healy, 'A Great Man's Fancies, Some Reminiscences of Charles Stewart Parnell', *Westminster Gazette*, 2-3 Nov. 1893.
Healy, *Why Ireland Is Not Free*	T. M. Healy, *Why Ireland Is Not Free. A Study of Twenty Years in Politics* (Dublin, 1898).
Letters and Leaders, Proofs	Galley Proofs for *Letters and Leaders*, Beaverbrook Papers C/167, House of Lords Records Office.
Healy, *Letters and Leaders*	*T. M. Healy, Letters and Leaders of My Day* (2 vols., London, 1928).

II Other Works and Sources

Bew, *Parnell*	Paul Bew, *C. S. Parnell* (Dublin, 1980).
Byrne, *Parnell*	Edward Byrne, *Parnell: A Memoir*, ed. Frank Callanan (Dublin, 1991).
Chamberlain, *Political Memoir*	Joseph Chamberlain, *A Political Memoir 1880-92*, ed. C. D. H. Howard (London, 1953).
Cooke and Vincent, *Governing Passion*	A. B. Cooke and John Vincent, *The Governing Passion* (Sussex, 1974).
Davitt, *Fall and Feudalism*	Michael Davitt, *The Fall of Feudalism in Ireland* (London and New York, 1904).
Foster, *Parnell*	R. F. Foster, *Charles Stewart Parnell: The Man and his Family* (2nd ed., London, 1979).
Frederic, 'The Ireland of Today'	'The Ireland of Today', by 'X', in *Fortnightly Review*, no. 323 (1 Nov. 1893), pp. 686-706).
Frederic, 'The Rhetoricians of Ireland'	'The Rhetoricians of Ireland', by 'X' in *Fortnightly Review*, no. 324 (1 Dec. 1893), pp. 713-27.
Frederic, 'The Ireland of Tomorrow'	'The Ireland of Tomorrow' in *Fortnightly Review*, no. 325 (1 Jan. 1894), pp. 1-18.
Hammond, *Gladstone*	J. L. Hammond, *Gladstone and the Irish Nation* (London, 1938).

Harrison, *Parnell, Chamberlain, Garvin*	Henry Harrison, *Parnell, Joseph Chamberlain and Mr. Garvin* (Dublin and London, 1938).
Harrison, *Parnell Vindicated*	Henry Harrison, *Parnell Vindicated: The Lifting of the Veil* (London, 1931).
Irish Party Minutes	Minutes of the Irish Parliamentary Party: (1) 7 Apr. 1880-5 May 1885, TCD MS. 9223; (2) 11 Jan. 1886-4 Dec. 1890, Dillon Papers, TCD MS. 6500; (3) 11 Dec. 1890-24 June 1895, Dillon Papers, TCD MS. 6501.
Kettle, *Material for Victory*	Andrew J. Kettle, *Material for Victory*, ed. L. J. Kettle (Dublin, 1958).
Larkin, *Fall*	Emmet Larkin, *The Roman Catholic Church in Ireland and the Fall of Parnell 1889-91* (Liverpool, 1979).
Leamy, *Parnell's Faithful Few*	Margaret Leamy, *Parnell's Faithful Few* (New York, 1936).
Lucy, *Salisbury Parliament*	H. W. Lucy, *A Diary of the Salisbury Parliament 1886-92* (London, 1892).
Lyons, *Dillon*	F. S. L. Lyons, *John Dillon: A Biography* (London, 1968).
Lyons, 'Economic Ideas of Parnell'	F. S. L. Lyons, 'The Economic Ideas of Parnell', *Historical Studies* ii, ed. Michael Roberts (London, 1959), pp. 60-78.
Lyons, *Fall*	F. S. L. Lyons, *The Fall of Parnell* (London, 1960).
Lyons, *Irish Parliamentary Party*	F. S. L. Lyons, *The Irish Parliamentary Party 1890-1910* (London, 1951).
Lyons, *Parnell*	F. S. L. Lyons, *Charles Stewart Parnell*, paperback ed. (London, 1978).
Lyons, 'Political Ideas of Parnell'	F. S. L. Lyons, 'The Political Ideas of Parnell', *Historical Journal*, xvi. 4 (1973), pp. 749-75.
McCarthy and Praed, *Book of Memories*	Justin McCarthy and Mrs. Campbell Praed, *Our Book of Memories* (London, 1912).
Book of Memories, Draft	Draft of *Our Book of Memories*, including original of many typescript letters, NLI MS. 24958.
MacDonagh, *Home Rule Movement*	Michael MacDonagh, *The Home Rule Movement* (Dublin, 1920).
Moody, *Davitt*	T. W. Moody, *Davitt and Irish Revolution 1846-82* (Oxford, 1981).
Morley, *Gladstone*	John Morley, *The Life of William Ewart Gladstone* (3 vols., London, 1903).
C. C. O'Brien, *Parnell and his Party*	Conor Cruise O'Brien, *Parnell and his Party* (Oxford, 1957).

R. B. O'Brien, *Parnell*	R. Barry O'Brien, *The Life of Charles Stewart Parnell, 1846-91* (2 vols., London, 1898).
Sophie O'Brien, 'Recollections'	Sophie O'Brien, 'Recollections of a Long Life', unpublished typescript, O'Brien Papers, NLI MS. 14,218.
W. O'Brien, *Memories*	William O'Brien, *Evening Memories* (Dublin and London, 1920).
W. O'Brien, *Olive Branch in Ireland*	William O'Brien, *An Olive Branch in Ireland and its History* (London, 1910).
W. O'Brien, *Parnell*	William O'Brien, *The Parnell of Real Life* (London, 1926).
W. O'Brien, *Recollections*	William O'Brien, *Recollections* (London, 1905).
O'Broin, *Parnell*	Leon O'Broin, *Parnell, Beathaisnéis* (repr., Dublin, 1955).
O'Connor, *Memoirs*	T. P. O'Connor, *Memoirs of an Old Parliamentarian* (2 vols., London, 1928).
O'Connor, *Parnell*	T. P. O'Connor, *Charles Stewart Parnell, A Memory* (London, 1891).
O'Connor, *Parnell Movement*	T. P. O'Connor, *The Parnell Movement* (2nd ed., London, 1886).
F. H. O'Donnell, *The Irish Party*	F. H. O'Donnell, *A History of the Irish Parliamentary Party* (London, 1910), 2 vols.
O'Hegarty, *Ireland Under the Union*	P. S. O'Hegarty, *A History of Ireland Under the Union* (London, 1952).
O'Shea, *Parnell*	Katharine O'Shea (Parnell), *Charles Stewart Parnell: His Love Story and Political Life* (2 vols., London, 1914).
J. H. Parnell, *Parnell*	John Howard Parnell, *Charles Stewart Parnell: A Memoir* (London, 1916).
Robbins, *Parnell*	Alfred Robbins, *Parnell, The Last Five Years* (London, 1926).
Special Commission Brief	Special Commission Act 1888. Brief on behalf of Mr. C. S. Parnell M.P. and other Irish M.P.s against whom charges and allegations may be made. Lewis and Lewis Solicitors (including instructions, witnesses, proofs, etc.) NLI ILB 348, p. 8.
S.C.P.	*Special Commission Act, 1888: Reprint of the Shorthand Note of the Speeches, Proceedings, and Evidence taken before the Commissioners appointed under the above named Act* (12 vols., London, 1890).
Donal Sullivan, *Room 15*	Donal Sullivan, *The Story of Room 15* (Dublin, 1891).

Maev Sullivan *No Man's Man*	Maev Sullivan, *No Man's Man* (Dublin, 1943).
Maev Sullivan, 'Tim Healy'	Maev Sullivan, 'Tim Healy', annotated typescript, Healy-Sullivan Papers, UCD MS P6/E/3.
Maev Sullivan, *No Man's Man* Sequel	Maev Sullivan, Notes and Scripts for a second part of Healy's Life (c. 1950-60) never completed. Healy-Sullivan Papers, UCD MS 65/E/5.
T. D. Sullivan, *Recollections*	T. D. Sullivan, *Recollections of Times in Irish Politics* (Dublin, 1905).
Thorold, *Labouchere*	Algar Labouchere Thorold, *The Life of Henry Labouchere* (London, 1913).
Tynan, *Memories*	Katharine Tynan, *Memories* (London, 1924).
Tynan, *Middle Years*	Katharine Tynan, *The Middle Years* (London, 1916).
Tynan, *Twenty-Five Years*	Katharine Tynan, *Twenty-Five Years: Reminiscences* (London, 1913).
Ulysses	James Joyce, *Ulysses,* ed. H. W. Gabler (London, 1986).
Under Which Flag?	*Under Which Flag? Or is Mr. Parnell to be the Leader of the Irish People?* by 'A Gutter Sparrow' (Dublin, n.d.).
Words of the Dead Chief	*Words of the Dead Chief: being extracts from the public speeches and other pronouncements of Charles Stewart Parnell, from the beginning to the close of his memorable life,* compiled by Jennie Wyse Power, with an introduction by Anna Parnell (Dublin, 1892).

III   Newspaper Abbreviations

B.D.P.	*Birmingham Daily Post*
D.E.	*Daily Express*
D.N.	*Daily News*
D.T.	*Daily Telegraph*
F.J.	*Freeman's Journal*
I.C.	*Irish Catholic*
I.D.I.	*Irish Daily Independent*
I.N.	*Irish News*
I.T.	*Irish Times*
I.W.I.	*Irish Weekly Independent*
K.M.	*Kilkenny Moderator*
L.W.	*Labour World*
M.G.	*Manchester Guardian*
N.P.	*National Press*

N.Y.T.	*New York Times*
P.M.G.	*Pall Mall Gazette*
T.L.S.	*Times Literary Supplement*
U.I.	*United Ireland*
W.F.J.	*Weekly Freeman's Journal*
W.N.P.	*Weekly National Press*

IV Other Abbreviations

BM	British Museum
DDA	Dublin Diocesan Archive
HC	House of Commons
NF	Irish National Federation
NL	Irish National League
NLI	National Library of Ireland
RIC	Royal Irish Constabulary
TCD	Trinity College Dublin
UCD	University College Dublin

INTRODUCTION

I asked one day, when I was travelling alone with him [Parnell] from
Holyhead to London, 'why public men are so vain'. It was not any
act of his which prompted me to put the query, and I cannot at the
present moment recall ... what had; but I remember distinctly his clear-
cut reply — 'Out of the necessity of the case, sir', said he, addressing
me by my name.

Edward Byrne[1]

When the strong silent man was at hand he organised their people,
and they looked like a heroic people ... The party was like a hollow
shell, but Parnell did not show the crack in it. When his organising
hand was gone the hollow shell was turned round and round, and
looked at from behind.

W.B. Yeats, 5 October 1892.[2]

In the split of 1890-91 fell Charles Stewart Parnell, the greatest Irish nationalist leader of the late nineteenth century, who had transformed the Irish
question into the pivotal issue of British politics, and brought Ireland to
the threshold of statehood under home rule. After a decade of hegemony,
Parnell found his leadership forfeit within three weeks of the granting on
17 November 1890 of a divorce decree nisi to Captain W. H. O'Shea in
proceedings in which he was named as the co-respondent. Opposed by the
leadership of the British Liberal Party, a majority of the Irish Parliamentary Party, and the Catholic Church in Ireland, he fought fiercely to
reconstitute his leadership. He lost three bitterly contested by-elections in
Ireland. On 25 June 1891, after the divorce decree which had set his fall
in train was made absolute, Parnell married Katharine O'Shea. His fragile
health was unable to withstand the rigours of his Irish campaign, and he
died at Brighton on 6 October 1891 at the age of forty-five.

1

The Parnell split tore Ireland apart. With his death, the controversy shifted key but did not abate. A bitter sense of his lost promise suffused the ensuing years of nationalist disenchantment. His memory endured through the medium of his myth, the posthumous working through of the split's thwarted dialectic. As he receded in time, physical remembrance yielded to political distortion in the evolution of the myth. Elusive in life, he remained unassimilable in death.

To modern historians, as to many contemporary observers, Parnell's campaign in the split has appeared a regrettable lapse which travestied his antecedent historical achievement. In this interpretation, the ten months of the split are treated as a biographical aberration, severed from the two phases of Parnell's career deemed classic: the phase of heroic opposition — of agrarian agitation and of parliamentary obstruction and non-alignment 1875-85, — and the high parliamentarianism of his career in mid-phase, of the Liberal-Nationalist home rule alliance. The Parnellism of the split is considered a demeaning sequel to the high politics of the Liberal alliance, a wanton, almost parodic, regression to the early obstructionist phase. Thus Conor Cruise O'Brien wrote in 1945 of 'the irrelevant catastrophe amid which his life ended'; F.S.L. Lyons characterised the split as 'the last disastrous coda to his career', and as 'the final paroxysm'.[3]

Historical understanding of Parnell's final endeavour has suffered disproportionately from the neglect of the course of the split in the country at large. His campaign of 1890-91 has never been subjected to sustained historical analysis. Cruise O'Brien's masterly *Parnell and his Party* (1957), by virtue of its terms of reference, did not extend beyond the schism in Committee Room 15. F.S.L. Lyons' *Fall of Parnell* (1960) extended the modern historiography to cover the period to the death of Parnell, but, in applying to the split the evaluative criteria and methodology of the preceding phase of parliamentary high politics, tended to disregard the course of the split in Ireland, and to discount Parnell's campaign in reducing it to an opportunistic disturbance of the equilibrium of the Liberal-Nationalist alliance.

The severing of Parnell's campaign in the split from the remainder of his career has distorted perceptions of Parnell and permitted an appropriation of the Parnell of the split by extreme nationalist ideologues, who misconstrued his purpose. The severe cropping of Parnell's politics in the split from his former career, and its linkage by implication with the eventual failure of the Irish Parliamentary Party, has facilitated an anachronistic projection of the later nationalist malaise on Parnell's politics in the split. The history of the Parnell myth after his death in its political aspect has come to resemble the theft by nationalist ideologues of the remains of a medieval saint, which modern liberal historians then fastidiously disdained to reclaim.

Analysis of the split by modern historians has tended, much like contemporary comment in the course of the split itself, to be conducted in terms of Parnell's mortal flaws rather than by reference to the frailty of the nationalist polity. The skilfully cultivated nationalist myth of Parnell's omnipotence in the preceding decade masked a deepening crisis of governance within nationalism which the split starkly exposed. Parnell's boldness and resolve concealed the fragility of his political endeavour: his seeming insouciance up to the divorce crisis in part reflected the sang-froid which the audacity of his purpose required.

Conor Cruise O'Brien has discerned in the Parnell of the split 'something of the romantic hero, dazzled by his own myth, preferring a tragic ending to self effacement and the continuation of his policy', so breaking with the rational and unromantic policy which marked the time of his power.[4] The suggestion that Parnell succumbed to a kind of mythic self-infatuation underestimates both the trenchancy of Parnell's campaign in the split and the rationality of the Parnell myth. Rather than a primitive charismatic phenomenon, that myth was a subtle contrivance of state, pitted against nationalist society as well as against the Westminster party system. The myth mediated the nexus of the Union: as Parnell brought Irish power to bear on the British government and on the party system, he in turn availed of the constraints of the Union to shape the Irish polity. In what was the astonishing and deceptively fragile *trompe l'œil* of Parnellism, his coercive power was directed back within nationalism. This provided the essential circuitry of Parnellism, its feedback mechanism. In 1890-91 the myth's simple but delicate artifice was shattered, as Parnell found himself emperilled by a disturbance of both the internal and external equilibria on which his authority relied.

Inevitably, Parnell's success in marshalling the forces of nationalism against the British party system has distracted from the immensity of the difficulties he faced in maintaining his authority in Ireland in the longer term. The balance of forces within nationalism had shifted decisively across the decade of his hegemony. By the late 1880s the land movement had acquired an increasingly conservative direction. Parnell by 1890 was, as the split so devastatingly revealed, far more vulnerable to an attack from the emergent nationalist right than from its enfeebled and directionless left. Ideologically, he had more to fear from proprietorial Catholic nationalist reaction than from revolutionary radicalism (even though the deliberate exaggeration of the latter threat continued to be integral to his political strategy).

The split's personal drama belied the depth and complexity of its engagement in Ireland. Beneath the acrid personal contest between Parnell and T. M. Healy, erstwhile master and apprentice, there was enacted a sophisticated and trenchant debate in which the themes and contradictions of nationalism were starkly elucidated. Healy was the most acute Catholic nationalist intelligence of his time. His insistent social realism set him apart from Parnell's other leading lieutentants, Dillon and O'Brien, and from Davitt. Alone of the split's main actors, Parnell and Healy fully comprehended the implications of the split. Each perfectly comprehended the other's purpose. Both accepted the inexorability and completeness of the split's conflict.

It was on the issue of land that Healy's opposition to Parnell acquired its most dangerous form in the period prior to the split. Healy had a lucid apprehension of the full implications of land purchase for nationalist politics. Firmly astride the pig's back of nationalist historical inevitability, he was the first nationalist leader to grasp that an irreversible shift in social power through the unfolding evolution of land purchase had reshaped the terrain of Irish politics. Within those altered contours the contest of the split was enacted. While Healy looked to the entrenchment of a conservative Catholic nationalist order, Parnell struggled to reshape the configuration of power within the nationalist democracy. He sought to contain precisely those tendencies which Healy sought to exploit.

Healy brilliantly strove in the split to achieve the dissolution of Parnell's former myth. In a rhetoric of astonishing comprehensiveness and demotic vigour, he assailed Parnell as a monomaniac, traitor and libertine. In Healy's revisionist discourse the attributes of the Parnell myth were thrown into reverse. Parnell's regal mystique in nationalist politics was denounced as an aristocratic confidence trick. Parnell's much-vaunted calmness (itself compromised in the split's critical opening stages) was discovered to be callousness, and his qualities of judgement to reflect an arid cynicism. Healy imputed to Parnell a dishonesty and a depravity bred of caste. He denounced the 'inborn rascality' of 'Mr. Landlord Parnell'. He attacked him as an Anglo-Irish aristocrat and a Cromwellian settler. He rendered the campaign against Parnell an extension of the nationalist struggle for the land. Against this devastating onslaught, Parnell throughout the split struggled to stabilise his decline.

At a Land League meeting in October 1881 Parnell had declared that 'in every movement of this kind it is most desirable that there should be a large section considerably in advance of the rest', and that having himself been 'during several years of my political life considerably in advance of the rest of the country', he was now pleased to find that the rest of the country was considerably in advance of him, and 'I do not in the least object to find men a long way beyond me — in fact, I like it exceedingly'.[5] This was Parnell's favoured equilibrium, that of the progressive constitutional leader reining in the radicals.

Caught awkwardly in the split, Parnell was obliged himself to define a radical agenda without compromising his claims to leadership. He was compelled to play at once the roles of agitator and leader. This doubling up frequently appeared crudely contrived, as he struggled to re-enact the politics of controlled menace which had served him so well in the earlier stages of his career, when directed against the English government and party system. The *Spectator* shrewdly observed that in 'resorting to the expedients of the ordinary agitator', Parnell was committing a serious blunder. Parnell 'does not make a good agitator ... and except when he suddenly turns a stream of invective to his enemies, he has no popular mood'. His power on the contrary resided in the belief that he could give effect to his commitments.[6]

In the split Parnell found himself compelled crudely to articulate the premises which had discreetly informed his political strategy in the period of his undisputed hegemony: as in his attack on clerical influence, his agrarian strategy, and his critique of the Plan of Campaign. On the central issue of the Liberal intervention, Parnell fiercely insisted that an issue of fundamental political strategy, as well as of principle, was involved, and frankly asserted his own indispensability. The split became a laboratory of his political technique, in necessarily coarsened form.

Yet what was most striking, and central to the retrieval of the lost integrity of Parnell's career, forfeit in the myth and historiography of Parnell in the split, was his enduring capacity to articulate radical positions without abrogating his constitutional purpose, his eschewal of commitments which could compromise him as a nationalist leader in the future.

Parnell responded to the challenge of the split with the audacity and fierce resolve which had marked his career. He treated as axiomatic the identity between his own restoration and the preconditions for effective governance within nationalism. In an endeavour to constitute a framework of effective political authority, and a viable home rule state, he challenged not merely 'Liberal dictation', but the configuration of social power in Ireland. It was a staggeringly ambitious undertaking for a politician circumstanced as was Parnell. In defeat he made tactical concessions, but refused to reduce the scale of his political enterprise. He continued to conduct himself as the Irish leader. In this lay the classicism and the hubris of Parnell's politics in the split, and the sense in which he truly was, in the fine epithet of James Joyce, 'strong to the verge of weakness'.[7]

References

1 Edward Byrne, *Parnell*, pp. 23-4.
2 *I.W.I.*, 12 Oct. 1892.
3 Donat O'Donnell (Conor Cruise O'Brien), 'Parnell's Monument', in *The Bell* (Oct. 1945), pp. 566-73; F. S. L. Lyons, 'Charles Stewart Parnell' in *The Irish Parliamentary Tradition*, ed. B. Farrell (Dublin and New York, 1973), p. 614.
4 C. C. O'Brien, *Parnell and his Party*, pp. 348-9.
5 Quoted *I.W.I.*, 7 Oct. 1893, C.H. Oldham, 'Parnell's Leadership'.

6 *Spectator*, 28 Feb. 1891. R. D. Edwards wrote that it was tempting to conclude
that Parnell's mistake was what he termed 'the Napoleonic one, of provoking,
immediately, issues which were essentially long-term ones when he attempted
to reverse the Liberal alliance in 1891' (R. D. Edwards, 'The Fall of Parnell:
1890-1, Seventy Years After', *Studia Hibernica*, vol. 1 [1961], p. 209). The proposition requires modification to the extent that Parnell, as he repeatedly insisted, sought to reverse not the Liberal alliance, but the enfeebling of the
independence of the Irish party to which it had conduced.

7 Joyce, *Ulysses*, p. 522.

I THE SPLIT

Figure 1 Parnell's re-election as chairman of the Irish party on 25 November 1890 (*Illustrated London News*, 6 Dec. 1890)

1

DIVORCE

Ireland had 'the Man' who could bring round 'the Hour'. Parnell felt
the hideous irony of fate which destroyed the first in the name of the
second.

Lionel Johnson[1]

On 17 November 1890, after two days of unchallenged evidence against
his wife and Parnell, Captain W. H. O'Shea obtained a decree nisi of
divorce. The evidence rendered Parnell ludicrous as well as dishonourable.
Two allegations in particular gained wide currency. The first, and most
damaging, was the unfounded surmise of a maidservant that Parnell to
avoid Captain O'Shea must have on several occasions fled by a fire-escape
from the house on Medina Terrace to reappear at the door asking for the
Captain. The second, true, allegation was that Parnell had made use of
several aliases, including those of 'Preston' and 'Fox'.[2]

Moralism and ridicule commingled in the Unionist response. Of the
evidence, the *Birmingham Daily Post* opined: 'There was about it no touch
of false romance which seeks to palliate, though not to excuse, a lapse from
virtue'.[3] A Tory peer, Brabourne, categorised it as 'a bad case in a bad
class of case, inasmuch as it showed an abuse of friendship, a habitual
depravity, and an elaborated system of deceit, which are happily of rare
occurrence even in such cases.'[4] Parnell's old adversary, *The Times*, hailed the vindication of Captain O'Shea's honour, and the implication of
the patrician Parnell in the squalor of illicit bourgeois venery:

Domestic treachery, systematic and long continued deception, the whole squalid
apparatus of letters written with the intent of misleading, houses taken under
false names, disguises and aliases, secret visits, and sudden flights make up
a story of dull and ignoble infidelity, untouched, so far as can be seen, by

9

a single ray of sentiment, a single flash of passion, and comparable only
to the dreary monotony of French middle-class vice, over which M. Zola's
scalpel so lovingly lingers.[5]

Perhaps more pertinently, Frederic Harrison, a Gladstonian sympathiser,
warned that 'a man who is made a public laughing-stock cannot be a leader
of men, even if he were an angel'.[6] The divorce decree, Brabourne wrote,
wrought in Westminster politics 'a change so strange, so sudden, and so
unexpected as to have almost paralysed men's faculties'.[7] The decree and
the divorce-court evidence left the Irish public stunned and incredulous.
The stock nationalist response to the initiation of the proceedings — to
dismiss them as a reprise of the Pigott forgeries — and the moratorium
on public discussion of the divorce proceedings which ensued, had left the
Irish public unprepared. The effect was to be compounded by the rapid
succession of shocks which followed.

   Parnell benefited initially from an instinctive closing of ranks in Ireland.
His mystique of invincibility at first held firm. One well-informed Dublin
commentator wrote that Parnell was 'to the imagination of Ireland an instrument of fate; a resistless glacier-like force moving on slowly and
relentlessly to its destination. He can be no more put aside than one of
the forces of nature.'[8] The *Freeman's Journal* remained staunchly, if
somewhat gauchely, Parnellite.[9] The two established papers which were to
lead the opposition to Parnell did not initially call for Parnell's resignation or removal. The *Nation* confined itself to noting 'the heinousness of
the offence'. The *Irish Catholic*, while noting that Parnell's offence affix-
ed 'a stigma of the utmost moral gravity and seriousness', conceded that
without him the existing Irish party would be an impossibility, while adding mysteriously that 'it does not follow that, if it were dissolved, another
would not take its place'. Although the maintenance of the existing party
precluded 'that free expression of an outraged public opinion which we
would like to see', the paper warned against any glorification of Parnell,
and declared that he owed an unspecified duty to make reparation to
Ireland.[10] Notwithstanding the call for Parnell's retirement made in
Davitt's *Labour World*,[11] the contemporary expectation that England
rather than Ireland would be the cockpit of the opposition to Parnell appeared to be borne out in the first critical weekend after the decree was
pronounced.

   At the time of the divorce hearing T. M. Healy lay seriously ill in Dublin
following an attack of typhoid.[12] This did not prevent him attending the
meeting at the Leinster Hall, Dublin, on 20 November, a meeting originally
convened to support the evicted tenants, but which became a public
demonstration in support of Parnell attended by a large contingent of the
Irish party. Healy not merely attended the meeting, but drafted the resolution in Parnell's favour. According to an unchallenged account of John
Redmond, some eight to ten nationalist politicians called at Healy's house

to avoid bringing him out in his illness. Healy declared that they would let the English nonconformists know that they would sooner lose a general election than accept their dictation as to the Irish leadership. William Redmond later recalled Healy saying that they would teach 'these damned nonconformists to mind their own business'.[13]

Healy's speech at the Leinster Hall was the definitive formulation of the case for Parnell. It was his last act as the master-propagandist of Parnellism, and contributed some of the stock phrases and images to Parnell's campaign in the split. He charted the transformation of the nationalist cause under Parnell and devised the image which Parnell was to make his own in asking: '... is it now in this moment within sight of the promised land that we are to be asked to throw our entire organisation back once more into the melting pot?' He concisely epitomised the logic of home rule to put succinctly the Parnellite case in the split: 'I say that the Irish party are sovereign in their own domain, and if the English people are willing to cede to us our rights and liberties upon domestic questions, I say of all questions that this is a domestic question.' Their English friends must remember 'that for Ireland and for Irishmen Mr. Parnell is less a man than an institution', who could not be ousted as a result of what he strikingly described as 'a temporary outcry over a case that in London would be forgotten tomorrow'.

Healy entered a caveat, warning that the duty the party owed Parnell was reciprocal: '... as we have to consider our position let him consider his, and as we are acting with sole thought to the interests of Ireland, so we may fairly demand that in every act and determination and resolution of his he shall act with equal singleness of purpose'. This however was not a substantial detraction from his endorsement of Parnell, but referred back to a veiled suggestion earlier in the speech that Parnell might resign and be re-elected for Cork ('were Mr. Parnell tomorrow to resign his seat for Cork he would be instantly re-elected ... and if he were elected for Cork would not his re-election to his former position by his colleagues follow as a matter of course?'). This was the course which Healy through Joseph Kenny advised Parnell to follow as a gesture of atonement.[14] Healy concluded to sustained and tumultuous cheering, enjoining his audience 'not to speak to the man at the wheel'.

It was an astonishing *tour de force*. Morley wrote to an increasingly apprehensive Gladstone that 'Healy's speech at the Dublin meeting was the best', adding, as if recollecting himself, 'I mean, best hit the sense of the audience'.[15] It was a speech which Healy would never be permitted to forget.

What then prompted Healy to endorse Parnell in such ringing tones? He later sought to justify his action on the untenable grounds that the attack on Parnell was believed at the time to emanate from hostile Tory sources. In an interview with the Liberal *Pall Mall Gazette*, after the break-up of

L. Hall *mtg*

-20/11/90

the party, Healy insisted that he adhered to everything he had said at the Leinster Hall meeting, and that it was only when it later became clear that the opposition to Parnell was not a 'Tory-cum-*Times* outcry', but came rather from sympathetic pro-Irish Liberals, that his view changed: 'The moment we saw that it was Liberal feeling — that the outcry represented not enmity, but the regrets of friendship — then our attitude altered ...'.[16] Healy went on to assert that, as a result of Parnell's treatment of him over the Galway election and of Parnell's deletion of his name from the list of counsel retained in the Special Commission, he felt 'I should examine my conscience more keenly, in order to make my determination depend solely on grounds affecting the country at large.' His Leinster Hall speech had in fact been explicitly directed to Home Rule Liberals. He had declared at the outset that he would endeavour to address himself to the head rather than the heart, and 'to keep myself as far as I can to argue this question with timid friends outside upon the cold granite of facts'.

What gave Healy's speech its force and tension was its exaggerated sensitivity to English opinion in its bearing on Ireland. It was only by pitting them against hostile English perceptions that Healy could contain and repress the inner promptings of his own animosity to Parnell. In what was the psychological crux of his speech, he furiously repudiated the charge levelled against nationalists of obsequious subservience to Parnell.

> I say in the first place with regard to servility of Irishmen and of the Irish part, a more independent people and a more independent party does not exist *(applause)*. Servile to Mr. Parnell? Who is servile to him? I am no man's man but Ireland's *(loud and prolonged cheers)*, and if I stand here tonight as I gladly do, to second this resolution I do so not for the sake of Parnell as an individual, but for the sake of Ireland as a nation *(applause)*. We are not sentimental politicians ...

As seasoned politicians, they would be 'foolish and criminal' if they 'at the first blast of opposition surrendered the great chief who has led us so far forward':

> ... and let me say this, and let me put it to our friends, which is the more decent attitude on behalf of the Irish people and of the Irish party if we who have been for ten years under the leadership of this man, and who have been accused of harbouring all kinds of sinister ambitions, of greedy desires to pull him down, if we joined with this howling pack would that be a noble spectacle before the nations *(cheers)*? Further let me put it to the meeting would it not be a most unhappy spectacle if we allowed ourselves to present the world the view of a number of men, taking advantage, rejoicing, I might also say the downfall of our leader, but furthermore if we gave our enemies the satisfaction of knowing that they could set each of us at each other's throats in the grasp and struggle of ambition to see which of us would take his place *(applause)*.

Healy then turned to attack Michael Davitt, the only prominent nationalist who had called for Parnell's resignation, to mock the social fragmentation and anarchy which would attend the 'dethronement' of Parnell.

Healy sought to define his position in terms of the tension between two conflicting hostile English characterisations of the Irish party: one of a ductile Irish party subject to Parnell's dictatorship, the other of a party riven by rivalries held only temporarily in check. The resonance of his Leinster Hall endorsement derived from this unstable tension.

T. D. Sullivan alone of Healy's kinsmen and allies was unreservedly opposed to Parnell. Donal Sullivan had endorsed Parnell on the evening of the divorce decree, declaring 'come weal, come woe, so long as he had the honour to represent Westmeath, he should fight by the side of their great leader, and should never falter in his ranks'.[17] Donal Sullivan, William Martin Murphy, and Arthur Chance — all of whom were shortly to become vehement opponents of Parnell — were present at the Leinster Hall, thereby participating in what one outraged cleric described as 'the grand chorus of Catholic gentlemen in the Catholic city of Dublin in praise of one of the vilest scoundrels ever disgorged from an English divorce court'.[18] T.D. Sullivan, in the United States on a fund-raising delegation of the Irish party, refused to join in an endorsement of Parnell to American reporters, for which he was magisterially castigated by John Dillon and William O'Brien: 'I do not remember ever having spent a more unpleasant quarter of an hour in my life.' Sullivan was obdurate, and alone of the American delegates did not sign the cable sent in support of Parnell to the Leinster Hall meeting. The unswerving Parnellite loyalist Tim Harrington wrote that Sullivan was 'bitter in the extreme and indulges in his most abusive style', describing Parnell as 'a base adulterer'. Isolated, he returned to Ireland. As Dillon wrote to O'Brien, he looked 'the picture of melancholy. It would have been cruelty to keep him here any longer'.[19]

The Leinster Hall meeting was the culmination of demonstrations of support for Parnell across the country. For Parnellite stalwarts and functionaries, the course of events since the divorce verdict could not have been more satisfactory. D. J. Hishon of the National League wrote to Harrington in the United States of the Leinster Hall meeting that 'the determination displayed in support of the Chief's leadership surprised even the most sanguine of us.' Meetings and conventions were proceeding across the country. 'The priests are acting splendidly in connection with the business. At every convention that has been held they have been well represented and a strong resolution in favour of the continuation of Mr. Parnell's leadership has been adopted unanimously', save in one instance: '... thank heaven the day of sentiment has passed and we are at last practical politicians and not sentimentalists.' In concluding that 'the unfortunate business will ... I am convinced do infinite good, as it will weed out from the home rule ranks weak-kneed creatures whose interest in it was never more than skin-deep', Hishon's comments disclosed the premature triumphalism of the Parnellite machine.[20]

The initiative thus remained with Parnell as the Irish party assembled at Westminster on the opening of the parliamentary session on 25 November to elect its chairman. The Irish leader strode through the lobby past coteries of anxious Liberals, 'looking better than is his wont, seeming perfectly at ease, and reciprocating with all his old coolness the friendly greetings accorded to him by some of his political friends'.[21]

Parnell's election as sessional chairman was moved by Thomas Sexton, and seconded by Colonel J. P. Nolan. It immediately became clear that the support for Parnell was concerted, while the opposition to him was without direction. Jeremiah Jordan, an obscure and habitually unassertive member of the party, intervened to urge that Parnell retire, even if only temporarily. This intervention was received in silence, and brushed aside as the party proceeded to re-elect Parnell. Parnell rose 'amid cheers and cheers again'. In returning thanks for his election, he alluded, as if *en passant* to the divorce proceedings, calmly assuring his astonished colleagues that 'in a short period of time, when I am free to do so, I will be able to put a complexion on this case very different to that which it now bears, and I will be able to hold my head as high, aye, and higher, than ever before, in the face of the world.' He denied he had shattered 'a sense of domestic bliss and felicity' or that O'Shea was his friend, asserting that he was on the contrary since first they met 'my enemy — my bitter relentless enemy'. He thus masterfully contrived to lift that 'corner of the curtain' which would permit the vindication of his own honour, without making any specific allegation against O'Shea which would have frustrated the making absolute of the divorce decree by prompting the intervention of the Queen's Proctor. He then requested his colleagues to keep their lips sealed 'as mine are' until the period after which he could vindicate himself had elapsed (by which he meant the efflux of the six months required before the divorce decree could be made absolute), and proceeded to the election of officers and the selection of bills which the party would promote in the course of the session. This speech, staggering in its boldness and dignity, delivered to a meeting which was as Donal Sullivan wrote 'hypnotised' under his personality, completed what his opponents were immediately afterwards to regard as Parnell's coup. It was the final, and in its way the most remarkable, essay in that placid audacity which characterised his career.[22]

To the Prime Minister that evening fell the doubtful honour of making the first divorce-court jibe. Speaking in the House of Lords, he observed: 'There is always some difficulty with Irish leaders. Their strong point just now is escaping. Some prefer to escape by water; some prefer fire escapes'.[23] Salisbury was linking the escape of Dillon and O'Brien to America with Parnell's supposed precipitate departures from Medina Terrace. It was not a very good joke (few of the divorce-court jokes were), but its significance as a foretaste of Tory election rhetoric was lost on neither

Nationalists nor Liberals. Gladstone responded glumly, when asked by E. W. Hamilton later that evening if he considered Salisbury's joke a lapse of taste: '... he was inclined to think it legitimate: it has got so that it is irresistible'.[24]

Among most of the Irish party, consternation reigned. The anti-Parnellites would later bitterly complain that Parnell's re-election was procured by the deliberate dissemination of rumours that Parnell, once elected, would retire.[25] Those accused were Parnell's secretary Henry Campbell, and the astute and *parti pris* London Correspondent of the *Freeman's Journal*, J. M. Tuohy. In Tuohy's case the allegation is hard to reconcile with the fact that he had written on 18 November that he had 'direct authority for stating that Mr. Parnell has not the remotest intention of abandoning either permanently or temporarily his position or his duties as leader of the Irish Parliamentary Party'. Similarly, on the morning of the meeting itself the *Freeman's Journal* published a column by Tuohy which dismissed reports of Parnell's intention to resign as 'absolutely unauthorised and unfounded'.[26] Yet there was almost certainly a measure of deception perpetrated by the Parnellite faction in encouraging the suggestion that Parnell intended to resign. The confusion as to Parnell's intentions alone served to disorientate the opposition to him. Alfred Robbins, of the *Birmingham Daily Post*, wrote that at the last moment before the meeting, the rumours of Parnell's resignation changed direction, to the effect that he would not now retire.[27] Whether induced by Parnellite disinformation, or persuaded by a naïve belief in Parnell's readiness to efface himself, a considerable number of the party unquestionably believed that Parnell was about to resign. A discomfited Donal Sullivan wrote to Healy that 'up to a minute before Parnell finished his address, I thought he would conclude by announcing his resignation. We all expected it'.[28] Arthur O'Connor declared that he had considered himself in the position of 'one of the Old Guard of Napoleon giving a parting salute'.[29] 'A fog appeared to envelop everything', Alfred Webb miserably recalled. 'We were being cajoled and humbugged and led to our doom with Machiavellian ingenuity.'[30]

Parnell's *coup* was at a price. If he had with ruthless adroitness seized an enormous tactical advantage in achieving his re-election in advance of Gladstone's declaration of opposition, he hastened the erosion of the trust reposed in him by those members of his party not unalterably committed to him. The belief that Parnell's election had been secured by at least passive false pretences merged with the well-founded suspicion that he had deliberately rendered himself incommunicado to the Liberal leadership to harden opposition to him. Thus William Martin Murphy, on the eve of the reconvened party meeting, assured Archbishop Walsh of Dublin that he need have no fear as to the result: 'I am all through satisfied since the issue of Mr. Gladstone's letter and the discovery of the trick played upon us on Tuesday last'.[31]

Parnell thus declined his last opportunity to retire gracefully in an un-forced gesture. In the wake of the calamity which overtook him, his deter-mination to persevere came to appear a hubristic error of judgement. Yet Parnell's course of conduct can be explained by considerations deeper than the promptings of an unyielding pride. The ferocity of Healy's rhetoric in the split, the unyielding antagonism of the Liberal party, and the in-creasingly overt and self-assertive hostility of the Catholic Church in Ireland, all beg the question as to whether his retirement could have been temporary. He had good reason to doubt whether a policy of moral ap-peasement would have silenced his critics or assured the temporary nature of his retirement. He had moreover an innate mistrust of sentimental gestures of atonement. Even had he returned to the leadership, it would have been on terms: the surrender and regrant of a diminished authority. His former power would not have been intact. It would no longer have been a hard-won, combat-hardened ascendancy, but a nominal or titular nationalist leadership. Parnell's determination, bred of the instinct of power, was to fight on.

Gladstone was by now poised to act, feeling impelled to abandon his careful reticence, and to intervene directly to undo Parnell's election. While John Morley was to be villainised in nationalist mythology for his role in the split — notably by William O'Brien — his initial response to the divorce-court evidence, in forwarding to Gladstone, who was sequestered at Hawarden, a newspaper report of the first day's proceedings, conveyed an inclination to let Parnell ride out the storm. He took care, however, to insert a somewhat formulaic expression of moral disapprobation:

> I dare say, the hateful thing will pretty quickly recede into the background, but what a perversion of character must have been worked by all that mean hiding, lying, and the rest of it. However, from a political point of view, and apart from the damage done to the cause for the moment, the great thing is that the Irish party should continue to speak with one voice — as, I am convinced, they wish it.[32]

Gladstone's response contrasted sharply. He was, from the outset, per-suaded that the divorce proceedings would eventuate in the end of Parnell's political career.[33] After the decree he awaited with mounting apprehension either Parnell's voluntary resignation or a move against him in Ireland. On the day after the decree he wrote to Morley expressing surprise at the ap-parent acquiescence of the Catholic Church in Parnell's leadership: '... but they may have tried the ground and found it would not bear. It is to the Irish Parliamentary Party, and that alone, to which we have to look ...'[34] The following day he wrote to Morley that 'the Irish have abstractedly a right to decide the question', and proceeded to reveal just how abstract that right was. 'We must be passive, must wait and watch'. He proposed himself to maintain 'an extreme reserve': 'But I again and again say to myself, I say I mean in the interior and silent forum "It'll na dee" '.[35]

On 21 November, while the annual meeting of the National Liberal Federation concluded at Sheffield, Gladstone at Hawarden further considered his response to the issue of the Irish leadership in the first of three personal memoranda. He reiterated that the leadership question was primarily a matter for the Irish, adding: 'It is no part of my duty as the leader of a Party in Parliament, to form a personal judgement on the moral conduct of any other leader or fellow member'. While personally 'with deep pain but without any doubt', adjudging Parnell's resignation necessary, he added: 'I have no right spontaneously to pronounce this opinion. But I should certainly give it if called upon from a quarter entitled to make the demand'.[36] In the second of two memoranda written the following day he wrote: '... there may be contingencies which would justify, or require my giving an opinion on Mr. Parnell's continuance in the leadership of the Irish party: but it is no part to bring about, or to take a share in bringing about, those contingencies.'[37]

These memoranda — extracted by Morley from the main corpus of Gladstone's papers but not used in his *Life of Gladstone* — reflect the conflict between Gladstone's conviction that Parnell's leadership of the Irish party was unsustainable and his shrewd determination — which it took Parnell's re-election as leader to break — not to intervene on the issue of the Irish leadership, as he looked despairingly to either Parnell's resignation or a spontaneous nationalist initiative against Parnell which never came.

Gladstone's reference to 'a quarter entitled to make the demand' and to the 'contingencies' which would justify his intervention (the shift from the former to the latter suggests an enlargement of the circumstances in which he would countenance intervening) were characteristically oracular. What he looked to was either a spontaneous split in Ireland, or alternatively a solicitation of his views from an influential body of nationalists prior to their deciding the question of the leadership (assuming that a soliciting of his views by a unanimous request of the party was out of the question). The second alternative was at once unrealistic and potentially more damaging than the mode of intervention Gladstone eventually adopted. A prior ascertainment of Gladstone's views could readily have been presented as an obsequious 'waiting upon Gladstone', and would have been harder to justify than the intervention which actually occurred. In the event, the anti-Parnellites were able to present their acquiescence to the Gladstone letter as a cruel necessity — the acquiescence in the *fait accompli* of Gladstone's declaration that the retention of Parnell nullified the prospects for a Liberal home rule administration, rather than a predetermined ascertainment of, and submission to, the views of the Liberal leader.

The hardening of Liberal opposition to Parnell increased the pressure on Gladstone to act. W. T. Stead on 20 November advised Gladstone that he had embarked on a campaign against Parnell, warning, 'I know my

Nonconformists well, and no power on earth will induce them to follow
that man to the poll or you either, if you are arm in arm in [*sic*] him'.[38]
John Morley warned Gladstone on 22 November of the intensity of Liberal
hostility to Parnell which he had encountered at Sheffield.[39] Arnold
Morley the same day wrote that Liberal opinion required at least the temporary retirement of Parnell.[40] Harcourt pointed to the overwhelming
sense of the Sheffield meeting to urge 'a clear and authoritative declaration' from Gladstone against Parnell. E. W. Hamilton the following day
found Harcourt in 'one of his anti-Gladstone tantrums'. Harcourt insisted
that something had to be done at once and a decision taken before Parliament met '... for if Parnell was in his usual place in the House and rose
to speak as Irish leader, half the English and Scotch members on the opposite side would get up and walk out of the House. And yet Mr. Gladstone
would not come up to town an hour before he chose'.[41] Gladstone had
already resolved to move. He wrote to Arnold Morley on 22 November asserting that his own opinion was constant from the start '... and I conceive
that the time for action has come. All my correspondents are in unison'.[42]

On the afternoon of 23 November the Radical Henry Labouchere called
on Justin McCarthy. He was sent by Harcourt and John Morley. He said
that they thought that Parnell should give up the leadership for a time 'and
they wanted to know whether a letter of advice from Gladstone would have
the effect if it could be got to Parnell in time'. McCarthy responded that
the Irish party would not throw Parnell over, but that if the wish to withdraw
came from Parnell himself, it would be a different matter: he was sure that
a letter from Gladstone would have more effect on Parnell 'than a million
letters from the world in general'. All he could give Labouchere was the address of the club to which Henry Campbell, Parnell's secretary, belonged.[43]

Gladstone reached London on the afternoon of 24 November, the eve of
the opening of the parliamentary session and of the Irish party meeting.
That evening, he interrupted a conference with Granville, Harcourt, John
Morley and Arnold Morley, to meet Justin McCarthy. In his eagerness to
respect Irish susceptibilities, Gladstone failed to convey his position clearly
to McCarthy, and McCarthy failed to draw the intended inference from the
oblique proposition that Parnell's retention of the leadership would entail
the loss of the next election and the postponement of home rule beyond
the span of his political career ('I cannot expect of Providence with any
confidence, I may say, with any decency, that my life will be spared eight
or nine or ten years, for the furtherance of Home Rule'). The *mésentente*
was no doubt compounded by Gladstone's tribute to Parnell's 'splendid and
altogether unrivalled services to Ireland', and by his unguarded comment
as McCarthy left: '... the thing that bewilders me is this: how on the face
of that evidence any jury could have found that O'Shea had not connived'.[44] The confusion played into Parnell's hands. Tuohy, the partisan
London correspondent of the *Freeman's Journal* reported that McCarthy

only saw the Gladstone letter an hour after it was read to Parnell, and that Gladstone's oral statement to McCarthy had fallen short of a threat of resignation: '... the gist of Mr. Gladstone's oral statement was that if Mr. Parnell retained the leadership the general election would be lost, in Mr. Gladstone's opinion'.[45]

The next day John Morley failed to locate Parnell — who was almost certainly keeping out of his way — before the meeting of the Irish party to apprise him (as he failed also to apprise McCarthy) of the text of a letter from Gladstone to Morley, which included the statement that Parnell's retention of the Irish leadership 'would render my retention of the leadership upon the prosecution of the Irish cause, almost a nullity'.[46] By the time Morley found him, Parnell was able to state 'in a casual way' that he had been re-elected chairman of the Irish party. In Gladstone's room in the Commons, Morley read the letter to an unyielding Parnell, who insisted that feeling against him was a storm in a teacup and would soon pass. In the face of Morley's warnings of an electoral rout in England, Parnell calmly reiterated his determination to hold to his course. 'He answered, in his slow dry way, that he must look to the future ... that if he gave up the leadership for a time, he should never return to it; that if he once let go, it was all over.'[47] Gladstone joined Morley minutes after the interview to be advised of Parnell's resolve. Exasperated as much by the pusillanimousness of the Irish party as by the intransigence of its leader, he decided to publish his letter to Morley immediately, through the medium of a special edition of the *Pall Mall Gazette*. Morley sought out Parnell to alert him, and as they strolled round the lobby, Parnell calmly observed: 'Yes, I think Mr. Gladstone will be quite right to do that; it will put him straight with his party'.[48]

Parnell returned to the chamber, determined to forestall nationalist panic on the publication of the Gladstone letter. Sitting beside Sexton, he advised him with studied nonchalance that Gladstone was about to issue a manifesto to secure his own position. The information spread rapidly among the Nationalist members opposed to Parnell's retention of the leadership, who congregated in coteries about Westminster, still reeling in confusion from Parnell's re-election *coup*. Parnell calmly, but emphatically, rebuffed two approaches to reconsider his position or reconvene the meeting of the party. Justin McCarthy then for the first time informed the Irish members of his interview with Gladstone. McCarthy was despatched — too late — to prevent the publication of Gladstone's letter.

Alone of the Liberal leadership, Earl Spencer openly doubted whether the Liberals 'were right in putting any screw at all upon Parnell, and he pressed earnestly that Parnell was the only man who could drive the Irish team'.[49] The exigencies of Liberal politics prevailed. E. W. Hamilton noted: '... however narrow-minded and illiberal people may be, it is impossible to disregard the Puritanical frenzy of the nonconformists who form so important a factor in the Liberal party'. A month later Hamilton, who had misgivings at the time, expressed doubts to Morley about the wisdom of the Gladstone letter, wondering whether the Parnell divorce might not have been eventually forgotten. Morley replied bluntly that had no steps been taken to depose Parnell 'the storm about their heads would have been tremendous, and the difference would have been that, instead of division in the Irish party, there would have been division in the Liberal party of Great Britain'.[50]

T. P. O'Connor later wrote that '... the rapidity with which the letter followed the meeting of the Irish party made the whole thing look like an exchange of pistol shots'. Auberon Herbert commented of Gladstone's 'dismissal' of Parnell:

> Never was there a more summary exercise of authority, a scantier exercise of ceremony. Mr. Parnell is not invited to confer with Mr. Gladstone; the difficulties are not put before him; neither he nor the Irish party are presumed to have any volition in the matter; but Mr. Parnell is simply told through a third person in a letter that it is published within — how many hours? — of the date on which it was written, that he must go ...[51]

Yet the significance of Gladstone's decision to publish his letter to Morley has been exaggerated. It is difficult to accept that 'from this vital decision, rather than from the initial action of the Irish party in re-electing Parnell, came the real impetus to disaster'.[52] It had always been intended that the letter would be communicated to the Irish party members if Parnell did not resign.[53] Once the letter had been shown to Parnell, it could not have been suppressed. Whether published by Gladstone or not, Parnell was in a position to assail every step thereafter taken against him as the consequence of the Liberal leader's fiat. If it might have been wiser to avert the brutal and peremptory impact of the immediate publication of the letter, it is difficult to credit the fact of its publication with especial significance.

The play of sentimentality in the split was to negate the effectiveness of Parnell's *realpolitik*. While it gave Parnell his single strongest argument in the split, the fact that Parnell was re-elected before the release of Gladstone's letter was not without some compensating advantage from the anti-Parnellite point of view. It permitted the anti-Parnellites in one respect to get the best of both worlds. They had first consulted their hearts and elected Parnell in a gesture of sentimental allegiance. Then, advised *ex post facto* of Gladstone's putatively authoritative assessment of the electoral consequences for Home Rule in Britain, confronted by a cruel and ineluctable dilemma, they yielded to their political heads and regretfully deposed a great leader. This provided a potent theme in Healy's rhetoric; likewise William O'Brien in September asserted that the speakers at the Leinster Hall meeting had obeyed the generous instincts of their Irish hearts ... I know of nothing that shows better how completely Mr. Parnell has lost his grasp of Irish sentiment, I know of nothing that places his character in a less loveable light, that instead of being touched and melted by that generous action of his colleagues and of his countrymen ... he actually took advantage of their impulsive generosity to lure them, to entrap them, to a position of most deadly peril to the cause of Ireland.[54]

The benefit which Parnell derived from his election before the publication of the Gladstone letter lay as much in the demonstration of consummate mastery, in the ruthless and devastating outmarshalling of his opponents, which left him once again towering above them in demonstrated political capacity, as well as in the tactical advantage he thereby achieved of being able to point to 'Liberal dictation' in procuring his deposition. Yet in the aftermath of the achievement of the Liberal alliance the hard classicism of Parnell's political technique no longer attracted the premium it once enjoyed in nationalist politics. Under the sound and fury of the split's competing rhetorics, the issue of 'the only possible leader' had a profound significance. The question was less whether Parnell was the most ferociously capable of nationalist politicians (which even Healy's rhetoric largely conceded), than whether, in the apparently ameliorating conditions of nationalist politics under the Liberal alliance, there was the need for such a leader: Parnell was not dismissed by Gladstone so much as made redundant by operation of the 'Union of Hearts'. Parnell's strategic mastery was to prove decidedly double-edged. The superb professionalism of his political technique was all too readily cast as a ruthless cynicism subversive of the high moral ambience of the Liberal-Nationalist alliance. The Irish leader found himself a practitioner of *realpolitik* fallen among sentimental ideologues.

E. W. Hamilton, dining that evening at the home of Stuart Rendel, found the almost-nullified leader of the Liberal party in sombre, and somewhat pompous, form.

Mr. Gladstone though displaying his usual pluck has taken it much to heart. He feels that he has been betrayed by a man for whom he always had a liking and too fond a regard, and whose political veracity he never had reason to question. For Parnell had through J. Morley assured Mr. Gladstone that he would come out of the O'Shea trial triumphantly. In short Parnell had lied to Mr. Gladstone, and Mr. Gladstone could not forget or forgive that. He flattered himself that he like Sisyphus, had rolled the [home rule] stone to within an ace of the top of the hill; and now the stone was going to be rolled some way down the hill again. He was too old to go down and recommence the task. Therefore the *raison d'être* of his staying on as leader of the party was to a great extent at an end.[55]

On foot of a requisition signed on the evening of 25 November by thirty-one members, a meeting of the Irish party was convened the following afternoon; John Barry moved that a full meeting of the party be held on Friday

28 November 'to give Mr. Parnell an opportunity of reconsidering his position'. Parnell, still seated, replied, as recorded in the minutes, 'that he could not nor would not reconsider his position, in the light that he was unanimously elected by the party the day before. It was useless to ask him. Upon the Party should rest the responsibility today of its vote'. Parnell calmly maintained this position, against the sense of the meeting, and in the face of conciliatory appeals from Sexton, McCarthy and others. The meeting was adjourned to the following Monday 1 December.[56]

Though numerically superior, the nascent opposition to Parnell remained confused and outmanoeuvred. William Martin Murphy telegraphed plaintively to the Archbishop of Dublin on the evening of 25 November: 'Parnell determined to hold on and no one here strong enough to avoid catastrophe'.[57] His letter the following day conveyed the escalating panic of the anti-Parnellites at Westminster:

> From all that I can learn here there is no doubt that even with Gladstone at their head, the Liberals could not get a majority at the General Election which Tories would precipitate if Parnell is retained, and that being so Gladstone's retirement is a certainty, with the result of wrecking our movement for this wretched woman. It is revolting. The interval between this and Monday will be used by Parnell to strengthen his hand.

Murphy's last comment reflected anti-Parnellite fears that Parnell would use his control of the National League machinery to maintain his advantage by manipulating and misrepresenting opinion in Ireland. On the evening of 26 November, having secured the adjournment of the party meeting to 1 December, the Parnellites, in the phrase of Donal Sullivan, sent out across the country 'the fiery cross'.[58]

Against this background of disarray in the opposition to Parnell at Westminster, T. M. Healy bestirred himself in response to requests from his alarmed colleagues. While he had not attended the party meetings of 25 and 26 November, pleading ill health, he had nonetheless managed to travel to Derry to deliver an arbitrator's award in the case of the Drapers' estate on 22 November, on which he had been working for some months previously.[59] His absence from the party meetings was at least in part prudential. Having already expressed himself prematurely at the Leinster Hall, he could not afford to do so again, and he may not have trusted his judgement in the atmosphere of uncertainty and incipient bitterness at Westminster. He did, however, send a telegram to the meeting of 26 November to the effect that the maintenance of Gladstone's leadership of the Liberal Party should be a paramount consideration.[60]

Healy arrived in London on the morning of Thursday 27 November, still looking very ill, and went from the National Liberal Club to Westminster. In the chamber, he sat on the corner seat of the second bench below the gangway, where the leading Irish members habitually sat; Parnell later sat nearby, unwontedly absorbed in reading batches of telegrams and letters.[61] The two men did not speak. Healy complained in his memoirs that Parnell, poisoned against him by D. J. Hishon, had cut him 'stonily'.

The swiftness with which Healy on his arrival moved against Parnell belies the claim in his memoirs that he went to London hopeful of bringing Parnell round to his scheme of resigning and being re-elected for Cork. That day, with Thomas Sexton, he telegraphed to T. P. O'Connor in the United States that a large majority including the foremost party members would vote for Parnell's resignation, 'otherwise generation lost campaign ruined dissolution inevitable', and soliciting the support of the American delegates to achieve 'practical unanimity'.[62] The following day he moved to deprive Parnell of the opportunity afforded by the adjournment of the party meeting to rally his support in Ireland. He drafted a requisition that the party be convened that evening to pass a resolution against any speeches or public declarations 'to influence or overawe the deliberations of the Party pending its adjourned meeting on Monday next'. Parnell, advisedly, was not to be found, and the meeting aborted.[63]

The dissolution of the Irish party at Westminster had already began. On the first day of the session, in the wake of Parnell's re-election, the debate on the Queen's Speech was concluded without a division, for the first time since the Irish party was formed.[64] On 27 November the split was virtually engaged, when on a negativing amendment to Balfour's Land Purchase Bill, Parnell and some fifteen nationalists voted in favour of the bill, a few voted against, while most of the party including Healy and Sexton abstained.[65]

Parnell now embarked on the most startling *démarche* of a career which owed so much to its defiance of expectations. His address 'to the people of Ireland' was designed to convulse Irish opinion against Gladstone over the weekend prior to the party meeting, as he struggled desperately to maximise the advantage conferred by his incumbency of the Irish leadership, and by his myth. The manifesto, which appeared in the newspapers of 29 November 1890 was conceived as a direct appeal to the Irish public over the heads of the Irish Parliamentary Party, 'the integrity and independence' of a section of whose members had been 'apparently sapped and destroyed by the wirepullers of the English Liberal Party'. Gladstone, foremost among those Parnell described as 'the English wolves howling for my destruction', could not be allowed to exercise a veto on the Irish leadership.

Parnell unveiled a politically sensationalistic secret history of the Liberal-Nationalist alliance over the preceding year, centred on his meeting with Gladstone at Hawarden the previous December. He asserted that Gladstone intended to provide in the second Home Rule Bill for a drastic reduction in the Irish representation in the imperial parliament, and the reservation to the imperial parliament of the settling of the land question, together with control over judicial appointments for a period of ten to twelve years and

over the Irish constabulary for an indefinite period. If Gladstone at
Hawarden had touched on the points referred to, Parnell's presentation
of them was calculatedly misleading in relation to what had been a discur-
sive survey of the range of options open to the two leaders under shifting
political circumstances, in the course of which Parnell took no strenuous
exception to anything said by Gladstone.[66]

Parnell charged that Morley, on behalf of the Liberal leadership had
requested that the Irish party oppose Balfour's Land Purchase Bill, and
had expressed views on the evicted tenants prejudicial to nationalist interests. He added that Morley had asked him to assume the Chief
Secretaryship, or permit a member of his party to do so, and urged that
one of the law offices be filled by a legal member of the party (widely
construed, as Parnell intended, as a reference to Healy). An intemperate
farrago of abuse and tendentious and improbable allegation comprised
the bulk of the manifesto. Only in its concluding paragraph did the
manifesto achieve a classic political idiom:

> Sixteen years ago I conceived the idea of an Irish parliamentary party in-
> dependent of all English parties. Ten years ago I was elected the leader of
> an independent Irish parliamentary party. During these ten years that party
> has remained independent, and because of its independence it has forced
> upon the English people the necessity of granting Home Rule to Ireland.
> I believe that party will obtain Home Rule only provided it remains indepen-
> dent of any English party. I do not believe that any action of the Irish peo-
> ple in supporting me will endanger any home rule cause, or postpone the
> establishment of an Irish parliament; but even if the danger with which we
> are threatened by the Liberal party of today were to be realised, I believe
> that the Irish people throughout the world would agree with me that a
> postponement would be preferable to a compromise of our national rights
> by the acceptance of a measure which would not realise the aspirations of
> our race.[67]

Parnell wrote his manifesto from noon to late evening on Friday 28
November at the home of J. G. Fitzgerald, MP for Longford South, at
31 Eccleston Street, Chester Square. It was probably in the early part of
that day that Justin McCarthy was first brought to Eccleston Street by John
Redmond. He told Mrs Campbell Praed that Parnell was 'very quiet out-
wardly, but I could see was greatly excited ... He laughed and seemed quite
unconcerned'. Significantly, Parnell took the opportunity to apprise McCarthy of the defence he could not afford to make publicly, for fear of jeopar-
dising the making absolute of the divorce decree. It was one of his
exceedingly rare references to the circumstances of his relationship with
Katharine O'Shea. When the final divorce decree was obtained

> ... he meant to make a statement which would put him straight except for
> the actual crime. He would show that for twenty-three years of married life,
> O'Shea had in numbers of days, spent one year with his wife; that he had
> carried on with fast women, and had ill-used her; that he (Parnell) had found
> her a miserable woman, and that O'Shea had been quite willing to sell her

to keep his seat in Parliament. He said: 'If I had defended the case, I should have sacrificed the one person whose interests I am bound beyond everything in the world to protect'.[68]

Through the day Parnell drafted his manifesto. At about ten o'clock in the evening he summoned first his chief loyalists, including the Redmonds and J. J. O'Kelly, and then Justin McCarthy. His purpose was rather to implicate his supporters and bind them to the manifesto, than to solicit their views. When McCarthy arrived, they listened in silence as Parnell with slow deliberation read out the text of the manifesto. When he had finished, McCarthy, whose misgivings were almost certainly shared by Parnell's mute lieutenants, expressed his disagreement with the entirety of the manifesto. When McCarthy observed that Gladstone, whom he had already seen, would deny the allegations relating to the Hawarden meeting, Parnell quietly replied 'let him produce the memorandum'. Parnell remained immovable, and the text of the manifesto was given to a reporter from the *Freeman's Journal* where it appeared on Saturday 29 November.[69]

In the world of British politics, Parnell's manifesto elicited an astonished response. 'The manifesto published this morning came with the detonating force of a dynamite explosion', Harold Frederic cabled to the *New York Times:* 'It is a terrible thing to have to record the public suicide of a great public man'. Significantly, this friend of Healy and virulent critic of Parnell now reverted to the theme of his controversial article of July 1890 to raise one of the earliest public suggestions in the split of Parnell's insanity: 'There are reasons for thinking that the mental balance and faculties for cool weighing of vital questions, which have ever been Mr. Parnell's distinguishing qualities, have now completely broken down.'[70] Even allowing for Frederic's animosity to Parnell, his comment conveys the widespread sense among contemporaries of the irrationality of Parnell's initiative. Henry Labouchere (significantly, another of Healy's Westminster intimates) writing in *Truth*, diagnosed Parnell as suffering from a state of 'cerebral excitement': 'I have always perceived in Mr. Parnell a certain weirdness, which, under great stress, might develop'.[71]

Others discerned fiendishness rather than lunacy. Alfred Robbins wrote for the Chamberlainite *Birmingham Daily Post* that politicians were agreed that while Parnell's manifesto was 'diabolically clever ... its effect has been to shatter the faint opportunity that still remained to the member for Cork of proving himself worthy of continued trust'.[72] Gladstone's daughter Mary confided to her diary that Parnell's manifesto was 'defiant, dastardly, devilish'.[73]

For many nationalists it was as if the last thread of faith in Parnell had snapped. The immediate political effects were felt on two fronts. The first was on the nationalist parliamentarians in the United States. 'I find that the Parnell manifesto has embittered the feelings of my colleagues', Harrington disconsolately noted.[74] The delegates, with the exception of

Harrington, cabled a declaration of opposition to Parnell and his 'rash and fatal path'.[75] Secondly, the manifesto permitted the Archbishop of Dublin, who had been pursuing a temporising strategy to ensure that no odium attached to the Church by reason of a premature declaration against Parnell, to pronounce publicly against him for the first time.[76] Healy declared in Committee Room 15 that 'Mr. Parnell cannot get away from the manifesto. It is like a Nessus shirt — it will stick to him all his life'.[77] It was, the *National Press* later declared, 'a manifesto in the tone of Lucifer'.[78]

Parnell had elected to treat Gladstone's letter as an abrogation of the conventions of the Liberal alliance. If he regarded his retaliation as exactly proportioned to Gladstone's breach of protocol, it was to most nationalist observers a gross excess which placed him falsely on the offensive. The nationalist electorate in Ireland had no forewarning of either the abruptness or the vehemence of Parnell's change. Nurtured on the soothingly messianic rhetoric of the 'Union of Hearts', opinion in Ireland was unprepared for the violence of the sundering of the sentimental nationalist diptych of home rule, the intertwined portraits of Parnell and Gladstone. The manifesto was the earliest, and definitive, revelation of the flawed premises of Parnell's strategy in the split. Owing perhaps in part to his long absence from Irish political terrain (where he had not addressed a meeting in almost five years), he underestimated the depth of the impact of the Liberal-Nationalist alliance, and — what is at least as important — the complex social transformation wrought by the pervasive anticipation of peasant proprietorship. His perception was of a static Ireland, unchanged from that in which he had commenced his political career. He appeared oblivious to the revolution wrought by Gladstone's championing of home rule, and he underestimated the devastating backlash from an attack on the liberal leader. He misleadingly equated his campaign with that of 1880. It was no longer a question of Parnellites pitched conveniently against 'Whigs' and 'nominal Home Rulers', but against members of his own party, with demonstrated nationalist credentials.

It was difficult to attach credence to the allegations of the manifesto, and impossible to reconcile them with either Parnell's public expressions of satisfaction after the Hawarden meeting or his perseverance in the Liberal alliance thereafter. The denials of Gladstone and Morley[79] were almost unnecessary. He had moreover committed an egregious breach of political confidence. The rhetoric of the manifesto further suggested a disconcerting loss of that poised detachment which had marked Parnell's career, and a recourse to an extravagant patriotic idiom which he had habitually eschewed. He thereby compromised his greatest asset, his mystique of diffident reticence. It appeared as if his much vaunted composure had deserted him at the first moment that he found his own position threatened.

In retrospect it is difficult not to feel that Parnell's interests would have

been better served had he eschewed any tendentious reference to the
Hawarden negotiations, as well as any challenge impugning of the integrity of his colleagues, and confined himself to pointing to his record and
demonstrated capacity as a nationalist leader, and challenging the right
of the Liberals to dictate the leadership of the Irish party. The main advantage Parnell derived from the Hawarden allegations was to lay the
ground for the manœuvre of requiring the party to seek assurances from
the Liberal leadership in relation to the points at issue, both through the
Clancy amendment in Committee Room 15 and the Boulogne negotiations.
This was integral to Parnell's strategy of embroiling the Liberal leadership
in a predicament which he believed to be of its own creation. In terms of
the immediate impact of the manifesto, Parnell seemed to have disastrously
overplayed his hand: for many nationalists, Parnell now appeared as the
aggressor, Gladstone the victim. As T. P. O'Connor later wrote, Parnell
by his manifesto 'undid the impression favourable to him which had been
made by Mr. Gladstone's letter'.[80]

Yet it has been too readily assumed that the manifesto was dictated by
a paroxysm of affronted pride and fury, and by a gross overestimation of
his support in Ireland: that the 'uncrowned king' was dazzled by his own
regal aura. Faced with the opposition of the Liberal leadership, and, as was
already apparent, that of the majority of the Irish party, Parnell resolved
coldly on a strategy of unflinching audacity: to deploy his authority and
mystique; to throw into the scales the full force of his myth; and to impugn
the legitimacy of a home rule settlement sponsored by that section of the
nationalist party which was ready to dispense with his leadership. It was
a bid to affirm his status as the chairman of the Irish party and as the 'leader
of the Irish nation' — a politician uniquely possessed of the authority to
conclude a final treaty of peace with England. He sought to achieve a re-
sounding affirmation of his capacity as a nationalist leader through a coercive display of mastery: to demoralise, humiliate and overwhelm his
opponents within the Irish party, before taking the issue to Ireland.

Central to an appreciation of Parnell's strategy is the fact that his defeat
at the party meeting was, and was perceived by many members of the party
to be, foreordained. On 30 November, the eve of the party meeting, William
Martin Murphy telegraphed to the Archbishop of Dublin assuring him of
the outcome. While conceding that if 'a substantial rump' cleaved to Parnell,
'he could do an immensity of harm and say that they represented the Irish
people', Murphy was confident that with the declaration of the American
delegates, together with that of the Irish bishops which he anticipated,
'Parnell will not get five members to follow him anywhere'. It was a wild
exaggeration, which he subsequently moderated to a prediction that if it
came to a vote Parnell would lose by a margin of two to one:

> No one knows if he will 'cut up rough' tomorrow. My belief is that he will
> not, but either retire giving way to the inevitable or withdraw and refuse to
> recognise our action. Most of the men supporting him say they believe it would
> be better he should retire but will not vote against him nevertheless. These men
> would never follow in any subsequent action ... Some of the proverbial rats
> are already in motion ...[81]

Murphy, while correct in his (revised) estimate of Parnell's support, badly
underestimated Parnell's resolve and his capacity to marshal the support
of his more lukewarm adherents.

Parnell now set in motion his tactic of inviting assurances from the
Liberal leadership on the points raised in his manifesto, which he was to
reactivate twice more over the ensuing two months. The first deployment
of the tactic served its immediate purpose in averting a defection among
his own more hesitant supporters. Pierce Mahony was among a small group
of members — all of whom were eventually to vote for Parnell — who
wrote to him on Friday 28 November. While asseverating unconditional
allegiance, they urged him in the interests of party unity to retire. Parnell
the following day convened a kind of caucus at the Westminster Palace
Hotel, attended by some twenty of his future loyalists, together with four
future anti-Parnellites he had summoned.[82]

When Justin McCarthy, who was among those invited, arrived, he asked Parnell what he would do if deposed. Parnell replied: 'I will fight you
everywhere. I will go to Cork, and be re-elected. I will oppose you wherever
you put up'. When McCarthy asked did he not know this would lead to
something like civil war in Ireland, Parnell replied 'I am the chosen
representative of the Irish people. I will not be dictated to by that drunken
sweep Sexton'. He also denounced the Healys. He then said that if McCarthy could get an assurance from Gladstone, Morley and Harcourt on the
points at issue in the Home Rule Bill, which he wrote out, he would resign.
McCarthy protested in vain. He told Mrs Campbell Praed the following
day that Parnell was 'shuffling and evasive till that point, when he made
the proposal, and that then his manner became sweet and bland'. When
someone asked, what if the assurance from Gladstone was forthcoming,
'Parnell answered sweetly "then we can put it in a glass case and keep it" '.
This unguarded flippancy angered even the faithful Campbell, who interjected 'if you are going to talk like that, we shall never come to an
understanding'. When Parnell feebly protested that he only meant that they
would keep it as a document of historic importance, Campbell gruffly
retorted 'then we want no more talk of glass cases'. McCarthy found
Parnell's manner extraordinary, and believed he was out of his mind.[83]

The hapless McCarthy, who had already on 28 November put to
Gladstone the points which Parnell was then about to embody in his
manifesto, obediently met the Liberal leader again on 30 November. Determined not to be lured into the labyrinth of the manifesto, Gladstone declined to provide assurances on the grounds that he could only respond to

an approach authorised by the Irish Parliamentary Party, and that Parnell in his appeal to the Irish nation renounced the authority of the party. It was not an adroit response, and left him open to a formal request from the party during the debates in Room 15.[84]

William Martin Murphy wrote to the Archbishop of Dublin furiously denouncing Parnell's 'most insidious proposal', which he accurately characterised as 'intended to embarrass the Liberal party and to insult us by implying that we are not fit to make terms for the country when he retires'.[85] Yet Parnell's tactic served its purpose of consolidating the allegiance of his more hesitant adherents. '... for me, and I believe for others, it cleared the way', wrote Mahony. 'It showed that Parnell was fighting for principle and not for self.'[86]

Parnell marshalled his support. He canvassed members of the party. He used his control of the National League, his support among political activists, and his strength in the higher echelons of the National League organisation, to ensure a flood of resolutions in his support from National League branches across the country. As Healy later admiringly wrote: 'To the doubting he talked, he urged, he implored; and all the time the wires were going to the constituencies, where little groups were being rallied to declare in the name of Humanity, Patriotism and Ballyhooly, that their members should support "the only possible leader" '.[87] Parnell became unwontedly gregarious. When he took his seat in the Commons on 25 November, H. W. Lucy noted: 'Usually he sits silent, taking no notice of his neighbours. Today he talked almost effusively to members of his party sitting near him'.[88] Harold Frederic reported a rare sighting of Parnell in the House of Commons library which was largely abandoned to Irish members on Saturdays, appealing to each in turn of a number of anti-Parnellites present.[89] He played relentlessly on the susceptibilities of his colleagues. After an interview with McCarthy, he roguishly exclaimed 'Well, happen what will, you and I are always friends — God bless you, my dear old friend'.[90] Over the weekend canvassing grew intense and the party began to regroup into two opposing blocs. On Friday 28 November Healy wrote to his wife: 'In the lobby and corridors there is nothing but groups of Irish members talking and arguing ...', and observed in a strange coupling 'The buttonholing by the pressmen is awful. The attitude of the Liberals is friendly'. 'Lobbying goes on and on', he wrote the next day.

The division was already growing bitter. Healy complained he had been cut by W. J. Corbet MP, but rebutting a report that he saw Parnell in the lobby and conversed with him, himself wrote: 'How such rubbish is invented amazes me'.[91] Liberal involvement in the lobbying was to become one of the split's most acrimonious issues. Parnell later extravagantly denounced 'the extraordinary system that was carried on throughout the House of Commons for the purpose of sapping the courage and independence of my colleagues'.[92] The Liberal 'wire-pullers' whom

Parnell accused of actively subverting the independence of the party were Henry Labouchere and Professor James Stuart, together with Philip Stanhope, later Lord Weardale, whose involvement was more discreet. All three were Radicals, belonging to that fringe of the Liberal party whose support for home rule was bred out of a programmatic radicalism rather than any innate affection for the Irish.[93]

Labouchere showed himself a true utilitarian: having initially in *Truth* endorsed Parnell in an editorial entitled 'Measures not Women', in the next issue he insisted that Parnell had to go, pointing to Radical opposition and asserting that 'the question is one of expediency'.[94] Reginald Esher, unusual among Liberals in believing Gladstone's intervention against Parnell to violate the essence of home rule, wrote to W. T. Stead on 2 December: 'Perhaps if mischievous intriguers like Labouchere and J. Stuart keep quiet and Mr. Gladstone writes no more letters, in time there may be a rally'.[95]

If their lobbying exceeded the strict limits of legitimately advising Irish members of the degree of Liberal opposition to Parnell, it is doubtful whether it was as effective as Parnellite publicists subsequently asserted. Yet their ostentatious involvement sensibly enhanced the bitterness of the emergent divisions in the party. That the misery of those Irish members torn by a conflict of allegiance should have attracted the perhaps superfluous, but decidedly predatory, attentions of officious members of the Liberal party attested to the collapse of the Irish party. That the agonising of a once united Irish party should have thus been carried on in the view of the English parties was itself traumatic. A party which had claims to having invented the idea of party discipline in its modern form, which prided itself on the inviolability of its deliberations, was now in public disarray.

Healy wrote to his wife that John Redmond and Edmund Leamy were 'both sworn for Parnell', and that J. J. Clancy 'has gone round to him, as he is greatly embarrassed by his Leinster Hall declarations, but he is very wretched and wishes he was dead'.[96] J. G. Swift MacNeill had come to Healy and asked to be forgiven, as he had had a sleepless night and could not make up his mind: 'I told him he need not trouble, as his mind would be made up for him because his name would be so low down alphabetically that he could calculate beforehand that Parnell was dished, and would vote accordingly'.[97]

On Sunday 30 November, while too ill to attend an anti-Parnellite caucus in the chambers of Arthur O'Connor to concert the strategy to be pursued in Committee Room 15, Healy liaised with James Stuart. Stuart wrote to Herbert Gladstone that Healy said that John Redmond had gone that evening to beg Parnell to resign 'and that Redmond puts his following at fifteen. Mr. Healy would put it at twenty'.[98] Allegiances had set hard before the reconvened meeting of the party commenced. The scurrying of

William Martin Murphy's 'proverbial rats' was stilled. The party moved to schism with the ineluctability of classical tragedy. That the outcome was fore-ordained did not diminish the ardour of the debates in Committee Room 15. As Healy later perceptively wrote: 'When the hour for voting came every man on both sides was in his place, nobody wanted to be neutral, no-one who could be present was away. Trained politicians make splendid partisans'.[99] The fierce constancy of allegiance among the parliamentarians, once sides had been taken, was reproduced in the split in the country. It was to invest the Parnell split with its defining characteristics of passion and stasis.

Parnell would in the event be left in Committee Room 15, after the withdrawal of the forty-four anti-Parnellites, with twenty-seven loyalists. He had thus rallied his potential support to surpass the estimate of Healy as well as of Redmond, an achievement which should be set against the judgement of Parnell as a politician who in the split had forfeited his effectiveness.

On the eve of meeting the Irish party Healy wrote to his wife: 'It is after twelve, and I am going to get a little sleep so as to be fresh for tomorrow. I will have to say little, as I proposed that Sexton should undertake all the statement necessary'.[100] In anticipating a brief debate, Healy under-estimated the resourcefulness and tenacity of the chairman of the Irish party.

References

1 Lionel Johnson, ' "The Man Who Would be King" ', *The Academy*, 19 Nov. 1898.
2 *The Times*, 16 and 18 Nov. 1890; *N.P.*, 25 June 1891; O'Connor, *Memoirs*, ii, p. 276; Harrison, *Parnell Vindicated*, pp. 161-63, 298-303; Sir Alfred E. Pease, *Elections and Recollections* (London, 1932), p. 276.
3 *B.D.P.*, 18 Nov. 1890.
4 Brabourne, 'The Parnell Imbroglio' in *Blackwood's Magazine* (vol. 149, Jan. 1891), p. 143.
5 *The Times*, 18 Nov. 1891; in similar vein the *Speaker* of 13 Dec. wrote of Parnell's 'vulgar intrigue at Eltham'.
6 Frederic Harrison, 'The Irish Leadership', *Fortnightly Review*, n.s. vol. 49, p. 123 (1 Jan. 1891).
7 Brabourne, 'The Parnell Imbroglio', p. 142.
8 *F.J.*, 25 Nov. 1890, quoting an article by the Dublin Correspondent of the *Manchester Guardian*, J. F. Taylor.
9 *F.J.*, 18-21 Nov. 1890.
10 *Nation*, 22 Nov. 1890; *I.C.*, 22 Nov. 1890.
11 *Labour World*, 20 Nov. 1890.
12 *Nation*, 1 Nov. 1890; *U.I.*, 1 Nov. 1890; *F.J.*, 10 Nov. 1890; Healy, *Leaders and Letters*, i. 318-19.

13 11 May 1891, Healy to Redmond; 12 May 1891, Redmond to Healy, draft copy; 13 May 1891, Healy to Redmond; 14 May 1891, Redmond to Healy draft/copy Redmond Papers, NLI MS 15, 196; R. B. O'Brien, *Parnell*, ii. p. 242; *N.P.*, 30 Apr. 1891, speech of Joseph Kenny at National League; *U.I.*, 16 May 1891, speech of Harrington at Mullingar, 10 May 1891.

14 *Letters and Leaders*, i. p. 320; F. S. L. Lyons omits to note the narrow ambit of Healy's caveat: *Fall*, p. 74; *Parnell*, pp. 481-482.

15 *F.J.*, 21 Nov. 1890; Morley to Gladstone, 22 Nov. 1890, Gladstone Papers, BM MS 44256, f.82.

16 *P.M.G.*, 8 Dec. 1890. Healy likewise asserted during the Kilkenny election that the initial Tory outcry against Parnell was succeeded by a cry of 'genuine despair' from the Liberal party: *K.M.*, 20 Dec. 1890.

17 *F.J.*, 19 Nov. 1890, Central Branch NL.

18 *F.J.*, 19 Nov. 1890, Central Branch NL, speech of Donal Sullivan; *F.J.*, 21 Nov. 1890; Thomas Doyle to Walsh, 4 Dec. 1890, Walsh Papers, DDA.

19 *Weekly Nation*, 23 Oct. 1897; T. D. Sullivan, *Recollections*, pp. 20-22; Harrington Diary, entry for 4 Dec. 1890, Leamy, *Parnell's Faithful Few*, p. 230; O'Connor, *Memoirs*, ii, p. 192; Dillon to O'Brien, 13 Dec. 1890, NLI MS 13506 (9); see also R. B. O'Brien, *Parnell*, ii. pp. 241-42.

20 D. J. Hishon to Harrington, 22 Nov. 1890, Harrington Papers, NLI MS 8576 (23).

21 *B.D.P.*, 26 Nov. 1890.

22 Donal Sullivan, *The Story of Room 15* (Dublin, 1891), 1-6; Irish Party Minutes, 25 Nov. 1890; Donal Sullivan to Healy, 25 Nov. 1890, Healy-Sullivan papers, UCD P6/B/32; published in extenso in Healy, *Letters and Leaders*, i. pp. 322-23. For a further account, somewhat fragmentary and unreliable, but of interest as the stuff of Parnellite mythology, see J. G. Fitzgerald, 'Parnell's Desertion', *I.W.I.*, 6 Oct. 1894.

23 *Hansard*, vol. 349, col. 27 (25 Nov. 1890).

24 E. W. Hamilton Diary, entry for 25 Nov. 1890, Hamilton Papers, BM MS 48654; for nationalist reaction see Donal Sullivan, *Room 15*, p. 9.

25 Donal Sullivan, *Room 15*, pp. 2-4; *Letters and Leaders*, i. pp. 321-3; *Kilkenny Journal*, 17 Dec. 1890, speech of Healy, Castlecomer, 14 Dec. 1890.

26 *F.J.*, 18 and 25 Nov. 1890, 25 Nov. 1890.

27 *B.D.P.*, 26 Nov. 1890.

28 Healy, *Letters and Leaders*, i. p. 322.

29 *F.J.*, 2 Dec. 1891.

30 Alfred Webb, 'Memoir of the Parnell Split', 31 May 1906, Library of Society of Friends, Dublin.

31 William Martin Murphy to Walsh, 30 Nov. 1890, Walsh Papers, DDA.

32 Morley to Gladstone, 15 Nov. 1890, Gladstone Papers, BM 44256, f. 68.

33 Morley, *Gladstone*, iii. p. 429.

34 Gladstone to Morley, 18 Nov. 1890, Morley, *Gladstone*, iii. p. 430.

35 Gladstone Papers, BM Add. MS 44256, f. 75, part quoted in Gladstone to Morley, 19 Nov. 1890, Morley, *Gladstone*, iii. p. 431.

36 Memorandum dated 21 Nov. [1891] entitled 'The O'Shea Suit', and marked 'secret'; Gladstone Papers. BM MS 56448, f. 45.

37 Memoranda dated N[ov.] 22 1 890; Gladstone Papers, BM MS 56448, ff. 58, 59; In the first memorandum Gladstone, recalling the scrupulousness and honesty of Parnell's dealings when in opposition to the Liberal government, expressed his confidence that Parnell would act sensibly.

38 W. T. Stead to Gladstone, 20 Nov. 1890, Gladstone Papers, BM Add. MS 56448,

f.30. Stead enclosed an offprint of an article by him entitled 'Home Rule or Mr. Parnell', to be published in the following day's *Daily Chronicle*.

39 Morley to Gladstone, 22 Nov. 1890, Gladstone Papers, BM Add. MS 44256, f. 82.

40 Arnold Morley to Gladstone, 22 Nov. 1890, Gladstone Papers, BM Add. MS 44524, f. 56.

41 Harcourt to Gladstone, 22 Nov. 1890, A. G. Gardiner, *Life of Sir William Harcourt*, ii. pp. 83-84; Gladstone Papers, BM Add. MS 44202, f. 37; E. W. Hamilton, Diary entry for 23 Nov. 1891, Hamilton Papers, BM Add. MS 48654, f. 151.

42 Gladstone to Arnold Morley, 22 Nov. 1890, copy BM Add. MS 44524, f. 56.

43 McCarthy and Praed, *Book of Memories*, pp. 256-57.

44 R. M. Praed, notes on conversation with Justin McCarthy, 29 Nov. 1890, McCarthy and Praed, *Book of Memories*, Draft; McCarthy and Praed, *Book of Memories*, pp. 258-59; Lyons, *Parnell*, pp. 492-96.

45 *F.J.*, 27 Nov. 1890.

46 Gladstone to Morley, 24 Nov. 1890, Morley, *Gladstone* iii. pp. 436-37; Healy, *Letters and Leaders*, i. p. 322; Donal Sullivan, *Room 15*, pp. 3-4; see generally Lyons, *Parnell*, pp. 494-6. Labouchere claimed to have communicated to Parnell the day before parliament met that Gladstone intended to declare by letter that he could no longer act with him (*Truth*, 15 Oct. 1891, 'About Mr. Parnell'); Parnell was doubtless grateful to Labouchere for the tip-off.

47 Morley, memorandum dated 25 Nov. 1890, Morley, *Gladstone*, iii. p. 440. Hamilton made an entry in his diary some four weeks later after a conversation with Morley that 'when Morley read out Mr. Gladstone's letter Parnell declined to take Mr. Gladstone's threat of retiring seriously'; E. W. Hamilton, Diary, entry for 21 Dec. 1890, BM Add. MS 48654.

48 Morley memorandum dated 25 Nov. 1890.

49 Donal Sullivan, *Room 15*, pp. 6-8; R. B. O'Brien, *Parnell*, ii. pp. 250-51; Sophie O'Brien 'Recollections', i. p. 261.

50 Morley, *Gladstone*, iii. p. 436; E. W. Hamilton, Diary, entries for 23 Nov. 26 Nov. 21 Dec. 1890, Hamilton Papers, BM Add. MS 48654, pop. 51, 62, 104.

51 Auberon Herbert, ' "The Rake's Progress" ' in Irish Politics', *Fortnightly Review*, n.s. vol. 49, p. 134.

52 Lyons, *Parnell*, pp. 500-01; see also Lyons, *Fall*, pp. 93-94; Hammond, *Gladstone and the Irish Nation*, pp. 643-64; Healy, *Letters and Leaders*, i. p. 323; R. B. O'Brien, *Parnell*, ii. pp. 250-01; Robbins similarly describes the publication of the Gladstone letter as 'the crowning tactical error of all'; Robbins, *Parnell*, p. 159.

53 Morley, *Gladstone*, iii. p. 436; E. W. Hamilton, Diary entry for 25 Nov. 1890, E. W. Hamilton Papers, BM Add. MS 48654.

54 *F.J.*, 21 Sept. 1891.

55 E. W. Hamilton, Diary, entry for 25 Nov. 1890, E. W. Hamilton Papers, BM Add. MS 48654, pp. 59-60; for a similar expression of Gladstone's state of mind see Gladstone's memorandum of 26 Nov. 1891, Morley, *Gladstone*, iii. pp. 443-44.

56 Donal Sullivan, *Room 15*, pp. 6-11; Irish Party Minutes , entry for 26 Nov. 1890.

57 William Martin Murphy to Walsh, 25 Nov. 1891, Walsh Papers, DDA.

58 Donal Sullivan, *Room 15*, pp. 11-12.

59 *F.J.*, 24 Nov. 1890.

60 *F.J.*, 27 Nov. 1890, London Letter; see also *F.J.*, 28 Nov. 1890; Healy in his memoirs states he wired McCarthy: 'Think Parnell should defer to Gladstone',

Healy, *Letters and Leaders*, i. 324.

61 *F.J.*, 27 and 28 Nov. 1890; Healy's statement in his memoirs that he arrived on Friday (*Letters and Leaders* i. 324) is incorrect.

62 Sexton and Healy to O'Connor, 27 Nov. 1890; NLI MS 13506 (4).

63 Minutes of the Irish Parliamentary Party, 28 Nov. 1891, Dillon Papers, TCD MS 6501; Donal Sullivan, *Room 15*, p. 12.

64 Donal Sullivan, *Room 15*, p. 9.

65 *F.J.*, 28 Nov. 1890.

66 Lyons, *Parnell*, pp. 450-1; *Fall*, p. 107; Morley, *Gladstone*, iii. pp. 445-6. It is possible that Parnell at Hawarden did, as he insisted in the manifesto, object to any reduction in the number of Irish members during any transitional period prior to the vesting of the full range of powers in a home rule government (or in the case of the land question, its prior resolution). This is not necessarily inconsistent with Gladstone's contemporary memorandum to his colleagues stating that Parnell had 'no absolute or fore-gone conclusion' on the retention of Irish members at Westminster, and had agreed that judgement should be reserved until the time came for the introduction of a Home Rule Bill, in that Gladstone must be taken prima facie to be referring to the issue of the retention of Irish members at Westminster in the longer term.

67 *F.J.*, 29 Nov. 1890; the published text is reproduced in Lyons, *Fall*, at pp. 320-26. What survives of the original draft of the manifesto is a nine-page manuscript in Parnell's hand kept by C. P. Fitzgerald and presented to Eamon de Valera in July 1921. What then remained were nine foolscap pages, which contain the text of a little over half of the manifesto, continuous from the start. The missing pages had been stolen or mislaid (MS draft of Parnell manifesto [incomplete]; J. G. Fitzgerald to Griffith, 22 July 1921; J. G. Fitzgerald to De Valera 20 July 1921, NLI MS 21,933). The second page of the manifesto was reproduced to illustrate Fitzgerald's article in the *Irish Weekly Independent* of 6 Oct. 1894, and is also reproduced in Jennie Wyse-Power's *Words of the Dead Chief*. Parnell later asserted that the word 'apparently', qualifying the sapping of the independence and integrity of the Irish party, which had been omitted from some published versions, should have been included (*F.J.*, 4 Dec. 1891; R. B. O'Brien, *Parnell*, ii. p. 258). The qualifying adverb does not however appear in the manuscript. The manifesto originally opened with the words 'The machinations of the wirepullers of the Liberal Party and the evil associations of the National Liberal Club having sapped and destroyed the independence of a considerable section of the Irish party ...', for which is substituted in Parnell's hand the opening recital as published. The surviving leaves of the manuscript, in a firm hand and large script, have few corrections, and conform closely to the text published.

68 R. M. Praed, note of conversation with Justin McCarthy, 29 Nov. 1890, McCarthy and Praed, *Book of Memories*, Draft. Mrs Campbell Praed's note refers to Parnell making a statement when the decree nisi was made, but it is clear from the context that what she was referring to was the final, absolute, decree of divorce. McCarthy's further observations suggest he was not reassured, and reflect how the prevalent perceptions of Parnell's relations with Katharine O'Shea were shaped by the anecdotes — and professional breach of confidence — of Katharine's former solicitor: 'George Lewis tells me that they are absolutely happy and devoted, and all day together — he smoking cigarettes, she by him, never wearying of each other. Parnell said to Lewis what seems rather pathetic, when Lewis said something about "Mrs. O'Shea's friends". "Mrs. O'Shea", said Parnell, "has not one friend in the world except myself, and we neither of us care what anyone thinks" '.

69 J. G. Fitzgerald gave two newspaper accounts of the drafting of the manifesto on which I have relied. The first and more reliable appeared in an interview in the *Evening Herald* for 28 Dec. 1891, in rebuttal of the allegation of Donal Sullivan in his account of the split that the manifesto was drafted in committee. The second was a commemorative article entitled 'Parnell's Desertion' on the third anniversary of Parnell's death, in the *Irish Weekly Independent* of 6 Oct. 1894. An account published in early 1892 by an anonymous *Freeman's Journal* journalist summoned to Eccleston Street (probably J. M. Tuohy) substantially corroborates the relevant part of Fitzgerald's account (*Evening Telegraph*, 3 Jan. 1892, republished *F.J.*, 4 Jan. 1892). The assertion by Katharine Parnell that Parnell began drafting the manifesto at Brighton on the evening of 26 Nov. appears incorrect, unless referring to something in the nature of a preparatory draft (Katharine O'Shea, *Parnell*, ii. p. 162). Ironically Parnell probably did not write the concluding paragraph. According to the account furnished by Justin McCarthy to Mrs Campbell Praed, as Parnell completed the drafting of the manifesto, one of the Parnellites suggested there should be a flourish at the end about all he had done for Ireland. Parnell said wearily 'I'm not good at that sort of thing. Let Leamy finish it'. McCarthy, sadly ironical, suggested they use Grattan's saying about the Irish parliament, 'that he had watched over its cradle, and was following its hearse'. Parnell answered gently: 'No, we won't say that, Justin'. McCarthy and Praed, *Book of Memories*, p. 261, see also Donal Sullivan, *Room 15*, p. 12.

70 *N.Y.T.*, 30 Nov. 1890, cable dated 29 Nov.

71 *Truth*, 4 Dec. 1890.

72 *B.D.P.*, 1 Dec. 1890.

73 Mary Gladstone, *Diaries and Letters*, ed. Lucy Masterman (London, 1930) p. 414, entry for 27 Nov. 1890.

74 T. C. Harrington, Harrington Diary, entry for 29 Nov. 1891, in Leamy, *Parnell's Faithful Few*, p. 223.

75 *F.J.*, 1 Dec. 1890, cable dated 30 Nov.

76 *F.J.*, 1 Dec. 1890, interview with the Central News Agency.

77 *F.J.*, 5 Dec.

78 *N.P.*, 11 Jun.

79 *The Times*, 1 Dec. 1890.

80 *Weekly Sun*, 28 June 1896, 'Reminiscences of My Public Life V'.

81 Murphy to Walsh, 30 Nov. 1890 (2), Walsh Papers, DDA.

82 Donal Sullivan, *Room 15*; *I.W.I.*, 7 Oct. 1893, Pierce Mahony, 'Parnell's Resolution'.

83 R. M. Praed, notes of conversation with Justin McCarthy, 30 Nov. 1890, in McCarthy and Praed, *Book of Memories*, Draft. Both in the draft and in the published text (at p. 262) Mrs Campbell Praed conflates the meeting(s) of 28 November at C. P. Fitzgerald's home at Eccleston Street, and that of the following day at the Westminster Palace Hotel after the publication of Parnell's manifesto. She confusingly relates the 'glass case' dialogue to 'his [Parnell's] secretary Harrington'. This must be taken to refer to Henry Campbell, Parnell's secretary. Tim Harrington did not leave New York until 13 December, and the remark is not characteristic of his taciturn and resolutely Parnellite brother, Edward.

84 Gladstone note dated 28 Nov. 1890; McCarthy to Gladstone, 29 Nov. 1890; Gladstone note dated 30 Nov. 1890; all in Gladstone Papers, BM Add. MS 56446.

85 Murphy to Walsh, 30 Nov. 1890, Walsh Papers, DDA.

86 *I.W.I.*, 7 Oct. 1893.

87 Healy, *Rise and Fall*, p. 201; of the resolutions Healy observed in Room 15 '... I say we know the machinery. We hear the creaking of the cranks. Every winch and pulley that could be employed has been gathered together to set them in motion'; *F.J.*, 5 Dec. 1891.

88 H. W. Lucy, *Salisbury Parliament*, p. 315.

89 *N.Y.T.*, 30 Nov. 1890.

90 McCarthy and Praed, *Book of Memories*, p. 260.

91 Healy to Erina Healy, 28, 29 Nov. 1890, *Letters and Leaders*, Proofs, B131-32, passages deleted from published texts, *Letters and Leaders*, i. pp. 326-8.

92 *F.J.*, 23 Mar. 1891, Navan.

93 See in particular Robbins, *Parnell*, pp. 171-72; for a remarkable, and erroneous, attack on the involvement of James Stuart, see two articles by T. P. O'Connor (*Sunday Sun*, 8 and 15 Nov. 1891), and Stuart's denials (*P.M.G.*, 9 and 10 Nov. 1891); for a mocking, but interesting, assessment of Stuart's role see *St. Stephen's Review*, 13 Dec. 1890. For a Parnellite account, see *I.W.I.*, 6 Oct. 1891, 'Parnell's Desertion', by J. G. Fitzgerald. In relation to the National Liberal Club see C. C. O'Brien, *Parnell*, pp. 321, 330-32; see also speech of William Redmond, *F.J.*, 3 Dec. 1890.

94 *Truth*, 20 and 27 Nov. 1891.

95 *Journals and Letters of Reginald Viscount Esher*, ed. M. V. Brett, 2 vols. (London, 1934), p. 147.

96 Healy to Erina Healy, 29 Nov. 1890, *Letters and Leaders*, Proofs, B132.

97 Ibid, 30 Nov. 1890, B133.

98 Donal Sullivan, *Room 15*, p. 17; J. Stuart to H. Gladstone, 30 Nov. 1890, Gladstone Papers, BM Add. MS 56449.

99 Healy, *Rise and Fall*, p. 200.

100 Healy to Erina Healy, 30 Nov. 1890, *Letters and Leaders*, Proofs, B133.

2

COMMITTEE ROOM 15

When the Committee Room meeting was going on it was perfectly
plain that all the arguments and all the invective that were being launched at his head were only strengthening his resolution, and that all
the appeals made to him by his own friends had the effect rather of
refrigerating than thawing his iron will. Whatever chance there may
have been of a compromise on the first day, there was less on the second, and I doubt if there was any at all on the third. When the first
day's proceedings were ended I remember asking Mr. Parnell what had
been done, and he answered 'They are getting into a cast iron position from which, so far as I can see, there will be no escape'. No leader
could ever have gone through a more fiery ordeal than he had to face
in the Committee Room, but though he was occasionally provoked
into violent displays of passion, he almost instantly recovered his self-
control, his face resumed that most ominous look of composure, and
he never for an instant gave any sign that indicated the least faltering
in the pursuit of the purpose he had in view.

> J. M. Tuohy of the *Freeman's Journal*[1]

Parnell attacked meant Parnell immovable.

> Pierce Mahony[2]

Well of course you may get another leader to succeed me, but you'll
find it very hard to get a leader who takes so much killing as I.

> Parnell, during an adjournment
> of the debate in Room 15[3]

At noon on 1 December 1890, the members of the Irish party assembled
in Committee Room 15 of the House of Commons, a high oak-panelled
room overlooking the Thames. Parnell took his place at the head of the
large horse-shoe table, with his secretary Henry Campbell to his left, and

McCarthy, Sexton and Healy to his right. Over by the window sat Parnell's irreconcilable opponents, dominated by John Barry and Arthur O'Connor, dubbed by Henry Campbell in the course of the debates as 'the caucus in the corner'.[4] Too ill to walk the few hundred yards, Healy drove to the House of Commons and sat shivering by the fire in Room 15, trying to get warm before the meeting assembled.[5]

Before the meeting, an ugly, if somewhat farcical, scene was enacted at the Westminster Palace Hotel. Parnell asked Justin McCarthy, referring to Gladstone: 'And what answer have you brought from your shuffling friend? I will hear it with no shuffling'. McCarthy replied that he would give an account of the interview, but that he expected to be listened to without interruption, and 'with good breeding'. Parnell's furious retort — 'I have more good breeding than you' — provoked Huntley McCarthy to observe 'that's a lie'. 'Parnell rushed at him, and was held back. There were cries of "withdraw". Huntley said "I will not withdraw. He insulted my father; and I say he is a liar" '. Justin McCarthy asked his son to withdraw the comment, which he did and left. He followed. While Parnell later apologised to both, it was an ominous prelude to the party meeting.[6]

In Committee Room 15, Parnell, menacingly composed, signalled from the outset his determination to wrest the maximum procedural advantage from his chairmanship of the meeting. It opened with the reading at Parnell's direction of a great number of endorsements and resolutions of support for Parnell, dismissed by the anti-Parnellites as emanations from the Parnellite political machine rather than as genuine expressions of Nationalist opinion. Parnell then calmly took what was an evidently prearranged amendment to Barry's resolution convening the meeting by the Parnellite Colonel Nolan, that the meeting be adjourned to permit the views of the constituencies to be ascertained, and then reconvened in Dublin.

Healy in reply openly articulated for the first time his highly developed reductionist critique of the mystique of Parnell. It disclosed his temperamental incapacity to concede to Parnell any substantial credit for the political progress achieved under his leadership. The party, he asserted, had stood by Parnell not only on account of his parliamentary services, 'but because of the great value of his name as a magnet and centre for Irish patriotism ... but let us retain Mr. Parnell, and of what value is that name to us?' Healy proceeded to develop the image of the electromagnet, which recurred through his speech, into a dramatic Victorian metaphor of power:

> I say to Mr. Parnell his power is gone. He derived that power from the people. We are the representatives of the people (*loud and prolonged cheers*). Place an iron bar in a coil and electrize that coil and the iron bar becomes magnetic. This party was that electric action. There (*pointing to the*

chairman) stood the iron bar. The electricity is gone, and the magnetism with it, when our support has died away.

He concluded by telling Parnell that 'if he has a sacrifice to make on the altar of his country there is yet time'.

Healy's speech was a formidable indictment of Parnell in terms of what he defined as the premises of constitutional action. He argued that constitutional progress had from the outset involved an abatement of nationalist demands, which Parnell had been ready to accept in the 1886 Bill. He then asked the question to which he would revert through the split: why had Parnell, instead of praising Gladstone, not declared his reservations immediately after the Hawarden meeting?

His assertion that 'either Mr. Parnell at Liverpool was false or his manifesto was false', was the first to draw blood. Amid cries and countercries, Parnell broke in to demand the withdrawal of the remark, declaring, 'I will not stand an accusation of falsehood from Timothy Healy'. Having achieved the desired effect, Healy withdrew his observation 'out of respect to the chair'. In rebuttal of the charge of acceding to English pressure, he audaciously cited his own support of Parnell at the Leinster Hall: 'Aye, we stood up for Mr. Parnell against the Bulls of the Pope of Rome *(cheers)*. It was not likely that we would allow ourselves to be influenced by the declarations of a single Wesleyan pulpit'. He insisted that 'having neither armies nor fleets we are bound to rely upon constitutional and Parliamentary methods', methods which his argument disquietingly equated with the Liberal alliance. To Parnell's taunt that the integrity and independence of his opponents had been sapped, Healy retorted that Parnell had stepped outside the pale of constitutional politics. The split's destructive dialectic was already evident.

It was an impressive and restrained speech, unmarred by the verbal savagery which he was to exhibit subsequently. Yet his letter to his wife, later that evening, already reflected the savage pugilistic intimacy of his attacks on Parnell: 'My speech broke Parnell a lot ... I faced him from five or six feet away, and he seemed to feel the argument'.[7]

That Parnell immediately rose to reply to Healy suggests, as well as an intention to undo the effects of his speech, a shrewd determination to dramatise the contest of the split in terms of their adversity. His retort skilfully cast Healy in the role of the ingrate, the soured apprentice, a charge which was to provide the thrust of his taunts against Healy through the split, while at the same time advertising the qualities of his own generalship:

Mr. Healy has been trained in this warfare, and who trained him? Who saw his genius? Who telegraphed to him from America to come to him and gave him his first opportunity and chance? Who afterwards got his first seat in parliament for him, rebuking and restraining and going past the prior right of my friend Jack Redmond? That Mr. Healy is here today to destroy me is due to myself.

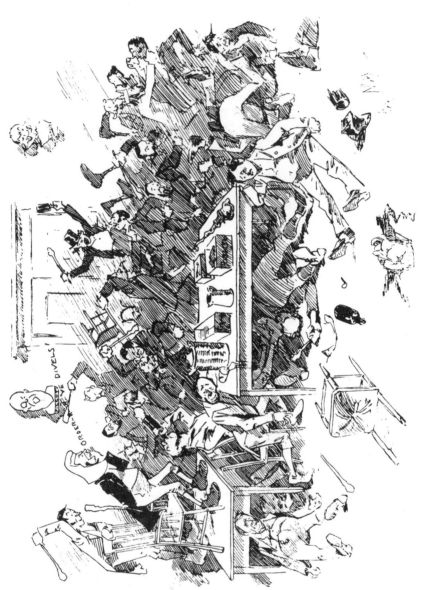

Figure 2　The Split (St. Stephen's Review, 13 Dec. 1890)

Having taunted Healy with his Leinster Hall speech, Parnell went on to posit a confederacy of disloyalty against him. He attacked John Barry by an oblique reference to 'the leader-killer who sharpens his poniard to stab me as he stabbed the old lion, Isaac Butt, in the days gone by', a characteristically audacious argument, given that he had been the principal beneficiary of Barry's attacks on Butt. He defended his manifesto in terms which laid the ground for the device of soliciting assurances from the Liberal party in relation to the points in contention, asking the party, 'Before you vote my deposition, to be sure you are getting value for it'. Parnell's voice uncharacteristically broke with emotion at the close of his speech, which culminated in his closing avowal: 'I should like — and it is not an unfair thing for me to ask — that I should come within sight of this "promised land" '.

After the strenuous passage of arms between Healy and Parnell, the debate wore on into the night, ending in acrimony just before midnight as Healy unavailingly tried to force Parnell to take a division on the proposal to adjourn to the following day.[8]

On this first night, the existence of a majority against him already discernible, Parnell told Robbins during a short pause in the proceedings that if defeated, 'I will go on fighting, and Ireland will be the battle ground'. Robbins wrote: 'He does not profess to forecast the future; he gives utterance to nothing in the nature of a prophesy, but that he feels sure of ultimate victory may be considered beyond a doubt'. Beyond 'a deep flush upon a face customarily extremely pale', Parnell betrayed no trace of agitation.[9]

Healy was increasingly drained. In the drama of the split his old admiration for the embattled Irish leader intermittently flared up before quickly guttering. He wrote to his wife on 30 November, 'At one moment I pity Parnell. At another, when I hear of his determination to wreck everything, I loathe his conduct'. The latter part of Parnell's speeches brought tears to his eyes, and he wrote to his wife that Parnell bore himself wonderfully: 'I cannot conceive of any other man going through such an ordeal with so much dignity. I feel sorry for him'. 'Apart from the technical rulings, he has acted the gentleman', he continued, but recollecting that his wife was a Sullivan before she was a Healy, tempered his concluding comment with a stern moral reservation: '... and no one, from a Pagan point of view, could help admiring him'.[10] Writing to his wife in shorthand during the debate at about 6 o'clock, and correctly anticipating that it could go on till midnight, he commented: 'You will be expecting a line from me, though I am so exhausted I hardly know what I am saying. No more trying time have I ever gone through'.[11]

On the following day, Tuesday 2 December, the debate dragged on, amid deepening acrimony as the existence of a substantial majority against Parnell became overwhelmingly evident. At about six o'clock in the evening Healy wrote his wife a running commentary on the debate:

> [J] F. X. O'Brien now begins to talk. Having said that the standard of Ireland
> fell in the divorce court, Parnell muttered, 'That is plain speaking anyhow'.
> There is a great tumult over it. O'Brien is speaking stoutly against Parnell,
> and with extraordinary courage. My admiration for our fellows has been in-
> creased by their temper and speeches.
>
> I am afraid that Parnell won't allow a vote to be taken tonight. Still, it looks
> as if their orators were exhausted, as three of our men have spoken in succes-
> sion, and nobody on their side has risen.[12]

Healy's fears were unfounded. Parnell drily, in one of his rare jokes,
signalled the exhaustion of the filibuster he had orchestrated from the chair,
by turning to his left and enquiring with a smile 'I say, Sexton, are you
fellows going to keep this thing up all night?' In the gathering darkness
illuminated by a few oil-lamps and candles, Parnell, his pallid face faintly
visible, put the question. When he declared the Nolan amendment carried, a division was called for. Parnell impassively called out the names
of the members of the party from a list. Towards the end came his own
name. He called 'Parnell' in a louder voice, and louder again responded
'aye'. His adherents cheered and banged the tables. The amendment was
lost by forty-four votes to twenty-nine.[13]

The parliamentary arithmetic thus inescapably clear, Parnell embarked
on the manœuvre for which his manifesto and speech had laid the ground
of seeking assurances from the Liberal leadership. The following morning, Wednesday 3 December, after the now ritual reading of telegrams, the
Parnellite J. J. Clancy moved a resolution that in view of the difference
of opinion between Gladstone and Parnell as to what had transpired at
Hawarden on the issue of the control of the constabulary and the settlement of the land question, the views of Gladstone, Morley and Harcourt
be ascertained by the whips of the Irish party. Parnell was absent, probably intentionally, at the critical point of the speech, when, before putting the amendment, Clancy declared: 'I have authority for stating that,
if assurances are given after the manner suggested in this amendment, Mr.
Parnell will retire'.

Healy immediately raised the issue of how the adequacy of any Liberal
assurances was to be determined. Sexton took up this argument and sought
assurances from Parnell that in the event of an outcome adjudged satisfactory, Parnell would resign. Healy, speaking with 'great emotion', rose to
make 'a personal declaration in your regard, Mr. Parnell'. If Parnell was
able to meet the party on the points raised by Sexton, 'my voice will be
the first, on the very earliest moment possible, consonant with the liberties of my country, to call you back to your proper place as leader of the
Irish race.' As the meeting broke into loud and prolonged applause, Healy
wept.[14] He again intervened to blunt the edge of diehard anti-Parnellite
opposition to the Clancy amendment, cutting off P. A. Chance by

declaring: 'If any voice is raised against a settlement proposed on the lines laid down by Mr. Sexton that voice, in my opinion, would be a vote contrary to the interests of the nation'. Even though Redmond and Clancy had already, in Parnell's absence, declared that they had authority to state that Parnell would resign if satisfactory assurances were forthcoming, Parnell pronounced Sexton's query as to who would be the judge of the adequacy of the Liberal response 'a very sudden question on a very important matter', which he would need time to consider, and procured an adjournment of the meeting for twenty-four hours.

The question of the sincerity with which Parnell embarked on the strategy of seeking to elicit assurances from the Liberal leadership has been widely canvassed. Assessments of Parnell's subjective sincerity perhaps miss the point. He probably proposed to await events and to let the initiative take its course, willing to resign in the abstract, yet all the while awaiting developments which would confirm his instinctive inclination to fight the question out to its conclusion, and to that end ready to avail himself ruthlessly of any tactical advantages which the seeking of the Liberal assurances afforded him. What can be confidently discounted is the pervasive belief that Parnell's hardening of his attitude the following day reflected the influence of Katharine O'Shea, the *bête noire* of Parnell's parliamentary opponents and supporters alike.[15] If any external influence stiffened Parnell, it was the declaration against him by the standing committee of the Irish hierarchy made the same day as Clancy proposed his amendment.[16] He was committed to the manœuvre of seeking Liberal guarantees, but sought to maximise his subsequent freedom of action. It is unlikely that Parnell believed that he would succeed without clarifying the issue of who would determine the adequacy of the guarantees. His bluff called on that aspect of the manœuvre, he reserved his position.

After his contemplative respite, Parnell returned to the fray on the morning of Thursday 4 December. Avowedly in response to Sexton's double query, he now sought to entrench his position by modifying in crucial respects the amendment of Clancy, his own supporter. He proposed that the party adopt two resolutions: the first pre-committing the party to reject any home rule measure which did not confer control of the police on the Irish executive and power to deal with the land question on Irish parliament; the second that a subcommittee comprising the whips, five of the majority and five of the minority, nominate three delegates from each side to confer with Gladstone, Harcourt and Morley 'for the purpose of ascertaining whether their views are in accordance with the views of the party on those points as above expressed, and whether they will agree to embody those views in their Home Rule Bill, and to make them vital to that measure'.

While Parnell's speech has been characterised as rambling, inconsistent and tactically inept,[17] it is possible to discern, in spite of some obscurities, Parnell's habitual clarity of purpose. He stated at the outset that he had been assisted by 'a consultation with my friends', to whom he was to refer twice more. The Clancy amendment contemplated ascertaining the views of the Liberal leadership:

> Mr. Sexton asks me before we have obtained this information to bind myself practically to accept without any further consideration of the question the definite judgement of the party upon the matter. Now, I wish to say with regard to that proposal at once that, having placed myself in the hands of my friends in regard to this matter at the commencement, I could not agree to surrender my responsibility or any part of my responsibility ... My position has been granted to me, not because I am the mere leader of a Parliamentary party, but because I am the leader of the Irish nation *(hear hear)*. It has been granted to me on account of the services which I have rendered in building up this party, in assimilating prejudices, in smoothing differences of opinion, and in keeping together the discordant elements of our race within the bounds of moderation all over the world. And you, gentlemen, know, and I know, that there is no man living if I am gone, who could succeed in reconciling the feelings of the Irish people to the provisions of the Hawarden proposals *(hear hear)*. I have explained to you why I cannot surrender my responsibilities in this matter . . . I claim that you, since you wish to take from me the responsibility which today is mine and which can only be surrendered by my act *(cheers)*, that you should state, for the information of your constituents and for my information, what your definite judgement is with regard to the two important questions of the control of the constabulary and the land question *(cheers)*.

Parnell thus proposed his first resolution. He proceeded to characterise Gladstone as 'an unrivalled sophist', and to observe ominously: 'My responsibility ceases when your responsibility commences. Consider well before you assume it. I will gladly divest myself of it'. He then outlined his second resolution, and stated in conclusion that if the party adopted his resolutions, and after the interview contemplated by his second resolution resolved that the views of the Liberal leadership conformed to the principles contained in the first resolution, 'then I shall place myself in the hands of my friends and retire from the position of the chairman of the party'. The reference to 'my friends' is here crucial: it signalled that Parnell's offer was not made voluntarily, but in deference to the insistence of his parliamentary supporters. Here, as elsewhere in the early stages of the split, Parnell's actions were shaped to the necessity to avert wholesale defections from his own parliamentary camp. He proclaimed his refusal to abdicate his responsibilities, but professed his willingness to permit a formal assumption of those responsibilities by the party.

The ensuing debate was dominated by the majority's querying of his sincerity, and its determination to establish that his undertaking was unequivocal and binding. While Healy correctly discerned a clear menace in his speech, Parnell's opponents did not attend to the precise terms of his commitment. He committed himself to retiring from the chairmanship: he did not commit himself to supporting the decision of the party. He left open his future policy, and reserved to himself the critical decision as to whether his retirement would be on the basis of boasting that he had secured the points in contention in the Home Rule Bill, or advising the nation of his dissent from the judgement of the party. He thereby left open the menacing possibility of his retiring under protest, impugning the sufficiency of the Liberal assurances and the judgement and capacity of the party. He was clearly signalling that he had maintained his defiance of Gladstone's 'dictation' until compelled by an alliance of his parliamentary allies and opponents to retire, so commending himself to 'advanced' nationalists and others outside the party.

Parnell contrived to couple minimum concession with maximum freedom of action. Even if the majority of the party adjudged the Liberal assurances satisfactory, and thus procured his withdrawal from the leadership, Parnell had still reserved to himself the last word. The finality of the decision of the party was thereby practically nullified, leaving Parnell in a formidable position to assail the adequacy of the Liberal guarantees, underwritten by the threat to resign under protest, or even to maintain a minoritarian campaign against almost the entirety of the party. It is most unlikely that he would have gone to the latter extreme. A resignation under protest, bowing to the inevitability of an alliance between the majority and a large body of his own allies, would have conformed to Parnell's fierce ethic of power — his sense of his 'responsibilities' — so that he could contemplate his withdrawal from the leadership with cold and lucid equanimity. It was an astonishing, even terrifying, demonstration of Parnell's acumen, and his uncanny tenacity under threat.

When Parnell finished, a momentary conference ensued between Healy and Sexton, in which Healy rejected Sexton's suggestion that they adjourn for an hour, and Sexton told Healy to reply. Healy rose and delivered a powerful speech accusing Parnell of cynical insincerity, which marked a sensible increase in the bitterness of the debates. The gravamen of the speech was an attack upon Parnell for his refusal 'to submit this matter to the judgement of the party', his failure to undertake by 'a straight answer' to be bound by the majority, and for shifting the ground of the Clancy amendment: 'Do you think we are children?' Parnell interrupted that his resolutions constituted his response, and by them he would stand or fall before the country. With Healy's retort to Parnell's interruption, the decorum of the debate for the first time fractured, and the party lurched closer to schism:

> Mr. Healy: Then you will fall Mr. Parnell *(loud cheers)* ; and now that both sides have made up their minds what is the use of further debate? *(cheers and interruptions)*.
>
> Mr. Clancy: Away with him. Away with him.

Mr. John O'Connor: Crucify him *(cries of 'Oh, oh')*.

Mr. Condon: I think that is an expression that should not be made use of *(hear hear)* ...

Mr. T. M. Healy: ... Now that a speech appealing to what a certain gentleman known to us all [Captain O'Shea], called in the Special Commission Court the hillside men, has been delivered *(cheers)*, our position is plain. It is unmistakable.

Mr. Parnell: Hear, hear.

Mr. Healy: It is unmistakable *(hear, hear)*. Let us come then to the issue *(cheers)*. You declare the country is for you — go to it *(cheers)*. Go to it *(renewed cheers)*.

Mr. Parnell: So we will *(counter-cheering)*.

Healy then provokingly and skilfully led Parnell through the terms of his endorsement of Gladstone on the occasion of the banquet on Parnell's birthday in June. When Parnell and his supporters chorused in reply to his question as to what had broken off the Liberal-Nationalist alliance, 'Gladstone's letter', Healy brutally riposted that the alliance had perished 'in the stench of the divorce court'. Nothing had transpired since Parnell had lauded Gladstone to change Healy's opinion of the English leadership: 'Nothing has occurred since these dates to turn me back into that course of hatred towards the English people out of which you led me'. Healy concluded by calling the Parnellite bluff, with a rallying cry to the anti-Parnellites to take the fight to the country:

I shall maintain my position. I shall invite my countrymen to do the same *(cheers)*, and I declare my belief is that though you, a Frankenstein, who having created this party, is able and determined to destroy it, I say you will discover that there is sufficient civic virtue and public courage among the men who are your comrades to prevent for their country any such hopeless and hapless consummation *(cheers)* ... we will go to our people and we will tell them what are the real issues in this matter, for though hitherto some of them have been covered up and enclosed, we shall not shirk, and I shall not shirk, stating them broadly and openly to the people, and with the people be the verdict *(loud cheers and counter-cheers)*. If you sir should go down you are only one man gone. Heads of greater leaders have been stricken on the block before now for Ireland.

Col. Nolan: Not by their own friends, not by their own allies *(cheers)*.

The intensification of the debate was reflected in the fact that Parnell interrupted Healy forty-four times, interruptions which Healy correctly judged to be the result of method and not of passion. In Healy's speech there was a clear foretaste of the split in the country. To the menace which Healy sensed in Parnell's speech, he responded by a strategy of polarisation, determinedly impugning Parnell's credentials as a constitutional politician. If Healy's speech was, as Sexton asserted, 'impregnated and possessed by the spirit of a great constitutional argument', that argument was infused with a partisan purpose. The split's bitter dialectic was under way.

After a more temperate speech from Sexton, Parnell skilfully ceded ground without compromising his underlying position, coolly pronouncing the dispute a storm in a teacup. To Sexton's urging that he withdraw his resolutions, Parnell declared that he had not moved them: having staked out his position, he had no need to do so. He continued: 'But I shall propose that the party should express its opinion upon the answer by resolution. I want simply to have an expression from the party either first or last, so that the responsibility should be thrown off my shoulders'. Parnell confirmed to Sexton that he would resign in the event of the majority by vote deciding that the answer of the Liberal leaders was satisfactory, adding, only half-disingenuously, 'You might have had that at the beginning, if you had not had Mr. Healy's speech'.[18] The original Clancy resolution was duly carried with the modification that a group comprising Parnell, McCarthy, Sexton, Healy, Redmond and Leamy, together with the two whips, be instructed to ascertain the views of the Liberal leadership. Only Barry and Chance voted against.

Gladstone's reaction must be set against the background of hardening Liberal opposition to Parnell, and dismay at what was perceived as the pusillanimousness of the anti-Parnellites. The spectacle of the Irish party torn between Parnell's mastery and Liberal pressure had already ominously revived the old, pre-Parnellite perception, of the Irish party as ineffectual, irresolute and suggestible. Even among hostile observers in England, there was an involuntary deepening of the perception of Parnell as the sole effective leader of the Irish party, which his fierce seizing of the initiative had affirmed.

Sensing he was in a minority, Unionist critics were quick to laud Parnell's 'unflinching stand against the pack of curs that are yapping round him, bent on his destruction'.[19] A reluctant admiration for Parnell extended to within the Liberal camp. The fiercely anti-Parnellite W. T. Stead wrote on 2 December that Parnell displayed throughout the crisis 'the supreme qualities which have enabled him to write his name indelibly on the history of his native land'. He had taken the chair in Committee Room 15 with 'that indomitable courage which has characterised him at all crises of his career'.[20]

At the end of the first day's debate the young David Lloyd George wrote to his wife that 'the Irishmen seem utterly unable to settle Parnell'. He was told by Cunninghame Graham (the MP for North Lanarkshire, and the only Radical publicly to support Parnell) that 'Parnell wiped his boots on them right and left at the meeting and that they stay there like a pack of dumb dogs'. Lloyd George, an admirer of Healy's style, registered his disbelief: 'I can hardly credit that when I know that daredevils like Healy are in the opposition. I don't believe he would stand any of Parnell's insolence'.[21]

On the eve of the Irish party meeting Harcourt had harangued Gladstone on the inadvisability of being seen to make any concession to Parnell, warning: 'It is a very dangerous thing to approach an expiring cat ... He is as lawyers say "in mercy" which means that he has none to expect, and if it were suspected even that you had let him march out with the honours of war it would create a very bad effect upon the public mind'. He insisted that it was essential that a decision was obtained on Monday, the first day of the party's meeting, adding that James Stuart was of the view that 'if P.'s friends could engage you in pourparlers it might be an excuse for postponing the final stroke'.[22] With the Clancy amendment Harcourt's bombardment of Gladstone took place daily. He warned on 3 December against any dealings whatever, commenting that, even if Parnell were to retire from the leadership of the Irish party, he would remain the head of the National League, 'rendering his professed abnegation of the Parliamentary lead a mere farce'.[23] By the following day Harcourt was so incensed as to discern in the Clancy amendment a collusive device between the two Irish factions at the expense of the Liberals ('what they call on the racecourse a "put up" job'). He warned Gladstone against embarking on negotiations before Parnell's retirement (an event he considered highly unlikely) so as to permit him to retire on his own terms: 'If so he will not only have triumphed over Healy and Co. but over us'.[24] He complained that 'Parnell's unscrupulous mendacity opposed to the miserable feebleness and vacillation of his antagonists gives him an immense advantage'.[25]

The debates in Committee Room 15 dragged on. Liberal exasperation mounted. Alfred Robbins for the *Birmingham Daily Post* quoted the comment of 'one of the keenest Radical wirepullers', probably Stanhope, that 'every hour's delay is an hour's gain for Parnell'.[26] James Stuart wrote a letter to Gladstone which is undated, but almost certainly refers to the Clancy amendment of 4 December. Stuart wrote that he had received the following note which evidently emanated from within Committee Room 15 from 'a friend', probably Healy: '2.35 p.m.: P. has exposed his *mala fides*, and we have determined to accept none of his compromises'. Stuart added by way of comment: 'All eaten up 3 hours later'.[27]

Healy looked to the Liberal assurances to resolve the dilemma of the Irish party, and used his good offices to ensure that they would be forthcoming. The influential Liberal James Stansfeld reported to Gladstone in the late evening of 4 December after a meeting with Healy. Cognisant of Liberal reservations, Healy was defensive ('He says the press is wrong; that we don't understand the situation; that Parnell is "cornered" and not they'), and anxious to ensure the success of the initiative. He wanted Gladstone to receive the deputation, and sought to concert the Liberal response with the anti-Parnellite strategy: 'They do not ask you to say anything about the judiciary. They want you to say two things only'. Those were that the agrarian situation could be left as it was, but would require to be fully dealt with by the imperial parliament, or failing time and opportunity there, by the Irish parliament; secondly the time period for the dissolution of the RIC was to be fixed in the Home Rule Bill, rather than subject to dissolution by the Lord Lieutenant as under the 1886 Bill.

Stansfeld's note suggests there had been a prior communication by Gladstone to the anti-Parnellite leadership. He wrote that 'they would be helped by some repetition of the concluding sentiments of your letter': as neither Gladstone's letter to the whips of earlier that day, nor his famous letter to Morley had concluded with sympathetic sentiments of any sort, it must be concluded that Gladstone had written to one of the anti-Parnellite leaders, probably McCarthy. From the tenor of Stansfeld's note, and from what is known about Gladstone's thinking from other sources, it may be surmised that the communication from Gladstone had advised of the embarrassment which the Clancy amendment would create for the Liberal leadership, rather than endeavoured to elucidate what form of assurance would satisfy the Irish party.

The conclusion of Stansfeld's note conveyed an attempt by Healy to overcome Gladstone's reservations: 'That you may understand the situation, they would beg you not to receive the deputation before reading the report of their meeting in tomorrow's paper'. Healy thus looked to the firm resistance proffered to the further resolutions contemplated by Parnell, and the vehemence of his own attack on Parnell, to impress Gladstone and those of his colleagues who believed that the anti-Parnellites were failing to stand up to Parnell. Ironically, Parnell probably inspired this last suggestion: at the end of the meeting, seated at a table with Parnellite and anti-Parnellite members amicably discussing the approach to Gladstone as if nothing untoward had occurred, Parnell had observed that they should go to Gladstone that evening, before he had read the following day's newspaper reports of Healy's speech 'over which he would be licking his lips'.[28]

The Clancy amendment took its doomed course. Gladstone first took a point of protocol, objecting that it entailed meeting an arbitrarily nominated group comprising himself, Harcourt and Morley. This was met by a revised request by the whips of the Irish party for a consultation with Gladstone alone or accompanied by any of his colleagues he wished. Gladstone then, in the unkind words of the Dublin *Daily Express*, 'after petting and pouting in a most ridiculous manner, like an elderly coquette', agreed to see the deputation of the Irish party. Healy, Sexton, Redmond and Edmund Leamy met Gladstone the following morning, Friday 5 December. Gladstone, reading from a written memorandum, refused to address the questions in issue. He raised as a 'preliminary bar' the linkage of the issues of policy to the conflicting versions of what transpired at Hawarden. He further made the argument which could admit of no compromise, namely that his authority from the Liberal party did not authorise him to open a policy discussion 'in connection with the question of leadership'.

The party was duly reconvened and substituted for the Clancy amendment a resolution which omitted all reference to the Hawarden interview. Gladstone, however, responded to the renewed request for an interview from the Irish whips with a letter late that evening whereby, having ascertained the views of his colleagues, he declined to treat of the two points raised 'in connection with the leadership of the Irish party'. The Liberal leadership thus firmly refused to provide assurances in relation to the issue of land and police in the context of the dispute over the Irish leadership.[29] So ended the Clancy amendment.

If Gladstone was inclined to give some form of assurances, he was overborne by the opposition of his colleagues. The version of events conveyed to Healy three days later almost certainly exaggerated the difference of opinion with the Liberal leadership: 'Gladstone tore his ex-Cabinet asunder on Friday night trying to get them to give "assurances" before Parnell was deposed. He almost cried, Campbell-Bannerman says, talking over the result "for those poor fellows, Healy and Sexton", after the fight we made'.[30]

Throughout the evening of 5 December Healy wrote intermittently to his wife a running commentary on the course of events, and a self-defence against her remonstrances over his support of the Clancy amendment. A portion of the letter omitted from his published memoirs reveals Healy's state of mind and physically depleted condition on the eve of the break-up of the party:

> I have just heard of your telegram to John Barry, and am glad you are such a stalwart, but you must remember there are forty-three others besides myself sharing the responsibility. Also that Parnell only required eight deserters from our ranks to turn his minority of twenty-nine into a majority for himself.
> Of course our men are solid, and not a hair of one of them has turned; still, we must not only be right, but we must appear to be right with our misguided countrymen. It will be a miracle if we succeed.
> There is a rumour tonight of a Dissolution next month, which I hope is true, as it would steady our people. If we fail the men most largely responsible for the mischief that will follow, as they backed Parnell all through are John Redmond and Dr. Kenny.
> Although it is not six o'clock the House is up, as nobody takes any interest in the proceedings of the Commons. In consequence our meeting is postponed until noon tomorrow, when I hope we shall be able to make an end of this business one way or the other. I don't think we can carry it on any further after Saturday, or that we could hold our men in London, so something must be done to terminate the racking suspense. I don't suppose I shall ever be the same man after this week. None of us will, perhaps. I should like to go away with you for a change. I am so tired.[31]

The letter was written before Gladstone's final refusal to offer the assurances contemplated by the Clancy amendment. Whatever his response, the debates had run their course and would not be prolonged beyond the following day.

Richard Power, one of the whips, brought Gladstone's final reply at 11.00 in the evening to the Westminster Palace Hotel, where the deputation, together with Parnell and McCarthy, assembled. Parnell asked the four members of the deputation to draw up and sign a minute of their interview, which they did. Sexton and Healy urged Parnell to retire. Parnell said that he would need the night to consider, and asked that they would return to see him the following morning. At 2 a.m. Healy and Sexton left to inform a caucus of anti-Parnellite members of Gladstone's response.

On the following morning, Saturday 6 December, Parnell told Healy and Sexton that the dictates of his 'responsibility' did not permit him to retire. A bizarre valediction followed. Parnell shook hands with Sexton and Healy. He took Healy aside and assured him that there was no truth in the story that he had fumbled with a revolver when speaking on Thursday, that he had not carried a revolver for the previous two years, nor would he think of bringing such a weapon into a meeting of his countrymen. So ended Healy's personal relations with Parnell.[32]

On Saturday 6 December 1890 the unbroken Irish party assembled for the last time. Much time was consumed in the preparation, at Parnell's insistence, of a formal report of the delegates. The meeting resumed in the afternoon, when Redmond read the memorandum. The party was now poised for schism. In the restrained partisanship of J. M. Tuohy's description from the *Freeman's Journal:*

> ... it was apparent from the demeanour of both sides that the crisis was at hand. There was an undercurrent of excitement that was with difficulty suppressed during the reading of the correspondence with Mr. Gladstone. Mr. Parnell looked a shade paler than usual, but quite self-controlled and determined, and with his inscrutable eyes fixed upon the desk before him, he smiled grimly to himself ... Mr. Healy was sitting back in his chair with his arms folded, with the air of one whose mind was made up and who was waiting for something which he expected to occur soon.[33]

When Redmond completed the reading of the memorandum, the unnatural calm ended, as the suppressed passions of the week broke through. William Abraham stepped forward to propose the resolution terminating Parnell's tenure of the chair. Parnell called upon John O'Connor, who had begun to rise to propose a motion condemning Gladstone's refusal to meet the delegates. The composure of Parnell and of the party cracked in a scene of exceptional bitterness. Pandemonium ensued for a quarter of an hour, as Parnell, 'showing signs of intense excitement',[34] and insisting on calling O'Connor, lost control of the meeting. Abraham advanced to within a few feet of Parnell and bawled out his motion, throwing the slip of paper on which it was written over the shoulder of Healy, who passed it to McCarthy. Parnell had already risen, and when McCarthy rose, holding in his hand Abraham's resolution, he snatched the paper and thrust it crumpled into his pocket, exclaiming repeatedly to McCarthy, 'You shall not dare to usurp my authority'. With uplifted arms and clenched fists, his face drawn and white, Parnell declared, 'Until the party deposes me from the chair I am your chairman', at which Barry cried, 'You are not our chairman'. Barry called Parnell 'a dirty little trickster', while Healy shouted at Parnell, 'Give us back our document'.

Parnell, erect, was confronted by the break-up of the party. Tuohy's account for the *Freeman's Journal* froze Parnell at the moment of the dissolution of his authority, fixedly contemplating the ebbing of his power, as if instantaneously subsuming Parnell into the statuesque figure of his myth:

> Mr. Parnell remained standing at his desk, looking straight before him, his face deathly pale, his eyes burning with a fierce light, and an expression of fixed and immovable resolution in his whole aspect that was more like a statue than a thing of flesh and blood, while he continued to cry, 'Order, order', 'I call Mr. John O'Connor', 'Silence, silence', in a crescendo scale.

As Parnell reiterated that he was the leader until deposed, Healy taunted: 'Allow us to depose you'. When Parnell again declined to put the motion, Healy declared that he would put it himself. The anti-Parnellite Arthur O'Connor made himself heard and urged his colleagues to respect Parnell so long as he retained the chair. There was a brief respite. O'Connor spoke, while Parnell conversed apologetically with McCarthy, smoothing out the crumpled paper on which Abraham's resolution was written which he returned to McCarthy. Parnell then turned sideways in his chair and tensely scanned the *Freeman's Journal*. It was Healy who shattered the fragile peace with an interjection whose obviousness served to accentuate its offensiveness. In the course of O'Connor's speech Redmond interjected, to cheers and counter-cheers, that Gladstone was 'the master of the party'. Healy rose, and leaning forward, with his hands on the table, 'jerked forward his long neck, his teeth showing in the sneer that parted his lips', scornfully to enquire: 'Who is to be the mistress of the party?' The scene which ensued is described in Michael MacDonagh's later account:

> Parnell violently flung the newspaper away and turned quickly round to the table. A spasm of pain contracted his face. He was again in a raging fury. Twice he half rose from his seat and twice fell back again. Then, grasping the arms of his chair, he raised himself up. He seemed so clearly bent upon striking Healy that a few of Healy's friends rapidly moved up and clustered round him. Among them was Arthur O'Connor. 'I appeal to my friend the chairman', said the suave O'Connor, as if interceding for Healy. 'Better appeal to your own friends', cried Parnell. His right arm was fully extended and his clenched hand was close to Healy's face. In his voice was that vibration which came from the quivering of his nerves. 'Better appeal', he exclaimed, 'to that cowardly little scoundrel there who dares in an assembly of Irishmen to insult a woman'.

McCarthy stopped pulling at his beard, and Sexton drew back his chair a little so as not to prevent Parnell striking Healy who 'sat with folded arms, unmoved either by Parnell's retort or threat, or the hostile roar that hurtled about his head'. The blow did not fall, and Parnell sank back in his chair, exhausted and breathing heavily.

Healy was impassive in his isolation. He made no reply to Parnell's attack, being, as he confided to his wife, 'content with the thrust, which will stick as long as his cry about Gladstone's "dictation" continues'.[35] He had given a forewarning of the brutal retaliatory scheme of his rhetoric in Ireland. A nervous peace was restored. When Parnell observed that Abraham's resolution could not be construed as an amendment to the O'Connor resolution, thereby signalling the further indefinite prolongation of the meeting, Healy cried 'Bravo, Bravo', to which Parnell responded 'Mr. Healy, I will not stand very much more from you'. Shortly afterwards, McCarthy rose, and after a short speech left Committee Room 15 at the head of forty-four anti-Parnellites. As they left, some members of the sundered party shook hands and said their farewells. The circumstances of the break-up of the party gave the successor parties their terms of mutual abuse. The Parnellites reviled the anti-Parnellites as 'seceders', while the anti-Parnellites condemned the Parnellites as 'pledgebreakers' in not abiding by the view of the majority. For the anti-Parnellites there was little alternative. As Healy later declared, 'Unless we had deposed Mr. Parnell in the way we did he would have kept us there proposing resolutions like repeating decimals until doomsday'.[36]

So, with an almost somnambulistic air of unreality, which only the fierceness of the split in Ireland was to dispel, the *cérémonie des adieux* of the Irish Parliamentary Party was enacted. Thus dissolved in tragic rancour the Irish party, which had been characterised by a compactness and effectiveness unprecedented in Irish history and Westminster politics alike, and was never to be reconstituted with the same fierce discipline of purpose.

The anti-Parnellite members moved swiftly to formalise their position. Proceeding from the Committee Room downstairs to the Conference Room, they passed a resolution declaring Parnell's tenure of the chair terminated. Healy proposed and Sexton seconded McCarthy's election as sessional chairman of the party. The new chairman, however, was to submit to a conciliar form of leadership as it was resolved that a committee of eight be appointed to exercise jointly with the chairman the powers and to discharge the functions hitherto attached to the chairmanship. The committee elected on the Monday following comprised William Abraham, Healy, Arthur O'Connor, T. P. O'Connor, and David Sheehy, together with the absent John Dillon and William O'Brien.[37] Later that evening the majority assembled again in Arthur O'Connor's chambers and passed a series of resolutions, the most important of which provided for the immediate moving of the writ for the vacant seat of North Kilkenny, and constituted

a committee to establish a daily national newspaper to challenge the
Parnellite *Freeman's Journal*.[38] The following day Healy advised his mili-
tant spouse, 'There is exultation in the Party at getting rid of Parnell'.[39]
The anti-Parnellites established in Dublin an interim organisation under
Healyite auspices, the 'National Committee in Sustainment of the Irish
Parliamentary Party', described by William Martin Murphy as 'a commit-
tee of public safety, to meet Mr. Parnell on his mad career', which solicited
the adhesion of 'clergymen and gentlemen'.[40]

The Parnellite members were summoned to the reconvened meeting of
the majority on Monday 8 December, when Parnell was on patrol against
defectors from his own ranks. Harold Frederic despatched to the *New York
Times* a suggestive description of the fallen leader in the tense hiatus between the schism at Westminster and the translation of the split to Ireland.
He had espied the 'weird figure' of Parnell roaming the passages in the vicini-
ty of Committee Room 15 and the library 'questing, suspicious, watchful
and determined ... an anxious jealous shepherd of his flock, roaming through
the passages like a sentinel, to see that none went over to the enemy'. He
described Parnell smilingly greeting the McCarthys *père et fils:* 'What a spectacle it was! And then as they passed away the impress of cold, ashen hatred
settled upon his haggard face, and again he went on patrol'.[41]

After the meeting, the anti-Parnellites entered the Commons in a ritual
show of strength. They occupied the first four benches below the gangway
where the Irish party sat, occupying seats where Parnellites habitually sat,
save that of Parnell, where he had taken the precaution of placing his
card.[42] Robbins noted that the fact that the Parnellites and anti-Parnellites
'met and chatted in their accustomed friendly manner' belied the depth
of the bitterness between them. With the immediate moving by John Deasy,
the anti-Parnellite whip, of the writ for North Kilkenny, the split was engaged. The anti-Parnellites thereby asserted their claim to be *the* Irish
Parliamentary Party, and moved the field of battle to Ireland.[43] As the
party dispersed from Westminster, its members to meet again in the bitter
acrimony of the North Kilkenny campaign, its obituaries were already being written.

> The great Irish faction which for six years has played such a part in our history
> and which captured Mr. Gladstone is no more [wrote the *Economist*]. There
> are only Irishmen as of old more or less hostile or discontented, but unable
> to agree as to what they precisely want, or which leader represents their
> wants'.

After the schism in Room 15, Parnell told the *Evening Telegraph* representative, 'Tell them I will fight to the end'. He was as good as his word.[44]

The course of the split in Ireland would follow the pattern of Committee Room 15. There, Parnell had outmanœuvred the opposition to him,
and had lost. Carrying the contest to the country, Parnell continued to

demonstrate his mastery, but victory eluded him. The widening rift between demonstrated political capacity and electoral success accounted for
much of Parnell's exasperated bewilderment, shrewdly heightened by
Healy's goading rhetoric, which asserted the redundancy — even the comical excess — of his strenuous statescraft.

As the hostilities commenced at Kilkenny, the Archbishop of Dublin
moved to close the rift. An 'entirely private and personal' meeting took
place between Walsh and Edward Byrne, the staunchly Parnellite editor
of the *Freeman's Journal*, on 16 December. A twenty-two point memorandum of that date headed 'Notes of Conversation' embodied Walsh's suggested basis for a resolution of the split.[45] The tenor of the memorandum
was strikingly sanguine. Walsh's starting-point was that whereas, in the
case of the Pigott forgeries (in the exposure of which he had played an
important part) there had been a public statement from Parnell of his competence to rebut the charges, which had permitted the archbishop and others
to stand by Parnell without exposing themselves to the charge of condon-
ing crime, in the divorce case there had been no such statement: 'The
statements made by others on Mr. P's behalf or in his defence in the present case are now declared not to have been made authoritatively'.

This line of argument was entirely consistent with the elaborately
qualified formula with which Walsh had broken silence on 30 November,
after the publication of the Parnell manifesto: 'If the Irish leader would
not, or could not, give a public assurance that his honour was unsullied,
the party that takes him or retains him as its leader can no longer count
on the support of the bishops of Ireland'.[46]

He continued to believe it possible that Parnell could have 'a satisfactory reply on the moral question'. He emphasised the extent of his 'friendly disposition', observing that so long as it was 'feasible for him to do any
good on Mr. P's side he had endeavoured to assist in that direction'. The
declaration of the hierarchy of 3 December had been based on the uncontradicted evidence and verdict of the divorce court, and delayed until the
last possible moment to afford Parnell an opportunity of meeting the difficulty either by resigning or by 'a reply satisfactory on moral grounds to
the case made in Court on behalf of Captain O'Shea'.

What Walsh proposed was an interview with Parnell immediately after
the Kilkenny election. If, after that interview, Walsh was unable to declare
Parnell's explanation satisfactory, Parnell would voluntarily retire on
patriotic grounds 'and with such provisos as the personages may agree upon
in their conversation'. If on the other hand Walsh was satisfied, he would
issue 'a Manifesto' [*sic*] declaring that after an interview with 'the Irish
Leader', he was satisfied as to the completeness of Parnell's answer to the
charges against him. Unspecified steps would then be taken to resolve the
'very grave difficulty' created by Parnell's account of the Hawarden interview with Gladstone. Yet more remarkably, Walsh indicated it would then

be his duty and the duty of the other bishops publicly to declare 'that the whole foundation on which the judgement expressed in their address and taken away', without impugning the earlier address, which had been 'based upon the verdict of a Court of law, the propriety of which had not in any authoritative public way been challenged by Mr. P.'

It is not clear what Walsh considered to be 'a satisfactory reply on the moral question', but it must be taken to have been equated with Parnell's assurance that his honour was unsullied, referred to in Walsh's first public statement on 30 November: presumably that the O'Shea marriage had already broken down and that Parnell had not deceived Captain O'Shea. One ground of mitigation was excluded: Walsh made clear that 'of course' connivance on the part of Captain O'Shea could not temper his judgement on the moral question. In response to a specific question put by Byrne, as to whether Parnell's marriage to Katharine O'Shea would present an insuperable bar to a final settlement on the lines indicated, Walsh 'stated that this in itself could not be so regarded'. Walsh's initiative revealed an extraordinary degree of goodwill towards Parnell, an intimation of the disaster which the split in the Irish party portended, and an anxiety to maintain the heroic axis of collaboration between the hierarchy and the party leadership which had evolved during the period of Parnell's leadership:

> ... the Archbp. is convinced of the necessity above all other political considerations of a Leader in the Irish Party of recognised political pre-eminence amongst his colleagues. The Archbp. deems this essential to keep the Party from being split into sections: he looks upon it as unquestionable that Mr. P. supposing the present difficulties he got over would hold, as he had hitherto held that pre-eminent position.

Byrne left for Kilkenny that evening.

The archbishop's proposals coupled a sophisticated view of the moral aspect of the case with astounding political naivety. Apart altogether from the peculiarity of the spectacle of the Protestant Parnell seeking a form of absolution from a Catholic prelate, a sphinx-like pronouncement from Walsh would not have sufficed to satisfy Parnell's moral critics in Ireland and would have further inflamed the 'nonconformist conscience', as well as exciting amused Conservative derision. In the unlikely event that Walsh's initiative was not repudiated by his brother bishops, it would have further embroiled the episcopacy with the Vatican. It would from Parnell's point of view have jeopardised the prospects for the O'Shea divorce going through, by almost certainly eliciting the intervention of the Queen's Proctor. In proposing to constitute himself at once a nationalist arbitrator and the confessor of a Protestant leader, Walsh had overreached himself. His *démarche* represented the last, and most striking, moment of quivering equipoise in the concordat between Church and nation which Parnell's fall was to shatter.

A letter from Croke of 16 December alerted Walsh to the isolation in which his proposals placed him: 'I do not like [William] O'Brien's attitude at all for some days past in reference to the fallen chief. He desires to patch up some sort of compromise. We cannot compromise with Parnell. He is dead and buried so far as leadership in Ireland is concerned'.[47]

Walsh had stipulated that the proposal would have to be accepted before the Kilkenny poll and even before the result became clear, and so looked to an immediate response from Parnell. In the absence of a reply the following day, his first flush of optimism waned, and he cabled Byrne at Kilkenny: 'Felt bound to give your suggestion every chance but anticipated its failure cannot of course give any sanction to further proceeding'.[48]

In an elegant, courteous, and unyielding reply on 18 December Parnell explained, in an evident allusion to the constraints placed upon him by divorce proceedings, that 'it is not at present possible for me to speak fully upon that subject, even to Your Grace'. He added that he did not wish Walsh 'to suppose that this reticence need be permanent as after a brief period I hope to be in a position to speak confidently'. He would always remember 'the kindness which has induced Your Grace to consent to receiving any confidential communication from me upon this subject'.[49] So ended the split's most bizarre peace initiative.

References

1 *F.J.*, 9 Oct. 1891, London Correspondence.
2 *I.W.I.*, 7 Oct. 1893, 'Parnell's Resolution'.
3 *U.I.*, 10 Oct. 1891, 'Some Recollections of the Chief, by One Who Knew Him'.
4 MacDonagh, *Home Rule Movement*, pp. 207-08. The Irish party had met until 1 Mar. 1886 in the Conference Room of the House of Commons (Irish Party minutes, 22 Feb. 1886 and 1 Mar. 1886).
5 *Letters and Leaders*, i. p. 330.
6 R. M. Praed, note of conversation with Justin McCarthy, 4 Dec. 1890; Justin McCarthy to R. M. Praed, telegram, 1 Dec. 1890: McCarthy and Praed, *Book of Memories*, Draft.
7 1 Dec. 1890, Healy to Erina Healy, *Letters and Leaders*, i. p. 331.
8 *F.J.*, 2 Dec. 1890.
9 Robbins, *Parnell*, pp. 168-69; *B.D.P.*, 2 Dec. 1890.
10 Healy to Erina Healy, 30 Nov. 1890, *Letters and Leaders*, i. p. 329; Healy to Erina Healy, 1 Dec. 1890, *Letters and Leaders*, i. p. 331.
11 Healy to Erina Healy, 1 Dec. 1890, *Letters and Leaders*, Proofs, B 134, deleted *Letters and Leaders*, i. p. 331.
12 Healy to Erina Healy, 2 Dec. 1890, *Letters and Leaders,* Proofs, B 135, deleted *Letters and Leaders*, i. p. 332.
13 *F.J.*, 3 Dec. 1890; MacDonagh, *Home Rule Movement*, pp. 213-15; Donal Sullivan, *Room 15*, p. 28.

14 *F.J.*, 5 Dec. 1890; T. P. O'Connor, *Memoirs*, ii. p. 224. The following day C. P. Fitzgerald would taunt Healy with this initial response to the Clancy amendment: 'You cried over it' (*F.J.*, 5 Dec. 1890). Harrington in Chicago noted in his diary, 'The report of the morning shows Healy's hysterical fits of insolence to his chief, followed by tearful professions of love. Such a spectacle in a public man is disgusting'; Harrington Diary, entry for 5 Dec. 1890, in Leamy, *Parnell's Faithful Few*, p. 232; see also *F.J.*, 1 May 1891, speech of Harrington at North Dock Ward NL.

15 Donal Sullivan, *Room 15*, p. 10, *Letters and Leaders*, i. p. 333; O'Connor, *Memoirs*, ii. p. 212.

16 *F.J.*, 4 Dec. 1891

17 C. C. O'Brien, *Parnell and his Party*, pp. 337-40.

18 *F.J.*, 5 Dec. 1890; Sullivan, *Room 15*, pp. 30-36; Healy, 'Rise and Fall', p. 198.

19 *St. Stephen's Review*, 6 Dec. 1891.

20 *Review of Reviews*, Dec. 1890, W. T. Stead, 'The Story of an Incident in the Home Rule Case', 2 Dec. 1890.

21 Lloyd George to Margaret George, 1 Dec. 1890, in *Family Letters of Lloyd George*, ed. Kenneth Morgan (London and Cardiff, 1973).

22 Harcourt to Gladstone, 30 Nov. 1890, Gladstone Papers, BM Add. MS 44201 f. 43.

23 Harcourt to Gladstone, 3 Dec. 1890, Gladstone Papers, BM Add. MS 44201, f. 45.

24 Harcourt to Gladstone, 4 Dec. 1890, Gladstone Papers, BM Add. MS 46649; see also Lyons, *Parnell*, pp. 524-25.

25 Harcourt to Gladstone, n.d., Gladstone Papers, BM Add. MS 56449 f.169 (perhaps postscript to Harcourt to Gladstone, 7 Dec. 1890, Gladstone Papers BM Add. MS 56449 f.167).

26 *B.D.P.*, 3 Dec. 1890, London Correspondence.

27 Stuart to Gladstone, n.d., BM Add. MS 56449, f. 112.

28 James Stansfeld to Gladstone, 4 Dec. 1890, Gladstone Papers, BM Add. MS 56449 f.70; Healy to Erina Healy, 4 Dec. 1890, *Letters and Leaders*, i. p. 333. Healy, flattered and nonplussed by Parnell's comment, wrote to his wife: 'I never knew of such a man, nor ever read of such a man'.

29 *F.J.*, 8 Dec. 1890; *D.E.*, 8 Dec. 1890; *The Parnellite Split: or the Disruption of the Irish Parliamentary Party*, from *The Times* (London, 1891), pp. 158-68.

30 Healy to Erina Healy, 8 Dec. 1890, *Letters and Leaders*, i. p. 339; see generally Lyons, *Parnell*, pp. 524-26; Larkin, *Fall*, pp. 142-45.

31 Healy to Erina Healy, 5 Dec. 1890, *Letters and Leaders*, Proofs B 136, omitted *Letters and Leaders*, i. p. 335.

32 Donal Sullivan, *Room 15*, pp. 38-39; Healy to Erina Healy, 7 Dec. 1890, *Letters and Leaders*, Proofs, B 138. This account of the leave-taking is omitted from the letter as published in *Letters and Leaders*, but substantially reproduced in the body of text at p. 336. It is a measure of the underlying tensions of the split that Healy's suspicions were not altogether allayed. The letter continued: 'Kilbride, however, gave me a thing called a "Skullcracker", which he took out of a topcoat near where Parnell was sitting, but he won't say whose the coat was. I returned it to him, but am promised it as a souvenir when things have quieted a little. I have since learnt it was Henry Campbell's'.

33 *F.J.*, 8 Dec. 1890. The account which follows is based on the reports of the *Freeman's Journal*, including J. M. Tuohy's London correspondence (*F.J.*, 8 Dec. 1890), on the account of Michael MacDonagh, present as a journalist, written in 1920 (MacDonagh, *Home Rule Movement*, pp. 215-21), and on Donal Sullivan's account (*Room 15*, pp. 35-43). Tuohy conceded the insufficiency of the *Freeman's* official report: 'The speeches cannot be relied on to convey a

thorough conception of the tone and temper of the proceedings, when speeches and argument gave place to general excitement and to exclamatory interchanges between both sides which no reporter could record with sufficient rapidity, and of the general effect of which no report could possibly give a proper impression'. The sheet with Abraham's resolution written upon it, crumpled and partly torn across, is in the National Library of Ireland (MS 4572).

34 *F.J.*, 8 Dec. 1890.

35 Healy to Erina Healy, 6 Dec. 1890, *Letters and Leaders*, i. p. 336.

36 *N.P.*, 11 Mar. 1891, National Federation inaugural meeting.

37 *F.J.*, 8 and 9 Dec. 1891. The previous night, the McCarthys *père et fils* and Richard Power, the Parnellite whip, had dined, and drunk champagne, 'for the last time'. The abrogation of old civilities was signalled in the comment of the atrocious M. J. Kenny when the anti-Parnellites had assembled in the conference room: 'Well, we will now hold out the flag of Ireland; and Parnell is left to stretch out Kitty's petticoat' (R. M. Praed, note of conversation with Justin McCarthy, 7 Dec. 1890, McCarthy and Praed, *Book of Memories*, Draft).

38 Minutes of the Irish Party, 1890-95, Dillon Papers, TCD MSS 6501; Sullivan, *Room 15*, pp. 44-45; Healy to Erina Healy, 7 Dec. 1890, *Letters and Leaders*, i. p. 338; *F.J.*, 8 and 9 Dec. 1890.

39 Healy to Erina Healy, 7 Dec. 1890, *Letters and Leaders,* Proofs, B 138, deleted in *Letters and Leaders*, i. p. 338.

40 'Suppressed' *United Ireland*, 15 Dec. 1890; *Insuppressible*, 24 Dec. 1890, speech of W. M. Murphy at first meeting of National Committee; W. M. Murphy to Walsh, 12 Dec. 1890, Walsh papers, DDA; Minutes of National Committee II, 12 Dec. 1892, Dillon Papers, TCD MS 6503; *I.C.*, 13 Aug. 1892.

41 Sullivan, *Room 15*, p. 45; *N.Y.T*, 9 Dec. 1890.

42 *F.J.*, 8 Dec. 1891; signed House of Commons prayer cards of the anti-Parnellite members, with inscription by Tuohy, NLI MS 3882.

43 *B.D.P.*, 8 Dec. 1891; *F.J.*, 8 Dec. 1892, Sullivan, *Room 15*, pp. 45-46; Healy, *Why Ireland is Not Free*, p. 31.

44 Quoted, *Words of the Dead Chief*, p. 138.

45 Memorandum marked and headed 'copy', 'Notes of Conversation, December 16th 1890', Walsh papers, DDA. The memorandum is in a hand other than Walsh's, and is couched in terms of the archbishop's responses to an 'intermediary'; it is endorsed with a comment in another hand: 'this intermediary was Byrne the editor of the *Freeman* and he left for Kilkenny that night (16.XII.90)'. This memorandum, extracted from the main body of the Walsh papers, was not formerly available to historians. F. S. L. Lyons correctly deduced from Walsh's letter to Byrne of 17 Dec. and Parnell's letter to Walsh of 18 Dec. the general tendings of the 'highly secret exchange' between Walsh and Parnell (Lyons, *Parnell*, pp. 540-41). I am indebted to David Sheehy, archivist of the Dublin Diocesan Archive, for drawing this memorandum to my attention. Walsh's diary contains an entry for 16 Dec. 1890, for 12.30, which refers to 'Conference, Parnell case' (Walsh Papers, DDA).

46 *F.J.*, 1 Dec. 1890.

47 Croke to Walsh, 16 Dec. 1890, Walsh Papers, DDA.

48 Walsh to Byrne, 17 Dec. 1890, Walsh Papers, DDA.

49 C. S. Parnell to Walsh, Victoria Hotel Kilkenny, 18 Dec. 1890, Walsh Papers DDA; quoted F. S. L. Lyons, *Parnell*, pp. 539-40.

3

THE SPLIT IN IRELAND

You are now amongst us. Of the result we have no fear. The manhood of Ireland is with you. Go on! Fight! Let the issue be Gladstone or Parnell.

Parnell Leadership Committee, Address
to Charles Stewart Parnell[1]

The very men who told them all that, and who less than a month ago at Leinster Hall, Dublin, decided to stand by him, are the men who now tell the voters that Mr. Parnell is a small man, a heartless self-seeker, a fraud whose success meant ruin to the country. I shall not forget the expression of bewilderment that passed a certain farmer's face when, on hearing a canvassing MP describe Mr. Parnell in the former terms, he exclaimed, 'Well, well! Now is that a fact, sorr!'

Daily News Special Correspondent,
North Kilkenny[2]

So far as I can yet see the big towns are on the whole for Parnell but a country and small towns are dead against him — Tipperary as a whole is dead against him, while the City of Dublin, up to this time, is for him. The really abiding elements in Irish society, the clergy and the farmers, are dead against him.

Richard Adams Q.C.[3]

Parnell's predicament was of unnerving proportions. He returned to fight a campaign in a political terrain which was considerably altered from the Ireland in which he had begun his career. It was a changed society, transfigured by the revolution in expectations among tenant farmers of a substantial measure of land purchase, and by the pervasive and confident anticipation of home rule. Parnell's buoyant predictions of immediate and decisive victory in Ireland, reversing his defeat in Committee Room 15, should not be taken at face value. In spite of his bombast, he is unlikely to have had any illusions about the fierceness of the contest he faced. He was gambling heavily on his mystique, in a furious but calculated attempt to take the country by storm in the crucial first stage of the struggle in Ireland, against a background of deepening rural opposition to him. If he was to fight at all, he had to do so on the grand scale.

Even so, Parnell was unprepared for the magnitude of his defeat or the intensity of the opposition he encountered. He was oblivious to the full extent of the transformation of nationalist Ireland during the years of his supremacy, and underestimated the extremely disadvantageous situation in which the disclosures of the divorce court and his repudiation by Gladstone combined to place him, bringing into play his vulnerability as a Protestant landlord leader of a Catholic peasantry. The split in this respect contained a cruel irony. Parnell believed that his twin achievements in furthering the issues of home rule and the land purchase would ensure him wide support in Ireland. Yet it was precisely the belief in the imminence of a settlement of the national and agrarian questions which had transformed public opinion in nationalist Ireland and rendered Parnell at once vulnerable and seemingly dispensable. He was to fall victim to his own achievements.

Parnell was to lose the split's three by-elections, which comprised a staggered plebiscite on his leadership. While he attracted what might otherwise be considered a respectable 36 per cent of the aggregate votes, the results were disastrous for a politician of Parnell's stature, and threatened his elimination from the equation of nationalist power. The split became an essay in his response to a defeat far greater than he had allowed for. There are two Parnells in the split. The first is Parnell defiant in Committee Room 15, carrying the issue to the country; the other is the 'discrowned king', encountering defeat in Ireland, shorn of his mystique of invincibility, struggling to stabilise his decline and fight his way back.

On the evening of 9 December John Barry escorted the Healy brothers to Euston where in 'a fantastic scene' Parnellites and anti-Parnellites congregated at opposite ends of the Holyhead train. From their carriage the Healys watched the tumultuous departure of Parnell for the fight to recover his lost domain.[4] Alfred Robbins wrote on 9 December that Parnell had gone to Ireland that night 'in the highest spirits', and added that he had 'excellent reason' for stating Parnell had not the slightest fear of not carrying the country. Parnell had outlined to Robbins the thrust of his Rotunda speech:

> If he is charged with being a dictator, he is likely to retort that his only fault — if fault it has been — is to have trusted too much to his lieutenants, and to have failed to keep them duly in hand; and he may be expected to seek to demonstrate that the movement against him is no sudden uprising of

outraged feeling, but that it had been designed for months, and that only a favourable moment was awaited for its execution.[5]

That Parnell's professed optimism was calculated bravado is suggested by his tentative opening up of what was, if not a fall-back position, certainly a second front. In the brief respite between Committee Room 15 and the return to Ireland, the *Freeman's Journal* urged a peace initiative under which John Dillon and William O'Brien would return from Paris to confer with the two sections of the Irish party to avert 'the utterly fatuous course of the destruction of the party'. The same day Parnell responded to a cable from O'Brien with the ominous words 'now too late for me to rescue seceders from false position', but stating that he would consult with O'Brien when he reached Europe.[6]

On the evening of 10 December, Parnell passed triumphantly through the thronged streets of Dublin from the Mansion House to the Rotunda to make the speech which inaugurated his campaign in Ireland. His entry into the Round Room was greeted with 'a scene of the most frantic enthusiasm'.[7] The wild cheering lasted for ten minutes. This was Parnell still at his height, his power as yet unbroken by an Irish constituency, in what was to prove his only triumphal moment in the split. It was on Parnell's part a calculated lifting of the severe mask of command, permitting himself a show of personal emotion unique in his career. It was the stuff of myth. Katharine Tynan wrote four years later:

> One remembers the tall, distinguished-looking man, slender to attenuation, standing there and looking with outward calm at that roaring crowd of faces half-mad with enthusiasm and love of himself . . . That night, despite his calm, pale face, the hand inside the breast of his frock coat clenched till the nails bit in the flesh and made it bleed.[8]

The *Freeman's Journal* commented: 'The marvellous power of self-control and self-repression which distinguish Mr. Parnell was never more apparent than at that moment, when he faced that extraordinary enthusiasm without a movement in his countenance to denote emotions which must have been surging within him'. The *Evening Telegraph* wrote that Parnell had seldom, if ever before, spoken with such oratorical vehemence and contrasted the 'impassioned declamatory eloquence' of the speech with his House of Commons manner.[9] M. M. O'Hara, who had last seen him in 1885, thought he had aged perceptibly.

> He was less studied in his attire than formerly. His face was paler, his hair more meagre, and it was unkempt and long at the back, curling slightly over his collar. He was thin. His features were those of a man who had been recently sick. That he was excited was evident, but he still gave evidence of that unconquerable self-command which was so marked a feature of his personality. His eyes glistened with fire and feeling. He spoke with fluency, yet with deliberation. His voice sounded with thrilling clearness. He put passionate

vehemence into some of his words. He hissed others in a note of scathing defiance. There was a splendid confidence in his tone. He was unusually lavish of gesture.[10]

Parnell at the outset defended himself against the charge of neglecting his parliamentary duties by invoking his state of health:

> I have been absent from the fight it is said *(no, no)*. Oh, gentlemen, when Wellington retired into winter quarters within the lines of Torres Vedres, his lieutenants and officers did not seek to fix a halter round his neck *(loud cheers)* ... God knows it was not a time when I was crippled in strength, when it was doubtful whether I might ever again come before you — God knows it was not the time to confront me with a movement of mutiny stronger, more vindictive, more disgraceful, and more cowardly *(tremendous cheering and groaning for 'Healy')* than any commander-in-chief has been called upon to face *(cheers)*.

According to the close commentary in the *Evening Telegraph*, when referring to his health, Parnell stamped his feet. Tears glistened in his eyes, and he finished in a tone of emotion quickly suppressed. He declared in the strangely mortal idiom of the split: 'Ah, yes. They bided their time, and they thought that I was dead *(cries of 'No, No')*, and that they might play round my corpse and divert the Irish nation from the true issues involved'. Parnell 'wrung his hands with almost overwhelming nervousness: "But they reckoned without you", he shouted fiercely, "and without me"'.

He insisted that the integrity and independence of the Irish party had to be maintained in the face of Gladstone's intervention, and warned of the consequences of the breaking and discrediting of the party for constitutional politics in Ireland. He staked out his political constituency, pledging himself to pursue the settlement of the land question, and appealing to the labouring population to whom he looked for 'the recruits in the grand army of the Irish Nationality which I hope to lead in the near future'.

On the divorce issue, Parnell observed simply and impenitently, 'My defence will be known some day'. In a profession of humility which breathed defiance, he declared he could not have come amongst, and looked his audience in the face,

> ... did I not know that there is another side of this question . . . and if you will wait to hear that other side *(cheers)* before you decide that, unworthy as I am *(cries of 'No')*, I am too unworthy to walk with you within the sight of the promised land, which, please God, I will enter with you *(loud cheers)*.

At the conclusion of his speech to the overflow meeting, Parnell movingly reverted to this theme, linked to an invocation of Grattan by whose statue he had passed earlier:

> I could still, in looking upon the marble of that imperishable name, say in a different sense that I have followed the hearse of the enemies of Ireland *(loud cheers)*. I have watched by the cradle of the birth of Irish independence, and I know that having come this far with me you, our warm-hearted race,

will not forbid me to lead you to this promised land and that you will not declare me unworthy to share with our nation the future joy, happiness, prosperity, and freedom of our race *(loud and prolonged cheering)*.

It was an electrifying speech, which, if it did not carry through to the Irish countryside, confirmed Dublin in its Parnellism, and signalled the fierce tenacity with which Parnell would wage his campaign in Ireland.

Parnell had resolved to oust Mathias Bodkin who, as editor of *United Ireland*, had opposed his leadership. On the morning of his return to Ireland, observing to Edmund Leamy that 'this is going a little far, to be denounced in my own paper!', he had taken possession of the offices of *United Ireland* in Lower Abbey Street. He summarily dismissed Bodkin, and installed Leamy as editor. Healy and other anti-Parnellites urged Bodkin to reassert his authority. Bodkin, protesting that if he did so he would certainly be ejected again and might on the second occasion get his head broken, reluctantly agreed. While the Rotunda meeting was in progress, Healy and a handful of supporters re-entered the office. Before departing for Cork the following morning, Parnell resolved to retake *United Ireland*. In the extraordinary scene which ensued, the habitually placid Irish leader was alarmingly metamorphosed in a public display of wild and violent fury.

Parnell, his face, according to *Suppressed United Ireland*, 'distorted with mad passion', led the attack on the building, plunging his shoulder against the door. When the door proved resistant to battering, Parnell, in the words of James O'Connor, who was in charge of the small anti-Parnellite garrison within, 'baffled and like a raging lunatic tried to leap over the railings'. He had to be restrained by his supporters, who took the cue and, clearing the railings, broke in from below at the same time as the door gave way.[11] Parnell's loss of composure compromised one of the central attributes of his political repute, that of extreme self-control. The widespread perception of Parnell in the split as furious and frenzied, if not actually deranged, drew heavily on this incident as well as on his demeanour in the ensuing Kilkenny election. Healy's blood was up in turn. After recapturing *United Ireland*, he had written in reply to 'a slashing letter' of Croke: 'We must fight this Lunatic inch by inch at whatever personal cost, and for my part I will not give him any quarter now'.[12]

And so Parnell retained control of *United Ireland*, 'a by no means by the by appropriate appellative', as Leopold Bloom was to observe in *Ulysses*.[13]

Parnell's journey by rail to Cork was the first venture into the *terra incognita* of rural Ireland. The pattern of response was confused, but gave a misleading impression of the strength of support for Parnell in rural areas. At the early stops through Kildare Parnell was cheered, and responded with short polite speeches. At Monasterevan there was the first note of opposition from a divided crowd. At Maryborough and through Tipperary to Thurles, the crowd was Parnellite. Remarkably, the crowd of some 2,000 on the platform at Thurles, seat of Archbishop Croke, whose roars were at first assumed by those travelling on the train to betoken opposition to Parnell, turned out to be enthusiastically in his favour. The large crowd at Tipperary town was divided, but from the anti-Parnellite section there was the first threat of violence from a band of men carrying a banner for 'Mr. O'Brien and New Tipperary'. By now Parnell was exhausted, sitting in the corner of the carriage, speaking rarely and in a hoarse voice, and declining to make speeches at stops. At Mallow, William O'Brien's home town, the response was hostile and menacing. When Parnell opened the window, a hostile address was thrust into his hand, and he was coarsely abused by a man on the platform. Parnell slammed the window shut, and the curtains were pulled down. Amid cries of 'Bring him out', the crowd laid siege to the carriage with such force that the door broke. All the while a priest excitedly paced the platform denouncing Parnell as a blackguard and a libertine. Parnell remained calm and helped in holding back the door. He arrived exhausted to an enthusiastic reception in Cork. After his speech, he looked ominously aged, ill and distressed, his face pallid and with a restless look in his eyes.[14]

The anti-Parnellites needed to improvise not merely an organisation, but a rhetoric. The campaign in North Kilkenny found Healy still handling the issues of the split with some awkwardness, particularly in his treatment of the issue of 'Liberal dictation'. A rhetoric based on the supposed exigencies of the Liberal alliance, or on sentimental paeans to Gladstone — 'a poor old man in his eighty-first year who had worked and slaved for Ireland as a lusty youth'[15] — could not suffice to assure the majority of victory in Ireland. The character of the controversy changed as the split was translated to Ireland. As Healy wrote to his wife from Kilkenny, 'Little regard is paid to the arguments in Room 15!'[16]

The anti-Parnellites needed a more visceral political idiom, which Healy began to devise in the course of the Kilkenny election. He was determined to frustrate, by a ceaseless reiteration of the facts of the divorce court, Parnell's purpose of casting the issues of the split in a high patriotic vein. Healy later wrote of Parnell: 'His friends boasted that he would "sweep the country", and at the outset most people believed it. If he could have eluded the Divorce Court issue nothing could have beaten him'.[17] It was through ridicule rather than moralism that Healy achieved the dissolution of Parnell's mystique. If this purpose informed Healy's campaign from the outset, his rhetoric in North Kilkenny was not fully developed: he had yet to cast the stylised anti-Parnellite rhetoric of peasantry, which short-circuited the issue of 'Liberal dictation' by reducing Parnell's politics and morals to his landlord provenance and deriding his pretensions to leadership as invidiously anachronistic in an era in which the 'native' Catholic peasantry was poised to inherit the nationalist earth.

Healy vowed 'so long as life lasted, that he would meet this once respected chief at every twist and turn'.[18] This he did through a rhetoric of sexual allusion. The tenor of his campaign was set from the outset. Entering his hotel in Kilkenny on his arrival, he turned to a jeering crowd to call for 'three cheers for Mrs. O'Shea'.[19] At Freshford he declared to a hostile crowd:

> We were within a kick of the goal of Home Rule. What prevented it? It was because Mr. Parnell had disgusted every woman and child in England *(noise)*. He has neglected his business in the House of Commons. He could never be had when wanted. He was always down with Mrs. O'Shea *(noises)*. We never complained of his absence *(interruptions)*. I believe all England is ashamed of Mr. Parnell. The bishops and priests are ashamed of him.

To a heckler who cried 'shut your mouth about the woman', Healy retorted that Katharine O'Shea was 'a bad woman who hates Ireland, who cares nothing for Ireland, who has been spending the money of the Irish people and ruined Parnell'.[20] 'From the Tory point of view, Mr. Parnell was the saviour of the Tory party, and Mrs. O'Shea was the Tory Joan of Arc.' Referring to Parnell's seizure of *United Ireland*, Healy said: 'He played cuckoo in the nest of William O'Brien, and I have to say that a good election cry in this constituency upon all grounds is the cry of cuckoo'.[21]

Healy was not alone in his sexual allusions. He was rivalled by Charles Kearns Deane Tanner. A medical doctor who sat for mid-Cork, he was by any reckoning the most unstable member of the Irish party, accurately characterised by Harold Frederic as 'a madman — obstinate, vulgar, eccentric, violent in speech and action'. North Kilkenny afforded Tanner a unique opportunity to display these qualities, for which he was lauded by Davitt's *Labour World*.[22] Tanner announced it was the duty of every man in Ireland 'to hunt Mr. Fox with the cry of "Tally-ho" ', eliciting the chorus of the crowd while he and Davitt pointed at Parnell. He continued:

> Tally-ho! Who put O'Shea into Galway as the price of his scheme? What has become of the Tenants' Defence money? Was Parnell marrying Mrs. O'Shea for love or for her two hundred thousand pounds? ... Parnell would crucify his country to cover his shame. Parnell was a man who would set 'God Save Ireland' to the tune of 'Such a getting downstairs I never did see'.[23]

As throughout the split, Parnell conducted a highly personalised and old-fashioned campaign, in archaic reliance on his mystique. He made a series of rapid sorties from his base in Kilkenny town through the constituency. He dissolved his election committee of six in favour of one director and an assistant, the latter a Fenian: the deficient campaigning calibre of many of his supporters is reflected in the fact that he found it necessary to veto the service of breakfast in the hotel after 9.30 in the morning. Parnell's restless personal dominance of his campaign and his profligate expenditure of his own energies rendered understandable the confusion of the electors, a good majority of whom, according to the shrewd Sergeant Hennessy of the local Royal Irish Constabulary, believed that 'it is Parnell himself who is going for the elections'.[24]

The claims of Michael Davitt, correctly described by the Liberal *Daily News* as 'the organiser of this victory',[25] as the architect of Parnell's defeat at Kilkenny, take precedence over those of Healy. Healy, temporarily reconciled, credited him with a central role: 'He has kept doggedly on Parnell's track and much of the victory should be credited to him. Only for him we should not have energised the constituency as we are doing'.[26] The anti-Parnellite campaign, masterminded by Davitt, was in contrast to Parnell's, a triumph of organisation and intensive campaigning. The constituency was divided into eighteen polling districts, to each of which was assigned one or two MPs matched by as many local priests. At the same time Davitt sought to engage Parnell's canvassing sorties by a band of anti-Parnellites led by Davitt himself and Tanner (incessantly crying 'Tally-ho Mr. Fox!') which gave Parnell pursuit. It was, he explained, 'a sort of flying column. Our plan was to dog Parnell's footsteps, to anticipate his movements, and to confront and answer him wherever he showed his nose'.[27]

Davitt's 'flying column' actualised Healy's rhetoric of physical confrontation with Parnell. It invested the North Kilkenny campaign with its Leveresque aspect of galloping cars chasing at high speed between market towns, and contributed to the ugly incidents which marred the election — at Ballinakill, where Davitt himself was assaulted, and at Castlecomer, where Parnell was struck in the eye by what he claimed was a preparation of lime.[28]

In accounting for their defeat, Parnellites stressed the illicit influence of the clergy. Barry O'Brien wrote that it would 'be idle to deny that the struggle at Kilkenny was a fight between Parnellism *plus* Fenianism and the Church'.[29] Heavy clerical influence was deployed against Parnell. Although for fear of an election petition the priests tried to avoid door-to-door canvassing, they facilitated anti-Parnellite meetings after masses and many spoke from anti-Parnellite platforms.[30] Among the bishops, the fear of an election petition ran deep. Brownrigg, the Bishop of Ossory, wrote with some relief to Walsh, after the election, that no petition was likely, although what he intriguingly described as 'one little spiritual threat' had been uttered from the altar by a curate at Ballyragget.[31] Healy wrote to his father 'the priests are working hard and if they didn't they would but little appreciate what defeat means for their influence'. According to the local RIC sergeant, Healy had successfully courted a wavering priest at Paulstown 'and poisoned him against Mr. Parnell and his party on account of having a band of Fenians going through the country with him', so that the priest chaired Healy's meeting the next day.[32] In the event Parnell got a majority only in Kilmanagh, where the parish priest Nicholas Murphy held out for him in what his bishop denounced as 'studied deliberate and treacherous contempt of ecclesiastical policy'. In every other district, with the parish priest opposed to him, Parnell was beaten. 'Were it not for Fr. Murphy's action and that of two more curates', Brownrigg fulminated to Archbishop Walsh, 'the defeat would have been an annihilating one'.[33]

The by-election conformed to the pattern of support which would become familiar in the split. Parnell commanded the support of a coalition of social extremes, and was at his weakest in the middle stratum of middling and small tenant farmers. The local sergeant reported that Parnell had the support of the influential Smithwicks family, brewers and large employers in Kilkenny, of the doctors of the city and county, and on the other extremity of many of the voteless poor. Assessing Parnell's meeting of Johnstown, he reported that while he had seen only about twenty voters in the crowd, they were 'some of the biggest and most influential men in the parish'. The missing median group of farmers was lost to Parnell. Parnell, he concluded, 'has the villages and the educated people, and [Pope] Hennessy has the country farmers'. The latter group was not amenable to the blandishments of Parnellite campaigners, of either the parliamentary or Fenian orientation: 'They are of no use in the country. It is only in towns and cities they could use influence with the people'. McDonald for the *Daily News* observed of Parnell's meeting at Johnswell that 'it was almost entirely composed of corner boys and loafers from the town of Kilkenny'. He wrote that 'the big farmers have been against us, the middle ranks for us' (the 'us' being the anti-Parnellite-Liberal alliance).[34] Healy's report to his wife from the battle front that 'if the mob had votes we were dished' attested to the depth of the split's sociological schism: 'The city has nothing to do with the county ... Parnell's hotel is opposite ours. He was hoarse last night and only said a few words, but he is to speak again today, although there is not a county voter amongst his followers'.[35]

The daily reports of Sergeant Hennessy to the Chief Secretary's office chart the sharp decline of Parnellism from an initial position of perceived strength. On 15 December he noted that the odds were on Parnell among those who betted. By the following day the bookmakers had grown nervous and closed their books: no money was to be got on Parnell. Hennessy shared the expectation that Parnell would carry the constituency 'with the exception of Castlecomer and its surrounds where they would assault you for speaking of him'. By the 21st, Hennessy anticipated a narrow anti-Parnellite win: 'The betting is even and the excitement is increasing. The money is going on freely'.[36] At least the bookmakers of Kilkenny had cause to feel gratitude towards Parnell.

Davitt had predicted at the outset: 'Parnell ... has the start. He has the money, he has the dash, and he is backed up by unscrupulous followers. It will be a desperate contest, but I think he will go down in the end'.[37]

Healy's confidence likewise never wavered. He wrote to his brother on 15 December: 'We shall win. Parnell has got the rabble because of drink, money and P. N. Fitzgerald, but we shall beat him'.[38] By the eve of the poll, Davitt estimated they would win by a majority of at least 1,500. The *Daily News* correspondent noted that 'Parnell ... might have "rushed" North Kilkenny less than two weeks ago. He cannot "rush" it now'.[39] The Bishop of Ossory observed that the Parnellites were 'quite crestfallen' by the close of poll, and that the 'disgraceful sympathy' shown to Parnell in the city had abated, adding repulsively, 'his followers are like spaniels at the feet of the priests, watching for a token of forgiveness'.[40] Parnell on the eve of the poll commented to the *Daily News* correspondent, 'We are only at the beginning of our troubles'; on the night of the poll he told Barry O'Brien that they had lost, but that he would fight while he lived.[41]

The following day at the courthouse, Parnell listened impassively to the declaration of the poll, in which his candidate was defeated by 2,527 to 1,326. The *Daily News* correspondent wrote:

> Bandage or no bandage, and in spite of his commonplace, almost slovenly attire, you would have picked him out of a crowd of ten thousand men. He stood proudly erect. Not the shadow of emotion or feeling of any sort passed over Mr. Parnell's face when the figures were read out. The face was as calm and fixed as the face of a marble in the British Museum.

From the balcony Parnell addressed the crowd outside and declared that he would appeal to the country 'when a familiar voice cried out swiftly and cruelly "You have made your appeal and you have been whipped"'. It was Healy, who had emerged behind Parnell. He took off his hat and bowed ironically to the hooting crowd as the police sought to contain a rush at the balcony. Parnell declared that 'strengthened by the repulse I shall press forward amongst every Irish constituency, as the opportunity serves'.[42]

'To Catholic Irishmen', declared their namesake journal, 'it seemed as if that Providence which watched over our country and its faith, had again, by an inscrutable decree, ordained that the gates of hell shall not prevail against them.'[43]

North Kilkenny was a disaster for Parnell. The magnitude of his defeat in a rural Irish constituency considered reasonably representative (it was designated by *The Times* a 'priest-ridden agricultural constituency'[44]) shattered his mystique of electoral invincibility. The Parnellite Pierce Mahony wrote from Listowel to Harrington, 'There is no doubt the Kilkenny election has had a very bad effect in these parts. From all directions I am hearing of the change it has made in the feelings of the people.'[45]

Yet more damaging was what was widely perceived as Parnell's forfeiture of his mystique of self-control and reticence. As Healy wrote, 'It shocked the public when his success seemed certain, that, surrounded by bands and

banners and a roaring mob, to whom he foretold an assured victory, he
should have so badly lost his temper'[46].

Parnell's speeches at Kilkenny, Healy asserted, had reached 'a level almost
of intellectual imbecility'.[47] His speeches did show the traces of exhaustion and of the illness he was suffering,[48] and his rhetoric exhibited
disconcerting lapses from its former tautness. Thus he could declare:

> I feel it within me that the day of our victory is near, and that this is the
> last bitter and dreadful struggle before Ireland, and that the gates of darkness
> are open before us, and that we are even now walking in the valley of the
> shadow of death. Yet the light will surely come, the light of the Irish
> sunburst.[49]

Addressing the Kilkenny crowd from his hotel window after he had been
injured at Castlecomer, Parnell, debilitated and unnerved, was at once Sam-
son and Sarsfield:

> I was dumb last night, and I am blind tonight, but I have some sense left
> yet *(cheers)* to interpret the voice of Ireland, and the voice of Kilkenny. I
> do not intend to, and I will not, pull down the pillars of the temple. I will
> not allow Ireland to sink into the ruin that her enemies have prepared for her
> ... As Sarsfield went to Aughrim, as our forefathers went to the walls of
> Limerick, as they trod the causeway on the plains of the Boyne, we will go
> together, you and I, to victory *(cheers)*, or, believe me, we will go to the death
> together *(cheers)*.[50]

At Castlecomer Parnell spoke of himself in an alarmingly biblical third
person: 'As long as Ireland supports me, and as long as Charles Stewart
Parnell has breath to stand up for your cause, he will be with you'.[51]

Most notoriously, as a hearse passed while he was addressing a crowd
in Kilkenny, Parnell exclaimed: 'There goes the hearse of Pope Hennessy
and British misrule in Ireland to their doom'.[52] It was an alarming lapse,
which Healy in later years plausibly explained in terms of Parnell, prompted by his 'irrepressible horror of funerals', having 'merely stumbled into
the ejaculation as a kind of counterspell to avert the disaster which he
thought it foreshadowed and transmit the bad luck to his opponent'.[53]
Parnell's references to his former colleagues, to Davitt as 'a jackdaw', Tanner as 'a cock-sparrow', and to Justin McCarthy as 'a nice old gent for
a tea-party' shocked expectations more than taste. He succeeded in violating
even the extremely robust conventions of Irish elections in suggesting that
Tanner's bungled surgery caused the death of a celebrated Cork MP under
his care (a reference to J. P. Ronayne, an early practitioner of obstruc-
tionism who died after an amputation in 1876), an allegation he was forced to withdraw after Tanner issued a writ.[54]

Healy wrote that 'the inroad of Mr. Parnell's stoicism at Kilkenny was
probably only temporary', observing sardonically that 'for a man of limited
vocabulary to have to make three or four speeches every day for three weeks
is sorely trying'. The Kilkenny incidents 'arose not from faults of character,

but from mere mistakes of judgement. These will not be repeated'.[55] Yet the damage done to Parnell's political repute by his excesses at Kilkenny proved enduring.

It was Parnell's demeanour, as much as anything he said, which made the deepest impression on public opinion in Ireland and England. John MacDonald, the perceptive correspondent of the *Daily News*, memorably described Parnell speaking to the deeply hostile audience in the gathering twilight at Castlecomer, shortly before his eye was struck. MacDonald took as his point of departure Parnell's declaration that 'I am the same man — as good a man as I was ten years ago':

Alas, Mr. Parnell is not the same man he was ten years ago. The change in the 'uncrowned king's' mien and manner was positively startling. It was no longer the dignified, self-possessed Charles Stewart Parnell of old, the great leader who ever disdained to use personal abuse. The contrast between Mr. Parnell as I last saw him and as I now saw him in this spot, was to me at least profoundly touching. He had just said he would not stoop to per- sonalities, but he forgot his promise. 'Gutter sparrows like Dr. Tanner!' he exclaimed, contemptuously. 'Hounds like Davitt!' And the white teeth gleamed, the words came forth harshly, ferociously. It was not the low, refined, gentle voice of the House of Commons and the Parnell Commission, but the hard cruel voice of one hungering for vengeance ... Mr. Parnell's face was thinner than ever I had seen it. The lustre of the eyes was gone. They seemed tired and dazed. He smoked, or rather half-smoked numbers of cigarettes, throwing one away and lighting another. His gesticulations, his familiarities with his followers, were utterly different from anything I have ever seen in his demeanour before. The 'uncrowned king' is breaking down.[56]

Parnell's dignity was not enhanced by the retreat from Castlecomer: 'Mr. Parnell's car filled with his own followers — and himself among them — came rushing down the street at a wild gallop, while the yelling, cursing crowd pursued it with mud and gravel. The whole line of Mr. Parnell's cars was in full flight'.[57] His donning of a melodramatically large head bandage after his eye was struck aggravated the eccentricity of his appearance and excited the contemptuous amusement of his opponents. MacDonald thus described Parnell at his eve of poll meeting at Johnswell:

'The uncrowned' or 'discrowned' 'king' was pale, and instead of the small neat bandage he wore in the morning, he now wore a big, heavy, one cover- ing half his face, but the sharp frost necessitated precautions unneeded within doors. His headcovering was a grey hunting cap with peak before and behind, and its two flaps, one falling on either side of his face, were secured by a black tape tied beneath his chin. Dark trousers, woollen cardigan jacket, and a black frock coat completed his attire.

The tramp-like appearance was belied by the refined tones of what was Parnell's best and most dignified speech of the by-election, if still marred by rhetorical excesses. 'Mr. Parnell's speech sounded like the knell of a lost cause. Now and again in the course of its delivery the harsh grating, vengeful tone of his view grew dominant, the dry lips quivered and the thin hands tightened until their knuckles grew white ... It was the speech of a defeated leader'.[58]

The Parnell myth was fast unravelling. For English commentators, Parnell could at last be assimilated to a recognisable Irish stereotype. The *Spectator* noticed 'the strange revelation of Mr. Parnell's inner self, the "impassive statesman" roaring like a tub-ranter, the cool strategist hurling insults at the party chiefs whom, if he is to win, he must bind together again', thus bringing to an end his 'long course of histrionic moderation':

> Nothing in the recent Irish explosion has amazed us so much as Mr. Parnell's sudden dropping of his assumed character. It was so inexpedient. He is clearly an Irishman at bottom, though an Irishman of a peculiar temper; and his original assumption of what we may call the English character, the note of which is chilling reserve, and, as foreigners say, superciliousness, must have been quite deliberate.

It noted that the violence of Parnell's campaign, even if it succeeded with the Irish, was destroying his hold over the English.[59]

Frederic Harrison wrote perceptively, if complacently, of the dissolution of 'the legend of the personal grandeur of Mr. Parnell', to which thoughtful Gladstonian Liberals had refrained from subscribing:

> For ten years he has certainly shown himself a consummate tactician, of great sagacity, and marvellous self-command. He now chooses the part of the half crazy firebrand, the conspirator wildly fighting for his own hand. Which is the true Parnell may be a matter for ultimate judgement. But for all questions of practical politics, the actual Parnell has completely effaced the historic and legendary Parnell.

The English journalist E. W. Pitt, who covered the opening of the struggle for the Press Association, commented sadly to Alfred Robbins: 'He's not the Parnell you and I have known. That Parnell is dead'.[61]

The astute E. W. Hamilton, his sardony tempered by admiration, noted in his diary that Parnell was bent on combat 'with great bounce and swagger. He is a metamorphosed man'. Yet the charisma was shading into comedy: 'There is certainly a splendid audacity about the man which one has rarely seen equalled; the figure he is cutting is almost pantomimic'. Three days later he wrote that 'one cannot help thinking that the next place in which he may, not unsuitably, find himself is a lunatic asylum'. A week later he mused: 'One can't help thinking sometimes he is mad though there is no doubt method in his madness'.[62]

The perception of Parnell as deranged gained wide currency. W. T. Stead wrote:

> Pale and haggard with what seemed the fierce light of incipient madness flashing in his eyes, he hurried from town to town, from village to village,

from hamlet to hamlet, breathing out threatenings and vengeance against the men who dared to oppose him. He spoke as if he had been the heir of a hundred kings insulted by the treachery of a miscreant mob.[63]

'Well may it be asked, "is Mr. Parnell mad?". That there are evidences of insanity in his actions no one can doubt', wrote Davitt's *Labour World*.[64]

Labouchere wrote to Herbert Gladstone that the anti-Parnellites said that Parnell 'is getting so mad, that he may soon have to be restrained'.[65] Writing in *Truth*, Labouchere deemed Parnell's attacks on his former colleagues and on the Liberal party 'entirely inconsistent not only with his own past, but with his sanity'. Parnell had made the error of descending from his pedestal:

> He had the reticence and the calm which are generally believed wanting in the Irish character, and the Irish believed in him because he possessed those negative qualities which they are without. Since the divorce decree, he has descended into the arena, and fought for his own hand. What has been the result? He has shown himself utterly destitute of ability, and made it clear that his stock-in-trade is mendacity and low cunning.[66]

The *Spectator* was prompted to wonder whether, except in the management of men, Parnell had any originality at all, and whether Parnell's campaign in Kilkenny did not disclose 'the sterility of brain often found in aristocrats who can govern'.[67]

By his attack on the *United Ireland* office, and his excesses in the Kilkenny election, Parnell damagingly compounded the adverse impression created by the manifesto. The image of the Parnell in the split as in the grip of an irrational frenzy, if not actual insanity, derives from the impressions created in the brief period of two weeks between his return to Ireland and the Kilkenny poll. While Healy wrote in March that 'Mr. Parnell has resumed his native demeanour and soared home into the trackless altitudes of statecraft',[68] the memory of Parnell at Kilkenny was never effaced. It was sedulously cultivated by Healy in his newspaper writings and speeches, and above all in the depiction of Parnell in *National Press* cartoons as frenzied, hunted and possessed, caught in the dementia of frustrated ambition. Healy's propaganda froze the image of Parnell in the first moment of vehemence as his leadership stood forfeit.

Parnell was not the only casualty of the Kilkenny election. The by-election offered to English opinion a welcome restoration of a reassuringly comic vision of Ireland, reinstating the burlesque Ireland of Carleton and Lever which Parnellism had banished. In Kilkenny the caricature nationalist was made flesh. Conservative publicists hailed the recrudescence of electoral bedlam in Ireland, and the revival of the forgotten hilarity of Irish political engagement.

The Tory *Saturday Review* after the schism in Committee Room 15 complacently predicted: 'The genius of the place in which the Irish party met, with years of sobering contact with English and Scottish members, have perhaps tamed the wild spirits of the Irish orators, but on Irish soil, and in the Irish environment, they would soon awaken from their dreams of decorum'.[69] The same journal was not disappointed, and, in an article significantly entitled 'The Return of the Irishman', celebrated the turbulent epiphany of the market place at Ballinakill, and welcomed the restoration of 'the true Irishman, the Irishman whom we loved and whom we all thought we had lost'.

> ... Englishmen in general were settling down, we imagine, into the fixed con-
> viction that the typical Irishman of Lever — the 'Rollicking' Irishman —
> had never, at any time, a flesh-and-blood existence, when lo! a sudden flood
> of light upon the market square of Ballinakill, and we find, not merely that
> he had existed, but that he still exists, and in the fullest vigour of abounding
> and cudgel-playing life. He is still there in all his varieties; every portrait in
> the delightful Leverian gallery seems to have started from its frame, the 'bhoy',
> the comic and pugnacious priest, the wild but beloved squireen, who plunges
> with such hearty good will into an electoral struggle; even the stock villain
> of Irish fiction, the wicked and treacherous lawyer, who fawns upon his patron
> in prosperity and insults him in adversity — even he, too, is represented ...[70]

The comparison, if envenomed by racial animus, was irresistible.

For Unionists Irish parliamentary nationalism was losing at last its former inscrutable severity. The strain of discipline and reticence had finally proved too much for Irish tempers, and the nationalists were reverting grati-fyingly to type. The Irish question was mercifully receding, and what was more important, appeared to be doing so in such a manner as to inflict the maximum damage on Gladstone.

One of the most important consequences of the fall of Parnell was the collapse of public interest in Britain in Irish affairs, after the immediate drama of the divorce, of Committee Room 15, and North Kilkenny. With the seemingly irreversible vanquishment of Parnell and the failure of the Boulogne negotiations, English press coverage of Irish affairs diminished sharply, only to flare again briefly on the death of Parnell. It was the first alarming indication of the loss of the primacy of the home rule question in British politics. It was as if the fall of Parnell in its early stages was the last convulsive engagement of the Victorian political imagination with the Irish question, of which Gladstone's introduction of the second Home Rule Bill in 1893 was a nostalgic recapitulation.

There is also discernible in the Kilkenny election the first manifestation of the phenomenon which was to confuse and embitter nationalist opi-nion in the split: the oppressive sense of the split as a demeaning exhibi-tion enacted before an English audience. This was more complex and elusive than the narrow political arguments: of Parnell on the one hand having emperilled home rule, or of the majority on the other having succumbed to Liberal 'dictation'. Each side blamed the other for the sense of nationalist degradation: the split became the theatre of an exaggerated nationalist self-consciousness.

The sense of spectacle was pervasive. Unionist politicians and apologists provokingly played on the nationalist sense of discomfiture. Salisbury, the Conservative Prime Minister, at Rossendale woundingly insinuated that Irish nationalism had ceased to be a cause and had become a spectacle. He observed that while the debate in Committee Room 15 was progressing:

> To us who take a deep interest in its human aspects there is a flavour of amusement as we look on the drama that is being unfolded at Westminster, and I have no doubt that in this sporting county some of you have already got bets for or against Mr. Parnell.

The professedly Hibernophile W. T. Stead wrote unhelpfully that the Kilkenny election had

> all the excitement of the race for the derby with some of the cruel fascination of gladiatorial shows thrown in. It was a great drama in which the irresistible drollery of Irish humour was mingled with something of an awe of the Greek tragedy.[71]

The sense of spectacle was to endure. Healy wrote in March that 'we often hear of the eyes of the civilised world being fixed on certain situations, and without exactly claiming the attention of all humanity, it is certain that the cockpit in Ireland will command a "good gallery" for some time to come'.[72] The sense of the split as an externally witnessed spectacle gives Yeats magnificent and complex accusatory stanza, from *Parnell's Funeral*, its troubling resonance:

> An age is the reversal of an age:
> When strangers murdered Emmet, Fitzgerald, Tone,
> We lived like men that watch a painted stage.
> What matter for the scene, the scene once gone:
> It had not touched our lives. But difficult rage,
> *Hysterica passio* dragged this quarry down.
> None shared our guilt; nor did we play a part
> Upon a painted stage when we devoured his heart.

Yeats's distinction was too sharply drawn. The intricate interrelationship between the 'popular rage', and the acute nationalist awareness of the 'strangers' as onlookers, was to invest the split with much of its peculiar and unassuagable bitterness.

The souring of Irish opinion on both sides in Kilkenny was marked. Parnellite anger at defeat, and resentment of the treatment of Parnell at Castlecomer ran deep. The ugly jollity of Davitt's observation, in the course of a complacent interview with the Liberal *Pall Mall Gazette* that 'this fight at Kilkenny was full of fun and Irish good humour throughout'[73] still rankled over twenty years later to prompt the retort of James Joyce in 'Gas from a Burner':

> 'Twas Irish humour, wet and dry,
> Flung quicklime into Parnell's eye

The issue of the split was now sharply joined in Ireland. The already exiguous prospects of peace were blasted: the attitude of the anti-Parnellite right wing towards Parnell was hardened by triumph, while Parnell's temperamental receptiveness to a settlement, already limited, had sharply diminished.

References

1 *F.J.*, 11 Dec. 1890.
2 *D.N.*, 23 Dec. 1890.
3 Richard Adams QC to John Morley, n.d., part of letter forwarded by Morley to Gladstone 19 Dec. 1891 (BM Add. MS 44256 f. 88).
4 *P.M.G.*, 10 Dec. 1891, *F.J.*, 10, 11 Dec. 1891; *The Times*, 10 Dec. 1891; *Letters and Leaders*, i. p. 340.
5 *B.D.P.*, 10 Dec. 1890.
6 *F.J.*, 8 and 9 Dec. 1890; draft of press release containing O'Brien to Parnell, 7 Dec. 1890, Parnell to O'Brien, 8 Dec. 1890, Dillon Papers, TCD MS 6736, f.44.
7 *F.J.*, 11 Dec. 1890.
8 *Evening Telegraph*, 11 Dec. 1891; *F.J.*, 11 Dec. 1891. Katharine Tynan's description quoted both in R. B. O'Brien's *Parnell* (ii. pp. 291-93), and in her own *Twenty-Five Years* (pp. 326-27), is taken from her article 'Parnell, a Retrospect', published in the *I.W.I.*, 6 Oct. 1894.
9 *F.J.*, 11 Dec. 1890; *Evening Telegraph*, 11 Dec. 1890. The text of the speech here quoted is from *F.J.*, 11 Dec. 1890.
10 M. M. O'Hare, *Chief and Tribune: Parnell and Davitt* (Dublin and London, 1919) pp. 316-17.
11 'Suppressed' *United Ireland*, 15 Dec. 1890; *Insuppressible*, 5 Jan. 1891, James O'Connor to editor n.d.; A. M. O'Sullivan, *Old Ireland: Reminiscences of an Irish KC* (London, 1927), pp. 52-54; R. B. O'Brien, *Parnell*, vol. ii, pp. 293-97; Margaret Leamy, *Parnell's Faithful Few*, pp. 38-40; Parnell to Bodkin, telegram, 2 Dec. 1890, Gill papers, NLI MS 13506(7).
12 Healy to Croke, 11 Dec. 1890, quoted Mark Tierney, 'Dr. Croke, the Irish Bishops and the Parnell Crisis, 18 Nov. 1891-92', *Collectanea Hibernica*, 1956, p. 121.
13 Joyce, *Ulysses*, p. 534. This is the point which Joyce chooses for the intersection of the destinies of Parnell and Leopold Bloom in a fastidious pastiche of the Parnell myth, to which the issue of Parnell's composure is central: 'His [Parnell's] hat a silk one was inadvertently knocked off and, as a matter of strict history, Bloom was the man who picked it up in the crush after witnessing the occurrence meaning to return it to him (and return it to him he did with the utmost celerity) who panting and hatless and whose thoughts were miles away from his hat at the same time all the same being a gentleman born with a stake in the country he, as a matter of fact, having gone into it more for the kudos of the thing than anything else, what's bred in the bone instilled into him in infancy at his mother's knee in the shape of knowing what good form was came out at once because he turned round to the donor and thanked him with perfect aplomb, saying: Thank you sir ...' (pp. 534-35). Dr. Dominic Mangianello is surely correct in suggesting that Joyce inserts Bloom in history not merely as the man who returned Parnell's hat, but as the author of the

account given to R. B. O'Brien by 'a gentleman wholly unconnected with politics, who happened, by the merest chance, to be in the neighbourhood when the final battle over *United Ireland* was fought': Dominic Mangianello, *Joyce's Politics* (London, 1980), p. 23; R. B. O'Brien, *Parnell*, ii. p. 296.

14 *M.G.*, 12 Dec. 1890, 'From Our Own Reporter', Cork, 11 Dec. 1890; Margaret Leamy, *Parnell's Faithful Few*, p. 54.

15 *'Suppressed' United Ireland*, 15 Dec. 1890, Speech of Healy to Kilkenny Election Committee.

16 Healy to Erina Healy, 13 Dec. 1890, *Letters and Leaders*, proofs, B 141.

17 Healy, *Why Ireland is Not Free*, p. 34.

18 *K.M.*, 17 Dec. 1890, Kilkenny; speech 12 Dec. 1890.

19 *K.M.*, 13 Dec. 1890.

20 *F.J.*, 13 Dec. 1890.

21 *F.J.*, 15 Dec. 1890, Election Committee, 12 Dec. 1890.

22 H. W. Lucy, *Nearing Jordan* (London, 1916, 3 vols.), iii. pp. 223-4; *Vanity Fair*, 4 Aug. 1888; *N.Y.T.*, 7 Aug. 1887, *L.W.*, 14 Dec. According to a pleasing story of A. M. Sullivan, Parnell once informed a group of colleagues that 'that fellow Tanner is out there in the lobby declaring that he is about to commit suicide. Can none of you fellows persuade him to do it?' (A. M. Sullivan, *The Last Serjeant* [London, 1952], p. 236).

23 *D.E.*, 17 Dec. 1891.

24 R. B. O'Brien, *Parnell*, ii. p. 302; *D.N.*, 23 Dec. 1890; Reports of Sgt. John Hennessy RIC, to the office of the Chief Secretary, 15-21 Dec. 1890, CBS, SPO 116.2219 S (hereafter cited as 'Hennessy').

25 *D.N.*, 24 Dec. 1890

26 *D.N.*, 24 Dec. 1890; Healy to Maurice Healy snr., 17 Dec. 1890, Healy-Sullivan Papers, UCD, p. 6/A/14; see also Healy to Erina Healy, 15 Dec. 1890, *Letters and Leaders*, Proofs, p. B141.

27 *P.M.G.*, 1 Jan. 1891, interview with Davitt; *D.N.*, 16, 20 Dec. 1890.

28 Parnell's admittedly partisan doctor J. Byrne Hackett affirmed his contention that he had been struck by a preparation of lime (*K.M.*, 20 Dec. 1890); see also *I.W.I.*, 6 Oct. 1894, J. Byrne Hackett, 'Castlecomer Lime'; *I.W.I.*, 7 Oct. 1893, E. Haviland Burke, 'The Days of Kilkenny'. The anti-Parnellites insisted that Parnell was pelted with flour and mud (*F.J.*, 1 Jan. 1891).

29 R. B. O'Brien, *Parnell*, ii. p. 305.

30 *D.N.*, 24 Dec. 1890.

31 Brownrigg to Walsh, 24 Dec. 1890, Walsh Papers DDA; see also Croke to Walsh, 9 Jan. 1891, ibid.

32 Healy to Maurice Healy snr., 17 Dec. 1890; Healy-Sullivan papers, UCD MS P6/A/16; Hennessy, 21 Dec. 1890.

33 R. B. O'Brien, *Parnell*, ii. pp. 206-7; Brownrigg to Walsh, 24 Dec. 1890, Walsh Papers, DDA.

34 Hennessy; *D.N.*, 22, 23 Dec. 1890.

35 Healy to Erina Healy, 13 Dec. 1890, *Letters and Leaders*, Proofs, pp. B 140-1

36 Hennessy.

37 Davitt to McGhee, 12 Dec. 1890, Davitt papers, TCD MS 9328.

38 Fitzgerald was a prominent Fenian supporter of Parnell in the split and possibly the assistant director of his Kilkenny campaign. Healy to Maurice Healy, 15 Dec. 1891, *Letters and Leaders,* Proofs, p. B141, deleted *Letters and Leaders*, i. p. 343.

39 *D.E.*, 22 Dec.

40 Brownrigg to Walsh, 22 Dec. 1890, Walsh Papers, Dublin Diocesan Archives; see also Brownrigg to Walsh, 24 Dec. 1890.

41 *D.N.*, 22 Dec. 1890; R. B. O'Brien, *Parnell*, ii. p. 307; *Westminster Gazette*, 30 Sept. 1896 'Letter from Ireland'. An unidentified 'old Fenian' later quoted Parnell as saying to him on the eve of poll: 'We are beaten. They [his supporters] don't think it, but we are ... It will take a long time to pull Ireland together again. But I will pull her together. England is not done with me. Perhaps her next humiliation will be greater than her last' (*I.W.I.*, 10 Oct. 1896).

42 *D.N.*, 24 Dec. 1890; *K.M.*, 24 Dec. 1890; *F.J.*, 24 Dec. 1890.

43 *I.C.*, 27 Dec. 1890.

44 *The Times*, 24 Dec. 1890.

45 Pierce Mahony to Harrington, 31 Dec. 1890, Harrington Papers, NLI MS 8576 (29).

46 Healy, 'Rise and Fall', p. 194.

47 *K.M.*, 20 Dec. 1890, Urlingford, 18 Dec. 1890.

48 R. B. O'Brien, *Parnell*, ii. pp. 301-3; Leamy, *Parnell's Faithful Few*, pp. 55-6.

49 *D.E.*, 22 Dec. 1890, Kilkenny 20 Dec. 1890.

50 *K.M.*, 20 Dec. 1890.

51 22 Dec. 1890, Castlecomer; see also Ballinakill, ibid.

52 *F.J.*, 22 Dec. 1890.

53 Healy, 'A Great Man's Fancies II'. Standish O'Grady similarly surmised, recalling 'the hilarity and jocosity displayed by Hamlet after his interview with the Ghost', that 'Parnell's nerves were unstrung at the time and his mind disordered, and probably his thoughts were set in motion and his words flowing by one of his numerous superstitions' (*K.M.*, 1 Feb. 1899).

54 *D.N.*, 22 Dec., Kilkenny; *D.E.*, 12 Jan. 1891, *F.J.*, 24 Jan. 1891; Healy, *Rise and Fall*, p. 195.

55 Healy, 'Rise and Fall', pp. 194-5. Davitt later patronisingly and absurdly ascribed Parnell's excesses to the influence of his coarser supporters, in an annotation of R. B. O'Brien's *Parnell:* 'Educated by chance and surroundings. After his fall influenced by the low manners and instincts of P(atrick) O'B(rien)s Ned H(arrington)s, Dr. Fitz(gerald)s and other lower still ... It was from these who flocked to him he borrowed his scurrility at Kilkenny election'. (Davitt, Notes on R. B. O'Brien, *Parnell*, i. Davitt Papers, TCD MS 9377).

56 *D.N.*, 17 Dec. 1890. McDonald's excellent reports did much to shape perceptions of the Kilkenny election. MacDonald had first been despatched to Ireland by Labouchere on behalf of the *Daily News* in January 1886 (Labouchere to Gladstone, 6 Jan. 1886, Viscount Gladstone Papers, BM Add. MS 46014, f. 142). He subsequently reported on the Plan of Campaign, and exhaustively covered the Special Commission (*F.J.*, 26 Sept. 1888); John MacDonald, *Diary of the Parnell Commission* (London, 1890).

57 *D.N.*, 17 Dec.

58 *D.N.*, 22 Dec. 1890. Parnell's attire had always been notoriously unpredictable and frequently eccentric. H. W. Lucy wrote of Parnell's curious attire on one occasion in 1885 that 'the dress is a triumph of laborious art giving Mr. Parnell an appearance which is a cross between Oscar Wilde and a scarecrow' (H. W. Lucy, *Diary of Two Parliaments*, [2 vols, London, 1886], ii. p. 498, dated 5 Aug. 1885).

59 *Spectator*, 20 and 27 Dec. 1890.

60 Frederic Harrison, 'The Irish Leadership', *Fortnightly Review*, n.s. vol. 49 (1 Jan. 1891), p. 125.

61 Robbins, *Parnell*, p. 181.

62 E. W. Hamilton Diaries, entries for 11, 14 and 22 Dec. 1890, Hamilton Papers BM Add. MS 48654, pp. 80-99.

63   W. T. Stead, 'North Kilkenny and Its Moral', *Paternoster Review*, vol. 1, no. 4 (Jan. 1891), p. 337.

64   *L.W.*, 20 Dec. 1890. The editorial is not, as suggested in Lyons, *Parnell* (pp. 541-42), by Davitt, who was campaigning in Kilkenny, but by Charles Diamond (the article in the *Labour World* file in the Davitt Papers is marked 'Diamond').

65   Labouchere to Herbert Gladstone, 17 Dec (1890), Viscount Gladstone Papers, BM Add. MS 46016, f. 146.

66   *Truth*, 25 Dec. 1890, 1 Jan. 1891.

67   *Spectator*, 27 Dec. 1890.

68   Healy, 'Rise and Fall', pp. 194-95. The *Brighton Gazette*, a close observer of Parnell's railway deportment, noted his temporarily altered behaviour during the divorce crisis and its immediate aftermath. Before the divorce he travelled down quietly from Victoria, shrinking from observation as much as possible: 'But after his private life was laid bare, he assumed an air of reckless ostentation for a time to which he was wholly unaccustomed and which he soon abandoned'. On the day of the manifesto's publication Parnell went up to London during the afternoon: 'Instead of seeking some quiet corner as usual, he stepped boldly into a Pullman, drew from his pocket a large cigar (although it was by no means his habit to smoke en route), and with a nonchalant air marched jauntily towards a central seat' (*Brighton Gazette*), 10 Oct. 1891.

69   *Saturday Review*, 13 Dec. 1890.

70   *Saturday Review*, 20 Dec. 1890. An article of strikingly similar import entitled 'The Fun of the Fair' appeared in the *Spectator* of the same day. On Irish electoral practise, see K. Theodore Hoppen, *Elections, Politics, and Society in Ireland 1832-85* (Oxford, 1984), pp. 341-423 *et passim*.

71   *F.J.*, 4 Dec. 1890. W. T. Stead, North 'Kilkenny and Its Moral' in *Paternoster Review*, vol. 1, no. 4 (Jan. 1891), p. 332.

72   Healy, 'Rise and Fall', p. 194.

73   *P.M.G.*, 1 Jan. 1890.

4

BOULOGNE

Healy returned to Dublin to confront a challenge which threatened to undo the victories in the Committee Room and at North Kilkenny: the pursuit of a negotiated settlement with Parnell at Boulogne. William O'Brien had left New York for France on 13 December with the authority of the remaining American delegates to procure Parnell's retirement on extremely favourable conditions. The terms contemplated his withdrawal in consideration of an acknowledgement of the informality of McCarthy's election as chairman, together with an indication to Parnell that his personal influence would remain ascendant, and that his retirement would probably be temporary. Parnell was to continue as President of the National League, and would be appointed one of the party's joint treasurers. He was also to be given a special role in the negotiations for any future Home Rule Bill.[1]

John Dillon on 18 December despatched to O'Brien a strikingly bleak assessment of the political prospect, suggesting that they should resign as Parnell had attracted a level of support sufficient to ensure defeat of the home rule alliance at the election, and possibly to precipitate a Liberal abandonment of the commitment to home rule. The argument recast the Parnell myth in terms of his destructive potential:

> ... If the election is lost, and still more if the Liberals throw over Home Rule, Parnell having done all the mischief will escape all the responsibility of his action, and will be able to cast the odium on us ... Our one chance is to unite on the Home Rule platform and I confess that after what has occurred and in face of the revival of the revolutionary party which I now regard as inevitable, and the sort of language which is sure to [be] copiously used here and in Ireland over the next year, without our having the slightest power to check it, I confess there is *no* chance of winning, unless Parnell retires, and when retiring issues a *strong* appeal to the Parliamentary Party. Without

this, I am convinced that by undertaking to carry on the movement we should
enter on a path which could only end in ignominious failure, and that after
a short period of weakness and helplessness, all eyes would be turned once
more to Parnell and men would say — well whatever were his faults, when
he was at the head we were united and strong, and since he went nothing
has gone right. Prestige in matters of this kind is an enormous power, and
whereas Parnell had reached the position that men were blind to all his faults
and failings ... with us in the country the slightest failing would be exaggerated and criticised.

On the conduct of the North Kilkenny election, he was scathing: 'The
whole thing is sickening. It is as if the whole people had been seized with
madness. Our friends have continued to manage their affairs as badly as
possible — could human folly go further than to send Tanner, Healy and
Davitt to carry on that election?'[2]

Parnellite appeals to O'Brien played blatantly on his susceptibilities
through pathetic evocations of the beleagured Parnell. In a letter, a fragment of which has survived, V. B. Dillon wrote to O'Brien of Parnell:

He seems to have [lost] that calmness and dignity which were his
characteristics and is now an ordinary man but what provocation he has had
coming after a time when his mode of life must have enfeebled him. It was
a sad sight to see him, defeated at Kilkenny, speaking at twelve o'clock at
night to a small [crowd] outside the National Club [his head] still
bandaged.[3]

Harrington invoked the deteriorating atmosphere in Dublin: 'Old friends
pass me without speaking, members of the same family have quarrelled
and fallen out, and in the mad zeal of partisanship no man's character
is free from the aspersions of the unscrupulous among his opponents'. Of
Kilkenny he wrote, 'No abandoned prostitute could have used language
as low as that of Tim Healy and Tanner'. The election had widened the
breach horribly: 'goaded on by language and abuse of the foulest kind
Parnell lost his usual dignity and used language of men who had been loyal
colleagues of his which every rational man must condemn'.[4]

As he crossed the Atlantic — 'over the desolate water the wind howls
stormily' — O'Brien wrestled with a resurgence of his old allegiance to
Parnell. His conflicting emotions are reflected in the rough draft of a 'battle
song', one of the most curious texts of the split and of the Parnell myth.
Remonstrating with Parnell for his initial response to Gladstone's letter,
he revealingly adopted the lupine imagery of the manifesto:

> Why did the howl of wolves for an instant
> your soul affright,
> And drive you back from the high heroic purpose,
> the path of right.

Parnell knew the depth of allegiance to him ('I have loved you, chief as
I have loved no man, as a leader and, aye, a king'): 'Why did you ask us

at the howl of the wolf then the one thing we dare not do, to write our lives down a lie?' Had Parnell resigned, 'the people's love would have mounted higher and higher', and the recall to the leadership of 'their hero of heroes' would have swiftly followed:

> And Prompt would the vindication come, and
>   passionate in grief
> Would the people cry 'give back to us now our
>   own born chief,
> O give us back our peerless one,for his right it
>   comes from God.
> He has proved it by his own great deed', and
>   all nations would applaud.

Instead Parnell had chosen to divide the country — 'you have torn our souls asunder'.[5]

Parnell met O'Brien at Boulogne on 30 December. O'Brien conveyed to him the terms he had agreed with Dillon, Harrington and O'Connor. Parnell immediately responded that he could not consider resigning, unless O'Brien himself was elected to the chairmanship and declined the chairmanship of the company to establish the *National Press*. He revived in modified form the scheme of soliciting Liberal assurances in relation to the provisions of the Home Rule Bill. Exploiting the fact that since McCarthy had been elected chairman of the party, Gladstone's objection to providing assurances in response to the Clancy amendment in Room 15 had been technically met, Parnell now proposed that McCarthy meet Gladstone and obtain a confidential memorandum stating his intentions regarding the disputed provisions of the Home Rule Bill. If the assurances were satisfactory to Parnell and O'Brien, Parnell would retire, and O'Brien would take the chair. The memorandum would be published only in the event of the introduction of a Home Rule Bill which fell short of its terms; otherwise it would be published by Parnell after the Bill's enactment. The ensuing weeks of negotiation were dominated by the evolution of Parnell's proposal: at their most developed stage the negotiations envisaged public assurances from the Liberal leadership in lieu of Parnell's elaborate mechanism to conserve secrecy, and the chairmanship of Dillon rather than O'Brien, to which Parnell had reluctantly acquiesced.[6]

Healy spoke in Dublin on Christmas Eve, the day before O'Brien's arrival in Boulogne, in a pre-emptive strike against the Boulogne negotiations. He insisted that Parnell had, by virtue of the manifesto and his campaign in Ireland, placed his leadership beyond recall:

> Once that man issued his manifesto; once he revealed himself in his true guise, once he made those speeches; once he acted as he did throughout Ireland — once he broke into the United Ireland office — the scales fell from my eyes, and I saw the mokanna we had to deal with — a man who would sacrifice not only his eighty-six followers, but the millions of the Irish

population to satisfy his purpose and ambition. I say we will have no dealings with him *(no, no)*. We will have no compromise with him *(hear, hear)*.
We will have nothing with him except combat and we will give him nothing
but defeat.

Describing Kilkenny as one of the most difficult of Irish constituencies
for the anti-Parnellites, Healy declared: 'There we have beaten him, and
will hunt him wherever he shows his head'.[7]

Healy now sought to bring his influence to bear directly on O'Brien.
On 4 January he left Dublin for Paris, in the company of the diehard John
Barry, fortified by a request of Archbishops Croke and Walsh to
remonstrate with O'Brien. Their immediate purpose was to procure
O'Brien's agreement to act as the editor of the *National Press* and chair-
man of the Irish National Press Company, in the prospectus of which
O'Brien had already been unguardedly described as chairman and editor.[8]

Henry Labouchere, who saw them off from London en route to Paris,
immediately wrote Gladstone an account of his conversation with Healy.
Healy had said that O'Brien's action was doing the anti-Parnellites great
harm in Ireland, and that they intended to protest strongly to him. In his
interview with Parnell, O'Brien had insisted on Parnell's retirement, 'and
since then has sent them over various propositions, the one more silly than
the other' — including the proposal that O'Brien should become leader.
The anti-Parnellites had had difficulty restraining the two archbishops from
putting out a statement condemning the negotiations. 'If O'Brien were
made leader, they say that the result would be disastrous. He would be
perpetually trying to make up with Parnell, and the appointment would
be most distasteful to the clergy.' Healy had asked Labouchere to assure
Gladstone that there was not the slightest prospect of the party coming
to terms with Parnell.[9] Labouchere's intervention was viewed with
justifiable scepticism by Morley, who wrote to Gladstone returning a letter of Labouchere with the comment that 'I see the latter worthy pretty
often, and have no confidence whatever in his hairy stories from Paris.
But there is no doubt that Parnell has got hold of O'Brien'.[10]

Healy and Barry reached Paris on the evening of 5 January and talked
with O'Brien into the small hours. Healy wrote to his wife that O'Brien
impartially blamed both sides. He believed him to be 'at heart ... sympathetic to the man we have been fighting', unwilling to endorse any action taken by the majority, and preferring to go to jail. In the conclusion
of the letter, deleted from the published version, Healy bitterly asked: 'Have
we all been fools, are they the only wise men? Words O'Brien uttered show
his feelings were against those who risked infamy to battle for their country, and all his reproaches were for us. He had no phrase against the other
side'. Healy did not know what the 'Boulogne chieftains' would do, but
feared an attempt to present a *fait accompli*: 'In order to bluff us they
may publish the result of their deliberations without communication with

us in a series of "protocols", which we shall be asked to assent to. O'Brien treats the Party, *minus* Dillon and himself, as of small account, but he will find this a mistake'.[11]

Healy wrote to his brother that Parnell had 'thrown a fly' over O'Brien the offer of the leadership, 'so that his friendship and consideration are for Parnell, and his criticisms for us'. He later wrote that 'O'Brien's treatment of the Party is as arrogant as Parnell's is, and I told him so in those exact words'. O'Brien overestimated Parnell's support in Ireland, but could not be argued with: 'Indeed it makes him angry, as he tells you he is much better able to gauge Irish feelings than you are. Having taken a partisan line all his life, he now figures as a "moderado" when partisanship and determination are needed'.[12]

Healy despatched to Labouchere an account of his interview with O'Brien, which as he intended Labouchere forwarded to Gladstone. While resolute for Parnell's retirement, O'Brien was inclined to retire himself if Parnell did not, or, as Healy prophetically added, 'at any rate to go straight to jail, and leave us to "mop up the mess" '. Against O'Brien's estimate that the anti-Parnellites would win no more than fifty or sixty seats, he thought that the Parnellites would take only six seats: 'Really outside Dublin county and city I doubt if he can be *certain* anywhere of a seat'. Healy attributed O'Brien's attitude to a reaction against his own and Davitt's opposition to Parnell ('as Davitt troubled us by free criticism all along since 1882, and O'Brien thinks personal antipathy to Parnell guides Davitt's action and coloured mine'); and to O'Brien's anti-clerical feelings, or at least his fear of 'a division of Ireland into a Clerical Nationalist Party and a Fenian Party'.

Healy's anger was mitigated by lingering personal affection for O'Brien, and by concern at the degree of Liberal animosity towards him, particularly in the press. He was at pains to stress O'Brien's bona fides, and to portray him sympathetically as a well-intentioned sentimentalist defenceless against Parnell's cynical mastery.

> In fact Wm. is a transparently honest man who believes everyone will play fair like himself and that he can appease our tiger into ceasing to gnaw the bone. You may judge when I tell you that he said it would have been easier to deal with P. if we hadn't beaten him so heavily and that precipitating Kilkenny was a profound mistake! ... It is no good arguing further with O'Brien, though his attitude hampers us very much so that we can't dress Parnell properly just now. All our men are disgusted with O'Brien's going on ... Your people should get out of their heads that there is any fear that we shall take P. back. *We won't* and O'Brien is as much against him as anyone — only he is awash with big oceans of Christian charity.[13]

Labouchere himself crossed to meet O'Brien, and furnished virtually identical accounts of his interview with O'Brien to Gladstone and to Healy. In spite of Labouchere's untrustworthiness as a rapporteur, there is reason to believe that his account is accurate: Healy wrote that Labouchere's account described Parnell's attitude with 'photographic accuracy', and, forwarding the account to Maurice, added that O'Brien had made several of the remarks quoted to him.

O'Brien, in Labouchere's account, could not express too strongly his disgust with those who were trying to hound down Parnell. He characterised Healy's conduct as monstrous (an observation Labouchere discreetly omitted from the account of the interview he furnished to Healy). He insisted that Parnell was neither bitter nor influenced by personal animus but 'as cool as ever'. He quoted Parnell as saying: 'O'Brien, you and I are still young. If the General Elections go against us we can still carry on the fight in Ireland for another ten years or longer'. O'Brien commented:

> He is a man to stick to his word. I have no doubt that we could easily gain general elections against him, and in spite of him, but such a victory would be worse than a defeat, for we could carry it by resorting to means which would be obstruction to Ireland and to you. We should require the help either of the priests or the Fenians. God help our country from their influence.

O'Brien looked for understanding from the Liberals, claiming he had a prospect, albeit doubtful, of succeeding in his negotiations with Parnell: 'If I fail it will be all up with Ireland. It will be a Donnybrook fair with priests and Fenians fighting each other. I would rather have even Balfour than this'. He insisted that he was not prey to a sentimental tenderness towards Parnell, but rather sought to preserve the Liberal alliance. When Labouchere put it to O'Brien that Parnell seemed to have an extraordinary hold over all the Irish members, O'Brien rose heatedly to his feet and declared: 'We cannot forget all he has done for our nation. Yet we are willing to sacrifice him. It is a great sacrifice, and you English should be willing to take it into consideration'. Labouchere's conclusion — 'I am convinced that all argument will be lost on Mr. O'Brien' — can only have hardened Gladstone's resolve.[14]

For his part, O'Brien correctly discerned a Healy-Labouchere axis, and cabled to Dillon, 'Labby intriguing furiously with Tim against the Liberal party'.[15] Healy left Paris exasperated, empty-handed, and little the wiser. As anticipated O'Brien cabled to Healy at the National Liberal Club on 7 January refusing the chairmanship and editorship of the *National Press*.[16] It was never explained how O'Brien was supposed to edit an Irish daily newspaper from either of his prospective residences, Paris or Galway Jail. Had O'Brien accepted Healy's invitation, he would have found himself in the invidious position of the titular editor and chairman of a newspaper whose direction was entirely under Healy's control.

After Healy and Barry's visit, O'Brien cabled Dillon, 'they insanely believe Parnell beaten', and characterised the attitude of the anti-Parnellite party in Ireland as shocking.[17] Just as he overestimated Parnell's support,

O'Brien erroneously discounted Healy's influence in Ireland, writing to Bodkin, 'Tim did his worst at Nenagh but he does not count and will be mightily sold when he learns the real proposal'.[18]

In old age, William O'Brien wistfully exaggerated the significance of Healy's opposition to the Boulogne negotiations, and the possibility of having reversed it. He lamented his failure to confide in Healy, and fondly imagined that had Parnell given way 'Mr. Healy's objection would have yielded to an impulse of generosity as compelling as that which caused him to break down sobbing in the midst of one of his brainstorms in Committee Room 15, to hold out a hand of peace to his broken chief'.[19] It was a characteristically naïve belief, born of O'Brien's later espousal of conferences as a medium of political progress, his obsession with the 'Parnell Tragedy of Errors', and his eventual rapprochement with Healy. It was not merely that the enmity between Parnell and Healy had passed beyond the possibility of sentimental reconciliation. The split could not be reduced to their mutual adversity: O'Brien's excessively biographical perspective, so characteristic of nationalist memoirists and chroniclers, led him to disregard less tractable political realities.

Parnell throughout the Boulogne negotiations contrived to maintain his freedom of manœuvre by continuing to address meetings in Ireland. To O'Brien's remonstrances, he replied that a cessation of meetings would be a one-sided arrangement,

> as it would leave the seceders practically in full usage of any effective powers they possess, which are chiefly the private exertions of the priests and the circulation of the *Insuppressible* with your name on the imprint, while depriving us of the most effective means of ascertaining and guiding public opinion.

He assured O'Brien that 'at the same time I shall continue to be guided by a sense of my responsibility, and shall avoid any personal attack upon the seceding members or any exasperating reference to Mr. Gladstone'.[20]

Over the weekend of 10-11 January 1891 Parnell spoke in Limerick. He taunted the hierarchy as well as the majority with failing to condemn his leadership until after Gladstone's intervention, and reiterated the arguments of his manifesto, relying in corroboration on his letter to Cecil Rhodes of 1 March 1890, from which he quoted selectively. He denounced the evasiveness of Gladstone's denial of the allegations of the manifesto, and challenged him to publish his memorandum of the Hawarden meeting. He re-emphasised the four points raised in his manifesto:

> These four points are the points of your charter. Hold firm to them. Be sure to get them before you surrender your leader *(cries of 'never')*. When you have got them you have got the power over your own future, and you can be as civil as you like to the Grand Old Man *(laughter)*. But until then remember the old Irish proverb. 'Beware of the dog's tooth, the bull's horn, and the Saxon's smile *(cheers)*, and even though the Saxon's smile of

yesterday may be turned into the frown of hate depend upon yourselves until you have got beyond yea or nay the rights you are looking for *(cheers)*.

This lapse into an unwontedly populist idiom was ill considered: the
reference to the 'Saxon smile' was particularly unguarded and would be
savagely retorted upon him by Healy with reference to Katharine O'Shea
throughout the split. Parnell shamelessly lauded William O'Brien, his
patriotism 'and deep friendship for myself — deep, lasting, long-
continuing, and fervent', and, waving his hat, called for cheers for O'Brien,
whom he calmly declared had 'traversed the ocean to consult with me as
to the course to be taken'. Speaking on the evening of his arrival from the
window of Cruise's Hotel in the blaze of torches and tar barrels, Parnell
concluded with a variation on a practised image:

> I shall attempt to imitate even at a long interval, the devoted patriotism and
> supreme courage which the Irish people have shown from time immemorial
> in defence of the nationality of Ireland *(cheers)*. If I falter, if I am weak,
> if I do not realise the ideal of you, patriotic Irishmen, I ask you to believe
> of me that I shall fail, not by intention, not from my heart, that I have desired
> to accompany Ireland to the gate of freedom, and within the gate of freedom,
> and if it should not be permitted for me to enter with you within that gate
> I shall, whether you like it or not, fight with you outside that gate until I
> have secured your interests and your independence *(prolonged cheering)*.

It was a declaration characteristic of Parnell in the split, the deceptive
hint of apology overwhelmed in his pride and combativeness of utterance.
The following weekend found Parnell in Tralee where he for the first time
warned of the consequences of clerical intervention in the split on
Irish Protestant attitudes to home rule; the weekend after he was in
Waterford.[21]

By negotiation in France and combat in Ireland, Parnell was regaining
lost ground. He was also recovering some of his fractured poise. The *Spectator*, while no doubt actuated in part by the unionist determination to
level the odds of the contest in Ireland, in contrasting his speech in Tralee
with those in Kilkenny, discerned a change in his demeanour: 'He has lost
his air of desperation, he has put off or suppressed the bravo, and he speaks
once more as a leader who at all events intends the world to accept him
as a statesman'.[22]

As Healy later wrote, the anti-Parnellites 'could not afford to stand,
wringing their hands, while, in the intervals of negotiations, Mr. Parnell
was sweeping through Ireland like a prairie fire'.[23] Healy proceeded with
an engagement at Nenagh on the weekend of 10-11 January, where he
dissociated himself from the Boulogne negotiations, for whose success he
entertained 'no hope whatever': 'His opinion was that Mr. Parnell was playing at Boulogne the game of Committee Room No. 15 all over again. His
policy had been the policy, first of delay, then of deception'. O'Brien had
not been present in the Committee Room and was consequently

susceptible to 'a whole litany of "ifs" ' recited by Parnell. Parnell's policy was of 'Rule or Ruin'. Healy charged that in demanding the disclosure of the terms of the Home Rule Bill Parnell was 'playing the same game as Chamberlain's Liberal Unionists', who had since the defeat of the Home Rule Bill harassed Gladstone to declare the terms of the next Home Rule Bill 'so that they might declare it worse than the one before'.

In a calculated evocation of O'Shea's involvement in the Kilmainham treaty, Healy declared that the Irish people would allow the Irish party 'to make no backstairs treaty behind their backs'. He cast a cruel and effective aphorism: 'When Mr. Parnell was on the fire escape at Eltham, Mr. O'Brien was on the plank bed at Tullamore'. Healy's closing peroration awkwardly disclosed the anti-Parnellite predicament of debilitating reliance on Liberal goodwill without any means of holding the Liberals to the bargain of the split:

> They would send Gladstone this message from that meeting today: 'Be true to Ireland and Ireland would be true to you' *(cheers)*. They declared to the English Liberal Party that never should Charles Stewart Parnell be allowed to lead their race or nation again *(cheers)*. But ... they should insist upon the full measure of their rights, a free and independent Parliament in College Green *(renewed cheers)*.[24]

To his constituents at Edgeworthstown the following week, Healy announced that 'he was there to declare that he would not tolerate by act or deed, secretly or openly, the leadership, covert or open, of Mr. Charles Stewart Parnell'.[25]

What was most galling to O'Brien was that the most persistent and vehement opposition to the Boulogne negotiations came from the anti-Parnellite *Insuppressible*, provokingly subtitled 'William O'Brien's Paper'.[26] While notionally under O'Brien's control through the medium of the editor Mathias Bodkin, *Insuppressible* was from the outset imbued with the spirit of Healyite opposition to Parnell. The hapless Bodkin, instructed by O'Brien to hold firmly but temperately to Parnell's retirement, and to write everything on the subject himself, had difficulty resisting the anti-Parnellite fury raging around him, and eventually gave up trying. After he had rejected the most vigorous contributions to the first issue, a subscription was got up by the Healyites to despatch him to Boulogne to confer with O'Brien. For the period of his absence *Insuppressible* was produced by a collective, with Healy, according to the young A. M. Sullivan, contributing the best and wittiest paragraphs. On his return, Bodkin wrote to O'Brien on 5 January, feebly insisting that he had throughout been a moderating influence, and that the objectionable paragraphs were not Healy's but D. B. Sullivan's.[27]

With Healy's return from Paris, the editorial policy of *Insuppressible* achieved a new stridency, which must be taken to reflect his direct inspiration. While professing unctuous allegiance to O'Brien, the *Insuppressible* could hardly have been more subversive of his peace-making efforts. Rather than directly condemn the Boulogne negotiations, *Insuppressible* espoused maximalist anti-Parnellite objectives in terms calculated to submit Parnell to the greatest possible provocation. On 10 January it affirmed the necessity of Parnell's 'absolute surrender' at Boulogne, by which it meant his permanent withdrawal: 'The retirement of Mr. Parnell from the chairmanship of the Irish Party, which we assume was the first article of the Boulogne settlement, is by its very nature irrevocable'. To Davitt's initial moderate demand in the *Labour World* that Parnell retire for a period of six months, Parnell had responded with a denunciation of Gladstone: through this and his subsequent conduct Parnell 'has built up walls of brass which forever bar him from the leadership'. On 12 January, anticipating Dillon's arrival at Boulogne, *Insuppressible* declared that Parnell knew that Dillon and O'Brien, in alliance with the forces already arrayed against him 'would chase him from Ireland like a mad dog ... we are convinced that he will submit to whatever terms they think proper to impose. He may shout or kick a bit in the beginning; but he will "go quietly" in the end'. Two days later, in an editorial entitled 'Kilkenny to Boulogne', the paper wrote provokingly: 'It would have been very humbling to have crept away after a bad beating ... the interval has allowed Parnell to move with a certain assumption of grace and dignity towards the wings ...' It looked to the curtain falling on Parnell's 'final exit'.[28]

O'Brien's attempts to moderate from Boulogne the newspaper war in Ireland, telegraphing in turn Bodkin and Byrne of the *Freeman's Journal*, proved unavailing. Increasingly angered at his failure to control *Insuppressible*, he fired a warning shot, publicly discountenancing 'the unwarrantable use that is being made of my name in expressions of opinion tending to perpetuate strife in Ireland'. Bodkin unconvincingly defended himself, asserting that, while 'the people who find money for the paper are constantly urging me to show more vigour', he was trying to steer a middle course.[29] Healy's policy was to inflict the maximum damage on the Boulogne initiative before O'Brien's inevitable repudiation of the *Insuppressible*. Finally disavowed by O'Brien on 23 January, *Insuppressible*, with a parting shot at 'the unsuspecting magnanimity of Dillon and O'Brien', ceased publication.[30]

At a meeting of the National Committee to establish the National Federation, held on the evening of the receipt of O'Brien's telegram repudiating *Insuppressible*, Healy nonetheless took care to rein in the diehards and stave off the threat of a schism between Dillon and O'Brien and the anti-Parnellite organisation in Ireland. The majority, he declared, had laid down as a basis of settlement 'the recognition absolute and decisive of the deposition of Mr. Charles Stewart Parnell', subject to which there was 'hardly any secondary plan to which we would not go very far in endeavouring to accommodate ourselves to'. As to the proposition that Dillon and O'Brien possessed no mandate from their party, Healy declared it would be taking 'entirely too high a ground to hold language of that character is any part of the country'. He at the same time reiterated his opinion that the negotiations should never have been undertaken, and adapted a quip he ascribed to the Parnellites to declare that 'Mr. Parnell was hanged in Kilkenny, but was cut down again in Boulogne'. To the protocols of Boulogne Healy opposed the imagery of Brighton, repudiating the idea that 'the Boulogne conference will end in any form of "fire escape", whereby, having thrust Mr. Parnell through the window, Mr. Parnell will be allowed to get through the halldoor'. He seized the pretext of McCarthy's absence to propose the adjournment of the meeting, and so pre-empted any resolutions openly repudiating the negotiations at Boulogne.[31]

The Boulogne negotiations took place against a background of uncertain relations between the anti-Parnellites and the Liberal leadership, as they struggled to reconstitute the Liberal-Nationalist alliance. At the end of December Healy had made to Gladstone a proposal fraught with hazard for the home rule alliance. The proposal, contained in a letter Labouchere forwarded to Gladstone, who received it on 30 December 1890, has not survived, but from Gladstone's reply it is clear that Healy had solicited formal Liberal endorsement of anti-Parnellites, so as to solemnise the split and constitute the anti-Parnellites *the* Nationalist party for the purposes of the Liberal-Nationalist alliance, an endorsement intended to forestall the Boulogne negotiations.

Gladstone from the outset was alive to the delicacy of the issue of relations between the Liberal leadership and the anti-Parnellites. On the day after the split in the Irish party, he wrote to Morley that they must now hope that 'our friends will find backing in their own country'. 'It will need infinite discretion on their part and ours to avoid the suspicion — which for good reason comes so naturally to Irishmen — that they have in any sense become the tail of English "Whigs" ', which he correctly anticipated would be Parnell's cry. He doubted the expediency of public or private relations with the majority before the opening of the House of Commons in January.[32]

While Healy's letter struck Morley as not unreasonable, Gladstone immediately realised its perilous implications, and responded with a letter to Labouchere marked 'Private but may be sent or shown to Mr. Healy', which judiciously mingled effusive flattery with extreme circumspection. He lauded the course taken by Healy from the Committee Room to his denunciation of the Boulogne negotiations at the National Committee on 24 December. He had read Healy's letter 'as I read his noble scalping speech, and as I have watched his conduct ever since the Clancy amendment, with deep sympathy'. His first impulse when the vote had been taken against Parnell was to communicate 'in warm terms' with McCarthy 'and those nearest to him in the party, such as Mr. Healy and Mr. Sexton'. 'A motive of prudence restrained me, lest Parnell should make fatal use of anything I did or said by the cry of English dictation, which he had raised from the first. Therefore I turned the cold shoulder and remained silent, while my whole soul was profoundly interested.' His first duty had been to get the sense of his party, and to afford Parnell the opportunity of spontaneously accepting the fact of his deposition: 'Remember this has been a revelation to me, I had no idea of the depths of the disgrace, no, not even after the Court, to which he could descend'. Of the reception of the deputation appointed pursuant to the Clancy amendment, he wrote that he had seldom spent a more painful hour or hour and a half: 'I told my colleagues that evening that my heart bled for them — for those I mean who have worked in the majority'. In relation to the anti-Parnellite majority, the Clancy amendment would 'have riveted the yoke of Parnell on their back'. Parnell had not given a real pledge to retire. Gladstone described his own speech at the Bassetlaw election as 'stingily guarded', but he had spoken 'in fear and trembling lest it should be laid hold of'. In conclusion, he held firmly to his course of reticence, and declined to accept Healy's invitation: 'In a word, if there is a desire for to say more I am quite ready to communicate with — I must not choose the person — but with the new Irish Leadership on the matter'.[33]

Healy's dangerously ill-judged proposal afforded a perfect, almost parodic, vindication of Parnell's strictures against the majority. Evidently alarmed at the prospect of the advantage gained at Kilkenny being dissipated at Boulogne, he was moving to consolidate the ascendancy of the hardline domestic opposition to Parnell by eliciting from Gladstone an endorsement (the consequent deepened estrangement of Parnellite nationalists would have been by no means inimical to his purpose). Healy — as Gladstone was quick to apprehend — was acting on his own initiative without the sanction of the other anti-Parnellite leaders, and his suggested mode of intervention, evidently by a communication from Gladstone to Healy, would have served as an acknowledgement of his *de facto* hegemony within the majority. His initiative bore all the hallmarks of a collaborative enterprise with Labouchere, a reprise of their politically inept intervention in the critical prelude to home rule, 1885-86.

Gladstone ruminated further on Healy's request in a letter to Morley of 12 January. Of Parnell he wrote that 'it has been plain for some time that he was either mad, or incredibly deprived of both principle and shame', and that his Limerick speeches went to the latter alternative. He feared that Parnell would strike a posture of opposition to any Home Rule Bill which would be produced: 'I expect that this will be Parnell's game against the adverse majority; and that he will succeed not in restoring himself, but in baulking and in baffling them, and us with them, by arguing, whatever they accept, that it is manifestly not enough'. In two months Parnell had done enough mischief to negate his 'years of splendid service', 1882-89. Gladstone remained acutely alive to Parnell's acumen and tenacity:

> It is certainly another question what to say and what not to say; the Nationalist majority halfthrottled in his strong grasp seem to ask (if Healy is a voice from them) for express support from us. He, on the other hand, watches like a lynx for anything that can be called English dictation. Hereupon counter arguments arise. On which side are they stronger? And, who should answer the question I have just put?
>
> In my opinion, the Irish Nationalists should answer it — with a full sense of its delicacy, as well as its weight. If they make a corporate i.e. authoritative request in the sense of Healy, I suppose we ought to comply with it. Till then, we, I mean the ex-Cabinet ought probably to be silent. Evidently *he* means to fight a desperate battle, and he will probably show that he has nine lives, like a cat.[34]

The awkwardness of Healy's request was precisely that it raised the full implications of Liberal intervention: a contemplated response by Gladstone expressed in terms of a readiness to respect 'the free agency of Ireland' begged the issue of the split.

The Liberal leader however spared the anti-Parnellites the consequences of Healy's misjudgement. Healy's request can only have borne in upon him a realisation of the want of capacity of the leadership of the domestic opposition to Parnell, and the slackening in the necessarily tense equilibrium of the Liberal-Nationalist alliance brought about by the fall of Parnell, which threatened to substitute for the formal order of the alliance Gladstonian tutelage of a nationalist client party.

Healy's letter to Labouchere of 9 January forwarded by Labouchere, must have served to deepen Gladstone's apprehensions. Healy's principal concern was now to allay Liberal fears that the Boulogne negotiations would be permitted to result in the *de facto* restoration of Parnell, and to warn against the adverse effects which attacks on the negotiations in the Liberal press were producing on opinion in Ireland. He explained that he and Barry had warned O'Brien of the effect of delay and 'friendly negotiation with Parnell' on English opinion. O'Brien replied that he trusted Gladstone. 'As I was equally strong in that opinion I turned my batteries on some of Mr. G.'s colleagues and Wm. replied that he had faith in the English democracy keeping their leaders straight.' The letter culminated in an intriguing outburst, against the excesses of the 'nonconformist conscience' and of the Liberal press which revealingly overreached the immediate argument:

> What a horror the whole thing has been. Yet your Noncoms [*sic*] at their ease recommended us to exorcise our demon as if we had only to say 'Begone,

Satan', while I have not the least doubt that Stead will be amongst the first to howl for the chucking of Home Rule. I confess I have not O'Brien's faith in British Democracy, nor in any Democracy or cracy. I think the Irish must rely on 86 votes and that if anything happened to Mr. Gladstone we should be in Queer Street. We therefore are fighting P. haunted and weakened by the terrible possibility that in the end he may turn out to have been right ... it will be a poor consolation to men like me to know when Parnell chortles 'I told you so' that he himself was the cause of the catastrophe. He will always be able to say that if we took his advice, it would have been all right and we cannot disprove this, while many must swallow it. In fact nothing could justify us except success and I am far from hopeful of the General Election now, thanks to Parnell & Co. ... The last state of Ireland will be worse than the first. However, if your Liberals will only not go screeching like geese we shall carry on and make a thorough fight, but if we be stabbed in the back by your Atherley Joneses it were better for men like me to 'up Killick' as the sailors say and seek my bread elsewhere. P cannot detach one vote from our side, but Stead & Co. may detach several and articles in the P.M.Gazette against O'B. are purely mischievous. We all know O'B. to be an honest man and why should he be ridiculed? [35]

Healy's irascible and inconstant vehemence marked a sharp break from the classic idiom of Parnellism. It reflected the altered condition of nationalist power, and starkly illumined the anti-Parnellite dilemma. The majority's leverage vis-à-vis the Liberals now lay exclusively in the risk that Parnell might gain the political advantage. For the creative equilibrium of Parnellism before Parnell's fall was substituted a weak appeal to elective affinities within the Liberal-Nationalist alliance.

Gladstone's course, as he struggled to salvage what *The Times* unkindly called 'the dream of his old age', was shaped by his acute sense of how formidable an adversary Parnell remained. In a memorandum written on 29 December 1890, his eighty-second birthday, he glumly ruminated on Parnell's 'scandalous exhibition of political resistance', which he believed would give rise to doubts among the weak-minded as to the Irish capacity for self-government. In surveying the political prospect, it is significant that he reverted to the perception of Parnell he had held prior to the Kilmainham treaty as the enemy of constitutional order, and erroneously equated Parnell's stance in the split with a rebellion against parliamentary democracy:

The cause is not that of Parnell as the accepted leader: he has been deposed. But his desperate struggle to retain the post, and his pretended appeal to the people have received countenance sufficient to make him at the moment a formidable rebel against Parliamentary Government, and supported by about as many members as he had in 1880.

Parnell, Gladstone thought, might have postponed home rule for a further five or six years [36] (and so beyond his likely tenure of the Liberal leadership).

After the defeat of the Liberal candidate at Bassetlaw, which he attributed either to a reaction of the English peasantry against the Liberals after 'the momentary favour shown us in '85', or to 'dismay and perplexity caused by Parnell', Gladstone wrote to E. W. Hamilton of Parnell: 'For political guilt, I know nothing in history like his conduct. But the man has a genius'. A month later he confided to Hamilton that he believed Parnell still had the Irish party completely in his hands.[37]

The containment of the damage wrought by the divorce crisis on the Liberal-party had nevertheless gone exceedingly well from Gladstone's point of view. Schnadhorst, the Liberal party organiser, wrote of the Bassetlaw result that while the Liberal vote was down 200, it was 'impossible to trace any loss to the recent events'. Although much depended upon the outcome of by-elections in Ireland, he did not believe that they had sustained a loss and rather that there was 'probably a check in the progress we have been making thro' the year'.[38] Even though predicated on the ouster of Parnell from the Irish leadership, Schnadhorst's assessment may suggest a greater robustness on the part of the Liberal-Nationalist alliance than the Liberal response to the divorce crisis had allowed for. It was a view formed from the narrow perspective of a party manager. While the general election of 1892 returned Gladstone to office, the compelling urgency of the demand for home rule under Parnell was gone, and the strength of the home rule alliance did not suffice to carry the issue beyond the defeat of the Home Rule Bill by the House of Lords in 1893.

In his letter to Morley of 7 December, warning against any formal relations with the anti-Parnellite party 'before the opening of parliament in January, Gladstone had addressed the extremely sensitive issue of anti-Parnellite finances: 'There will be good reasons for raising money for some of the forty-five — most of them in fact. Here again the utmost reserve will be necessary. Any *public* English fund for their salaries will have the worst effect in Ireland, and the raising and conveyance of such a fund will need much consideration'.[39] Gladstone's willingness to contemplate discreet private funding of the Irish majority was tempered by his fear of the risk of disclosure of anything which could be construed as Liberal subvention of the majority. The matter continued to concern him: three days later he wisely cancelled a letter he had drafted to Arnold Morley directing that 'when the effort is made to raise money for Irish Parliamentary purposes, in order to make up for the delinquencies of Mr. Parnell, please to put me down for £500'.[40] As the issue of Liberal funding of the majority passed into unofficial channels, the ubiquitous — and affluent — Henry Labouchere came to the fore. He wrote to Gladstone on 17 December that the anti-Parnellites would appreciate a good subscription in England for the evicted tenants. On 3 January Harcourt wrote to Gladstone that he heard from Labouchere 'that the key to the struggle in the Irish camp is the money chest'. On 11 January, Labouchere as the writer had unquestionably intended, forwarded to Gladstone Healy's letter of

9 January, which contained the pregnant question, posed in the context of a possible general-election defeat for the Liberal-Nationalist alliance: 'Where are we to get the funds to carry on a campaign thereafter? And if not the Irish representation will go back to the Tories who alone seem to have money to spend'. It is difficult to construe this other than as a pitch for funds — the idea of the Irish representation reverting to the Conservatives was patently absurd. The financial position of the anti-Parnellites was the main subject of Labouchere's covering letter to Gladstone: 'The real difficulty now is the financial one. They have hardly any money'. Labouchere proceeded to advise Gladstone that the 'difficulty has been met, but inadequately. It is not desirable, perhaps, that you should know much about this, as Parnell is capable of asserting that his opponents are on English pay, on the chance of its being true'.[41]

Evidently a financial contribution had been arranged from sympathetic Liberals to tide the anti-Parnellites over, of which Labouchere could not resist archly advising Gladstone. In a letter to Harcourt after Parnell's death, Labouchere stated that funds had been given after the Kilkenny by-election to John Barry 'without it being possible to say that they came from the Liberal party', which led F. S. L. Lyons convincingly to surmise that what appeared in the ledger of the anti-Parnellite fund as a loan of £1,550 from Barry represented a concealed contribution from English sympathisers.[42]

Parnell had already, in Labouchere's phrase, suggested that his opponents were on English pay 'on the chance of its being true'. At the Rotunda he had declared, 'We are in a position to estimate the magnitude and depth of our opponents when we have fathomed the depth of the purse of Henry Labouchere and Professor Stuart'.[43] The procuring of funds from sympathetic Liberal sources did not inhibit Healy from charging that Parnell's Kilkenny campaign was financed by monies from the Carlton Club and the English secret service.[44]

English press comments on Boulogne reflected amused Conservative gratification and mounting Liberal unease. *The Times*, celebrating the comic inconstancy of the Irish character and the sentimental passions of Irish politics, discerned in the Boulogne negotiations evidence for its belief that the split was in the main a collusive exercise between the Nationalist factions: 'Irish patriots are of so divine an essence that like Milton's angels, they heal their scars and join their severed limbs with instantaneous rapidity'. The anticipated settlement at Boulogne after 'the howls, the tears, the vituperation, and the shillelaghs of the "patriots"' would provide 'a ludicrous but perfectly appropriate termination to the burlesque that began with Mr. Parnell's manifesto'.[45] Of greater concern to Nationalists was the hostility of the Liberal press. The *Daily News* warned of the disastrous consequences of an O'Brien leadership, while the *Pall Mall Gazette* denounced 'Mr. O'Brien the Unionist hope', and in a leading article on 'the Boulogne harlequinade' warned that if the nationalists agreed to a reconciliation under the leadership of a nominee of Parnell, 'to us brutal Saxons it would show the Patriots to be as maudlin as Mr. Parnell himself be mad'.[46]

Of the Liberal leaders, it was John Morley who displayed the deepest understanding of the Irish predicament. In a memorandum to Gladstone before the Kilkenny poll, dated 21 December 1890, he detected a worsening of the split and noted that, as Parnell was now an enemy, there was no longer an authoritative Irish leader with whom to deal. The spectacle of 'faction in Ireland' had revived old English misgivings, deepened by ecclesiastical intervention: 'The dependence, now made patent, of the Parliamentary Nationalists on the Catholic clergy will worsen our case in Great Britain, to say nothing of Ulster'. The adverse political consequences of the split could be decisive in marginal constituencies. He made the striking assertion that 'a divided Ireland would be a negligible quantity in our affairs. I would rather see Ireland Parnellite than divided for her own sake'. He canvassed the possibility of Dillon and O'Brien achieving a reconciliation on the basis of Parnell going to America for the coming session, or at least absenting himself from the Commons. Even in the absence of reconciliation Morley asked, 'Will not the tendency to common action in Parliament on the Land Bill and other Irish matters make for reunion?'.[47]

While considering Parnell's proposed secret memorandum containing the terms of the Liberal Home Rule Bill of the future 'a desperately childish sort of device', Morley favoured public clarification of the points raised by the manifesto.[48] He was acutely cognisant of the obligations under which the Liberal leadership had placed itself in requiring the termination of Parnell's leadership of the Irish party:

> I don't think our party at all realise the immense responsibility they have incurred, when they insisted on the cashiering of Parnell. They write — or some of them do — as if we English had nothing to do but veto Parnell, or veto Dillon, and all would be plain sailing in Ireland. They little know the currents and undercurrents of faction in the country.

If no assurances were forthcoming, he warned that Dillon and O'Brien would submit to imprisonment 'and will come out to find the whole movement in pretty complete collapse, or else Parnell practically master of a demoralised party'. Morley's memorandum reveals the deepening realisation of the lieutenant most sympathetic to Gladstone of the implications of the Liberal response to the divorce crisis. He much later experienced intimations of remorse, suppressed in his public utterances and published works, in relation to the Liberal stance, on which he blamed the subsequent malaise of the Liberal-Nationalist alliance, if not the larger failure of the Gladstonian legacy in British politics.[49]

The debate within the Liberal leadership over Boulogne was reflected in conflicting personal preferences for Irish politicians. Gladstone favoured Healy, while Morley looked to Dillon and O'Brien. Gladstone wrote to Granville that Healy was 'of stiffer material' than Dillon and O'Brien, and to Harcourt that 'Healy and his friends have the strongest claims, political and moral, on both our consideration and our support'.[50] Morley had written to Dillon that 'if you and O'Brien should only have taken your part in the front of the fight, I should have no fear of the result'.[51] Morley disputed Gladstone's assessment of Dillon ('you think Dillon somewhat wanting in stoutness of heart'), and badly underestimated, if not Healy's stature, at least his capacity for mischief: 'It is well enough for Healy to flourish his tomahawk, but he has no weight in Ireland; he is a mere *gamin*'.[52] Harcourt regarded the Boulogne negotiations with unwavering suspicion, and the Irish leaders with impartial hostility. He discerned an objectively collusive purpose between the Irish parties.

> You know I have not a high opinion of Irish human nature [he wrote to Gladstone on 1 January], and I think it not at all improbable that they will in spite of all that has passed kiss and be friends and 'go for the money', for which they care a great deal more than they do either for Home Rule or the English alliance.

He wrote of the Boulogne negotiations on 7 January, 'I am afraid my opinion of these gentlemen is not at all on the mend'.[53]

On 26 January, after a conversation with Thomas Sexton, Labouchere wrote to urge Gladstone to furnish the assurances sought at Boulogne. While doubting the correctness of Sexton's belief that Parnell would withdraw if the assurances were satisfactory — 'for the man seems lost to all honour' — he continued: 'If he does not, however, many of his followers will leave him, and the best card will be taken out of his hand, for the Irish really do believe that they are to have control neither of the Police nor of the Land'.[54]

Even Healy had by now begun to accommodate himself to the possibility of a successful outcome of the Boulogne negotiations. He was, however, imperfectly informed of the terms under discussion. He had been left under the impression that the sufficiency of the assurances were to be adjudicated upon by McCarthy as well as by Parnell and O'Brien, and that there was a commitment on the part of a body of Parnell's parliamentary followers to abandon his cause if he showed bad faith.[55] He wrote to Walsh on 4 February that 'it seems as if P. were thinking of giving in ... Of course he may be "foxing" but I write assuming the Boulogne expectations'. The prospect of a settlement increased his determination to consolidate his own position. He wrote that it would take a fortnight to procure the meetings of the party necessary to have Dillon elected chairman 'and delay is useful for the new paper will be nearer starting every day and Parnell I gather

will address no more meetings in Ireland'. Against the possibility of the
negotiations succeeding, Healy was preparing himself for the second phase
of the split which Parnell's withdrawal would inaugurate — the war for
ascendancy within the anti-Parnellite camp, which was inseparably linked
to his purpose of blocking off any future resumption of the leadership
by Parnell.[56]

On 28 January the Liberal leadership provided written assurances, which
Dillon and O'Brien believed sufficient to ensure the satisfactory outcome
of the negotiations with Parnell. The negotiations had now come so close
to success that their failure would serve sensibly to accentuate the bitterness
and exasperation of the split. When an exhausted Parnell reached Calais
he took furious exception to an objection taken by Dillon to his proposal
to lodge the Paris Funds in their joint names, on the ground that this would
permit Parnell to incapacitate Dillon's leadership financially. More seriously, when Parnell returned to London, T. P. Gill ineptly gave him to understand that the Liberal leadership had made it a condition that O'Brien was
to be the sole arbiter of the adequacy of the guarantees.

Parnell now sought two modifications to the assurances. The first was
that the Royal Irish Constabulary should be abolished by a provision of
the Home Rule Bill itself; the second was to provide for the retention of
the full complement of Irish members at Westminster in the event of imperial Parliament reserving to itself the resolution of the land question.
Parnell further wrote to Gill on 5 February protesting against his supposed exclusion from adjudicating on the Liberal assurances, and mysteriously
asserting that information had reached him to the effect that it was intended that the existing number of Irish members would be retained at
Westminster, thereby detracting from the sufficiency and finality of the
home rule measure.

The fate of the negotiations was sealed by the refusal of the Liberal
leadership, abidingly mistrustful of Parnell and determined to avoid any
course which could be construed as negotiating with him, to amend the
assurances offered. O'Brien on 8 February wrote despondently to Redmond
that there was 'not the smallest use in prolonging the agony', and that
Parnell's action would make Healy 'the happiest man in London': 'I sadly fear that, whereas his acceptance of these conditions would have left
him the most potent man in the Irish race, he is now entering a conflict
which at the very brightest can only end in making the country a hellfire
of discord and defamation ... I suppose every man has always had to do
whatever fate ordains for him'.[57] As Gill and O'Brien struggled to con-
vince Parnell that his new concerns were groundless, they had also to advise him of the Liberal refusal to amend the guarantees.

Parnell cited the Liberals' refusal as the reason for breaking off the
negotiations, declaring his regret that it had not been possible for him to
conclude that there was no danger to the cause 'in my surrendering the

responsibility which has been placed upon me and which I have accepted at the hands of our nation and our race'.[58]

Parnell's refusal of the extremely favourable terms offered him at Boulogne — terms designed to entrench his pre-eminence, with the hope of ensuring that his retirement would only prove temporary — appeared profligate and hubristic, and also to suggest that he never intended to conclude a settlement at Boulogne, however generous the terms. Yet the ambassadorial ambience of the Boulogne negotiations was fundamentally deceptive. O'Brien and Dillon were, for all their considerable prestige, self-constituted envoys. Neither were they plenipotentiaries of the anti-Parnellite party, nor were their views representative of anti-Parnellite sentiment in the country: from the outset the *Irish Catholic* had warned that O'Brien had no mandate to participate in the 'farce' at Boulogne.[59] While almost any terms which entailed Parnell's resignation and did not impugn the legitimacy of his deposition and the election of McCarthy would have commanded acceptance in Ireland, Dillon and O'Brien were in no position to assure Parnell the reversion of the Irish leadership. As Archbishop Walsh warned Dillon, 'No matter what arrangement the party may come to, the opposition to him will go on'.[60]

The mounting evidence that Healy's rhetoric reflected the views of the socially dominant strata of rural nationalist society, including the Catholic Church, overcast the parleys at Boulogne. The negotiations had elicited an intensification of anti-Parnellite moral vehemence. The *Nation* emphasised that the country had already rejected 'an adulterer who prefers his passion to his country', while the *Irish Catholic* described as 'sickening' the idea of compromise with 'a convicted adulterer'.[61] Archbishop Logue wrote to Walsh from Rome on 27 December, ominously categorising Parnell's campaign as a challenge to the Church ('the anti-clerical crusade foreshadowed by the *Freeman* will be his death-knell') and warning that it would be a mistake to make peace. They should rather fight Parnell 'for fight him we must in the long run'.[62]

As the negotiations progressed, it was increasingly clear that the depth of anti-Parnellite sentiment in Ireland militated against Parnell reserving the kind of abiding pre-eminence and likely reversion of the Irish leadership contemplated at Boulogne. During the period of the negotiations, the lines of the split had hardened. Parnell cannot have failed to realise that he had gone too far down the road of confrontation to permit a reconciliation with his hardline opponents and their clerical backers. Moreover, there was no prospect whatever of an abatement of Liberal hostility to his resumption of the leadership. All that had happened since the split had served to deepen the conviction he had expressed to Morley on 25 November: '... if he gave up the leadership for a time, he should never return to it; that if he once let go, it was all over'.[63]

Parnell's decision to refuse the terms offered him at Boulogne is

explicable politically in terms of his perception of the necessity of confronting the coalition against any restoration of his leadership, and of facing
down the gathering challenge of an assertive Catholic nationalism. Thus
in his first draft of the letter breaking off further negotiations at Boulogne
(prudently suppressed, on John Redmond's advice), Parnell had alluded
to the hostile pastorals of several of the Irish bishops as creating 'great
doubts in my mind as to whether the peace we are struggling for is at all
possible, and as to whether we are not compelled to face even greater and
larger issues than those yet raised in this struggle'.[64]

The failure of the Boulogne negotiations subsequently became the subject of bitter acrimony and interminable speculation. For William O'Brien,
who had systematically underrated both Parnell's strength of will and the
immensity of the forces arrayed against Parnell in Ireland, the Boulogne
failure became the central episode in what he called 'the Parnell tragedy
of errors'. T. P. Gill likewise wrote to Morley in a naïve and superficial
assessment of the negotiations in 1892 that Parnell was not 'only consistent ... but ... he was perfectly frank and simple', and that 'all the dark
mystery' originated in the minds of those who regarded Parnell as having
been suddenly transformed 'into some venomous snake whom to touch
was to be poisoned. Parnell at the last realised how he was being treated
and it stung him fiercely. With that and the whole plague of misunderstanding ends the whole thing'. Gill lamented 'the bungling, fuss and fretful
impatience, the crosspurposes, the paltry fears, suspicions and misunder-
standings that supervened at a certain stage' and caused the negotiations
to miscarry.[65]

What was significant in terms of Parnell's psychology was, however, not
any sense of personal hurt, but the fact that the scale of opposition to
him detracted from the voluntary character of any withdrawal, and gave
it the aspect of an acceptance of the inevitability of defeat were he to fight
on. Interviewed after the end of the negotiations, Parnell 'with much emphasis' declared: 'One thing I am determined upon — that I will not retire
under compulsion, no matter from what quarter it comes'.[66]

Parnell throughout the split invoked the struggle for supremacy through
which he had first achieved leadership, reflecting his awareness that he had
prevailed by a course of challenge and audacity. He cannot have failed to
realise that even if a settlement at Boulogne were to eventuate after a period
in his resumption of the leadership, neither his former mystique nor his
power would remain intact. If recalled to the leadership at all, it would
be as a figurehead, a leader on sufferance, drawing on depleted reserves
of public gratitude for past achievements: in short, he would have been
precisely the kind of titular leader that Healy taunted him with having
been for the preceding decade. He was thus starkly confronted with the
constraints on effective nationalist leadership in Irish politics which he had
so skilfully evaded in the period of his hegemony, and to which he remained

unwilling to submit. To have agreed to withdraw in such circumstances would have been at odds with the entire course of his antecedent career.

Manifestly Parnell was not, as he had described himself with ominous menace at the Rotunda, 'a man whose heart delighted in compromise'.[67] Yet Healy's charge that Parnell's participation in the negotiations was of an entirely cynical character, and that he was resolved from the outset to repudiate any compromise, was too simplistic. Parnell engaged in the negotiations, ready to see whether a settlement which reserved to him an enduring pre-eminence in Irish politics could be achieved, but he remained throughout watchful and suspicious, all the while awaiting confirmation of his inclination to fight out the issue of the split. Against a background of hardening opposition in Ireland and Liberal intransigence, he reverted to the line of action he had instinctively favoured from the outset, and from which, by continuing to campaign through the negotiations, he had never desisted — the quest for victory in Ireland.

In the event Parnell did derive some tactical advantages from the Boulogne negotiations, though not remotely to the extent suggested by Healy in his later tirades against O'Brien and Dillon. He had recovered some of his lost aplomb, and showed once again his tactical supremacy. He had moreover consolidated the allegiance of his parliamentary supporters, the need to maintain which he felt as a constraint on his political conduct through the early split. He told Andrew Kettle in Dublin in the course of the negotiations: 'I have a lot of poor weak men around me. In fact I have more trouble with them than with the other fellows'. Sophie O'Brien later wrote that Parnell during the negotiations 'once blurted out to my husband that his friends' weakness was his chief trouble'.[68]

Parnell had already bound his lieutenants closely to him. It is unlikely that any of them, in spite of the desperate hopes of Dillon and O'Brien, would have deserted him unless he showed the most flagrant bad faith. Significantly, by the end Redmond was so far reconciled to Parnell breaking off the negotiations as to advise him to do so on the grounds of the Liberal refusal to amplify the assurances.[69]

Dillon later in Galway Jail sought to stiffen O'Brien's resolve against further negotiations by invoking the conduct of Parnell's lieutenants at Boulogne. Parnell, he wrote, 'has been too clever, and he has bound them so that I cannot for the life of me see how they can escape from him'. In a suggestive evocation of Parnell's unyielding purpose, he recalled the abortive endeavours of Redmond, Harrington and the others during the negotiations at Boulogne to prevail on Parnell to accept the Liberal assurances:

> I cannot forget what happened that day in the Westminster P[alace] Hotel — when all these men including O'Kelly — undoubtedly went up to see Parnell with the conviction that he ought to accept the assurances and retire and when he trampled on them all and routed them with slaughter. Since

then he has bound them to himself with a hundred new ties, and for my part, I really don't see how they can leave him so long as he claims their support.[70]

In an article written three years after Parnell's death, Harrington provided a description of Parnell at Boulogne, which, while bearing the heavy impress of the posthumous Parnell myth, does suggestively evoke Parnell's demeanour within his own camp, of courteous but unyielding intransigence. Any history of the Boulogne negotiations would have to conclude, wrote Harrington, that Parnell was 'the one cool, calm and unemotional person in the whole proceeding'. While everyone about him was 'excited, feverish, emotional', he remained absolutely imperturbable 'and in many anxious conferences that took place he bore the mien of a man who was sincerely anxious to extricate his excited colleagues from some unpleasant difficulty in which they had placed themselves, rather than that of a man who was resisting the storm that raged about him'. He considered each issue on its merits. Harrington recalled pressing him on a particular line of compromise. Parnell responded that it was a matter for his own judgement. He said that nothing had impressed him more than the manner in which those he knew to be the best Catholics in the Irish party had stood by him against the clergy: 'If the views of anybody in the world could prevail with me, theirs would. But I feel that this is a matter which I alone should decide, and if there was not a single man to stand by me I should take my course all the same'.[71] The last comment, at least, has an authentically Parnellian ring.

After the breakdown at Bologne, Dillon and O'Brien proceeded to release statements which were not calculated to win them friends among the anti-Parnellites. Dillon denounced the manner in which the opposition to Parnell had been conducted by some of his most prominent opponents: 'Mr. Parnell has been assailed with shocking vindictiveness and brutality, and with an utter disregard to what was due to him in respect of his splendid services to Ireland in the past'. He blamed 'powerful influences ... at work on both sides against peace', and went so far as to declare that 'I cannot yet entirely abandon the hope that the good sense of the Irish people before long will assert itself and insist upon an end being put to this insane conflict, which will result in nothing but humiliation and ruin for Ireland'. O'Brien lamented that the 'irreconcilables of all sections have carried the day'.[72]

Dillon and O'Brien resolved to return to England, thereby submitting themselves to the six months' sentences for conspiracy to prevent the payment of rents imposesd after they broke bail the previous October.[73] Arrested at Folkestone, Dillon and O'Brien were taken to Charing Cross, where Parnell just missed the cab taking them to New Scotland Yard. There Parnell had an interview with them of some length, giving the valuable public impression of a continuing rapport, if not of unfinished business.

Dillon and O'Brien were subsequently visited by Healy, Sexton, McCarthy and others, including John Morley: 'The prisoners held quite a *levée* in the bare white room of New Scotland Yard'. The following day they were taken to Ireland.[74] Their arrest placed them *hors de combat* for the duration of their sentence.

Their relations with the majority were now severely strained. At a meeting of the party on the day of their return, 12 February, Sexton, McCarthy and Healy at the request of the party drew up a memorandum on Boulogne, conceived as a riposte to Dillon's and O'Brien's public letters on the collapse of the Boulogne negotiations. In the event the party confined itself to a statement dealing with the points raised by Dillon and O'Brien, and withheld the memorandum. Healy advised the meeting that Dillon and O'Brien in their interview with him stated that they had no blame to attach, and that Dillon had strongly protested against the leadership of Parnell; McCarthy and Condon said that Dillon had declared that he would never again serve under Parnell and would rather retire to private life.[75]

Conspicuously Dillon and O'Brien had refrained from an endorsement of the majority, permitting the Parnellites to taunt the anti-Parnellites by asserting that they had deliberately chosen to go to jail rather than act in concert with the majority.[76] It did not pass unnoticed that the parliamentarians who awaited Dillon and O'Brien at Charing Cross and later on their arrival in custody at Dun Laoghaire were Parnellite.[77] Healy and his associates never forgave Dillon or O'Brien for having facilitated through the Boulogne negotiations what Healy described as 'the culminating cleverness' of Parnell's career. T. D. Sullivan wrote that they returned from Boulogne 'outwitted, bamboozled, and empty handed'.[78] The Boulogne failure left Healy strengthened. The correctness of his hardline strategy appeared to be affirmed. During the five-and-a-half-month period of Dillon's and O'Brien's imprisonment from mid-February to the end of July Healy's supremacy in the opposition to Parnell was untrammelled. If they hoped to emerge from prison to find his influence diminished they were to be severely disappointed. On the contrary, they would find themselves on their release humiliatingly compelled to endorse and adopt Healy's course of action.

Parnell now calmly prepared for a resumption of the struggle, cabling Harrington to organise meetings at Galway, Newry and Drogheda in addition to those arranged for Roscommon and Navan for the following two weekends.[79] His termination of the negotiations and return to the fray was a fateful decision. He was aware that having failed in his first attempt to overwhelm opinion in Ireland, he was embarking upon a fierce and protracted struggle:

> But we are standing here at the parting of the ways. This fight is one which I should have gladly avoided. I endeavoured to avoid it. I should have cheerfully retired *(no, no)* from public life ... I exhausted my ingenuity, my

resources, and my brains to bring about this retirement, and I could not effect it. It was impossible ... But we are at the commencement of this fight, and let us not disguise it from ourselves that the result will be a severe and bitter struggle.[80]

References

1 Lyons, *Fall*, pp. 184-85.
2 Dillon to O'Brien, 18 Dec. 1890, Gill Papers, NLI MS 13506 (10); other parts of the letter are quoted and considered in Lyons, *Fall*, pp. 190-91.
3 V. B. Dillon to O'Brien (fragment) n.d., Gill Papers, NLI MS 13506 (12).
4 Harrington to O'Brien, 27 Dec. 1890, Gill Papers, NLI MS 13500 (19).
5 MS in O'Brien's hand, on the notepaper of the *S. S. Obdam*, d. 20 Dec. 1890, Gill Papers, NLI MS 13508 (110).
6 See Lyons, *Fall*, pp. 197-220. According to Healy, Parnell took care to enturban himself in the melodramatic bandage he had worn after the Castlecomer incident and then discarded: 'On approaching Boulogne ... Mr Parnell, to the delight of every unprejudiced onlooker, reassumed the bandage which had been thoughtfully packed in his portmanteau for use on Mr. O'Brien, and wore it, according to some newspapers, throughout the negotiations' (Healy, *Why Ireland is Not Free*, p. 37).
7 *Insuppressible*, 27 Dec. 1890.
8 *Letters and Leaders*, p. 346; *Insuppressible*, 18 Dec. 1890.
9 Labouchere to Gladstone, 4 Jan. 1891, Gladstone Papers, Add. MS 56449, f. 222.
10 Morley to Gladstone, 7 Jan. 1891, Gladstone Papers, BM Add. MS 44256 f. 109. Morley was presumably returning Labouchere's letter to Gladstone of 4 Jan. 1891 (BM Add. MS 56449, f. 222).
11 Healy to Erina Healy, 5 Jan. 1891, *Letters and Leaders,* Proofs, B 144; *Letters and Leaders*, i. pp. 346-47.
12 Healy to Maurice Healy, 6 Jan. 1891, *Letters and Leaders,* Proofs, B146, omitted in its entirety from *Letters and Leaders;* Healy to Maurice Healy, 9 Jan. 1891, passage omitted from published text, *Letters and Leaders*, i. pp. 349-50. For a further account of Healy's meeting with O'Brien, see Healy to Walsh, 5 Jan. 1891, Walsh Papers, DDA, extensively quoted Larkin, *Fall*, p. 244.
13 Healy to Labouchere, 9 Jan. 1891, enclosed with Labouchere to Gladstone, 11 Jan. 1891, Gladstone Papers, BM Add. MS 56449, ff. 232, 230.
14 Labouchere to Gladstone, 6 Jan. 1891, Healy to Labouchere, 9 Jan. 1891, Gladstone Papers, BM Add. MS 56449, f. 224, 232; Healy to Maurice Healy, 9 Jan. 1891 enclosing text of Labouchere interview with O'Brien, *Letters and Leaders,* Proofs, B 146-47 (deleted from the published memoirs). Labouchere characteristically represented to Gladstone that the interview with O'Brien had been conducted by an unidentified third party on the basis of questions he had prepared. By this transparent device he sought to avoid fixing Gladstone with formal knowledge that he had been in communication with O'Brien, and thus to insulate the Liberal leader from the imputation that he was even indirectly in communication with O'Brien.
15 O'Brien to Dillon, 8 Jan. 1891, Dillon Papers, TCD MS 6736, f. 67.
16 Healy to Erina Healy, 5 Jan. 1891, *Letters and Leaders,* Proofs, B145; Healy to Maurice Healy, 9 Jan. 1891, *Letters and Leaders*, i. p. 349; see also O'Brien's

notebook of outgoing correspondence, Gill Papers, NLI MS 13508 (1) which contains the text of O'Brien's two telegrams to Healy of 7 Jan. 1891. There was a curious and somewhat comical postscript to Healy's Paris visit. A paragraph appeared in the Liberal *Pall Mall Gazette* suggesting that O'Brien's in-laws, the Raffalovitches, had swayed O'Brien in Parnell's favour, reflecting French sympathies in the split ('our un-Puritanical neighbours have been for the most part warm adherents of Mr. Parnell'), and had received Healy and Barry coldly. In response to O'Brien's complaints, Healy proceeded to add insult to injury by a mischievous telegram denying the allegation, and asserting that O'Brien's wife and family sympathised deeply with the anti-Parnellites, and that O'Brien was himself 'as determined an opponent of Parnell's leadership as I am. An old friend of Mr. O'Brien's, *I protest bitterly* against insinuations against him'. O'Brien wrote furiously to Healy, implying that he was responsible for the original paragraph in the paper, and that instead of disavowing 'a piece of journalistic scoundrelism making indecent and lying references to my private affairs ... you drag before the public the private expressions of a woman, your hostess, in a private house, and by way of befriending me, you seek to make the prospects of a settlement with Mr. Parnell more difficult by a misleading reference to our private conversation'. (*P.M.G.*, 12, 15 Jan. 1891; Healy to Maurice Healy, 14 Jan. 1891, O'Brien to Healy, 15 Jan. 1891, both in *Letters and Leaders*, Proofs, B148).

17 Dillon to O'Brien, 6 Jan. 1891, Dillon Papers, TCD, MS 6736, f. 67.
18 O'Brien to Gill, 'Thurs night' (probably 15 Jan. 1891), Gill Papers, NLI. MS 13507 (2); see also Bodkin to O'Brien, 10 Jan. 1891, Gill Papers, NLI. MS 13507 (4).
19 O'Brien, *Parnell*, p. 204; see also O'Brien, *Olive Branch in Ireland*, pp. 39-40.
20 Parnell to O'Brien, 16 Jan. 1891, Gill Papers NLI MS 13507 (7). O'Brien had the previous weekend warned Parnell of McCarthy's acute sensitivity to any public insistence by Parnell on McCarthy's retirement: 'If you find guarded allusions to Boulogne conference necessary no objection but McCarthy declares any public statement your determination insist on his retirement fatal bar to his taking first step suggested': O'Brien to Parnell, 10 Jan. 1891, text of telegram in O'Brien correspondence notebook, Gill Papers, NLI MS 13508 (1).
21 *F.J.*, 12, 19, 26 Jan. 1891.
22 *Spectator*, 24 Jan. 1891.
23 Healy, *Why Ireland is not Free*, p. 33.
24 *Insuppressible*, 12 Jan. 1891; *F.J.*, 12 Jan. 1891.
25 *Insuppressible*, 19 Jan. 1891.
26 After Parnell's seizure of *U.I.*, the anti-Parnellites published a paper entitled *'Suppressed' United Ireland*. Parnell obtained an injunction restraining any use of the title *United Ireland*, after which on 17 Dec. the first issue of the new anti-Parnellite paper appeared entitled *Insuppressible*, a title inspired by a cable of O'Brien's after Parnell's congratulating Bodkin on the publication of *'Suppressed' United Ireland* in which he stated 'proud to know *United Ireland* continues insuppressible': *'Suppressed' United Ireland*, 13 Dec. 1891; *Insuppressible*, 17 Dec. 1891.
27 A. M. Sullivan, *Old Ireland* (London, 1927), pp. 54-55; Bodkin to O'Brien, 5 Jan. 1891, Gill Papers, NLI MS 13507 (3). Healy wrote to his brother on 14 Jan. that he had not written for *Insuppressible* since Bodkin's return (Healy to Maurice Healy, 14 Jan. 1891, *Letters and Leaders*, Proofs, B 148, deleted *Letters and Leaders*, i, p. 351). If this is true, the paper remained unwaveringly Healyite in tone and temper, and it is likely that Healy subsequently resumed his contributions. The issue of 20 Jan. 1891 is particularly replete with

Healyisms. Healy was clearly mistaken in his assertion to Maurice twenty years later that 'no-one but Bodkin wrote anything for the *Insuppressible* until O'Brien's telegram to shut it up arrived; and then Bodkin came to me to write the obituary notice!! Certainly that was the only contribution of mine therein' (Healy to Maurice Healy, 29 Oct. 1910, typescript correspondence for *Letters and Leaders*, Healy-Sullivan papers. UCD MS P6/E/2); see Lyons, *Fall*, p. 222.

28 *Insuppressible*, 10, 12, 14 Jan. 1891.
29 For the texts of several despatches by O'Brien to Bodkin and Byrne, see his correspondence notebook, Gill Papers, NLI MS 13508 (1); *Insuppressible*, 17 Jan. 1891; Bodkin to O'Brien, Gill Papers, NLI MS 13507 (1).
30 *Insuppressible*, 24 Jan. 1891; Healy, *Why Ireland Is Not Free*, p. 38. The National Committee in Sustainment of the Irish Party had already resolved that publication of the loss-making *Insuppressible* as a daily was to cease on 24 Jan. and would appear weekly thereafter. (*Insuppressible*, 24 Jan. 1891; Minutes of the National Committee, 20 Jan. 1891, Dillon Papers, TCD MS 6503; Healy to Maurice Healy, 22 Jan. 1891, *Letters and Leaders*, i. p. 353). O'Brien's repudiation had been anticipated by the announcement by the *Nation*, the old Sullivan organ, of the inception on 24 Jan. of a new series at the reduced price of one penny, which provided Healy's principal journalistic vehicle until the launching in March of the *National Press (Nation*, 17, 24 Jan. 1891).
31 *Insuppressible*, 24 Jan. 1891; *F.J.*, 24 Jan. 1891; *Nation*, 31 Jan. 1891; Healy, *Why Ireland Is Not Free*, p. 38. The supposed Parnellite quip was published in the *Insuppressible* of 22 Jan.: 'Parnellism has hanged in Kilkenny, William O'Brien had cut it down, and Mr. Dillon would restore it'.
32 Gladstone to Morley, 7 Dec. 1890, Gladstone Papers, BM Add. MS 44256, f. 86.
33 Gladstone to Labouchere, 31 Dec. 1890 (copy), Gladstone Papers, BM Add. MS 56449, f. 220 (the file contains papers extracted from the main body of the Gladstone papers by Morley when working on his biography of Gladstone); Morley to Gladstone, 2 Jan. 1890, Gladstone Papers, BM Add. MS 42256 f. 107. Labouchere, as contemplated, forwarded Gladstone's letter to Healy: Labouchere to Gladstone, 4. Jan. (1891), Gladstone Papers, BM Add. MS 56449, f. 222.
34 Gladstone to Morley (copy), 12 Jan. 1891, Gladstone Papers, BM Add. MS 56449, f. 114.
35 Healy to Labouchere, 9 Jan. 1891, enclosed with Labouchere to Gladstone, 11 Jan. 1891, Gladstone Papers, BM Add. MS 56449, ff. 232 and 230. Llewellyn Archer Atherley Jones was an avowedly pro-Home Rule Liberal who sat for Durham North West, who had called in question Liberal support for home rule in the wake of the divorce crisis.
36 *The Times*, 24 Dec. 1890; Gladstone memorandum, 29 Dec. 1890, Gladstone Papers, BM Add. MS 56449, f. 105.
37 Gladstone to E. W. Hamilton, 16 Dec. 1890, Hamilton Papers, BM Add. MS 48607 A; E. W. Hamilton Diaries, entry for 16 Jan. 1891, BM Add. MS 48645. As Gladstone watched events in Boulogne, he received a letter from Arnold Morley in Monte Carlo. Morley had met O'Brien at the railway station in Paris *en route*. A curious Anglo-French traffic in political scandal followed: 'I travelled down here with Clemenceau, who was most interesting about the Boulanger incident, and very anxious to hear about our own difficulties'. (Arnold Morley to Gladstone, 3 Jan. 1891, Gladstone Papers, BM Add. MS 44254, f. 69).
38 Schnadhorst to Gladstone, 21 Dec. 1890, Gladstone Papers, BM 44295, f. 233.
39 Gladstone to Morley, 7 Dec. 1890, Gladstone Papers, BM Add. MS 44256, f.86.

40 W. E. Gladstone to Arnold Morley, 10 Dec. 1890, draft endorsed 'cancelled W.G.', Gladstone Papers, BM Add. MS 44254, f. 58.

41 Labouchere to Gladstone, 17 Dec. 1890, Gladstone Papers, BM Add. MS 46014, f. 146; Harcourt to Gladstone, 3 Jan. 1891, Gladstone Papers, BM Add. MS 44202, f. 47; Labouchere to Gladstone, 11 Jan. 1891, enclosing Healy to Labouchere, 9 Jan. 1891, Gladstone Papers, BM Add. MS 56449, f. 230. It is very possible that Labouchere in a letter which deals in some detail with anti-Parnellite financial requirements, in advising Herbert Gladstone that 'that little matter about which I wrote to you is I think satisfactorily arranged' was alluding to the provision of private Liberal finance (Labouchere to Herbert Gladstone Papers, 17 Dec. 1890, Viscount Gladstone Papers, BM Add. MS 46014, f. 146.)

42 Lyons, *Fall*, p. 329, n. 4.

43 *F.J.*, 11 Dec. 1890.

44 *F.J.*, 26 Dec. 1890, National Committee. The provision of Liberal funding in 1890-91 exposes the hypocrisy of Healy's ruthless exploitation in August 1894 of the issue of 'the Gladstone cheque', the receipt by the anti-Parnellite party of cheques for £100 each from Gladstone and Lord Tweedmouth, for which Healy savagely attacked Dillon's leadership of the anti-Parnellite party (Lyons, *Irish Parliamentary Party*, pp. 40-50; Healy, *Why Ireland Is Not Free*, pp. 104-05).

45 *The Times*, 1 Jan., 10 Feb. 1891. The *Spectator* had from the outset professed its belief that the antagonism of the Irish parties was collusive (*Spectator*, 13 Dec. 1890, 31 Jan., 7 Feb. 1891).

46 *D.N.*, 6, 16 Jan. 1891; *P.M.G.*, 27 Dec. 1890, 8 Jan. 1891. 'Patriots' was the term by which the *Pall Mall Gazette* chose to refer to the anti-Parnellites. It is possible that Justin McCarthy, who was writing in the *Daily News* may have contributed to some of the editorials on Boulogne. (See T. P. Gill to O'Brien, 12 Jan. 1891, Papers, NLI MS 13507 [8].)

47 Morley to Gladstone, 22 Dec. 1890, enclosing memorandum dated 21 Dec., Gladstone Papers, BM Add. MS 44256, ff.94 and 96.

48 Morley to Gladstone, 12 and 19 Jan., 1891, Gladstone Papers, BM Add. MS 44256, ff. 115, and 112.

49 Morley's injunction to John Redmond, a year after Parnell's death — 'Remember always I am at least as much a Parnellite as an anti-Parnellite' — reflected a deep retrospective ambivalence as to his own role in the Gladstonian response to the divorce crisis (Redmond, memorandum of interview with Morley, 17 Oct. 1892, Redmond Papers, NLI MS 15207 [1].) In a remarkable and bitter outburst in 1895 standing at the door of the library in Stuart Rendel's house in Carlton Gardens, where Gladstone had written his letter against Parnell, Morley declared: 'I cannot forget that in this room was struck the most deadly blow to our fortune of the last nine years. I mean the cashiering of Parnell'. He went on to blame Gladstone for not coming up to London in time to permit an adequate discussion as to the appropriate Liberal response *(The Personal Papers of Lord Rendel*, ed. F. E. Hamer [London, 1931], pp. 125-26, 2 Nov. 1895; see also p. 26). The platonic regrets of politicians are to be treated with extreme circumspection. Morley, a difficult and cantankerous politician after the retirement of his mentor Gladstone, did not express these misgivings either in his biography of Gladstone (1903) or his *Recollections* (1917). G. W. E. Russell wrote shrewdly of Morley's susceptibility to Parnell: 'From Lord Morley Parnell received that reverent homage which a sedentary man always pays to a man of action' (G. W. E. Russell, *Portraits of the Seventies* [London, n.d., p. 211]). For Morley's reaction to the death of Parnell, see E. W. Hamilton's Diary, BM MS 48656 (18 May 1891).

50 Gladstone to Granville, 21 Jan. 1891, quoted Lyons, *Fall*, p. 232; Gladstone to Harcourt, quoted Lyons, *Parnell*, p. 564.

51 Morley to Dillon, 3 Jan. 1891, Dillon Papers, TCD MS 6798, f. 7.

52 Morley to Dillon; Morley to Gladstone, 22 Jan. 1891, Gladstone Papers, BM Add. MS 44256, f. 127.

53 Labouchere to Gladstone, 26 Jan. 1891, Gladstone Papers, BM Add. MS 56449, f. 234.

54 Harcourt to Gladstone, 1 Jan. 1891, Gladstone Papers, BM Add. MS 56449, f. 170; 3 Jan. 1891, BM Add. MS 44202, f.51. Harcourt wrote sententiously on 3 January: 'The people I really feel sorry for are the Irish themselves — surely the most unfortunate of nations — who get as badly used as ever mankind was by the gods of Olympus, who resembled I think a good deal in their ethics the Irish Parliamentary Party' (Harcourt to Gladstone, 3 Jan. 1891, BM Add. MS 44202, f.47). Such was Harcourt's belligerence that Morley would only meet him in the presence of colleagues, as he explained to Gladstone: 'Nothing shall induce me to tolerate the violences with which he regaled you and me last November and December' (Morley to Gladstone, 19 Jan. 1891, Gladstone Papers, BM Add. MS 44256, f.112).

55 Healy to Walsh, 31 Jan. 1891, Walsh Papers, DDA.

56 Healy to Walsh, 4 Feb. 1891, Walsh Papers, DDA. Healy's eventual analysis of the Boulogne collapse reflected both the incompleteness of his information and his incessant trivialisation of Parnell. Parnell's 'wretched point about the police' was a pretext, 'the real truth being that Parnell won't have Dillon for leader!', a point which the majority had been willing to concede. (Healy to Walsh, 10 Feb. 1891, Walsh Papers, DDA.) Much of this correspondence is cited in Larkin, *Fall*, pp. 251-3.

57 O'Brien to Redmond, 'Sunday night' (8 Feb. 1891), Redmond Papers, NLI MS 15212 (4).

58 Parnell to O'Brien, 11 Feb. 1891, NLI MS 13507 (15). The foregoing résumé is based on the exhaustive analysis of the breakdown of the Boulogne negotiations by F. S. L. Lyons in his *Fall* (pp. 131-35), *Dillon* (pp. 131-34) and *Parnell* (pp. 560-71).

59 *I.C.*, 10 Jan. 1891.

60 Walsh to Dillon, 26 Jan. 1891, Dillon Papers, quoted Lyons, *Dillon*, p. 131.

61 *Nation*, 3 Jan. 1891; *I.C.*, 3 Jan. 1891.

62 Logue to Walsh, 27 Dec. 1890; see also Logue to Walsh, 23 Jan., 6 Feb. 1891, Walsh Papers, DDA.

63 Morley, *Gladstone*, iii. p. 440.

64 Parnell to O'Brien, 10 Feb. 1891, quoted and considered in Lyons, *Fall*, pp. 243-44.

65 W. O'Brien, *Olive Branch in Ireland*, p. 1; T. P. Gill to Morley (draft), 30 June 1892, Gill Papers, NLI MS 13507 (24).

66 *The Times*, 12 Feb. 1891, *P.M.G.*, 12 Feb. 1891.

67 *F.J.*, 11 Dec. 1890.

68 A. J. Kettle, *Materials for Victory*, pp. 94-95; Sophie O'Brien, *Recollections*, pp. 176-77.

69 Redmond to Parnell, copy, 'Monday night' (9 Feb. 1891), Harrington Papers, NLI MS 8581, quoted Lyons, *Parnell*, p. 244; see also Lyons, *Fall*, p. 241, n.I.

70 Dillon to O'Brien, n.d., O'Brien Papers, NLI MS 85555 (I).

71 *U.I.*, 6 O Oct. 1894, T. C. Harrington, 'Parnell's Obstinacy'.

72 *F.J.*, 12 Feb. 1891.

73 Lyons, *Dillon*, p. 111; Michael MacDonagh, *William O'Brien* (London, 1928), p. 119.

74 *F.J.*, 13, 14 Feb. 1891. According to O'Brien's wife, Dillon and O'Brien left Boulogne in a state of mind so despondent that they were troubled by the possibility that in the wake of the failure of the negotiations they would not be arrested, but left humiliatingly — and politically awkwardly — at large (Sophie O'Brien, *Recollections*, p. 179; *Golden Memories* [Dublin, 1929], p. 116).

75 Irish Party Minutes, 12, 13, Feb. 1891; *F.J.*, 13, 14, Feb. 1891. The *Freeman's Journal* of 17 Feb. alleged that Dillon considered the disclosure of his conversations with the anti-Parnellite members a breach of confidence.

76 *F.J.*, 25 Feb. 1891, speech of John Redmond at the Central Branch. NL; *F.J.*, 6 Mar. 1891, John Redmond, 'The Split in the Irish Party', first published in the *Melbourne Advocate*.

77 *The Times*, 13, 14 Feb. 1891.

78 Healy, *Why Ireland Is Not Free*, p. 35; T. D. Sullivan, *Recollections*, p. 295. An article by Harold Frederic, containing a polemical onslaught on the Boulogne negotiations and on all Irish politicians save Healy, includes an astute characterisation of William O'Brien: 'Exaggeration is said to be an Irish failing. With Mr. O'Brien it is almost a disease ... The innocent unconsciousness of his own vanity is almost past belief' ('The Rhetoricians of Ireland'). Arguably O'Brien never recovered from the Boulogne collapse. Years later, Davitt was compelled to agree with John O'Leary's characterisation of O'Brien as 'a historic lunatic' (Davitt to O'Leary, 12 May 1906. Davitt Papers, TCD MS 9377).

79 Parnell to Harrington, 13 Feb. 1891, telegram NLI MS 5385.

80 *F.J.*, 2 Mar. 1891, Navan. Lady Fingall saw Parnell speaking: 'My memory of Parnell that day is that he looked like a sick eagle. I have never forgotten his tragic face, while he was speaking, with obvious effort, for over an hour. It poured with rain, and the wet street of the grey country town made a sad background for the scene. The people seemed to me very apathetic' (Lady Fingall, *Seventy Years Young, Memories* (London 1937, repr. Dublin 1991) p. 204.

5

HEALY ASCENDANT

He says we have yielded to English dictation. Well he is not willing to
yield even to Irish dictation, (*applause and laughter*) because he says
that, after the next general election, if he had not one supporter, we
know he has declared he will go on, and on, and on, and on, until he
goes over the precipice.

T. M. Healy, 10 June 1891 [1]

In early March 1891, the campaign against Parnell in Ireland was consolidated by the launch of the anti-Parnellite *National Press* and the establishment of the National Federation. Early on the evening of 6 March the staff
and directors of the *National Press* assembled for its launch at the premises
in Abbey Street. After a benedictory visit by the Archbishop of Dublin and
a celebratory speech by Sexton, the presses started to roll. Watching the
newspapers come off the press at dawn, Healy malignly prophesied, 'This
is the winding sheet of Parnellism'.[2]

Healy wrote the first, as he wrote many later, editorials of the *National
Press*. In a pointed contrast with the *Freeman's Journal* he wrote: 'We shall
set up no idols. We shall swing no censer to make a smoke of sweet savour
in the nostrils of any chief'. He stated the paper's editorial policy with brutal
succinctness: 'The first great fact to be encountered on the very threshold
of inquiry is Mr. Parnell's responsibility for the controversy ... The shameful
revelation of the divorce court is the first cause, the *fons et origo malorum*'.
Parnell was 'the real, sole, manifest author of the evil': 'Should he efface
himself, or be effaced, dissension will disappear with him. While he remains
he must not complain if home truths are told which go to the very roots
of the controversy'. This ominous threat was amply fulfilled: the *National
Press* was to be distinguished by the unflinching savagery of its attacks upon
Parnell.[3] The influence of the *National Press* was amplifed by the

110

publication from 16 May 1891 of the *Weekly National Press*, whose 'large and splendidly coloured cartoon' invariably featured a savage caricature of Parnell's hunted face to provide a visual correlative to Healy's rhetoric. The *Evening Press* was launched on 26 September 1891 as a rival to the *Freeman's Journal*'s sister paper, the *Evening Telegraph*.

Sexton, who initally refused, eventually accepted the editorship of the *National Press*. His functions were those of a managing editor, and Healy retained control of the paper's editorial policy. Healy quickly fell out with Sexton, who he complained to his brother would not walk through the streets with him, except after dark: 'He is against attacking Parnell on the "moral question" '.[4]

The *National Press* marked a new departure in Irish journalism. The paper denounced Parnell and championed conservative Catholic nationalist values in a vigorously populist and idiomatic rhetoric. It carried to its logical conclusion, and redirected against Parnell with brutal humour, the agrarian rhetoric of the pre-split *United Ireland*. It was the vehicle of Healy's dominance of the anti-Parnellite forces in Ireland. Through it he pursued his vendetta against Parnell, as well as against the *Freeman's Journal*. He did everything possible to thwart Edmund Dwyer Gray's attempts to shift the editorial policy of the *Freeman's Journal* against Parnell; the *National Press* inflicted a wound on the *Freeman's Journal* which the subsequent amalgamation of the two papers from March 1892 was not to heal; neither did the amalgamation mark the end of what had become Healy's almost lifelong campaign to destroy the *Freeman's Journal*.

The launching of the *National Press* was followed three days later by the inaugural convention of the National Federation, in opposition to the Parnellite National League. Healy's speech was a précis of the case against Parnell. The rhetoric of crisis and struggle ('We have passed through trying times. Over there in London many a day our hearts were sore and downcast, thinking of what was before us. We had to wrestle with the wild boars of Ephesus') quickly yielded to the new tone of confidence in the opposition of Parnell. Against Parnell's pretensions to an absurd 'leadership of the Irish race' were ranged 'the thinking men of the community'. Impugning Parnell's conduct in Committee Room 15, Healy upheld the principle of majority rule:

> We will make that principle a potion which Mr. Parnell must swallow if it was gall and wormwood to him. I would never consent for one hour to remain in the party of which Mr. Parnell was the leader. I will never tolerate him. I will never consent to him in any shape or form ...[5]

The new organisation gave pride of place to its ecclesiastical supporters. 'Every priest who has been prominent in the national movement was present at the meeting', boasted the *National Press*. 'The four Archbishops blessed the infant in its cradle. Almost every bishop in Ireland concurred in its benediction.' Healy asked his audience: 'I wonder how many fireside hillsiders Mr. Parnell would give for the four archbishops?' The Dublin unionist *Daily Express* observed that 'the long rows of black coats gave the meeting quite the character of an ecclesiastical convention', while *The Times* claimed the convention signalled 'the formal and definite entry of the priesthood upon a struggle for the national movement', and described the National Federation as 'essentially the organisation of the Church for political purposes'.[6]

Less than two weeks later, on 23 March 1891, Michael O'Brien Dalton entered the Victoria Hotel, Tipperary, where Healy was getting ready for dinner. Bearing a candlestick in one hand, Healy went to meet him, only to receive what he afterwards described as a 'terrific blow in the face'. Healy was struck repeatedly, with fragments of his shattered spectacles driven into his eye, while his assailant muttered something about him betraying his country. O'Brien Dalton had already exhibited reckless patriotic ardour in imperilling his prosperity in the Plan of Campaign: indeed Healy had previously singled him out for praise among its leaders as a man 'who had as comfortable a house and as extensive a business as any merchant in Dublin'. He had just been released from prison, and professed to be outraged by Healy's allegation that a prosecution in Nenagh, in which he was one of the defendants, had been adjourned as a result of an arrangement between Parnell and Balfour. While Healy subsequently accepted the apology tendered by O'Brien Dalton, he was rendered *hors de combat* for the North Sligo election, and was understandably persuaded that the assault was instigated by Parnellites more calculating than O'Brien Dalton.[7]

The assault was the culminating incident of violence against Healy. He had shown unflinching physical courage in the face of repeated demonstrations of aggressive public hostility and even violence throughout the split. 'I have never left my house since this game began without being insulted in the streets of Dublin', he told a libel jury in July. After the split in Committee Room 15, a wigged and gowned effigy of Healy had been ritually burned in the Phoenix Park. The windows of his house on Mountjoy Square were broken, eliciting from Parnell at Boulogne the observation that 'people with glass windows ought not to throw stones'. He had his hat crushed in an attack in Abbey Street. Leaving mass on Christmas Day he was subjected to the indignity of being hooted 'on the very threshold of the church'. His hat saved him from injury when he was assaulted at Nenagh. At Edgeworthstown in his own constituency the platform mysteriously collapsed under him, an incident celebrated in Carletonesque detail by the *Freeman's Journal* under the headline 'Patriot Plunges from the Scaffold'. His meeting at Carrick-on-Shannon, along with his platform, was broken up by invading Parnellites from outlying districts, forcing Healy and anti-Parnellites inside the chapel yard whose gates were guarded by priests, where Healy addressed them from the steps of the church, declaring that 'ten drunken men could shout down Demosthenes or Daniel O'Connell'. After appearing against Harrington in a libel action, Healy was groaned and jostled in the Round Hall of the Four Courts, but flanked by friends, proceeded, in the words of the *Freeman* 'with as much dignity as was possible in the circumstances' to the Law Library.[8] Elaborate security arrangements did not prevent physical-force extremists causing a serious dynamite explosion at the *National Press* offices after Parnell's death, on 26 October 1891.[9]

Healy professed indifference to the attacks made upon him. He wrote to his wife from Johnstown during the Kilkenny election: '"Come one, come all". I don't care a tuppenny damn for them ... The attacks on me I have only regretted for your sake. I am wallowing in them'.[10] Characteristically, his bravery was spiced with provocativeness. Following a report of trouble at the inaugural meeting of the National Federation, he wrote from the *National Press* offices to assure his father that he was unharmed. He had encountered on leaving 'a gang of half a dozen cornerboys of the beeriest kind', and 'to annoy them I walked the whole way instead of taking a car'.[11]

Whether or not O'Brien Dalton had been put up to the attack, the crude and ugly Parnellite response revealed the depth of antagonism towards Healy. The *Freeman's Journal*'s condemnations were markedly tepid. At the National League Healy's former friend and doctor Joseph Kenny stated that at the time of alleging that he had been assaulted, Healy was 'in a condition of great mental disturbance'. John Clancy, sub-sheriff of Dublin, dissented from a statement by the chairman regretting the attack on Healy, bluntly declaring, 'he did not endorse sympathy with Mr. Healy no matter what happened to him'.[12]

The brunt of the anti-Parnellite campaign in North Sligo was borne by Maurice Healy and David Sheehy, aided by a number of lesser Parnellite MPs, and brief visits by Davitt and Sexton. The constituency straddled parts of three dioceses. While the bishops of Elphin and Achonry were anti-Parnellite, Killala declined to exert himself in the anti-Parnellite interest, and maintained a policy of neutrality which permitted the staunchly Parnellite Sligo priests of his diocese to canvass for Parnell.[13]

The diocese of Killala embraced the barony of Tireragh in the west of the county adjoining Mayo. Situate on the perimeter of the political nation, looking west to Ballina, the district had survived relatively unchanged. Remote alike from the reach of British power and the cultural hegemony of nationalism, it was largely untouched by the course of nationalism in the 1880s. In the polemical sociology of anti-Parnellite nationalism, the region was deemed socially backward and politically underdeveloped, affording high cultural as well as geographical resistance to the penetration of anti-Parnellite propaganda. The population of the district, the *National Press* wrote disparagingly:

> is of a type peculiar to Irish politics. They have taken no part in the movement of the past dozen years, have not joined the National League, and have lain practically quiescent during all the excitement and strife and persecution through which the the country has been passing. The district is the most remote in the country, near the seaboard, and probably because of its isolation was never organised.[14]

It was, Maurice Healy declared afterwards, 'a remote and backward district ... not traversed by railways, in which the means of communication were scarce, a district in which their literature and speeches in Parliament and public had up to the present not penetrated'. He and Sexton complained that the *National Press* had not penetrated into Tireragh.[15]

That the anti-Parnellites blamed the high Parnellite vote in the west of the constituency so heavily on the backwardness of the area in nationalist-political terms suggests that the receptivity to anti-Parnellite arguments and techniques of persuasion depended on a high degree of nationalist acculturation, and that the ascendancy of anti-Parnellism in rural Ireland was a function of the political and social transformations wrought in the preceding decade.

Ballina rather than the town of Sligo was the centre of operations for Parnell's campaign. Sexton charged that Parnell had imported hooligans from the west 'by means of the migration system', drawing on 'the spade-handled brigade from Mayo'. The *National Press* darkly alleged intimidation and personation as part of a 'reign of terror', while Healy wrote to Walsh complaining of the importation of 'bullies from Mayo and Ballina'.[16]

The Sligo campaign was thus heavily sectoralised, the constituency divided into two concentrated spheres of opposed allegiance. The major incidents of the campaign were occasioned by anti-Parnellite forays into Tireragh. Tim Healy later wrote to Walsh that Maurice had told him that 'when they went into the houses to canvass and argue with the voters, the very women took up stools and spade handles, and tried to assault them the moment they announced their mission!' On 29 March there were scenes of violence in Dromore West, the parish of John Kelly the most outspoken Parnellite priest, in which Maurice Healy and other anti-Parnellites were stoned out of the parish.[17] Parnell, with some temerity, entered into the spirit of the campaign in Tireragh by dismissing John Pinkerton, the anti-Parnellite member for Galway and formerly for Antrim North, as 'an Ulster Protestant'. He added that 'they thought the Protestants of Ireland were capable of looking after their own business, and they did not want any souping Presbyterian from Ulster to go in among the Catholics and instruct them on that point'.[18]

The anti-Parnellites carried the day by 3,261 to 2,493. The margin of
768 was the narrowest of the split's three by-elections.[19] North Sligo, exulted the *Nation*, 'is another spot of holy Ireland where the condoners
of adultery have no chance'.[20] The anti-Parnellites claimed that the
backwardness of Tireragh, western intimidation, and a perfidiously
Parnellite priesthood created uniquely favourable circumstances for Parnell
in the west of the constituency. Maurice Healy proclaimed the result a victory against Parnell on his strongest terrain, a constituency where prevailed 'a state of circumstances which would be impossible to reproduce in
any rural district in Ireland', and the Parnellite vote to represent 'the high
water mark of Parnellism in the rural districts of Ireland'.[21]

Tim Healy was, however, deeply unnerved by the clerical defections in
Tireragh. He wrote to Archbishop Walsh complaining about the local clergy
and about what he termed 'the Ballina party' presided over by the pro-
Parnell administrator of the diocese of Killala, MacHale, which 'ruined
the Barony'. In a passage replete with irony, which conceded the extent
of anti-Parnellite dependence on clerical support, Healy wrote:

> The whole thing is as unintelligible to me as it was wholly unsuspected. Who
> knows what pitfalls we may walk into in other districts if an election arises?
> To lend a sanction to violence and to encourage it by altar denunciations,
> after all that has passed about Parnell, argues an amazing spirit, which un-
> doubtedly is most formidable in election times. I don't believe we caught
> 5% of the Tireragh vote ... The wonder is that we won which we owe entire-
> ly to Sligo town. The whole affair has given our men an awful shake and
> has enormously encouraged Parnell. He can overawe or seduce the unthink-
> ing element easily enough Heaven knows, without the priests helping him
> to raise mobs against us.[22]

If North Sligo showed that Healy's declared object of completely van-
quishing Parnell continued to elude him, the fact remained that Parnell
had failed in favourable circumstances to break the cycle of defeat which
had dogged him since the publication of the Gladstone letter. He had lost
in a second Irish constituency, by a decisive, though not a crushing, margin.

'From the outset,' wrote Harold Frederic in the *New York Times* of 22
March of Parnell,

> cool men have seen that it could only be a question of time when, in the
> course of his desperate and wild struggle for political existence, he would
> commit some fatal error. In other words, the doctrine of chances is uniform
> against the success of crazy men. On Tuesday, misled by the vociferous cheers
> of a mob of Cork groundlings, he wandered off into the bog of insanity.[23]

Frederic was referring to Parnell's incautious declaration to his Cork
city constituents that he would resign and re-contest his seat if his fellow
member Maurice Healy did likewise. Maurice Healy took up the challenge
with alacrity. Parnell then declined to submit his resignation until Healy

had actually resigned. Healy called this feeble bluff by forwarding his resignation to the majority whip, to be submitted as soon as the Parnellite whip undertook to hand in Parnell's resignation concurrently.[24]

It was a demeaning retreat on Parnell's part, an open resiling from his own reckless challenge, which neither his own semantics, nor the *Freeman's Journal* warning of the danger of a three-sided contest in Cork giving the seat to the Conservatives, could conceal. 'His own worst enemy could not have devised a more ruinous calamity for him than this', gloated Frederic. 'His one remaining hold upon the Irish imagination was the belief that he was a good fighter. His own rude annihilation of this myth has sickened and disgusted his backers all over Ireland'.[25] Parnell's evasion added the charge of cowardice to the anti-Parnellite repertoire. In a speech at Queenstown in which, according to *The Times*, 'he attacked his late leader with a concentrated venom of which he has seldom before given so perfect an example', Tim Healy drew on the incident with superb sarcasm, insinuating in the mixed parlance of the duel and the boudoir a taunt of effeminate weakness against Parnell: 'All he said was: "If you resign so will I". Because we have dared to look crooked at this haughty beauty — because we have not sent him a letter in a kind of *billet-doux* in its scented envelope, forsooth he will not accept the challenge ...'. Healy asserted that Parnell had proved himself 'not merely a libertine but a coward and a sneak'.[26] He taunted that Parnell had not yet responded to Maurice's final challenge because 'he has not yet obtained the permission of the Brighton banshee', thus reiterating the charge that Katharine O'Shea was dictating Parnell's strategy throughout the split.[27]

Parnell's retreat from his challenge led to a galling incident in the Commons. On 15 April, after Parnell had spoken against an Irish Sunday Closing Bill, Maurice Healy, a temperance zealot as well as an anti-Parnellite, rose. Although as H. W. Lucy observed 'Mr. Healy's fragile, shrinking figure does not seem designed to brave the wrath of Mr. Parnell', his intervention was devastatingly effective:

> I only rise for the purpose of assuring the House that neither on this nor on any other public question does the hon. Gentleman who has just sat down represent the City of Cork. If the hon. Gentleman wishes to test the truth of my words let him keep the promise which he made to his constituents.

Cheering burst from the Conservative as well as the Liberal sides of the House, swelled by Gladstone's baying tones, 'amid which Mr. Parnell sat pale and defiant with folded arms, looking straight before him as if he had heard nothing'. Gladstone was much gratified, and wrote commending Maurice Healy's action both to Tim Healy and to E. W. Hamilton. To the latter he wrote: 'The little episode of Maurice Healy and Parnell on Thursday was most remarkable. A body of the Tories, much to their credit, could not help cheering Mr. Healy loudly. He did it admirably'.[28]

It was thus Maurice who realised his brother's cherished objective of humiliating Parnell in the House of Commons.

In March Andrew Kettle had sought to redefine the role of the Parnellite party, and moderate its pretensions. He sanguinely looked to an evenly divided nationalist representation after the general election, with Parnell and 'the Bishops' holding thirty-five to forty seats apiece, with twenty-five to thirty Unionists. He asserted that both nationalist factions were together 'on the high road to success', and believed that Parnell's pre-eminence in council would assert itself in the ensuing equilibrium. While Ireland had many lesser officers, she had 'only one real statesman or commander in chief'. Undeterred by the North Sligo defeat in April, Kettle renewed his centre-party concept, envisaging three parties in Ireland 'an intensely Protestant party, an intensely Catholic party, and an independent party'.

Parnell himself, briefly and unconvincingly, argued the virtues of dissent, declaring at Mullingar in mid-May that 'a nation without two parties would not be a nation — it would simply be a flock of sheep'. (He went on to dissipate any conciliatory effect by declaring, more characteristically, 'he would rather be the leader of a good minority than of a rotten majority.') It was not a line of argument which Parnell advanced again, and Kettle later defined the mission of the party as that of a principled minoritarian party.[29]

Healy wrote of Parnell to his father two days after the inauguration of the National Federation that 'the man is dead and gone politically, save for a small but active party'. This mortal idiom recurred with disquieting frequency in Healy's rhetoric. The *National Press* proclaimed in a curious construction 'Mr. Parnell personally is politically extinct'.[30] Healy published in the London *New Review* for March 1891 a remarkably poised essay, a stylised political obituary entitled 'The Rise and Fall of Mr. Parnell'. Surveying his persisting course of decline, Healy wrote 'the delirium is now over', and predicted that Parnell would take eight seats at the general election as against his current tally of thirty-three parliamentary supporters.[31]

Healy's rhetoric was increasingly triumphalistic, as he flouted Parnell with his inability to break the cycle of defeat. Part of his purpose in avowing as his objective the extirpation of Parnell and Parnellism was to ensure that the campaign against Parnell did not slacken in victory so as to permit moderate deviations within anti-Parnellism. He sought in particular to frustrate the adhesion of Gray and the *Freeman's Journal* to the anti-Parnellite cause, and to pre-empt any conciliatory initiatives by Dillon and O'Brien on their release which might threaten his hold on the direction of anti-Parnellite policy.

There was in Healy's rhetoric a troubling excess even in terms of his own objectives. His insistence that Parnell was irretrievably vanquished rendered the intensifying ferociousness of his attacks upon him hard to justify. His rhetoric disclosed a disquieting fanaticism, a perverse psychological rhythm whereby his implacability grew with every victory. His supremacist rhetoric became, as the split wore on, a shriek in the void of nationalist power. Its resonance derived from the fractured coherence of Irish politics as well as from the defects of his own temperament.

The *National Press* sharply contrasted the exaggerated pretensions of the myth of Parnell with his continued reversals in the split:

> No politician, it must be remembered, has ever given himself out as an invincible warrior in the same way as Mr. Parnell has continually since the Divorce Court ... Mr. Parnell's unhappy position, however, has led him to vice after vice in the matter of public policy, while his slavish supporters in the press and on the platform felt bound to spout hosannas to his wisdom.[32]

Healy fastened on the seeming transformation of Parnell's personality in the split, by which he asserted Parnell had compromised his mythic stature. The *National Press* emphasised 'the change in Mr. Parnell — the transformation of the divorce court which changed the languid leader into the restless and reckless firebrand', and, using a favourite quotation of Healy's, opined: 'We cannot and will not believe that Mr. Parnell of a few years back is Mr. Parnell of today! "Character", as George Eliot has finely said, "is not cut in marble"'.[33] In a withering *National Press* editorial in his unmistakable style of 13 April, entitled 'Mr. Parnell's Sunday Off' (Parnell had not campaigned in Ireland the previous weekend), Healy mocked the ineffectuality of Parnell's restless commuting. He contrasted Parnell's frenzied campaigning with his absence from Irish platforms in the preceding five years, which he ascribed to slothful concupiscence. Parnell's Irish campaign, he taunted, far from salvaging his cause, had served merely to dissipate the remnants of his mystique. At the mid-term of the split, Healy drew together the themes of his rhetoric to survey Parnell's decline in a characteristic moralising idiom of decay:

> Yesterday was a day of rest for Mr. Parnell. It was the first Sunday he had at home for very many weeks and he spent it peaceably at Brighton ... If Mr. Parnell's Sabbath-rest musings at Brighton turned at all on the events of the past four months, he must have sadly been forced to the conclusion that having laboured hard Sunday after Sunday he has nothing for his pains. There is nothing to show but an ebbing tide, a bleak shore, and the uncovering of an unsavoury slob. Mr. C. S. Parnell, who would not quit his winter (and summer) quarters for five years to speak even on an English platform, to win an important election, or on an Irish platform to forward the patriotic cause, rushed to and from hillside to hillside in Ireland to publish his gospel of dissension. Sunday after Sunday since his deposition he has shrieked himself hoarse against old allies and former colleagues and well-proved policy ... Has he convinced the reflecting that he is a statesman, or has he not rather exposed the barrenness of the common clay of which he is composed? What nostrum of socialism or anarchy is it that he has not shown himself ready to swallow to catch votes, while cynical insincerity the while exposed its

cloven hoof through the loudest of his professions ... Open the cornucopia of Parnellism never so wide, is any dupe beguiled by the blowings of that plenteous horn ... Was it soul or body, patriotism or personalism, that prevailed with Mr. Parnell during all these weary years. Is the slave at Eltham to become the Achilles at Irishtown? ... Is the leader whose life for years has been a lie, a hypocrisy, and a varnished sloth, to be trusted to perform the promises extracted from him in the galvanised activity of a personal misfortune?

The contrast between Parnell's former neglect of Irish campaigning and his activism in the split was tellingly drawn: 'Today, however, when except as a power for evil, Mr. Parnell's influence has perished he and his organ are instinct with life and a-thrill with spurious patriotism'.[34]

Healy renewed his devastating onslaught in a rhetorically superb editorial the following day.

In modern European politics there is no parallel to Mr. Parnell's fall ... There have been many sudden and startling falls within our time: Thiers, Gambetta, Bismarck, Crispi, Castelar. But in most cases they carried their greatness with them into retirement and in no case did they sink to the level of a loud-voiced political quack with ready nostrums for all diseases.

Even Boulanger had taken himself away from a people 'disgusted with his heroic attitudinising and play-acting'.

But here is this deplorable man fighting an impossible fight, catching now at this straw and now at that, hurling brave challenges and then explaining them away, marshalling Gaels and Amnesty men, land nationalisers, and eight hour advocates — the blind, the lame and the halt — and he has a fit word for all. Suppose Mr. John O'Leary and Mr. P. N. Fitzgerald were yoked to the chariot with such fiery steeds as Mr. V. B. Dillon and Councillor James Shanks, soon again the lash of the dictator would flay their flanks if they dared to grow restive and unruly.

Hammering relentlessly at the futility of Parnell's campaign, the paper asserted that his haggard exhaustion evidenced the intractability of his predicament. The French and Americans got along without the services of 'a "matchless chief"', and so will Ireland when her "matchless chief" betakes himself to his much needed repose. His power for mischief is nearly over and no fresh Boulogne episodes should distract the mind of Ireland from the fast approaching *dénouement*'.[35]

Healy cunningly derided the Parnellites' endeavours to present themselves in a moderate light as an admission of weakness. The *National Press* wrote on 8 April that the imminent danger had passed:

The Parnellites no longer talk the wild language of their first frenzy of sweeping the country and exterminating all who set Ireland above the audacious pretensions of Mr. Parnell. They now sing in a minor key but a more melancholy air. Their music is no longer a march but a retreat.

It added woundingly: 'Parnell struggles for vengeance not victory'.[36] The *Weekly National Press* derided 'the dreary and fatuous drivellings of this man'. Of the Parnellites the *National Press* declared: 'The country is getting sick of them and their master. The alternative threats and whines are nauseating. Their farce is nearly played out'. The country was 'a little tired of the Parnell fiasco'.[37] Healy at the same time moved to deepen his agrarian attack on Parnell, mounting a linked attack on Parnell's support of Balfour's Land Purchase Bill and on his alleged betrayal of the Plan of Campaign tenants.

Healy was increasingly concerned to frustate any pacific initiative on the part of the *Freeman's Journal*. The main shareholder in the paper was now, along with his mother, Edmund Dwyer Gray, who altogether lacked his late father's seasoned acumen. With the fading glamour of Parnellism after the Sligo defeat, and the mounting commercial threat posed by the *National Press*, Gray embarked on a protracted and graceless struggle to distance the paper from, and eventually to disavow, Parnell. Immediately after the Sligo defeat, the *Freeman's Journal* ostentatiously, if platonically, moderated its editorial policy, and espoused a negotiated settlement of the split and 'a truce to scurrility'. This elicited a predictable retort from the *National Press*: 'The time for negotiation is over and past. The fight must go on. It will be a bitter one, but is most unlikely to be a long one'.[38]

Gray persevered in his inept intrigues, approaching McCarthy, Sexton and Cardinal Manning. He despatched an unctuous missive to Leo XIII in which he proclaimed himself a '*figlio fedele della Chiesa Cattolica*', emphasised the Catholic credentials of his paper, and declared his readiness to submit himself entirely to the guidance of the Church.[39]

Healy had a profound and irrational loathing of the young Gray, whom he was to describe in 1892 as 'a horrible scoundrel, and . . . probably the worst thing in human nature that now exists since the death of Parnell', and determined to thwart him. He wrote to Maurice that 'young Gray has been telling all the priests that he is coming round on conscientious grounds, and I think the best way to land him and put him out of pain amongst the furious partisans surrounding him is to name him'. In an illuminating revelation of his polemical technique, he declared he would not regard it as any loss 'if the effect is to send him back to Parnell, as this will drive him into a denial of the story, with the result that of course he will give us the opportunity of being more specific. Neither the youngster nor the paper deserves the slightest consideration'.[40]

The *National Press* of 14 May duly reported rumours that Gray was about to defect. The tactic worked perfectly. Gray frantically cabled Parnell denying the report: 'As you know contemplated reconciliation not desertion'. The retreat became a rout. Gray wrote a public letter to his editor declaring that he had been 'under an unaccustomed strain' and was departing on vacation, and looked now to 'the two great Irishmen who are now in Galway jail'. The *National Press*, which venomously had declared 'we desired to do Mr. Gray a favour . . . we watched with sympathetic interest his movements for weeks past', proceeded to deliver the *coup de grace* by revealing that Gray had submitted what it described as a formal letter of contrition to the Vatican.[41]

Even as Gray struggled to tear himself from the Parnellite hook, Healy pressed the barb deeper, deriding the *Freeman's Journal*'s increasingly desperate attempt to couple its Parnellism with an espousal of conciliation. Healy through the *National Press*, with his habitual faculty of turning Shakespeare to polemical purpose, mocked 'it hath two voices — a most delicate monster'.[42] During the long process of the conversion of the *Freeman's Journal* — which took place finally, with extraordinarily unhappy timing, only on 24 September, two weeks before Parnell's death — Healy devastatingly maximised its discomfiture.

Healy further sent a clear signal to Dillon and O'Brien in Galway Jail with a public warning against 'any attempt now to patch up a compromise on the basis of the recognition of Mr. Parnell's leadership'. He pointedly dismissed 'any attempt which may be broached to induce us to go into a conference with Parnellism as another effort to revive the fatal Boulongdering which went on some months ago'.[43] His relentless determination to entrench his position prior to the release of Dillon and O'Brien evinced an intimation of his vulnerability centred on the future of the *National Press*.[44]

In a further intensification of hostilities calculated to thwart any peace initiative by Dillon and O'Brien, the anti-Parnellite party resolved that at county conventions in aid of the evicted tenants, candidates were to be nominated to contest seats held by Parnellites. This step — described by Healy as furthering 'a weeding out and a closing up of our ranks' — formalised the irreparability of the split. William Martin Murphy now looked to the 'utter defeat' of Parnell, while the *National Press* confidently predicted that Parnell 'will be wiped out so far as any following in the House of Commons is concerned', and would be reduced to the position of an ordinary private member.[45]

Healy further salted the bitterness of the split with a sequence of highly provocative articles, taking as their point of departure a speech of Archbishop Croke calling for an audit of national funds, in which Healy accused Parnell of embezzlement, or colloquially, theft. The initial article, entitled 'Stop Thief', in the *National Press* of 1 June was the first in a series of seven consecutive leading articles, the titles of which convey Healy's goading rhythm:

1 June	'Stop Thief'
2 June	'"My Action as a Statesman"'
3 June	'No Writ Yet'

4 June	'The Cold Facts'
5 June	'What Explanation?
6 June	'A Crowd or a Jury?'
8 June	'Breaking Covert'.[46]

The articles were a calculated aggravation of Croke's call for an audit: 'His Grace nowhere suggested that Mr. Parnell pocketed the money. We did ... He never suggested that Mr. Parnell was a thief. We say so'. The *National Press* charged that Parnell had 'for years ... been stealing the money entrusted to his charge'.[47] Healy's strategy was to force Parnell to institute libel proceedings, or submit to public humiliation. The first editorial asserted that 'he must plead to the indictment', and savagely concluded: 'the coils at the end of the harpoon will, however, soon be paid out, for there is an end to men's patience'.[48] The following day the *National Press* returned to the attack. No writ had been received in respect of an article written 'advisedly and with full deliberation of ... Mr. Parnell's peculation'. A sustained incitement to litigation ensued, culminating in a quotation, appropriately from *Othello*:

> Our act was plain, our charge was plump. This is an unmistakable word. We called Mr. Parnell a thief. We now repeat that epithet ... Should the disgraced man fail immediately to cite us before a jury, we will ring the charge in his ears so long as he persists in thrusting himself on public notice. Let there, then, be no misunderstanding. This charge, if he fails to face it, has come to stay. It will haunt Mr. Parnell on platform and in parliament, at bed and board, for the remainder of his career. We will force him to face it or, amidst the contempt of his own supporters, 'lash the rascal naked through the world'.[49]

The third editorial maintained the purpose of taunting Parnell into litigation and looked forward to '... when we have scourged the Fund-grabber into confronting us before a jury. Sooner or later we will drive him into Court, and when he leaves it, there will be few of his present serfs abject enough to do him reverence'.[50]

The central issue of the actual application of the funds by Parnell was left deliberately blurred. The only specific suggestion was that Parnell had applied monies subscribed to the pre-split nationalist movement to the partisan purposes of his campaign in the split. 'The rabidest [*sic*] Parnellite', asserted the *National Press*, could not pretend that those who subscribed had 'entrusted their money to the Chief in 1889 for expenditure in 1891, or even that if they did they are disentitled to a balance sheet'.[51] Yet the articles artfully conveyed the innuendo that Parnell had diverted money to purely personal purposes. Healy knew that Parnell could not possibly institute libel proceedings: irrespective of whether he could demonstrate the propriety of the application of money subscribed to the united Irish movement to his own campaign, he could not have exposed himself to an array of subsidiary allegations and issues or permitted the political issue of the split to become submerged in litigation.

The 'Stop Thief' series revealed how possessed Healy was by the split's mad logic. The articles were conceived in part as a riposte to what he denounced as the spurious metaphysical distinction between politics and morality drawn by Parnellite apologists. If adultery did not touch on the political domain, the paper asserted, the theft of public money manifestly did, so exploding the Parnellite argument: 'If Mr. Parnell debauched Mrs. O'Shea one of the commandments delivered by Moses called that "adultery". If he appropriated the monies left in trust with him, and we are prepared to prove that he did, the same old fashioned law-giver called that "theft" '.[52] Of what Parnell referred to as his record as a statesman, the *National Press* charged 'theft touches that record, if adultery does not'.[53]

Healy's insensate provocativeness renders the 'Stop Thief' sequence unique in the annals of Irish vituperation. He coupled the ruthlessly selective rationality of the advocate with the exhilarated vehemence of a leader-writer. Determined to entrap Parnell into litigation, his attacks combined the form of a prosecution with the idiom of a hunt. Barrister and politician, Healy sought to align the forensic with the polemical to achieve a political approximation to legal process.

Parnell, unnerved, replied abusively at Inchicore on 7 June, declaring his readiness to submit a balance sheet to O'Brien on his release. In a spirit of ghastly sanguineness, he expressed himself confident of 'ultimate victory'. Playing on the fact that Healy was not briefed before the Special Commission, he asserted:

> But our position grows stronger as the days go by. You see the desperate exertions which they are making to trump up fresh charges against me. They recognise that the old charge has lost its force, and they are seeking for fresh fields and pastures new, and the pasture that Tim Healy *(groans)* has selected for his spring grazing *(laughter)* is the only one of the many pastures which there have been which Ireland refused to allow his teeth to pollute *(laughter)*. That defence fund was the only fund out of the whole of them that he did not get a bite out of, and consequently it is one of the very few funds there is any balance left in.[54]

Healy retorted '... when he says that the old charge is getting stale, I tell him it is not but that the new charge is getting overwhelming'.[55]

It may be doubted that the 'Stop Thief' sequence brought about any significant further diminution of Parnell's support, yet it served Healy's purpose in deepening the rifts of the split, both between Parnellites and anti-Parnellites, and between hardline and moderate anti-Parnellites. The Parnellites were driven in their exasperation to evidence that 'mobology' of which Healy accused them. Joseph Kenny declared that the author of the 'Stop Thief' article was 'the stuff that traitors and informers were made of', and 'must be dealt with as an enemy of his country, and an enemy of the human race'. The *Freeman's Journal* condemned 'a lie before which the appalling perjury of the degraded suicide Pigott pales'.[56]

Healy persisted in his attempts to ensnare Parnell in the coils of litigation. Parnell's secretary, Henry Campbell, brought a libel action against the *Cork Daily Herald* arising out of an article which stated that he had discharged 'the degrading duty of hiring houses for the immoral purposes of his master'. Healy, instructed by his brother for the defence, applied unsuccessfully for liberty to issue and serve subpoenas on Parnell and Katharine O'Shea. The defence thereafter endeavoured to serve Parnell personally while he was within the jurisdiction. The *National Press* alleged that Parnell had sought to avoid service by returning from his Balbriggan meeting on 21 June by carriage rather than by train, and by lurking in the post office van of the train to Kingstown before emerging at Kingstown 'surrounded in circular form by a bodyguard'. The paper invoked 'the picture of the famous descent of the fire escape, and the hiding holes of Mr. Fox', and mocked the 'ludicrous precipitation' with which Parnell avoided the witness box.[57]

Campbell's libel action succeeded, but in circumstances which could hardly have been more embarrassing to Parnell. The evidence established that Katharine O'Shea had written letters in his name in 1886 to an Eastbourne estate agent without Campbell's authority or knowledge. The *National Press* hailed the result as a verdict against Parnell, and exulted in the opportunity to couple in denunciation Parnell and Katharine O'Shea: 'There is and can be no doubt that Mr. Charles Stewart Parnell and the wretched woman whose name he has brought, and persists in keeping, so prominent before the public, share this shame between them'.[58]

Parnell broke silence with a public letter to Campbell's solicitor written on 24 June to the effect that Campbell had agreed to permit Parnell to use his name but had been unaware that this was in relation to the purchase of a house. The blame accordingly lay with Parnell himself: 'I write this to you in order to vindicate this lady from the most unjust suggestions made against her at the recent trial, and to give the defendants the opportunity to reopen the case if they think this statement discloses any matter the withholding of which was prejudicial to them'. Healy did indeed motion to set aside the verdict and obtain a new trial, but the application was refused.

Parnell, however, went on in his letter to make a veiled allusion to the role of Katharine O'Shea as an intermediary in his dealings with Gladstone: 'I asked Mrs. O'Shea to conduct the negotiations because I was going to Ireland, and for the same reasons I have frequently charged her with the conduct of vastly more important matters and negotiations'.[59] Parnell thus recklessly contrived to vindicate, and to pay public tribute to, Katharine O'Shea, on the eve of his marriage to her. It was a protective gesture towards her charged with menace for his adversaries. It was a signal to Gladstone that he had refrained from disclosing the involvement of Katharine O'Shea in their earlier negotiations, a fact which, while it could quite conceivably have finished Parnell's campaign in Ireland, would have inflicted incalculable political damage upon Gladstone. Parnell's statement was calculated to preclude Healy's habitual retorsion in personal vilification of every reference he made to his relations with Katharine O'Shea. It was as if Parnell was at last acquiring the knack of the split's perverted mode of controversy.

While the Dublin unionist *Daily Express* observed that Parnell presented Katharine O'Shea as 'a great diplomatist who in some mysterious way played the part of a benefactor to Irish nationalism',[60] it was a line of enquiry which neither anti-Parnellites nor Liberals could afford to pursue. John Dillon in Galway Jail wrote aghast to O'Brien of Parnell's letter:

> To me it seems a most indecent document. It is hardly possible to believe that P. is sane on this subject to flourish this wretched woman in the face of the country for such is plainly the significance of the letter — that Mrs. O'Shea has been entrusted by him with important political business. It is revolting and indeed I must say the revelations at the Campbell trial were very disgusting.[61]

Dillon's response expressed the deep mistrust of Katharine O'Shea shared by almost all the Parnellite as well as anti-Parnellite members. Parnell could ill afford such an incautious tribute to Katharine O'Shea which lent credence to the widespread suspicion that she exercised significant political influence.

Healy looked to Parnell's marriage to administer the *coup de grace* to Parnellism. The *National Press*, on 18 May, malevolently celebrated the elapse of six months from the pronouncement of the decree nisi, on which the O'Shea marriage stood dissolved:

> Mr. C. S. Parnell is now therefore free to become in law the wedded husband of Mrs. Katharine O'Shea. The subject is not a pleasant one, but who created it? If at any time since the divorce decree the unhappy man had bowed his head and sought for pardon, pity and oblivion, would there be one voice today uplifted against him? Is not the very essence of Christianity and Catholicity comprised in the words charity, sorrow and atonement? Would even the heathen talk of 'my fault, if it has been a fault', in the awful circumstances? If Mr. Parnell has committed 'no fault', how long must his followers await for his vindication? They were promised before many days that the only leader would stand out pure as the moon, dazzling as the sun, and terrible as an army with banners. How long must they still tarry? Will it come with the release of the Paris fund for the evicted or with the marriage of the ex-wife of the whilom dragoon?

The paper added, 'The time is now ripe for the issue of another manifesto'.[62]

In the early morning of 25 June 1891, two days before his forty-fifth birthday, Parnell married Katharine O'Shea at the registry office in the town of Steyning, near Brighton. Parnell gave one of his rare press interviews afterwards in which he declared: 'I and my wife are perfectly happy. As for myself I can truly say I am now enjoying greater happiness than I have ever experienced in the whole of my previous life'.[63]

Parnell's public avowal of private felicity was highly uncharacteristic and, set against the débâcle of his Irish campaign, had a hollow ring. It was a brave but nervous romantic gesture, shot through with apprehension, as he braced himself for the torrent of abuse which his marriage would unleash. In the exact phrase of a later writer, he 'did not propose to flinch'.[64] He added that he intended to visit the United States in the autumn. Reflecting his unyielding determination to brook no compromise on any issue touching on his private relations, he expressed his wish to bring his wife to Ireland.

If Parnell had at the outset of the split believed that his marriage to Katharine O'Shea would dispose of the moral issue, the course of the split in Ireland had rudely disabused him of any such naïve expectation. He could readily have deferred his marriage until after the Carlow election. His refusal to do so cannot be explained by any lingering belief that his marriage would assist him politically. Rather he was determined not to depart from the course he had pursued from the outset of the split, and to which he was precommitted by his decision not to contest the divorce petition. He pointedly refused to subordinate to immediate political considerations what he considered to be his, and more particularly his wife's, vindication. He proposed to finish what he had started.

Nor was it an irrational gesture of infatuation. Parnell's entire campaign was based on a refusal to acknowledge any conflict between his political and his personal life. His fierce and demanding political professional ethic as a politician coincided with his commitment to Katharine O'Shea. His marriage was a deliberate gesture central to the logic of his stance in the split. He unflinchingly faced giving a further impetus to his decline, by marrying immediately before a critical by-election. He was in any event now committed to the belief — by instinct as well as out of necessity — that his support would have to contract and harden, and then be rebuilt on sound foundations.

Parnell's marriage served only to aggravate his moral offence. To excitable Catholic moralists his marriage to Katharine O'Shea was a hideous simulacrum of a Christian marriage. To them Parnell had profanely affirmed his depravity in solemn form, and showed himself resolute in vice. With the marriage, the split's bitterness was again deepened, as the moral opposition to Parnell attained a new ferocity.

The *National Press* predictably declared that 'the Pagan ceremony which

the fallen man has gone through only sinks him deeper in his disgrace ...
in the eyes of every man who values home, hearth, wife and children, the
husband of Mrs. O'Shea is now an even less reputable object than the co-
respondent of the divorce court', while the *Weekly National Press* denounced 'the empty mockery of marriage by which Mr. Parnell legalised his relations with the wealthy though degraded partner of his guilty pleasures'.
The *Nation* published the entry in the Steyning register beneath the words
of Matthew 14: 'And he that shall marry her that is put away commiteth
adultery'. The overwhelmingly anti-Parnellite provincial press excelled itself
in moral vituperation. The *Kilkenny Journal* declared that Parnell had
'damned himself beyond redemption', and in an observation which revealed
how widely imitated was Healy's rhetoric, coupled the taunts of adultery
and avarice to observe that 'Mrs. O'Shea is now the proud possessor of
her hero's name, and the ex-leader of the Irish Parliamentary Party is the
proud possessor of another man's wife, and in all probability, a considerable
sum of money!' The *Clonmel Nationalist* responded with a shriek of
moralistic exhilaration:

> At last the revolting tragedy of guilt and shame is consummated, the film
> of mystification is flung to the winds and the Scarlet Letter, in unblushing
> nakedness, reigns over the 'Leadership' Committee! Charles Stewart Parnell
> has divorced himself from holy Ireland. After covering soul and body with
> hell-deep infamy, the misrepresentative of fair Cork has irrevocably sealed
> the bonds with the wife of Captain O'Shea, whom he has already disgraced
> beyond measure.[65]

Parnell's marriage thus carried him yet deeper into the sphere of moral
obloquy. M. J. Kenny declared, 'In the eyes of every Catholic in this country these wretched people had added sacrilege to adultery'. Archbishop
Walsh described Parnell's wife as 'his partner in guilt', and the marriage
'a public compact for the continuance of their shameful career'. O'Donnell, Bishop of Raphoe, declared that Parnell's marriage 'only caps a climax
of brazen horrors'. The marriage gave a new resonance to the declaration
against Parnell, made collectively by the Irish bishops for the first time
since the commencement of the split, that 'by his public misconduct' he
had disqualified himself from the leadership.[66]

For Parnellites, the leader's marriage was another tribulation of their
allegiance to be borne stoically, and wherever possible silently. The
Freeman's Journal gave minimal coverage to Parnell's marriage. Few ventured to argue publicly as Pierce Mahony MP bravely did at Carlow that
if Parnell had committed a fault 'he had done his best to remedy it', and
was now married in accordance with the law 'and according to the laws
of the Church to which she and Mr. Parnell belonged'.[67] The *National
Press* sought to deepen the dismay of Parnell's adherents by linking his
letter after the Campbell case with the seemingly reckless timing of his
marriage: 'His few remaining friends ... are now shaking their heads over

his want of tact and judgement, and feel that they can no longer rely on the good sense of a man who within a week can show such reckless defiance of the laws of tact and common sense'.[68] The savagery of Healy's reaction, had Parnell in fact postponed his marriage until after Carlow, defies imagining.

Parnell's marriage led to the loss of both his most naïve and his most cynical supporters. For those nationalists, on some accounts numerous, who had obstinately refused to believe the allegations of the divorce court which they had treated as a reprise of the Pigott forgeries, Parnell's marriage afforded unwelcome but incontestable verification of the allegations linking Parnell with Katharine O'Shea. In the words of one astute observer, Parnell's marriage did him 'incalculable harm in the eyes of the good Catholics, who regard it not as an act of reparation but as public admission that the worst was true'.[69]

The marriage equally afforded those who had miscalculated in backing Parnell from the outset an opportunity to withdraw their allegiance in a show of affected righteousness. Most prominent among these was Edmund Dwyer Gray who publicly repudiated Parnell on the grounds of his marriage, which as he candidly stressed to Archbishop Walsh was 'a good Catholic reason'.[70] It only remained now for Gray to assert himself over the recalcitrant Parnellite majority of the board of the *Freeman's Journal*.

The *National Press* sardonically exulted:

> We cannot doubt that many honest and honourable men whom at first blind fanaticism, and afterwards a pardonable obstinacy kept fixed in the Parnellite ranks whose
>
> > 'Honour rooted in dishonour stood
> > And faith unfaithful kept them falsely true'
>
> will rejoice in a favourable opportunity to return to the service of the country.[71]

For the anti-Parnellites, the marriage put their victory in Carlow beyond doubt. The *National Press* declared that 'the tragedy of Parnellism' had degenerated into farce and with defeat in Carlow would 'be hissed off the stage'. Healy celebrated Parnell's moral incapacitation in a revealing image: 'His power is gone, and he has as little power in politics as a suspected priest has in the Church'.[72]

The neglected Carlow election of July 1891 was Parnell's last, bringing to an end an electoral career which had commenced with his candidature for County Dublin some seventeen years previously.[73] Healy approached the campaign in ebullient form. His rhetoric in Carlow was a vicious epithalmion to Parnell and his wife:

> He tells us that he is now enjoying greater happiness than he knew in all his life *(laughter)*. I don't know will he be so beautifully happy after

Wednesday morning. I wonder what will be his feelings when Carlow kicks his kettles across the country, and sends his utensil to a place which is certainly a place, so far as this country is concerned, where there is no redemption *(cheers)*.[74]

The hint of infernal menace was not altogether jocularly conceived.

The marriage provided Healy with the opportunity to bring together the themes of his sexual rhetoric against Parnell, all the while insisting that it was Parnell who was responsible for the introduction of this distasteful subject:

When you hear this talk about English dictation, and the Saxon smile, just ask Mr. Parnell why did he introduce English dictation and the Saxon smile into this country in the shape of Mrs. O'Shea *(groans)*. He says he is going to bring her over to Ireland *(hisses and laughter)*. I don't like talking about Mrs. O'Shea *(A voice : 'Kitty and Parnell')*, because it is a nasty subject; but I did not invent Mrs. O'Shea, I did not create Mrs. O'Shea, I did not marry her *(great laughter)*. I did not run down the fire-escape for her *(more laughter)*. She is the sole invention and discovery of Mr. Charles Stewart Parnell. A man in the crowd, a Parnellite, said a while ago 'Why can't you let her alone?' Why could not Mr. Parnell let her alone *(cheers and laughter)*. It is a curious thing that what is good enough for Mr. Parnell cannot be mentioned in public *(laughter)*. The other day Mr. Parnell's secretary got quite indignant that anybody should ever suggest that he had ever met Kitty O'Shea.[75]

The spirit of the campaign was captured in Healy's lauding of the administrator of the cathedral in Carlow, who presided regularly at his meetings: 'There was hardly a night he did not send across to Kitty a new bit of bride cake'.[76]

The *National Press* whipped to fever pitch popular nationalist hostility to Katharine Parnell (invariably referred to by her former married name). She became along with her husband a co-equal target of Healy's rhetoric: 'Mr. Parnell and his party', asserted Healy, 'ask you to give up Mr. Gladstone for Kitty O'Shea'.[77] She was denounced not merely as the faithless wife of Captain O'Shea, but as the arbiter of Parnell's politics. In concluding the Kilmainham Treaty Parnell 'was only the instrument in her hands'. The anti-Parnellite candidate had been nominated by a convention, the Parnellite 'was selected at Brighton by Mrs. O'Shea'.[78]

The *National Press* twisted Parnell's desire to bring Katharine to Ireland, expressed in his 'infamous interview', into an intention to introduce her to the electors of Carlow: 'The crowning insult was the promise that the debased and shameless woman, whose name Ireland had so much reason to abhor, intended (weather permitting) to honour this country with a visit, and to exercise her blandishments on the electors of Carlow'. It warned that 'audacity has a limit'.[79]

While the anti-Parnellites nominated a prominent Carlow merchant, representative of what were infelicitously described as the 'substantial, solid-headed men of the county',[80] Parnell, faced with a dearth of suitable candidates, turned to Andrew Kettle, a maverick agrarian radical lacking in political weight. Kettle's intrinsic limitations were as nothing compared with his surname. The most unhappily named candidate in the history of Irish politics, his nomination brought Parnell's rout at Carlow to the brink of pantomime.

Kettle's name provided Healy with an inexhaustible source of inspiration. He derided Kettle as Parnell's 'utensil': 'Whatever way the compass at Brighton points, Kettle will look that way. He will go up and down the fire escapes, just as Parnell wants him, and he will be prepared to boil over in support, if necessary, of Mr. Balfour's elbow'. The next day he declared 'when we are done with all these old pots and kettles, we will send them across to Brighton as a wedding present'. The *National Press* devastatingly parodied the overblown prose of the *Freeman's Journal* by interspersing patriotic declamation with popular advertising jargon to refer to 'the pure-souled, fireproof, illustrious, copper-fastened, disinterested, solid-riveted, Heaven-sent, scalding-hot, brass-mounted Andrew J. Kettle'.[81]

It was not merely Healy's punning inventiveness which rendered Kettle's name a disastrous liability, but the occasion which it afforded for popular protest, often by women and children. The kettle, emblem of the hearth, became a percussive instrument — in part a kind of alarum at the cuckolding of Captain O'Shea — in a bleakly festive carousel of opposition to Parnell. 'The kettle', explained the *National Press*, 'has come into extensive use as a political weapon. It is exhibited everywhere, on trees, on lamp posts, over doors of houses, and as you pass along housewives wave it good-humouredly in your face.'[82] Introduced at a meeting in Carlow by the clerical chairman as 'Parnell's scourge', Healy replied: 'There is a worse scourge than I am going just now. It is the sound of those rusty "Kettles" that the old women have *(laughter)*. That is the music of tally-ho after Mr. Fox *(renewed laughter)*'.[83]

The kettle became the popular symbol of opposition to Parnell, and a raucous orchestration of Healy's rhetoric. Outside Rathmore an effigy of 'Kitty O'Shea' supporting a kettle was suspended from a tree; near Tynock a dead fox was hung with a kettle tied to its tail.[84] When Healy's statement in a speech at Carlow that Parnell had 'married Kitty' was met by the blowing of a horn, he responded, 'My friend, it is Captain O'Shea wants that horn'. The horn-blower's explanation of his 'bit of fun' revealed how deeply Healy's rhetoric had penetrated the popular consciousness: 'Parnell had given horns to another man, and I brought out my horn to find out how he would like the taste of it himself. The people of Carlow are hunting the fox and I want the horn to cry "tally-ho" '.[85]

The apparent spontaneous convergence between Healy's rhetoric and

popular peasant protest at Carlow poses in acute form the central interpretative dilemma of the split: the role of Healy's rhetoric in the formation of anti-Parnellite public opinion. The coincidence between his rhetoric
and popular protest at Carlow appeared to affirm the existence of the
transcendental and timeless nationalist moral tradition he proclaimed, as
well as evidencing the intensity of popular opposition to Parnell. Yet the
conjuncture is deceptive, and obscures a subtle but crucial shift within
nationalism. Bitter Parnellite complaints that the attacks on Parnell were
politically organised — *United Ireland* for example complained that the
anti-Parnellites had sent young girls to approach Parnell's carriage to deliver
themselves of 'unwomanly and shocking expressions'[86] — shied away
from the reality. By his marriage Parnell had overtly trespassed into the
domestic domain and it was to be expected that he would find himself
running a gauntlet of popular protest. What is of significance in terms
of the evolution of nationalism is the ideological exploitation of that
response by Healy and the popular moralists of anti-Parnellism, so as to
render it politically hard and enduring.

The popular protests at Carlow represent an ambiguous and poignant
moment of transition in Irish politics. What was in many respects an
apolitical folk response, the residue of an older Ireland, antedating the
revolution wrought by Parnellism in the 1880s, was harnessed to the anti-
Parnellite purpose. An old vernacular of complex popular morality, sexual allusion and casual jocularity was put at the service of modern nationalist ideology, and transformed into the axioms of nationalist politics and
moralism. A popular tradition which had theretofore existed apart from
nationalism was increasingly adapted to fit the configuration of power,
tenure and Catholicism in late nineteenth-century Ireland. The Carlow election is a study in the alignment of the nation as social reality to the nation
as ideological myth, in which the hardening lineaments of a putatively
nationalist moral order are discernible.

Parnell in Carlow encountered often highly offensive demonstrations
of hostility — 'He is freely insulted now by scores of peasants who seemed six months ago to feel that gratitude required them to be no worse than
sullen'.[87] Perhaps more alarmingly, he also found himself frequently
shunned, the victim of co-ordinated boycotting, either pointedly ignored,
or listened to in terrible and impassive silence.

At Rathvilly, the speakers at Parnell's meeting were inaudible: 'The
children marched up and down in compact bands beating kettles till not
a word was to be heard, and the women howled and groaned untiring-
ly'.[88] At Ballon Parnell found all the shops closed, and the villagers
gathered round a banner with an effigy of a woman with a kettle in her
hand which bore the inscription 'Kitty I'm scalded'. He was greeted first
in grim silence, then by sustained hooting and groaning.[89] The next day,
in the village square at Nurney, Parnell was confronted by the most

concerted silent boycott of the Carlow campaign. The villagers turned out, 'but succeeded better than those of any hostile village in the county in keeping absolute silence'. Parnell and those with him responded with polite speeches to the unnaturally mute crowd. As the meeting ended, however, and Parnell's brake moved off slowly down the hill out of the village, the discipline of the crowd broke. Men started to cheer and women ran after the brake to shake Parnell's hand, while young girls, blushing and confused, threw flowers in the brake. Parnell was much pleased. It was, wrote the *Manchester Guardian* correspondent, 'a triumph of tactful management applied to the feelings of gratitude and kindness towards Mr. Parnell that linger everywhere here even among his opponents'.[90]

The same correspondent, who had covered Parnell's campaign in Kilkenny, charted Parnell's decline at Carlow: 'His roadside popularity which never failed him in Kilkenny, is almost gone'. At fair day in Borris 'he walked slowly through the fair amidst perfect silence, and waited for a couple of hours at an inn till the business of the morning should grow slack'. Parnell's personality 'loses more of its interest every week. It was highest in the years when he never came to Ireland, but these Irish campaigns are cheapening it slowly but pretty effectively. On the railway nobody marks him. Very few will leave the hay to hear him speak'.[91]

Parnell persevered in the polite and temperate pursuit of his lost hegemony. Belatedly adjusting his political style, he ran a studiously moderate campaign. The *Manchester Guardian* correspondent noted that he eschewed the vituperativeness of Kilkenny, adding that

> ... it was in the last days of the Kilkenny affair that he came closest to Fenianism, but then there was a physical breakdown, whereas at present Mr. Parnell looks perfectly well, is in good voice, and shows more of that power of reticence and of stopping exactly where he means that distinguishes him at his best. [Parnell] no longer hints that he is the only possible Fenian, but says outright that he is the most capable of the Constitutionalists.[92]

The anti-Parnellite won by a crushing margin of 2,216 votes, receiving 3,755 votes against 1,539 for Kettle. It was for Parnell a heavy blow in a constituency which he had incautiously proclaimed the only one of the split he had a real chance of winning. The (still Parnellite) *Freeman's Journal* conceded that the minority was 'far and away larger than anyone could have anticipated'. *United Ireland* conceded they had been 'badly and overwhelmingly defeated'.[93]

Even after Carlow, Healy sought to twist the knife. A virulent editorial in the *Weekly National Press* of 18 July which asserted that Parnell's marriage was motivated by venality brought together the marriage, the 'Stop Thief' allegations, and the evicted tenants' issue. It posited a contrast between Parnell's prospectively opulent marital felicity with the wretched plight of the evicted tenants.

Mr. Parnell has secured ... the legal right to share the colossal fortune of the unhappy woman whose character he has ruined. The money which they will divide between them if they come safely through the ordeal of the Probate Court is estimated at nearly two hundred thousand pounds. Mr. Parnell has expressed unalloyed satisfaction at the result. In the interview with the Central News representative after the performance in the Registry Office ... he assumed the role of an enthusiastic bridegroom just embarked on his honeymoon. He gave unqualified assurances to his 'wife's happiness', and his own. 'As for myself,' he gushingly explained, 'I never was so happy in all my previous life' ... The rapture of registry office Benedict can scarcely be attributed to any new-found delight in the society of Mrs. O'Shea, which according to his own account, he had, since the year 1883, enjoyed, uncontrolled by any laws human or divine. The legal status conferred on him by the Registrar and its attendant pecuniary advantages are the only possible explanation of his unsophisticated rejoicing.

The evocation of the plight of the evicted tenants and the variation of the 'Stop Thief' allegations, were intended to give this virulent onslaught ostensible political pertinence. The accompanying cartoon depicted Parnell as a prancing cad emerging from the Registry office, his plump bride awaiting in a carriage, while across the Irish Sea a sentimentally rendered evicted tenant languished with his family: 'On one side is vice triumphant, on the other virtue depressed'.[94]

Healy was not quite done yet. The *National Press* of 18 July recalled that Parnell had 'half-promised to gratify the admiring eyes of the electors of Carlow with the vision of the golden prize he had secured'. The paper proceeded to run a series of entirely invented reports of a visit to Ireland by Katharine Parnell: 'The Saxon smile ... won't even confine itself to Brighton any more'. Healy's malice had achieved a surreal intensity. When Parnell's agent denounced the reports of the amorous grouse-shoot at Avondale as diabolical fabrications, the *National Press* mockingly anticipated a telegraph from Parnell: 'Would my agent, if he be my agent, leave my wife, if she be my wife, alone'. The paper referred to Katharine Parnell by a new sobriquet, with the cadences of a limerick, 'the registered lady of Steyning'. Reporting Parnell's arrival in Dublin rather than from Avondale, where it had alleged he was staying, the *National Press* insouciantly shifted the direction of its attack. Dilating upon 'this brisk cross-channel traffic', it proclaimed it strange that Parnell could not 'stay ten consecutive days in his own country but must darkly flit across the Channel — despite the dangers of contact with the Saxon and the seductions of that famous smile'. It repeated a week later: 'What is the man at? Cannot he stay in Ireland for two days running, without bouncing back to England to bask in the light of the Saxon smile ... is Brighton Mr. Parnell's Mecca, and who directs the Hegira? What has wrought all this change, and fevered with restless patriotism that sluggish heart?'[95]

Figure 3 'A Startling Contrast' (*Weekly National Press*, 18 July 1891)

References

1 *N.P.*, 11 June 1891, North Dock Ward NF.

2 *I.C.*, 14 Mar. 1891; *N.P.*, 7 Mar. 1891; Healy to Maurice Healy, 7 Mar. 1891, *Letters and Leaders*, ii. p. 357; M. McD. Bodkin, *Recollections of an Irish Judge* (London, 1914), p. 175.

3 *N.P.*, 7 Mar. 1891; *Letters and Leaders*, ii. 357.

4 Healy to Maurice Healy, 6 Mar. 1891, *Letters and Leaders*, i. p. 356; Healy to Maurice Healy, 14 Mar. 1891, *Letters and Leaders,* Proofs, p. 151 omitted from *Letters and Leaders*, i. p. 359. Sexton further dissociated himself by refusing point-blank to stay in Ireland to fight the Sligo election, and insisting on going to London to attend a Children's Bill, agreeing only to go down later to make one or two speeches.

5 *N.P.*, 11 Mar. 1891.

6 *N.P.*, 11 Mar. 1891; *D.E.*, 11 Mar. 1891; *The Times*, 11 Mar. 1891. There was a correspondingly high degree of clerical influence on the *National Press*. The hierarchy extracted a secret written undertaking from the board on 27 Jan. that nothing contrary to faith and morals would appear in the paper and that the paper would co-operate in the promotion of Catholic interests for a *quid pro quo* for clerical share subscriptions. See Larkin, *Fall*, pp. 254-57.

7 *N.P.*, 24, 26, 30 Mar. 1891; for Healy's original allegation, *F.J.*, 20 Nov. 1889, 26, 27 Dec. 1890.

8 *N.P.*, 8 July 1891; *F.J.*, 8 Dec. 1890; *'Suppressed' United Ireland*, 13 Dec. 1890; *F.J.*, 10, 11 Dec. 1890; W. O'Brien, *Olive Branch in Ireland*, p. 29, n. 1; *F.J.*, 10 Dec. 1890; *Insuppressible*, 12 Jan. 1891; *F.J.*, 19 Jan. 1891; *Nation*, 28 Feb. 1891; *F.J.*, 28 Feb. 1891. The destruction of Healy's hat determined a familiar feature of his apparel for the rest of his life. A substitute hat was despatched by American sympathisers: 'They had slightly misjudged the size, and he always wore it cocked a little over one eye because it fitted better that way; and nothing would induce him to wear any other' (Maev Sullivan, *No Man's Man, Sequel*, p. 43).

9 *N.P.*, 27, 28 Oct. 1891.

10 Healy to Erina Healy, 18 Dec. 1890. *Letters and Leaders,* Proofs, B143.

11 Healy to Maurice Healy, *F.J.*, 12 Mar. 1892, Healy-Sullivan Papers, UCD P6/A/N.

12 *F.J.*, 24, 25, 27 Mar. 1891.

13 Larkin, *Fall*, pp. 263-8.

14 *N.P.*, 21 Mar. 1891.

15 *N.P.*, 8 Apr. 1891, speech made by Healy, Cork; speech of Sexton, Central Branch MF.

16 *F.J.*, 27 Mar. 1891; *N.P.*, 4, 8 Apr. 1891; Healy to Walsh, 4 Apr. 1891, Walsh Papers, DDA.

17 Healy to Walsh, 4 Apr. 1891, Walsh Papers, DDA; *N.P.*, 30 Mar. 1891; *Sligo Herald*, 4 Apr. 1891

18 *F.J.*, 31 Mar. 1891, Tireragh.

19 *N.P.*, 24 Apr. 1891.

20 *Nation*, 11 Apr. 1891.

21 *N.P.*, 8 Apr. 1891.

22 Healy to Walsh, 4 Apr. 1891, Walsh Papers, DDA.

23 *N.Y.T.*, 22 Mar. 1891.

24 *F.J.*, 18, 23, 24 Mar. 1891.

25 *N.Y.T.*, 22 Mar. 1891.

26 *The Times*, 24 Mar. 1891; *N.P.*, 23, 27 Mar. 1891.

27 *N.P.*, 23 Mar. 1891, Queenstown.

28 H. W. Lucy, *A Diary of the Salisbury Parliament 1886-92* (London, 1982), p. 369; Hansard, vol. 352, col. 635. MacDonagh, *Home Rule Movement*, p. 229. Healy to Maurice Healy, 26 Apr. 1891, *Letters and Leaders*, ii. p. 361; Gladstone to E. W. Hamilton, 18 Apr. 1891, Hamilton Papers, BM Add. MS 48607, f.200. There is nothing to corroborate Michael MacDonagh's assertion (*Home Rule Movement*, pp. 229-31) that Parnell returning after the division found the bench which included his seat occupied by a compact phalanx of anti-Parnellites and was driven to take refuge in the Liberal benches. Healy wrote Maurice on the publication of MacDonagh's book that he could not recollect such an incident and urged Maurice to contradict it. Healy to Maurice Healy, 19 Aug. 1920, typescript copy, Healy-Sullivan Papers, UCD P6/E/2(4).

29 *F.J.*, 19 Mar. 1891, Kettle to *F.J.*, 16 Mar.; *F.J.*, 2 May 1891, NL; *F.J.*, 11 May 1891, Mullingar; *F.J.*, 15 July 1891, NL.

30 Healy to Maurice Healy snr., 12 Mar. 1891, Healy-Sullivan Papers, UCD P6/A/17. The phrase is tastefully modified to read 'politically gone' in the published version (*Letters and Leaders*, i. p. 358). *N.P.*, 9 May 1891.

31 Healy, 'Rise and Fall'; see also his speech at Carrick-on-Shannon, *Nation*, 28 Feb. 1891.

32 *N.P.*, 11 May 1891.

33 *N.P.*, 18, 21 Apr. 1891.

34 *N.P.*, 13 May 1891.

35 *N.P.*, 14 Apr. 1891.

36 *N.P.*, 8 Apr. 1891.

37 *W.N.P.*, 16 May 1891; *N.P.*, 16 May 1891.

38 *F.J.*, 7, 8, 11, 13 Apr. 1891; *N.P.*, 8 Apr. 1891.

39 Manning to Walsh, 24 Apr. 1890; E. D. Gray to Leo XIII, copy, 27 Apr. 1891, Walsh Papers, DDA. For Walsh's caustic attitude, see his undated draft observations in the Walsh papers.

40 Healy to Maurice Healy, 31 Mar. 1892; Healy to Maurice Healy, n.d. Both the foregoing are from transcriptions of correspondence prepared for *Letters and Leaders* subsequently deleted from the proofs. Healy-Sullivan Papers, UCD, P6/E/2.

41 *F.J.*, 15, 18 May 1891; *N.P.*, 15, 19 May 1891.

42 *N.P.*, 31 July 1891.

43 *N.P.*, 21 May 1891.

44 Healy to Maurice Healy snr., 10 May 1891, Healy-Sullivan papers, P6/A/18; part quoted in *Letters and Leaders*, ii. p. 361 and misdated 'June'.

45 *N.P.*, 12 May 189; *N.P.*, 21 May 1891, speech of Healy at Central Branch NF; *N.P.*, 19 May 1891, speech of Murphy at Saggart; *N.P.*, 16 May.

46 Healy's authorship is beyond doubt. Quite apart from the uniqueness of his animus and the inimitability of his style, his authorship of the series was almost a matter of public knowledge. Attacks which charged Healy's authorship, such as Harrington's (*N.P.*, 3 June 1891) went uncontradicted. Healy took responsibility for the articles (*N.P.*, 11 June 1891, North Dock Ward NF).

47 *N.P.*, 1, 5 June. 1891.

48 *F.J.*, 1 June 1891.

49 *N.P.*, 2 June 1891.

50 *N.P.*, 3 June 1891.

51 *N.P.*, 1 June 1891; see also Healy's speech at Tynock, Co. Carlow, *N.P.*, 6 July 1891.

52 *N.P.*, 4 June 1891.

53 *N.P.*, 2 June 1891.

54 *N.P.*, 8 June 1891; see also Parnell at Leighlinbridge, 7, 29 June 1891.

55 *N.P.*, 11 June 1891, North Dock Ward NF.

56 *F.J.*, 3 June 1891, NL; *F.J.*, 2 Jun. 1891. See also *U.I.*, 6, 13 June 1891. Having served their purpose the attacks were not systematically renewed. The taunting of Parnell by the *National Press* of 13 Aug. with failing to submit the promised balance sheet to William O'Brien after his release is likely to have been the inspiration for Dillon's intervention against any further references to the subject: see Lyons, *Fall*, p. 276.

57 *N.P.*, 23, 24 June 1891. See also *Nation*, 27 June 1891. The *W.N.P.* cartoon depicted a frantic and distracted Parnell being pursued by a process server into the sorter's van: *W.N.P.*, 4 July 1891.

58 *W.N.P.*, 25 June 1891.

59 *N.P.*, 24 June 1891, letter from Parnell to P. C. McGough, d. 24 June; *N.P.*, 29 June 1891.

60 *D.E.*, 26 June 1891.

61 *D.E.*, Dillon to O'Brien, 'Thursday', with postscript marked 'Friday' (26 June 1891) containing the above, O'Brien papers, NLI MS 8555/1. Katharine O'Shea in an interview on the publication of her memoirs said that during the split 'I was sorely tempted to give to the public the true story of the sudden virtue of those English statesmen who had thrown him over at the hour of trial!' (*Daily Sketch*, 18 May 1914). She was constrained however by an awareness of just how counterproductive that would have proved to be from Parnell's point of view (Katharine O'Shea, *Parnell*, ii. pp. 163-64). Those close to Gladstone in 1882 had been deeply apprehensive at his being in receipt of communications from Katharine O'Shea: as Spencer wrote Gladstone: 'I quite dread the fact of her communications leaking out' (Spencer to Gladstone, 25 Sept. 1882 in *The Red Earl, Papers of the Fifth Earl Spencer 1835-1910* 2 vols. [Northampton, 1981, ed. Peter Gordon] i, p. 233).

62 *N.P.*, 18 May 1891. See also *N.P.*, 1, 8 June 1891 and W. M. Murphy at Saggart (*N.P.*, 19 May 1891).

63 *N.P.*, 26 June 1891; *F.J.*, 26 June 1891. Parnell himself telegraphed that evening from Walsingham Terrace to J. M. Tuohy in the London office of the *Freeman's Journal:* 'Kindly announce that I was married this morning nine o'clock to Mrs. O'Shea at Steyning before Registrar and superintendant of District'. He added that the marriage would shortly be solemnised in a London church, 'there having been delay in obtaining licence for this' (Parnell to J. M. Tuohy, 25 July 1891, NLI MS 5934, reproduced in Noel Kissane, *Parnell, A Documentary History* (Dublin, 1991), p. 98. On Parnell's death, the *Daily Telegraph* reported that Parnell and Katharine had planned a religious ceremony at St James's Church, Marylebone, and were waiting the licence of the Bishop of London; the Bishop of Chichester was reported to have refused to sanction a marriage by the vicar of Steyning (*DT*, 8 Oct. 1891).

64 Elizabeth Bowen, *Bowen's Court* (London, 1942). The phrase was used in relation to Parnell's response to the original divorce decree.

65 *N.P.*, 27 June 1891; *W.P.*, 4 July 1891; *Nation*, 4 July 1891; *Kilkenny Journal*, 4 July 1891; *Clonmel Nationalist*, 4 July 1891.

66 *N.P.*, 29 June, speech of M. J. Kenny, Tullow; *I.C.*, 8 Aug. 1891; *N.P.*, 27 June 1891; *N.P.*, 2 July 1891.

67 *F.J.*, 27 June 1891.

68 *N.P.*, 27 June 1891.

69 *M.G.*, 2 July 1891, A 'Broken-Hearted Parnellite' from Kilkenny wrote to the Leinster Literary Society disavowing his allegiance after the marriage, and

sarcastically urging the convening of a special general meeting to draft an address to Parnell on his marriage: 'The address should be illuminated, signed, framed and forwarded as soon as possible (per special train) to Our Only Chief and his "peerless" bride' (anon. letter to Secretary, Leinster Literary Society, 26 June 1891, NLI MS 22,223). Robert M. McWade, in his *The Uncrowned King. The Life and Public Services of Hon. Charles Stewart Parnell* (Philadelphia, 1891, at p. 403) heroically ventured that 'it is but simple justice to Mrs. O'Shea and to our departed friend and leader to say that there are grave doubts among well-informed parties as to their guilt. Both of them proud, high-strung, and, to a large extent, imperious in their natures, disdained to go before a divorce court, either to explain or palliate the alleged questionable transactions in which Captain O'Shea declared they were guilty participants'.

70 *F.J.*, 31 July 1891; Gray to Walsh, n.d., Walsh Papers, DDA.
71 *N.P.*, 29 June.
72 *N.P.*, 30 June 1891; *N.P.*, 29 June 1891, Healy's speech at Carlow.
73 Mar. 1874.
74 *N.P.*, 6 July 1891.
75 *Nationalist*, 29 June 1891, Carlow.
76 *N.P.*, 11 July 1891, Potato Market, Carlow, 5 July.
77 *N.P.*, 6 July 1891, Carlow.
78 *N.P.*, 6 July 1891, Tynock, 4 July.
79 *N.P.*, 27 June 1891; *W.N.P.*, 4 July 1891.
80 *N.P.*, 24 June 1891.
81 *N.P.*, 6 July, 1891 Healy's speeches at Tynock, 4 July; and at Carlow, 5 July; *N.P.*, 25 June 1891.
82 *N.P.*, 30 June 1891. See also *M.G.*, 2 July 1891.
83 *N.P.*, 6 July 1891.
84 *N.P.*, 6 July 1891.
85 *N.P.*, 20, 30 June 1891.
86 *U.I.*, 11 July 1891.
87 *M.G.*, 2 July 1891.
88 *M.G.*, 2 July 1891.
89 *N.P.*, 4 July 1891; *M.G.*, 4 July 1891.
90 *M.G.*, 6 July 1891; *U.I.*, 5 Oct. 1895, 'A Day at Carlow' by 'J.M.G.'.
91 *M.G.*, 2, 3, 4 July 1891.
92 *M.G.*, 4, 6 July 1891.
93 *M.G.*, 9 July 1891, quoting Parnell interview of 27 June; *F.J.*, 9 July; *U.I.*, 11 July 1891.
94 *W.N.P.*, 18 July 1891; see also the cartoon captioned 'A Heartless Refusal', *W.N.P.*, 29 Aug. 1891.
95 *N.P.*, 17, 18, 19, 18 Aug., 8 Sept. 1891; *W.N.P.*, 22 Aug. 1891.

6

THE FINAL PHASE

I am happy, he [Parnell] says, because whether Mr. Gladstone gives
Home Rule or not I am rejoiced. If he gives Home Rule then my feelings as a patriot will be gratified; if he refuses Home Rule then my intellect as a prophet is amply justified *(laughter)*. So that as it is remarked
in *Othello* 'whether he kills Cassio or Cassio kills him either way makes
my gain' *(cheers)*.

T. M. Healy, 26 Aug. 1891[1]

The Irish Parliamentary Party is the product of the people. It is the
instrument framed and fashioned by the people. It is the engine and
weapon of the people, yet the first man to snap it across his knee was
the sword-bearer himself — the leader of the Irish nation *(applause)*.
Putting aside mere insult and outrage I say in the language of
Shakespeare, 'for in this I shall exact a special vengeance'.

T. M. Healy, 22 Sept. 1891[2]

In the wake of the Boulogne collapse, William O'Brien professed a desire
to hold aloof from the split's controversy: 'No matter who attacks me or
how, I desire simply to be out of this business, and ... I am firmly determined that nothing shall draw me into partisanship in what I regard as a
fatal struggle'.[3] From Galway Jail, he watched Healy's course of action
with mounting abhorrence. He scribbled to his fellow prisoner:

H. has deliberately started this diabolical system of filth-throwing in the hope
of daunting us from attempting peace, or making the spirit on both sides so
poisonous as to make it hopeless to propose anything. Loathing is the only
word that can express my feeling every time I open the *National Press*. If that
spirit is to triumph, National politics will be turned into a privy and no man
can escape the filth. I regard H's conduct as surpassing everything for
downright treachery and low cunning at the expense of the National cause
in the interest of his own malignity against Parnell.[4]

Dillon warned O'Brien against an over-sanguine assessment of the prospects of bringing about a peace by detaching Parnell's moderate supporters, and an underestimation of Parnell's furious resolve:

> Now with reference to P[arnell] himself everything I have seen during the
> last five months has confirmed the opinion I formed at Boulogne — from
> reading his speeches — that his master passion now is to have revenge on
> Gladstone, the Radicals and his enemies in general. And I am firmly con-
> vinced he will sacrifice every other consideration to the achievement of this
> purpose. Believe me that is the nature of the man, so that I am firmly con-
> vinced we have nothing to expect from Parnell except implacable hostility
> to Gladstonian or other Liberals, and of course to us the moment we com-
> mit ourselves to any course calculated to preserve the alliance with the Liberal
> Party.

Dillon was no more optimistic about Parnell's adjutants: he went on presciently to remind O'Brien of their shared incubus, responsibility for the
fate of the Plan of Campaign tenants.

> Parnell is far too astute in general not to appreciate the extent to which this
> problem will embarrass us and he will of course hold like grim death to the
> Paris fund if we commit ourselves against him. And that damned nuisance
> Healy — by his idiotic manoeuvres has brought the tenants into a state of
> absolute distress I suppose by this time — so that we shall be assailed on
> this point the *moment* we get out.[5]

O'Brien retained a lingering susceptibility to Parnell, and saw in the anti-
Parnellite movement a vehicle for Healy's triumphalism, and the self-
aggrandisement of the Irish Church. He proposed that he and Dillon should
hold back, in the naïve hope of uniting moderate Parnellites so as to com-
pel Parnell to come to a compromise. Dillon's position was quite different.
His predominant purpose was to deprive Healy of his ascendancy in the
anti-Parnellite movement, which ruled out any delay in declaring against
Parnell on their release. It was essential that he carry O'Brien with him,
and he sought to convert him to the necessity of an initial declaration of
opposition to Parnell prior to parleying with moderate Parnellites, to be
followed by formal adherence to the National Federation in the event of
those parleys proving abortive.

O'Brien argued against an immediate declaration of opposition to
Parnell, on the grounds that without making 'a vigorous effort to reunite
the Party on the basis of Parnell's accepting the verdict of the country
... I for one cannot see any use in plunging into the conflict at H.'s heels'.
He advocated an approach to Parnell's followers on the basis of giving
the Liberals fair play at the general election and awaiting the introduction
of the Home Rule Bill: 'If the Bill is a good one, Parnell will get the credit
of having stiffened the Liberals; if it is a dishonest Bill, the anti-Parnellites
would be discredited and Parnell triumphantly called back to power'.

O'Brien looked to a meeting of the full party at which Parnell could make any statement he pleased reserving his right to criticise the Home Rule Bill, but would commit himself not to prejudice the nationalist party by persevering in the present conflict; on which basis there should be a freeze on the existing distribution of the nationalist seats between Parnellite and anti-Parnellite at the general election. He argued:

> I don't at all calculate on Parnell's approving such an arrangement — on the contrary I am satisfied he is determined not to disband his present forces on almost any terms — but if he knew that the most reputable of his followers were determined that the Liberals would have fair play and would leave him only the rump of a faction, he is astute enough to make the best of it.

O'Brien's proposals were quite unrealistic. He exaggerated the prospects for detaching moderate Parnellites, and underestimated the fierceness of Parnell's resolve, as well as the furious opposition which such a proposal would elicit from the anti-Parnellite parliamentary party and from the Liberals. His premise was nonetheless more convincing than his tactics. He could not envisage the enactment of a Liberal-sponsored measure of home rule without at least Parnell's passive acquiescence: 'If Parnell retains his present forces — no matter how the elections may go — it is to me clear as daylight that no Liberal government could carry a Home Rule Bill in the teeth of their enmity, nor would an Irish Parliament so inaugurated be worth fighting for'.[6]

In suggesting that, in the event of a satisfactory Home Rule Bill being introduced, Parnell would be credited with having 'stiffened' the Liberals, O'Brien had touched an exceedingly raw nerve. He argued that Parnell's presence in the background of a reunited party would have 'a wholesome effect on weak-kneed Liberals' in the all too probable event of Gladstone's death. Dillon refused to be a party to any public declaration that Parnell's action had strengthened the Liberals' commitment to home rule, and considered it would be 'very hurtful' for the Parnellites to return to the party with 'an emphatic public declaration that they still mistrusted Gladstone'.[7]

While Dillon and O'Brien shared an abhorrence of Healy's ascendancy, they differed radically on how it should be challenged. Dillon considered Healy to be 'a most formidable element in the situation'[8] and believed it essential that he be challenged from within the anti-Parnellite camp. For O'Brien, Healy's ascendancy underscored the necessity for an initiative to retrieve the fight from 'its present character as a struggle for vengeance for H. and power for the bishops'. He agreed with Dillon that 'Tim is now looking to the leadership as his legitimate spoils of battle. The bishops and priests are certainly delighted with him, and not being specially interested in the success of Home Rule would probably be content to see him elected knowing he had no strength but in their support'. He deduced from a recent *National Press* article tacit acceptance of the inevitability of a Dillon leadership, indicating that Healy did not believe himself sufficiently strong to mount a challenge in his own right.[9] Dillon in reply agreed that Healy did not feel strong enough to seek the leadership himself: 'Of course we have to count on the very utmost opposition from him that he thinks it safe to offer — and I have no doubt he has a considerable following in the party now — but nevertheless, if the feeling in the country is sound — as I believe it is — we shall have no difficulty in overcoming him, always provided we play our cards well'.[10]

Dillon warned O'Brien that by holding aloof they would 'increase Healy's power with the party and with the bishops, and lessen the chance of our being able to induce the majority to accept a conciliatory attitude'. He observed that 'the effect of Parnell's recent blunders and of the Carlow election ... may have been much greater than we suppose'. He was hopeful that they could rally a large measure of public support so that Parnell's party 'would begin to crumble away, and if a movement of that kind set in, it would be extremely rapid': a scenario at least as improbable as O'Brien's, and one in which Dillon probably did not genuinely believe.

Against O'Brien's preference for laying down peace terms as a first step, and only adhering to the majority if this failed, Dillon insisted they should see Redmond as soon as possible (he feared the response of Harrington and Joseph Kenny would be 'outrageous'), and only put peace proposals to the majority if a considerable number of Parnell's supporters had already accepted them: '... I am *strongly* of the opinion that after what took place at Boulogne we have no right to call upon McCarthy's men to agree to any terms, unless we come with full authority from the other men'. Any other course would put Dillon and O'Brien into the position of making terms for adhering to the majority and would make them 'a target for Tim's leaders. I believe it would be fatally bad policy to place ourselves in such a position, and that it would be simply playing T[im]'s game'.[11]

On the day of Dillon's release, T. P. O'Connor wrote advising that he had sought to persuade what he described as some of the decent Parnellites, but that they were 'pretty hopeless and indeed going from bad to worse', and warning against any criticism of Healy:

> You will know, of course, that I do not sympathise with much that Healy has said, but looking back on the whole struggle, I believe that his method, though rough, was made necessary by the action of Parnell, and that judging his conduct as a whole we owe him a debt of gratitude for the extraordinary moral and physical courage he displayed in the struggle.

O'Connor was careful to suggest that Dillon would be acclaimed as leader if he desired: 'That is as much the conclusion of Sexton and Healy as it is of McCarthy and myself'.[12]

Through July, the *National Press* maintained, in what was a veiled warning to Dillon and O'Brien, a barrage of invective against the compromise espoused by the *Freeman's Journal*. Three days before the release of Dillon and O'Brien from Galway Jail, the *National Press*, faithful to its strategy of escalation, affirmed that 'Parnellism must not merely be defeated. It must be annihilated'.[13]

Immediately on their release, Dillon and O'Brien declared their opposition to Parnell, while avowing their willingness to entertain any peace initiative. Dillon had prevailed over O'Brien's reservations, and the split embarked on its final bitter phase. They travelled on by rail to Dublin, where they found at the station, in O'Brien's later mournful recall, a Parnellite crowd 'in that impressive self-collectedness of a multitude that has ceased to cheer and has not yet commenced to hoot'.[14]

It may be doubted whether Dillon and O'Brien's final and unequivocal declaration of opposition to Parnell had any significant effect on popular allegiances, so unalterably were the battle-lines of the split drawn by the time of their release. The accession of Dillon, and more particularly of O'Brien to the anti-Parnellite cause, did, however, constitute a severe blow to Parnellite morale. There was commensurate satisfaction on the anti-Parnellite side. Harold Frederic found Healy after an all-night sitting in the Commons 'in a state of wild delight' on hearing what he declared to be 'the greatest piece of news I have heard for ten years'. Frederic mordantly noted that while Dillon's opposition to Parnell was considered a certainty, there had been doubts about O'Brien: 'There was a fear lest Mr. Parnell should meet Mr. O'Brien at the prison door and fix him with the magic of the glance Parnellite'.[15] In an editorial remarkably entitled 'Peace and Goodwill', the *National Press* exulted: 'Parnellism was in its last agony before they spoke. Their speeches put it out of pain'.[16]

Parnell responded impassively to the news, brought to him on his arrival at Kingstown.[17] That weekend at Thurles, in a measured and subtle speech, with considerable sureness of emotional touch, he presented O'Brien's repudiation as a personal loss rather than a political reverse. He had not expected that O'Brien would join 'the seceders'. He had hoped to see O'Brien on his release and had sent a message that he would call on him on his way through Dublin the previous day, '... but that purpose was defeated', he continued somewhat ambiguously, 'because he didn't wait to receive the message. He made a pronouncement which it appears to me entirely alters the conditions under which I could have met him'. To cheers, Parnell declared it 'a terrible and a great blow to me personally to be severed from such a friend, but if it needs be so, it must be so'. In an adroit and moving tribute, Parnell went on to quote his description of O'Brien at the height of the party's fortune as 'the Strongbow of Irish Nationality', so as to extract what compensating advantage he could from the éclat of the desertion of the most fervent of his erstwhile loyalists.

In the same speech Parnell showed all his old mastery in responding to Dillon's proposal that Gladstone should be allowed introduce his Home Rule Bill, and that if it proved unsatisfactory he would be the first to declare against it and fight the Liberal party. Parnell retorted: 'Mr. Dillon says he will draw his sword again if the Liberal Party deceive him. But what if he has no sword to draw?' He appealed to Dillon 'not to throw away his sword, not to disband his army'.[18] The speech had the desired effect of drawing Dillon into public controversy with him on a straightforward matter of policy, thus permitting Parnell at last to escape the confines of Healy's strategy of refusing to engage in conventional political argument.

Parnell's train reached Kingsbridge from Thurles late on the Sunday evening. He was met by what the unionist *Daily Express* described as an 'astonishing reception'. No meeting had been announced, but 'the word went round from corner to corner, and from street to street', that the people of Dublin should rally to affirm their allegiance to Parnell after the defection of Dillon and O'Brien. As Parnell's brake emerged from Kingsbridge, a great cheering crowd lined the quays and the streets into the city, illumined by torches. The houses were lit up, and rockets launched, as he passed bare-headed acknowledging the acclaim. It was an affecting tribute, and his last triumphal passage.[19]

Parnell skilfully chose this moment to concede the extent of his predicament. Around midnight at the National Club, addressing his loyalists, he declared, 'We may lose elections; we may lose the majority of the elections; some of us may lose our own seats; but the loss of elections, the loss of seats, does not mean everything *(cheers)*'. He was now the acknowledged leader only of Dublin:

> I am proud to have had the opportunity of seeing this great demonstration in Dublin to-night, unequalled by anything in my experience in this city since, a few days before the year 1882, I was arrested and sent to Kilmainham by Mr. Gladstone *(groans)*. Dublin is stirred to its heart *(cheers)*. Dublin says with the instinct and knowledge which comes from experience, culture and reading, if this man is a traitor, why is he supported by the best of Irishmen? *(cheers)*. If this man is a traitor, and means to betray and destroy this country, why these desperate attempts from all sides to crush him? They have pondered over their lesson and the determination of this city has grown and mounted higher and higher during the eight months that this crisis and trouble have lasted *(cheers)*. I say what cannot be contradicted, what no man can contradict, that wherever the forces of intimidation in Ireland are useless and ineffectual, there the seceders have found no strength, comfort, or support *(cheers)*; whenever there is manhood, independent and courageous, there our people have stood firm, and will stand firm by the flag of freedom and Irish liberty *(enthusiastic cheering)*.[20]

The failure of Dillon and O'Brien to entice any of Parnell's parliamentary supporters away from him, or at least into a collusive endeavour to induce him to retire, led to bitter recriminations in the by-elections in Cork and Waterford which followed Parnell's death. In the Cork election, O'Brien wildly accused Redmond of having broken a commitment to withdraw his support from Parnell if he rejected the terms offered by Dillon and O'Brien at Boulogne, and charged that Redmond for months before their release from Galway Jail and for at least a month afterwards had shirked 'his part towards his colleagues and towards his leader'.[21]

Redmond in turn asserted that to his certain knowledge O'Brien went into Galway Jail 'almost as much a Parnellite as he was', and that Dillon and O'Brien had disregarded Redmond's warning not to permit themselves to be dragged at Healy's heels.[22] O'Brien's predictably furious reaction to what he characterised as 'a mean and wicked falsehood' revealed the intense trauma which Parnell's death had engendered. The charge of treachery did not lie in the mouth of 'a gentleman who, during our imprisonment in Galway Jail was notoriously and persistently bargaining behind Mr. Parnell's back to get rid of the leadership of Mr. Parnell'. Redmond had 'professed himself just as anxious as we were to secure Mr. Parnell's retirement from the leadership and to preserve the Liberal alliance'.[23] In a remonstrance to T. P. Gill, Redmond wrote that he was seriously considering bringing libel proceedings arising out of O'Brien's 'shameful statements'.[24] O'Brien in turn stated that he made the allegation only 'to point out that his calumny against me came with special audacity from a man who, in all our communications from first to last, accepted Mr. Parnell's retirement as the indispensable condition of peace, and professed himself as anxious as Mr. Dillon and myself to enforce it', adding woundingly that Redmond 'now poses as a fanatical Parnellite'.[25]

The suggestion that Redmond contemplated Parnell's retirement on other than voluntary terms as part of a settlement was unfounded: O'Brien's use of the word 'enforce' was a polemical mistruth. The fragmentary scraps of evidence from inside Galway Jail do not bear out O'Brien's version. Thus John Dillon advised O'Brien that he had received an 'important letter' from his cousin Valentine Blake Dillon in which he intimated 'that Redmond, Clancy, etc. are anxious to co-operate with us for peace, and asks us not to commit ourselves', which John Dillon was quick to add did not alter his view as to the course they ought to pursue.[26]

Gill, in response to Redmond's letter, wrote to John Dillon protesting against the William O'Brien version of the 'Galway overtures' of V. B. Dillon and Redmond, reasonably asserting that 'I rather thought it was mainly because you and William judged that R. and his friends would not bring themselves to go against P. in case P. did not agree to reasonable peace that you spoke in Galway without waiting to see'.[27]

A note from O'Brien to Redmond suggests that, most likely on 31 July, Dillon and O'Brien, having sought out but missed him, sent a message asking him to call up to Dillon's house in North Great George's Street that evening.[28] There is no record of Redmond having called, and it may be doubted that, had he received the communication in time, he would have made the journey to so compromising a venue.

Such negotiation as occurred in pursuance of what Healy later derisively called 'the task of converting the Parnellite members who were to come over *en masse* to the majority as soon as the ex-prisoners had taken that side', took place in London on which Dillon and O'Brien, as well as a watchful Parnell, converged for the last two days of the session.[29] Dillon and O'Brien met a number of Parnellites, who while friendly indicated that the precipiteness of their declaration against Parnell had destroyed any lingering hope of compromise.[30]

Inconclusive controversy surrounded the response of J. L. Carew, the Parnellite member for North Kildare and proprietor of the *Leinster Leader*. Healy later wrote that in Carew, Dillon and O'Brien had their sole ' "draw" ', and this afterwards turned out to be a blank'. According to Healy, Carew, having wavered for half a day, despatched to his paper an article renouncing Parnell, which he later stopped when prevailed upon by Redmond to return to the Parnellite fold.[31] O'Brien subsequently characterised Carew's conduct in the wake of their interview as 'disgusting' and deplored the weakness of his behaviour.[32] The hapless Carew, stung by a remark of O'Brien during the Cork election, wrote bitterly to T. P. Gill explaining that he had told O'Brien that if O'Brien could undo the effect of his precipitate declaration against Parnell, Carew would reciprocate: 'I assured him of my support and the support of my paper towards a reconciliation if he did so, but I distinctly told him I would never go against Parnell but that if he (Parnell) were unreasonable I would resign'.[33] William O'Brien's wife Sophie, in her unpublished 'Recollections', wrote that Dillon and O'Brien were lunching in the House of Commons with Carew, who had agreed to join them and bring over his paper: 'All was settled, when Parnell came into the room. Carew's face wilted, he grew taciturn and left. He did not alter the policy of his paper and remained a Parnellite'.[34] This anecdote, while perhaps apocryphal, vividly conveys the difficulty of conducting negotiations in Parnell's wrathful shadow.

O'Brien was now firmly caught in the coils of the strategy propounded by Dillon in Galway Jail. On 28 August, bewildered and irascible, he wrote to Dillon of their elusive moderate Parnellite quarry: 'I would not be for going a single yard further to coddle these men. They have put Healy completely in the right by their dishonest shilly-shallying'.[35] The only prestigious recruit whom Dillon and O'Brien could boast was Edmund Dwyer Gray. His, however, was a hollow and contrived conversion, having been delayed in concertation with Dillon and O'Brien until their release.[36]

To retrieve Parnell's clarity of purpose, it is necessary to dispel the commingled fumes of Greek tragedy, Catholic superstitiousness and nationalist mysticism which have clouded the closing months of his career. Parnell's campaign, which had commenced as a defiant and uncompromising bid to wrest back his leadership from what he denounced as the usurpation of the majority in Committee Room 15, had become a desperate struggle against political marginalisation. He was no longer engaged in a quest for the immediate reconstitution of his leadership, but was furiously struggling to shore up his support against the flowing tide of anti-Parnellism, to ensure his political survival until that tide ebbed. His was a fierce battle to ensure that he would be returned at the general election with a level of parliamentary support, which, however severely reduced, permitted the continued existence of a distinct Parnellite party.

Parnell displayed unremitting tenacity. He signalled his determination to fight the issue through to the end, rejecting, as he had at Committee Room 15 and at Boulogne, any course which would encroach on his jealously-guarded 'responsibilities'. He made the minimal tactical accommodation which his demonstrated minority status required. He embarked on the delicate transition from that of the 'Chief' bent on the immediate recovery of his leadership to that of the leader of a minoritarian opposition within nationalism, without compromising either his claims to be the sole legitimate interpreter of the principles of parliamentary nationalism or his ultimate pretensions to leadership.

In Healy's phrase, 'a more workable political creed in supplement to the narrower faith in an "only possible leader"' was evolved by the Parnellites.[37] The National League Convention held in Dublin on 23 July 1891 heralded an elaborate, but unconvincing, attempt to broaden the issue of the split and to articulate a distinctly Parnellite programme on a range of social and economic issues.[38] The *National Press* witheringly derided the unreality of the Convention's 'constitution-mongering'.

> Anything that was wanted in the way of legislation by anyone, delegate or not, was immediately accorded by Mr. Parnell who might have sung with the Lord Chancellor in *Iolanthe*
>
>> Thus I sit in my chair all day,
>> Giving agreeable measures away.[37]

Of greater significance were the narrowly political themes of Parnell's campaign in its final phase: his renewed insistence that the issue of the split was no longer simply a question of leadership; his attack on Dillon and O'Brien which charged them with failing to respect the principles of independent opposition and with responsibility for the débâcle of the Plan of Campaign; and a redeployment of his attacks on the Liberals away from the person of the Liberal leader to the waning in the Liberal commitment to home rule he prophesied under Gladstone's successors.

At Thurles in August Parnell declared: 'It is no longer a question of leadership. It is a question of whether our country is worthy of being a nation'. He added with simulated humility that he happened 'only to be the humble and unworthy instrument. I wish from the bottom of my heart that you had a better and more worthy leader *(cries of no no)*'.[40] At

Limerick en route to Listowel he declared:

> As I said to you in Limerick eight months ago, this is no longer a question
> of mere leadership — I don't covet or desire to lead these men who have
> betrayed the interests of Ireland *(cheers)*. I never wish to lead them again
> *(hear hear)*. Neither will I go under them *(cheers)*. Neither will the Irish people
> go under them *(cheers)*. That, fellow countrymen, is our position today, and
> it is not a question as has been sought to be made out a question of leader-
> ship. God knows I never desired the responsibility of leadership, and I am
> glad to be rid of it, but I would not ask you to take on your shoulders, neither
> will I take on my own, responsibility for Sir William Harcourt and the Liberal
> party *(cheers)*.[41]

At Listowel, Parnell made the ringing declaration which became for
Parnellites, and for Fenian Parnellites in particular, his epitaph:

> I said at the beginning that this was not a question of leadership. If I were
> dead and gone tomorrow, the men who are fighting against English influence
> in Irish public life would fight on still; they would still be independent na-
> tionalists; they would still believe in the future of Ireland a Nation, and they
> would still protest that it was not by taking orders from an English Minister
> that Ireland's future could be saved, protected, or secured.[42]

Parnell's abiding difficulty in restraining himself from vituperative attacks on his opponents even in the context of an argument designed to
sound a temperate note was revealed when, having declared that the issue
was not leadership but of 'a grave difference of opinion as to the means
by which the future of our country can be secured', he proceeded to denounce his opponents as 'traitorous and cowardly seceders'.

The *Freeman's Journal* struggled vainly to suggest that Parnell's observations on the issue of leadership bespoke a new temperateness, or even
evidenced a conciliatory spirit. It ventured that, since the sessional chairmanship of the Irish party for the session 1890-91 had expired, the original
issue in the split no longer arose.[43] Parnell was, however, accommodating
himself to the inevitability of defeat at the general election, rather than
moderating the underlying pretensions of his campaign.

At Cabinteely on 20 September Parnell sought to defend himself against
the charge of having sabotaged home rule. He insisted that the existence
of an independent Parnellite party would enhance the settlement obtained:

> Ireland cannot possibly lose anything because some of her sons will remain
> independent *(cheers)*. You remember the threats that were held out to you
> some six months ago that unless you fell into line and obeyed the whip of
> Mr. Gladstone that the chance of Home Rule would be lost to the country
> ... Ireland has today as good a chance of Home Rule as she ever had *(cheers)*.
> She has lost no ground on account of the creation of this great and indepen-
> dent party.[44]

He argued that, on the contrary, the measure of home rule achieved,
would be 'all the stronger, all the more powerful' because of the Parnellite

stance. This audacious line of argument, which drew heavily on the fact of his own defeat as removing the threat which Gladstone asserted to exist to his leadership of the Liberal party, was charged with a peculiar menace for the anti-Parnellites. It left Parnell at liberty either to attack a future Home Rule Bill, or to pronounce it sufficient in consequence of his own spirited resistance to Liberal 'dictation' in the split. If the flaccidity of the argument marked a lapse from the habitual astringency of Parnell's politics, it confronted the extirpationist logic of Healy and other hardline anti-Parnellites. Parnell skilfully sought to assuage the still-fevered temper of the split in Ireland by asserting that the threat to home rule, which he had never believed to exist, had, even on Gladstone's own logic, receded. Adumbrating a more politically effective oppositionist role, the argument revealed a more assured Parnell, determined to persevere beyond defeat at the general election, and served as a reminder of just how formidably resilient and tenacious a politician he remained.

The *National Press* in characteristic vein dismissed Parnell's contention that the existence of an independent Parnellite party assured a better home rule settlement:

> This means, if it has any meaning at all, that Mr. Parnell committed adultery with Mrs. O'Shea in the interests of Home Rule, and that the revelations of the Divorce Court, by which 'things were disturbed' was his crowning benefaction to his country. Mr. Parnell has made many strange boasts of his services, but this is, surely the strangest of all. We are half ashamed of wasting so many words on this fallen and degraded man. His power for good was lost long ago; his power for evil is almost at an end.[45]

Parnell came under pressure from his parliamentary followers to espouse the principle embodied in the catch-cry of giving 'fair play' to the Liberals, and to restrict attacks on the Liberals until after the introduction of a Home Rule Bill, so as to give the Liberals the opportunity to demonstrate their bona fides. Parnell's perfunctory references to the principle were in terms so ironically mocking as to convey a brutal rebuff to those who urged its adoption. At Maryborough Parnell pointedly addressed the issue in terms of 'fair play' not for Gladstone but for Harcourt, whom Parnell insisted — inaccurately as it transpired — would succeed Gladstone, and whose lack of enthusiasm for home rule was notorious: 'It is asked that we should give a chance to the Liberal party and its future leader, Sir William Harcourt, if they give legitimate freedom and liberty to Ireland, none will be more proud and more glad than we shall be'.[46]

In what *United Ireland* published as an interview with Parnell of 4 October, two days before his death, Parnell criticised the proceedings of the National Liberal Federation and the programme adopted by it, the 'Newcastle Programme'. He discerned an ominous dilution of the Liberal commitment to home rule in the elevation of more populist English reforms to parity with, and, he suggested, even precedence over, home rule. He accused Gladstone of a departure from his former principle of reserving his energies for home rule over subsidiary English reforms: 'He now engages with the utmost avidity in an examination of these various other subjects, and devotes three columns of his speech to five to their consideration'. Parnell was quoted as concluding, 'we thus see, as one of the first fruits of the subserviency of the Seceders, Home Rule sandwiched between allotments and parish councils'. The interview also contained an attack on Gladstone's speech for its failure to deliver 'the great declaration ... as to the character of his Home Rule declarations, which was to overwhelm all Parnellites with confusion', which anti-Parnellites had hinted at, and at the vagueness of his treatment of the provisions of the Home Rule Bill.[47] Parnell's argument, blatantly directed to Liberalism after Gladstone, presciently warned of the danger of the eclipse of Home Rule by passing political fancies in England of a vaguely progressive character.

At Listowel in mid-September Parnell retaliated against Dillon and O'Brien with immoderate ferocity, culminating in his declaration that he was unwilling to have the Paris funds 'dissipated by a parcel of idiots'. In response to an incautious criticism by Dillon of the idea of seeking pledges from Gladstone, Parnell observed that Dillon at Boulogne had been party to such an arrangement. He added the extremely menacing comment that O'Brien's opening gambit at Boulogne made with Dillon's approval comprised a set of proposals 'which I found so absurd and ridiculous, and so traitorous to the Liberal allies of these men that they were obliged to admit that they were utterly untenable and unsuitable'.[48] Parnell's veiled allusion was to the provision in the proposals put by O'Brien at Boulogne that all possible efforts were to be made to secure from Gladstone an acknowledgement of the mistake in precipitately publishing his letter and an admission that he had not taken sufficient account of national senti-ment in Ireland or of Parnell's position. Parnell renewed this cold and furious thrust in his last speech, at Creggs, derisively inviting O'Brien to publish the Boulogne proposals the text of which he added he had not burnt in spite of O'Brien's request that he do so.[49]

On 12 August Dillon took the chair at a meeting of the National Federa-tion in Dublin, and, in thus stepping into Healy's lair, completed his breach with the Parnellites. Healy availed himself of the opportunity to ensnare Dillon in the coils of his strategy. He declared that Dillon's speech 'spreads out like a great panorama of perfidy the performances of this man for the last eight months', and observed that 'the volley of grape-shot delivered from the chair today, will, I think, thin their ranks in the Parnellite regi-ment'. Most importantly, Healy restated the issue of the split in terms which placed it beyond the reach of Dillon's increasingly fatuous attempt to detach moderate Parnellite sympathisers:

What hope have we for the return of these men? If we are right they must be wrong *(applause)*. And if we are right in our position towards the Irish movement they must be traitors towards the movement, not, I grant you, with the guilt of intentional perfidy, but what matters to us whether the cause of Ireland be lost by a knave or a fool *(laughter)* ... I say this is no longer a time for dialectics ... I say that the present situation, in regard to Mr. Parnell's immediate followers — it is a case for the sweeping brush *(loud laughter and cheers)*.[50]

The final collapse of the course of conciliation espoused by Dillon and O'Brien on their release was signalled by a speech of John Redmond, the most influential of Parnell's parliamentary lieutenants, ending a period of conspicuous silence and reserve (which included his absence from the National League convention), in which he affirmed his Parnellism and dismissed Dillon and O'Brien as impotent.[51] The *National Press* seized on the 'concentrated gall and venom' of Redmond's speech, which it categorised 'politically speaking, as the shriek of a lost soul'. It asserted that Redmond had been rebuffed in his endeavours to return by the back door to the triumphant majority: 'He sinned deliberately and against the light'.[52] O'Brien wrote angrily to Dillon that while Redmond had behaved 'with miserable weakness', 'Tim's crow of delight at having goaded him into active enmity is lamentable'.[53]

In a speech on 22 September Healy carefully isolated Redmond for attack, distinguishing his position from 'the mere omadhaunery of Mr. Timothy Harrington'. Redmond he described as 'a callous, calculating, cool-headed, able, man ... the man who made the balls for others to throw':

While he has conducted himself with astuteness avoiding the odium and rancour which has gathered around the names of less skilful men, I say — and I hope I say it without vindictiveness, but with a knowledge of the secret springs of this entire movement — that the main share, the capital responsibility for the split in the Irish Party will always be found next to Mr. Parnell, on the head and shoulders of Mr. John Redmond.[54]

Healy continued to compose political obituaries of Parnell. Of Parnell's Westport meeting, in an editorial entitled 'A Pitiable Performance', the *National Press* declared that 'no one dreams now of treating Mr. Parnell's vapourings seriously', and charted Parnell's precipitate decline:

Surely, no man in so brief a space has sunk so low. Power, reputation, and self-respect have in turn deserted him. From the haughtiest and most reserved of living men, he has become the most obsequious. He, to whom the most prominent men of the Irish race could find no access when the most momentous crises of the movement demanded instant attention, now fawns upon Tom, Dick, and Harry who are willing to crack their own voices or their neighbours' skulls in his service. He, whom the sore need and suffering of the people called in vain to come from winter quarters to Ireland, now hurries from post to pillar to address any 'demonstration' which, by means of free tickets and free drinks, can be mobilised to demonstrate ... One might almost be inclined to pity his downfall and dishonour if it were not so thoroughly well deserved.[55]

Healy declared that the entire controversy arose 'simply and solely because Mr. Parnell could not keep away from the wife of one of his colleagues', and the paper asserted that 'Mr. Parnell's repulsive personality alone obstructs the unity of the national cause'.[56] Of the recent Parnellite assertion that the split was no longer a question of leadership, the paper commented that 'as for the belated afterthought that there is some question of principle to be maintained, that is an exhalation of the present summer arising out of the decomposing remains of Parnellism'.[57] The paper denounced the new Parnellite proposition as a last, desperate ruse: 'Hopeless of victory for the present, their minds run on the best plan for keeping the seeds of dissension alive for fructification and germination later on'. It went on to deride the spectacle of Parnell in defeat, humiliatingly compelled to dissemble his political pretensions in a frantic endeavour to keep his campaign alive:

> All the old jargon about the 'Leader of the Irish Race', the 'Only Possible', the 'Matchless One', suddenly disappears through the trapdoor, and, as if by magic, we are favoured instead with the modest vision of an ex-Sessional Chairman, a time-expired officer, standing with humble mien, without cockade or epaulettes, ready to recruit for service in the rank of the army which he once commanded ... Why were we not treated to a word of all this until the death-dews had gathered on the front of faction? Only when the last hope has fled does the wretched organ which has been the main cause of Ireland's misery squeak out a whie of surrender, with the death-rattle in its throat, and now only does the arrogant ex-Dictator, who, on the very day of the Kilkenny election boasted that he would 'sweep out of public life' every man of the 'forty-four rats' who had voted against him, and declared there was no one fit to take his place, condescendingly say he does not want to be leader any more. He and his 'staff' may indeed make their minds easy on that point. He won't. Never again will Mr. C. S. Parnell be received as a soldier in the National forces.[58]

Healy contrived to maintain the political initiative by embarking on what he presented as the final drive to efface Parnell and Parnellism, with the intention of nullifying Dillon and O'Brien's efforts to control the direction of the split's controversy. With brilliant cruelty he mocked the Parnellite dilemma, exacerbating the tensions between Parnell and his Parliamentary followers yet in such terms as to bind them yet more tightly to him. No possibility for heightening the split's conflict was left unexploited. Provoked by a Parnellite manœuvre whereby a parliamentary debate on a Parnellite motion on amnesty was closed before any anti-Parnellite could contribute, the *National Press*, faithful to Healy's retributive purpose, suggested that 'it would be an excellent object lesson for the constituencies if, whenever Mrs. O'Shea's registered husband rose in Parliament, the Nationalists quietly left their places and refused to take any share in the debate or division which he inaugurated'.[59] If this proposal for a parliamentary boycott of Parnell was not seriously pressed, it nevertheless

revealed Healy's disturbing urge to consummate the ritual demeaning of
Parnell by translating the split's spectacle to Westminster, the effect of which
could only have been to discredit Irish parliamentary nationalism as a
whole, by importing an Irish circus surpassing the most fertile imaginings
of parliamentary caricaturists.

It is possible to discern in the split's closing stages an ironic moment
of objective collusion between Healy and Parnell. Healy needed Parnell.
His continued ascendancy in the anti-Parnellite camp was heavily reliant
on an unyielding and impenitent Parnell refusing to resile from the course
he had pursued from the outset of the split. Reciprocally for Parnell, the
continued hegemony within the majority of a politician of Healy's virulence
and temperamental instability offered the prospect of political advantage.

A fortnight before Parnell's death, Dillon's campaign to wrest control
of the anti-Parnellite movement from Healy began in earnest. Immediately after quitting Committee Room 15, the majority had appointed a committee of eight members to exercise along with the chairman of the party
the functions which formerly had been the prerogative of Parnell alone.
The committee had not met in the interim. Its composition however, by
a majority of one, was favourable to Dillon over Healy, and when convened on 21 September, carried a resolution which accorded to the repentant
Freeman's Journal equal status with the *National Press* in officially
soliciting funds for the anti-Parnellite party.[60]

The temper of the meeting is conveyed by what O'Brien later described
as Healy's 'most wanton declaration the night of the meeting of our party
that he would go on even more offensively than ever — and that at a time
when he knows there is no question on our part of receiving back any of
the Parnellite M.P.s'.[61]

Thus after ten months of arduous travail Healy was already losing control of the anti-Parnellite party. Even before Parnell's death, it was apparent that his supremacy was unstable. From Healy's perspective, Dillon,
whom he had always loathed, stood to be the undeserving beneficiary of
Parnell's defeat. He was to be deprived of the spoils of victory: Parnell
was to be dragged at the back of another's chariot. Yet, while leadership
would continue to elude him, he had in the split laid the foundations of
an extraordinarily powerful refractory influence in nationalist politics,
through an intimate rapport with those individuals and sectors of nationalist society resistant to strong political leadership within nationalism,
whose withholding of full support from successive leaders of the Irish party
was to render enduring the destruction in the split of the Parnellite edifice
of power of the 1880s.

Dillon and O'Brien's apostolate of conciliation lay in tatters. Unnerved
by Parnell's menacing allusion in his Listowel speech to his opening gambit at Boulogne, O'Brien detected a relapse on the part of an increasingly
desperate Parnell into his former excesses:

The Listowel speeches show two things, first that he is almost as desperate and as incoherent as in the wildest of his Kilkenny speeches, and secondly that he will stop at nothing to split us by fair means or foul. It is plain that there was a complete cooling off in his reception thro' the country and that he is falling back more and more on the hillside boys. If Tim would only give us fair play the situation looks excellent.

Dillon likewise wrote in his diary of Parnell's Creggs speech: 'Parnell at Creggs yesterday, incoherent scurrility — sad, sad. He must positively be going mad'.[62]

Dillon and O'Brien found themselves increasingly trapped within the confines of Healy's policy. Their predicament was sharpened by the issue, which loomed large in September, as to whether Dillon should join Healy on a platform in his North Longford constituency. O'Brien was opposed to Dillon going to Longford. While 'we ought to do nothing to hamper Healy's freedom of action, much less say or do anything unfriendly to him', he objected to Healy dominating their freedom of action. He wrote again:

Parnell's friends have so completely played into his hands they deserve no consideration. All the same [Healy's] attitude is lamentable from the point of view of our being able ever again to make the country a place worth living in. His taunts at JER[edmond] are woeful, and as to myself every offensive thing said by every insignificant blackguard in the country — things so gross that they are suppressed in the *F[reeman]* — are embalmed in the *National Press*, as if they were most precious deliverances — always, of course, by way of defending me.[63]

While 'a refusal will undoubtedly be taken as a declaration of war on your part', O'Brien urged Dillon to go to Longford only if he could reach an understanding with Healy. The nature of the understanding plaintively urged by O'Brien was markedly nebulous: 'Is there any possibility of establishing a clear understanding with H.? If he would undertake to drop all unnecessary aggressiveness and offensiveness and not obstruct us in trying to conciliate the Parnellite rank and file, we leaving him at perfect freedom to fight as hard as he pleases, whenever and wherever attacked?'.[64] O'Brien's frantic and ineffectual grasping for a distinct line of action in an endeavour to impose on the fury and chaos of the split what were increasingly metaphysical gradations of policy, reflected the impasse which he and Dillon had reached.

Dillon was aware that a refusal to attend would incur 'the bitter hostility of Healy so far as he dares to carry it': 'I don't know how we could avoid even speaking of his career during the last year — and although I consider that our Parnellite friends have released us from all obligations in their regard — I confess I cannot see my way towards endorsing Healy'. He nevertheless inclined in favour of attending the meeting.[65] (When Healy eventually spoke — alone — at Longford in November, he fulfilled

Dillon's and O'Brien's worst apprehensions by his atrocious denunciation of Parnell's widow as a 'proved British prostitute'.[66])

Little remained in practice to differentiate the policy of Dillon and O'Brien from that of Healy, beyond their eschewal of the offensive scabrousness of his attacks on Parnell. It was a measure of Healy's ascendancy, and of the extent to which his rhetoric had set the anti-Parnellite agenda that neither Dillon nor O'Brien felt able to condemn sexual attacks on Parnell until after his death; at Carrick-on-Suir Dillon permitted the cry of 'Kitty' from a member of the audience to pass unrebuked, for which he was condemned by William Redmond.[67] In his determination to wrest the initiative from him, Dillon found himself humiliatingly compelled to submit to Healy's strategy in the split. He declared at Mallow on 9 August, 'I adopt every single action which my colleagues have taken in this case *(cheers and cries of "Healy")'*. The distinction between action and rhetoric was, as Dillon doubtless intended, lost on his audience. His statement in late September that 'I shall feel it to be my duty, and the duty of every one of my colleagues — painful as it is to me and many of them no doubt — to do everything in our power to drive from parliament every man who supports factionism' was enthusiastically hailed by the *National Press*.[68]

The contest followed the course which Dillon had adjudged necessary and inevitable from the outset, of a war for supremacy within the anti-Parnellite camp. Dillon and O'Brien did not engage in any serious attempt to alter the terms of the controversy. O'Brien in the event proved as dedicated an anti-Parnellite as Dillon. Confused and irascible, he vented his rage against the recalcitrant moderate Parnellites of his fond imaginings, whose failure to rally to himself and Dillon he was unable to comprehend, rather than against Healy.

The failure of Dillon and O'Brien to differentiate their position sharply from Healy's marked the collapse of their project of achieving a moderate, and vaguely conciliatory, mode of anti-Parnellism. Their espousal of an anti-Parnellite *via media* proved unconvincing and incoherent. A failure of nerve compounded a failure of judgement. The damage to their reputations was not confined to Parnellites, who would never quite forget that in the closing weeks of Parnell's life they had thrown their full weight into a campaign against him under Healy's auspices. The *Kilkenny Moderator*, admittedly unionist and subliminally Parnellite, gave voice to more generally held opinions in taunting on Parnell's death that the adherence to the majority of Dillon and O'Brien was 'the result of cool and callous calculation': 'We think better even of Mr. Healy and the rest of the Parliamentary "rats", for they ratted on chance; they revolted against their leader at the first blush of a quarrel between him and the Chief of the English Liberal party, on the chance that Ireland would sustain their action'.[69] The damage to the repute of the duo of 'Dillon and O'Brien', popularly conceived among nationalists as the natural successors to Parnell in the Irish leadership — subsequently aggravated by their own political sundering — completed the debacle of the split.

For O'Brien, the anti-Parnellite politician most strongly drawn to Parnell, the outcome was a psychological as well as a political disaster. The strange and volatile course of his subsequent career emblematized the lost direction of constitutional nationalism after Parnell. He remained haunted by the remembrance of Parnell. In his several memoirs he obsessively rehearsed the lost opportunities for compromise in what he persisted in absurdly designating 'the Parnell tragedy of errors'.[70] This reflected his inability to come to terms with the ferocity of the split's intellectual engagement, through his incapacity as a romantic nationalist to see the conflict in other than sentimentally biographical terms. His lifelong lament began on his first hearing of Parnell's death:

> The appalling news just to hand ends all controversy. If he had only let us save him at Boulogne, what a different fate his might have been! If even J.E.R.[edmond] and the rest had the courage of their convictions after our coming out of jail he might even then have been persuaded to save himself from his tragic fate. It is most woeful.[71]

References

1 *N.P.*, 27 Aug. 1891, Central Branch, NF.
2 *N.P.*, 23 Sept. 1891, Trinity Ward Branch, NF.
3 O'Brien to T. P. Gill, n.d., recd. 25 Feb. 91, Gill Papers, NLI MS 13507 (1).
4 O'Brien to Dillon, 'Sat.', Dillon Papers, TCD MS 6736, f. 75.
5 Dillon to O'Brien, n.d., O'Brien Papers, NLI MS 8555/1.
6 O'Brien to Dillon, 'Saturday' (probably 4 July 1891), Dillon Papers, TCD MS 6736, f. 79; see Lyons, *Fall*, p. 283.
7 Dillon to O'Brien, 'Sun.' (probably 5 July 1891), O'Brien Papers, NLI MS 8555/1; see Lyons, *Fall*, pp. 284-5.
8 Dillon to O'Brien, 'Sun.' (NLI MS 8555/1).
9 O'Brien to Dillon, 'Thurs.', Dillon Papers, TCD MS 6736, f. 80; dated by Lyons, 9 or 16 July: *Fall*, p. 286, n. 2.
10 Dillon to O'Brien, 'Sat.' (17 July 1891?), O'Brien Papers, NLI MS 8555/1.
11 Dillon to O'Brien, 'Monday', 8555/1; dated by F. S. Lyons as 20 July 1891, Lyons, *Fall*, pp. 286-8.
12 T. P. O'Connor to Dillon, 30 July 1891, Dillon Papers, TCD MS 6740, f. 4.
13 *N.P.*, 27 July 1891.
14 *N.P.*, 31 July 1891; W. O'Brien, *Olive Branch in Ireland*, p. 58.
15 *N.Y.T.*, 2 Aug. 1891.
16 *N.P.*, 31 July 1891.
17 Leamy, *Parnell's Faithful Few*, p. 83.
18 *F.J.*, 3 Aug. 1891. At the National Club in Dublin later that evening, Parnell applied to the 'bitter pain' of O'Brien's loss, the lines 'Of all the words of tongue and pen,/ The saddest are; "it might have been" '(ibid).

19 *D.E.*, 3 Aug. 1891; *F.J.*, 3 Aug. 1891; *I.W.I.*, 7 Oct. 1893, F. J. Allan, 'The Passing of the Chief'.

20 *F.J.*, 3 Aug. 1891.

21 *F.J.*, 29 Oct. 1891, 2 Nov. 1891.

22 *N.P.*, 1 Jan. 1892, National Club.

23 *N.P.*, 2 Jan. 1891, O'Brien to *N.P.*

24 Redmond to Gill, 14 Jan. [189(2)], Gill Papers, NLI MS 13,492 (12).

25 *N.P.*, 18 Jan. 1892, O'Brien to *N.P.*

26 Dillon to O'Brien, 'Tues', O'Brien Papers, NLI MS 8551/1.

27 T. P. Gill to John Dillon, 17 Jan. 1891, copy Gill Papers, NLI MS 13507 (19); see also V. B. Dillon to John Dillon 'Sat' (25 July 1891), Dillon Papers, TCD MS 6771, f. 171; V. B. Dillon to John Dillon, 'Sun' (26 July 1891), Dillon Papers, MS 6771, f. 172.

28 O'Brien to Redmond, 'Fri evg.', envelope marked 1 Aug. 1891; see Lyons, *Fall*, p. 296, n. 2.

29 Healy, *Why Ireland is Not Free*, p. 46; *F.J.*, 5 Aug. 1891.

30 *F.J.*, 5, 6 Aug. 1891.

31 Healy, *Why Ireland is Not Free*, p. 46.

32 O'Brien to Dillon, 28 Aug., 17 Sept. 1891, Dillon Papers, TCD MS 6736.

33 *N.P.*, 5 Nov. 1891; Carew to Gill, 23 Jan. 1891, Gill Papers, NLI MS 13507 (19).

34 Sophie O'Brien, *Recollections*, p. 195.

35 O'Brien to Dillon, 28 Aug. 1891, Dillon Papers, TCD MS 6736, f. 85.

36 Morley to Gladstone, 23 May 1891, Gladstone Papers, BM Add. MS 44256, ff. 141-2; Healy, *Why Ireland is Not Free*, p. 45. Irritated by an inept Gray *démarche*, Dillon in Galway Jail complained to O'Brien that 'Gray is foolish not to let the thing alone till we get out' (Dillon to O'Brien, 'Tues', O'Brien Papers, NLI MS 8551/5).

37 Healy, *Why Ireland is Not Free*, p. 46.

38 *F.J.*, 24 July 1891. Most of the additions or amendments to the old National League constitution adopted were drafted by Parnell himself: Parnell to Harrington, 20 July 1891, Harrington Papers, NLI MS 8581.

39 *N.P.*, 24 July 1891.

40 *F.J.*, 3 Aug. 1891.

41 *F.J.*, 14 Sept. 1891, Limerick, 12 Sept.

42 *F.J.*, 14 Sept. 1891. Parnell had used a similar formula earlier in the day in replying to addresses presented to him: 'If I was dead and gone to-morrow the men supporting me throughout Ireland would continue to support my principles *(applause)*. It is the future of our country that we are struggling for, because we believe in the legitimate independence of Ireland as a nation, and because we think the seceders have tampered with this chance of our future, and attempted to give away our powers and rights as a nation'. That Parnell may have regarded this as a definitive casting of the issue of the split is suggested by his closing of his public speech by citing the most classic of all his utterances: 'We assert today in this town of Listowel what we asserted in 1885 and the years before it, that no man has a right to fix the boundary of a nation — that no man has a right to limit the aspirations of our own people'.

43 *F.J.*, 14 Sept. 1891.

44 *F.J.*, 21 Sept. 1891, Cabinteely, Co. Dublin.

45 *N.P.*, 21 Sept. 1891.

46 *F.J.*, 3 Aug. 1891; on Parnell's view of Harcourt as Gladstone's likely successor, see R. B. O'Brien, *Parnell*, ii. p. 339.

47 *U.I.*, 10 Oct. 1891. It is by no means certain that such an interview took place. It is not referred to by Katharine O'Shea in her close account of Parnell's last

days, but she does refer to Parnell on Saturday, 3 Oct., the day after Gladstone's speech at Newcastle writing notes for a speech (Katharine O'Shea, *Parnell*, ii. p. 269). It may be that Parnell, ever anxious to conceal the full extent of his illness, despatched the notes to be made up as an interview. It is likely in any event that the published interview was composed at Parnell's direction and on the basis of suggestions by him.

48 *F.J.*, 14 Sept. 1891.
49 *F.J.*, 28 Sept. 1891; see Lyons, *Fall*, p. 220, n. 1.
50 *N.P.*, 13 Aug. 1891.
51 *N.P.*, 15 Sept. 1891.
52 *N.P.*, 16 and 15 Sept. 1891.
53 O'Brien to Dillon, 17 Sept. 1891, Dillon Papers, TCD MS 6736 100.
54 *N.P.*, 23 Sept. 1891, Trinity Ward Branch, INF.
55 *N.P.*, 7 Sept. 1891.
56 *N.P.*, 8 Aug. 1891, Arran Quay Ward NF; *N.P.*, 3 Aug. 1891.
57 *N.P.*, 14 Sept. 1891.
58 *N.P.*, 15 Sept. 1891.
59 *N.P.*, 1 Sept. 1891.
60 Healy, *Why Ireland is not Free*, pp. 48-9. For Dillon's and O'Brien's sensitivity to the contest between the two papers, which would come close to tearing apart the anti-Parnellite party after Parnell's death, see O'Brien to Dillon, 24 Sept. 1891 and Dillon to O'Brien (copy), 25 Sept. 1891 (Dillon Papers, TCD MS 6736, ff. 105-6).
61 O'Brien to Dillon, 28 Sept. 1891, Dillon Papers, TCD MS 6736, f. 110. The reference can only be to the meeting of the Committee as there had been no meeting of the anti-Parnellite parliamentary party since the release of Dillon and O'Brien or indeed since February (see Irish Party Minutes).
62 O'Brien to Dillon, Dillon Papers, TCD MS 6736, f. 99; Lyons, *Dillon*, p. 143; see also Dillon to O'Brien, n.d., Dillon Papers, TCD MS 6736, f. 115.
63 O'Brien to Dillon, 'Sun', n.d.; 13 Sept. 1891, Dillon Papers TCD MS 6736, ff. 87, 98.
64 O'Brien to Dillon, 28 Sept. 1891, Dillon Papers, TCD MS 6736, f. 110.
65 Dillon to O'Brien, n.d. (*c*. 28 Sept. 1891), Dillon Papers, TCD MS 6736, f. 115.
66 *N.P.*, 2 Nov. 1891. Dillon and O'Brien spoke with Healy at the Thurles convention on 6 Oct., the day of Parnell's death (*N.P.*, 7 Oct. 1891).
67 *N.P.*, 5 Oct. 1891; *N.P.*, 7 Oct. 1891, speech of Redmond at National League; see also speech of O'Brien at Louisburgh, *N.P.*, 24 Aug. 1891.
68 *F.J.*, 10 Aug. 1891; *N.P.*, 24 Sept. 1891.
69 *K.M.*, 14 Oct. 1891. Redmond, who had an obvious interest in the proposition, told Labouchere that Dillon and O'Brien had completely lost their popularity ('He ascribes this to their trying to "sit on the fence"') and that Healy was by far the most popular anti-Parnellite politician (Labouchere to Herbert Gladstone, n.d., Viscount Gladstone Papers, BM Add. MS 46016, f. 159).
70 W. O'Brien, *Olive Branch in Ireland*, p. 1. Auberon Herbert used the same term to advance a subtler and more tough-minded argument: 'We look back at the tragedy of errors of the last month — if I am to dignify it by the name of tragedy — and it seems by a sort of perverseness each actor in it has done just what he should not have done'. The argument was directed in the first instance against Gladstone, and against the Irish party: 'Had the Irish members simply remained constant and unmoved, they would have remained masters of the field, and probably relieved Mr. Gladstone of all his difficulties'. Less

convincingly he conjectured that Parnell, had he been treated with proper respect, would have resigned the leadership (Auberon Herbert, '"The Rake's Progress" in Irish Politics', *Fortnightly Review*, n.s. vol. 49, pp. 135-37).

71 O'Brien to T. P. Gill, 'Wed' (presumably 7 Oct. 1891), Gill Papers, NLI MS 13507 (22).

7

THE DEATH OF PARNELL

There is no error more common than that of thinking that those who are the causes or occasions of great tragedies share in the feelings suitable to the tragic mood: no error more fatal than expecting it of them.

Oscar Wilde, *De Profundis* [1]

Something evidently riled them in his death.

James Joyce, *Ulysses* [2]

The superb economy of effort which had characterised Parnell's former career was forfeit in the split. Once the master of delegation, Parnell felt obliged to take upon himself an exhausting burden of responsibilities. He appears to have sensed that the survival of Parnellism was dependent on his own exertions, and the ferocious purpose they demonstrated; it was as though he believed that if his own fierce pace once faltered, with it would founder all prospect of his restoration. In pitiless self-reproach for his own former mode of leadership, the indulgently tolerant political style which he blamed for much of his trouble, he expended his energies profligately in the split.

Throughout its course he applied himself directly to the organisational details of his campaign. In one of his last letters, of 11 September 1891, Parnell wrote to Harrington manifesting his habitual concern to contain the exorbitant costs of Irish elections, directing him to agree a reduced sum in respect of monies owed to the *Carlow Vindicator* and only then to make the payment he enclosed: 'It is necessary to make a stand against the monstrous charges for that election'. [3]

Parnell's last energies were thrown into the establishment of a Parnellite daily newspaper. The tortuous volte-face of the *Freeman's Journal*, *ic & J dail,*

finally achieved only on 24 September 1891, had been long anticipated. The previous month, observing that the young Gray lacked 'that fixity of purpose which alone can make talent successful', Parnell had plunged himself into the establishment of a 'great nationalist newspaper', to counter what he described as 'a journalistic defection of great magnitude and proportions'.[4] Parnell was now largely isolated in the press, sustained by a handful of provincial papers and by the militant Parnellite *United Ireland*, a state of affairs which provoked rumours in Dublin in late September of Parnell's resignation.[5] The establishment of a Parnellite daily newspaper was urgently necessary, if more for the credibility of Parnellism as a national force than for its anticipated persuasiveness as an organ of Parnellite propaganda.

The defection of the *Freeman* came when Parnell's political fortunes were at their lowest ebb. His difficulties were compounded by disagreements among his backers and the paper's staff. Writing to Katharine, he described the establishment of the paper as 'a very troublesome business' due to a dispute among 'different sections of my own friends' as to who would have the largest share in the management of the paper. Parnell chose the directors; the *National Press* chose to comment after his death on the 'curious fact' that he had ensured that the editor and a majority of the board were Protestant.[6]

A notice reproduced in Parnell's hand was widely circulated inviting advance offers to purchase shares in the company to 'establish a first class morning and evening newspaper to advocate the principles of home rule for Ireland and Independent Action in the House of Commons'. Parnell personally solicited subscriptions, and T. P. O'Connor wrote immediately after Parnell's death, with his usual vividness and unreliability, of Parnell's pursuit of a wealthy supporter whom he wanted to act as chairman of the newspaper company and who systematically avoided his calls: 'Think of it, ye gods! This strong proud man, who had defied British Parliaments and the most potent of British ministers and leaders, dogging the door of a Dublin bourgeois like a poor clerk looking for a situation'. The first issue of the *Irish Independent* was published after Parnell's death, on 18 December 1891.[7]

Parnell's harried sense of isolation was fed by his belief that insufficient allowance was made by his friends as well as by the public at large for the extraordinary pressures under which he was acting in the split. In a conversation in London in the later split, R. Barry O'Brien, remonstrating with Parnell over his abuse of Gladstone, elicited an angry *cri de coeur*: 'You all come to me to complain. I am fighting with my back to the wall, and every blow I hit is criticised by my friends. You all forget how I am attacked. You only come to find fault with me. You are all against me'.[8] In spite of the contemptuous and occasionally hilarious tenor of Parnell's public references to Justin McCarthy, their relations remained cordial, even affectionate. McCarthy wrote perceptively: 'He assumed, I have no doubt, that I could make allowance for the conditions under which he was carrying on his struggle and that I was not likely to take offence at every extravagance uttered during the passing of so bitter a controversy'.[9] Unfortunately for Parnell, few were possessed of McCarthy's urbanity.

Parnell's physical aspect and demeanour became in the split a political issue. Jasper Tully's fiercely anti-Parnellite *Roscommon Herald* wrote that expectations in Sligo of 'a great statesman, a man of commanding appearance and noble brow' did not survive Parnell's arrival. 'The men of Sligo ... were terribly taken aback when they caught a glimpse of his worn and dissipated features'.[10] This was the crudest and most lucid statement of the proposition that Parnell's features bore the mortal impress of moral decay. In anti-Parnellite propaganda, Parnell's ravaged appearance became a register of his political decline, most dramatically in the cartoons of the *Weekly National Press*. Formerly the stylised national hero, a semi-allegorical figure, Parnell was for the first time in the split vulnerable to hostile nationalist caricature. In nothing was the corrosion of the marble surface of a myth, once smoothly impervious to the cartoonist's art, more evident. The *Weekly National Press* cartoons of Parnell froze him in the initial moments of vehemence in the split. They perpetuated the Parnell of the attack on *United Ireland* and of Kilkenny, but now ravaged by his further reversals. The cartoons chart a rake's progress of Parnell as the cynical and dissembling Anglo-Irish villain. They converge on his face, prematurely aged, haggard and unkempt, wearing a fixed grimace of desperation, with a suggestion of madness in the staring eyes with which he contemplates the wreckage of his fortunes: the moral physiognomy of dissolute ambition. The *Weekly National Press* glossed its last caricature of Parnell, three days before his death: 'The wretched Impossible looks sad, hopeless and broken'.[11]

The *National Press* unremittingly emphasised Parnell's dishevelled and harried appearance. Thus, in lieu of reporting Parnell's speech at Cabinteely on 21 September, the *National Press*, to illustrate its contention that the Parnell of the split's latter phase attracted mere curiosity rather than serious political attention, furnished its readers with 'A Descriptive Account of the Performances' by 'an Impartial Observer'.

> Mr. Parnell, whom I had never seen before, sat and stood, by turns looking wild and weird, furiously smoking the cigar in his left hand, while his right hand was stretched out behind his back over the seat of the vehicle. In this posture he shook hands with his admirers. Who they were he did not know, for he did not turn to look at them, but smoked away, with his face in the opposite direction, while the hand thrust out behind him was being wrung by all — and they were not very many — who cared to touch it.[12]

In similar vein, T. P. O'Connor wrote of Parnell's reported demeanour at his Westport meeting that 'the smallness of the gathering, and the

Figure 4 'The Wrecker Wrecked' (*Weekly National Press*, 8 Aug. 1891)

complete absence of every element of respectability, are said to have told even on his iron nerves; and he was flurried, excited and angry'.[13] Parnell's ravaged appearance inspired the *Freeman's Journal* itself to describe him in February as 'now scarred with the wounds of battle and worn with the work of years'[14]

O'Connor wrote of Parnell's appearance in the split in overblown terms which cast his former leader as a latter day Ancient Mariner. Writing immediately after Parnell's death he professed to have discerned 'a hideous glitter in his eye ... Hate, fierceness, desperate determination, and a look of death — these were what I then saw'. Again, almost five years later, O'Connor wrote of the awful change which had come over Parnell's face: 'The cheeks were full, almost bloated; all colour had vanished from them; there was a dreadful look in the eye — the whole impression was of a man desperate, reckless, doomed'.[15] If the novelettish excess was typical of O'Connor, a sharp deterioration in Parnell's appearance was noted by other contemporary observers. His health had always been precarious and his appearance dramatically variable, particularly from late 1886 onwards; but many contemporaries, if their later comments are to be believed, suspected there was now something seriously wrong, and that the split was telling on his nerves. Most ominously, some thought Parnell had lost his old tranquillity of mind.

Justin McCarthy shortly after Parnell's death wrote finely of the man behind the severe mask of command: 'The Parnell I knew was a singularly sensitive and nervous man. He was all compact of nerves — like an Arab horse'.[16] McCarthy, who alone of the majority was in direct contact with Parnell through the split, wrote subsequently of a steady deterioration:

> As time went on, and the intervals during which we did not meet became longer, and Parnell threw himself more and more into the work of agitation in Ireland, I could not help observing each time that we met again how his face was becoming thinner and paler, his manner more nervous, and that a certain physical irritability was growing on him. I call it a physical irritability, because it did not appear to affect his ordinary demeanour or his manner of transacting business. He was just as quiet and good-tempered as usual in his conversation with me, but it appeared to me that he was wearing himself out with over-work, that he was taxing at once his mental and bodily strength too much, and I told him so more than once. He took my remarks in a most friendly spirit, and assured me that he was not working more than he could avoid, and that he was taking all possible care of himself.[17]

On meeting Parnell at the end of the first day's debate in Committee Room 15, Alfred Robbins had been struck by Parnell's quiet resolve, but as he wrote on Parnell's death, 'that quietness was subsequently dispelled, and during the last session, though he would talk as freely as before, there was not the same steady resoluteness as of old'. Parnell told Robbins during the summer that he felt somewhat stronger, but his appearance belied him.

In Robbins's opinion 'both physically and to some extent mentally he was a different man after the split'.[18]

H. W. Lucy, doyen of the English parliamentary correspondents, suggested that Parnell had during the split substituted for his habitual reserve a morbid gregariousness: Lucy wrote on Parnell's death, that he had in his last campaign 'amazed, even appalled, his associates by developing a jollity in public and a familiarity in private almost hysterical'.[19]In the adversity of the split, away from Brighton, Parnell was prey to a sense of loneliness, and had a need for company at odds with his former severe aloofness. Patrick O'Brien recalled him as often lonesome during the split, never wishing to be long by himself. Encountering Parnell intermittently through the split in London, R. B. O'Brien found him sometimes little disposed to talk, and on other occasions 'unusually conversational'.[20]

The effect of Parnell's death in the nationalist canon was to obscure his purpose in the split. His death stimulated later nationalist ideologues perhaps more than his life, and served to seal the misunderstanding of his politics in the split as an exalted adventure in romantic futility.

He was evidently worried by his physical condition. His wife later wrote: 'He was in no way unhappy in this last fight, and had only the insidious "tiredness" that grew upon him with such deadly foreshadowing of the end we would not see given him a little respite, he could, he said, have enjoyed the stress and storm of battle'.[21] He responded with marked coldness to remarks concerning his health. Alfred Robbins wrote that Parnell 'hated the suggestion of unfitness to stand the continued strain. More than once, when he would pass through the Lobby that spring and summer, looking harassed and weary and unlike his old self, he assured me he was enjoying the fight'.[22] Barry O'Brien remonstrated with Parnell in London during the Boulogne negotiations that he was overdoing it, but Parnell abruptly insisted he felt well and it did him good: 'There was nothing that displeased him more than the least suggestion that he could not stand this constant strain'.[23] This underlay the brusqueness of Parnell's response to T. P. O'Connor at their last meeting. When O'Connor on his return from the United States greeted Parnell in the House of Commons and said he hoped he was well, he was met by the reply 'better than you'.[24]

Parnell tried to make light of the fatigue of the campaign, joking that 'the only thing I am afraid of is the bad whiskey'.[25] Sophie O'Brien wrote of Parnell's meeting at Westminster with her husband after his release, that he looked wretched, 'but with a brave smile he declared that he had never been better in his life'.[26] Invited to sit for a portrait by Whistler, Parnell according to an unidentified nationalist MP, probably J. L. Carew, deferred the sitting on the grounds that he was too thin, until he got stouter.[27]

Allusions to death recurred in Parnell's public speeches with disconcerting frequency. In Committee Room 15 he made his celebrated declaration that he did not intend to die. During the Kilkenny by-election he exclaimed: 'Oh, they have elected my successor, I was going to say, before the breath had left my body'.[28] There were other allusions to his state of health, culminating in his speech at Creggs. At Mullingar in May he expressed his regret that 'a slight attack of the prevailing malady that is going prevents my voice from being as strong as it usually is'.[29] Such utterances were codified after Parnell's death in nationalist martyrology to recast the split in terms of the chronicle of a death foretold, imputing to Healy a murderous purpose in his rhetoric, and assimilating Parnell to the mystical cult of defeat and martyrdom which derived from the rebellion of 1916.

There were also the two incidents in the split which suggested Parnell's dread of death: his outburst at Kilkenny designating a passing coffin, that there went the corpse of Pope Hennessy; and his extreme unease at the crowded graveside at the O'Gorman Mahon's funeral in June 1891, which was deepened when he was cheered leaving the graveyard at Glasnevin. Parnell had attended the funeral, against his normal practice. Unnerved by the crush at the graveside, Parnell was quoted in the *Freeman's Journal* as saying to David Sheehy 'This is disgraceful. You ought to get into the man's grave'. From Redmond's evidence in the libel action brought by Sheehy in January 1892, it is clear that Parnell had inspired the report.[30] (Healy wrote to his brother in 1892 that Harrington had told P. A. Chance that 'it was Parnell who brought up the reporter to Dr. Kenny's, and dictated the libel on Sheehy. The Chief was a handy man!'[31]) Healy's later treatment of these incidents to emphasise Parnell's superstitiousness is, like the later extreme nationalist myth of Parnell which it complements, misleading in its imputed fatalism.[32]

Parnell's death was, as he had insisted in Committee Room 15, unintended (an obvious proposition, but one which the subsequent course of nationalist ideology renders it necessary to state). He had neither a mystical affinity with fate, nor a death-wish. He had no craving in the lines of his collateral ancestor Thomas Parnell to

> Clap the glad wing, and tow'r away,
> And mingle with the Blaze of Day[33]

He did not fail to appreciate the magnitude of the political calamity which had overtaken him, but there was nothing to suggest that he had succumbed either to a fatalistic despair or to the mystical *élan* anachronistically imputed to him. He did, however, embark on the split's fierce contest alive to the physical risk which it entailed for him, to which he made apprehensive allusions throughout.

Parnell was for good reason 'of a hypochondriacal temperament'.[34] He was fully aware of the fragility of his own health, and that of his family. What he termed 'fate' had much to do with the history of the Parnells. By the end of 1882 five of his ten siblings were already dead. Years before he had asked Harold Rylett, who contested Tyrone in 1881, whether he believed in fate. Rylett replied that he did not. Parnell disagreed, and said he did not believe he would live to be forty-eight.[35] It was the age at which his father had died. He remained affected by the death of his father. Katharine recorded that 'he often told me how well he remembered being sent for in his father's last illness to go to him at Dublin, and his last journey with his dying father back to Avondale'.[36] He was then just fourteen.

Rylett's comment may afford a critically important biographical insight into Parnell's behaviour in the split. The furious impatience of his political course may have owed something to a sense of urgency bred of a pressing intimation of mortality,and specifically a conviction that he would not live beyond his father's age: a rational belief bred of the fragility of his own health and his family medical history, rather than a mystical tenet or an aspiration to martyrdom. If Parnell was not unalterably persuaded that he was approaching the limit of his mortal span, he was certainly oppressed by a sense of physical vulnerability. As his frequent references to the subject suggested, he was more afraid of his health than of his enemies.

Quite apart from his health, the split represented for Parnell a bizarrely exact fulfilment of the apprehensions which underlay his sceptical response to the accolades he attracted at his political zenith, and informed his awareness of the fragility of his political position throughout his career. It is not altogether remarkable that his heightened prescience came to acquire an almost superstitious intensity. Parnell's comment to William O'Brien years previously, that Macbeth's mistake lay not in consulting the witches, but in only believing that portion of their advice which pleased him, suggests how much his superstitiousness was reducible to a profound sense of irony.[37]

Parnell could not have been indifferent to the attacks upon Katharine O'Shea which achieved a particular popular intensity and pervasiveness during the Carlow by-election in the wake of their marriage. She thus characterised the campaign in the split: 'From one end of chivalrous Ireland to the other ... the name of "Kitty" O'Shea was sung and screamed, wrapped about with all the filth that foul minds, vivid imaginations, and black hatred of the aloof, proud Chief could evolve, the Chief whom they could not hurt save through the woman he loved'. His detractors, she suggested, hurt him a little but not very much. After Kilkenny Parnell commented to her that it would really have hurt 'if those devils had got hold of your real name' (meaning 'Katie' or 'Queenie', as he referred to her privately, rather than 'Kitty' which he never used). A sensitivity to Healy's attacks was evident in their reaction to an alabaster clock in the shape of a ship's wheel received as a wedding present from Parnell's sister Emily: 'We were very gay over its coming', wrote Katharine, 'disputing as to which of us should henceforth be the "man at the wheel" '. The reference to Healy's celebrated injunction at Leinster Hall not to speak to the man at the wheel

suggested that Healy had not been wholly ineffective in his determination
to penetrate Parnell's privacy.[38] In contrast to his friendly bearing towards
McCarthy, H. W. Lucy noted that Parnell treated Healy with 'uncompromising displeasure', taking no notice of him when they chanced to encounter at Westminster.[39]

Yet the effectiveness of Healy's calculated encroachments upon Parnell's
private domain can easily be exaggerated. The attrition of the split on
Parnell occurred more through physical fatigue, and the oppressive
awareness of the scale of the opposition to him, than the emotional impact of attacks on his relations with Katharine O'Shea. That the attack
led by Healy wounded Parnell to the quick may be doubted, but it inevitably
became the stuff of the bitter myth of the dead Parnell. Thus Harrington
wrote in 1898: 'It was this impotence to stem the tide of filth that was
unloosed against the lady whom he loved, and who became his wife, that
led him to eat his heart out in proud and silent mortification'.[40] It may
be surmised that Parnell's frustration was more political than personal.

What Harrison noted as Parnell's graciousness, his kindness, gentle
humour and unaffectedness,[41] did not desert him in the split. In private,
he retained his old tranquil charm, and his capacity for quiet, comic observation, which suggested that he had not succumbed to morose self-regard,
or fatalistic exhilaration. At a meeting in Limerick, where a local working
man of Fenian views stretched out from a balcony with a very low railing
was being urged by the chairman to 'keep within the constitution', Parnell
approached the chairman and said gravely: 'Perhaps it would be better
for himself, and for us all, if you advised him to keep within the window'.[42] Rather more bleakly, confronted by a former supporter who had
seized on the issue of his marriage to defect, and accused him of having
led his country through the divorce court, Parnell responded with acid
equanimity: 'No. I have tried to do so, but I greatly fear Mr. Gladstone
has barred the door at last'.[43] To a friend who, on the return of William
Redmond, Tim Harrington, and Henry Harrison from a fundraising expectation in the United States, asked whether he would kill the fatted calf,
Parnell was supposed to have enquired with a smile 'Which of them?'[44]

Even at his nadir in the Carlow election, he was capable of deriving considerable amusement from trying to embarrass Patrick O'Brien into sing-
ing an election ballad at a meeting. Dining with O'Brien, Parnell was highly
amused at an English lady whose dog barked on being asked to cheer for
the queen: 'This tickled Parnell very much. He would wink at me and say
in his quiet, shy, way: "I think this is intended for us" '.[45]

In early August, returning to Westminster with McCarthy after they had
settled some business concerning the evicted tenants, it occurred to Parnell
that they should alight together at Westminster Hall, and pass through
the Members' entrance as if there had never been a split: 'The idea amused Parnell and he was in one of those moods of quiet observant humour

which were not uncommon with him and when they came were always delightful to his companions'. He 'positively lingered' on emerging from the cab, relishing the surprise of a policeman. 'We got out of a hansom,' he told William O'Brien, 'to the admiration of all beholders'.[46]

Parnell's temperate graciousness in private was in marked contrast to his public lapses into vituperation. Pierce Mahony wrote: 'I have seen him since Committee Room 15 say a good word for even the bitterest of his foes; and to a friend I have seen him with almost a woman's tenderness make reparation for a passing harsh word'.[47]

Those closest to him in the split saw a different Parnell to the dominant public perception in the split of the unquiet, demented Parnell, the monster of cynical calculation limned in Healy's rhetoric. This contrast informed the uncharacteristically emotive passage in John Redmond's speech on the unveiling of the Parnell monument twenty years later, in which he rejected the caricature of Parnell as 'a cold, sinister personality — hard, unsympathetic, almost forbidding moved by hate, but not moved by love', to reinstate Parnell as 'one of the tenderest, gentlest, and most sensitive hearts I ever knew'.[48]

There was among Parnellites a fierce exhilaration of allegiance, and an actual affection which had previously been experienced only by very few. Parnell in the split was divested of his mask of forbidding severity. A new sense of his humanity partially compensated for the damage wrought by the split to his mystique of invincibility. Katharine Tynan, writing in chaste rapture of Parnell at the Rotunda, surmised that before the split he had discounted popular acclaim:

> But the Parnell crisis was a sifting, and he knew that those who remained to him were genuinely his. He manifested that great quality of a few great men in the world's history — he never forgot a face, nor a name, nor a record. When he came in to some of his great meetings in that last year of his life, does not one remember his quick flash of recognition over the faces all turned his way, his warm hand-clasp, his affectionate glance?[49]

The embattled minoritarian status of Parnellism contributed to its fierce solidarity of allegiance. *United Ireland* later wrote of: 'we few, we happy few, we band of brothers'. Tynan wrote: 'No adherent of the big battalions can ever know the joy of fighting against immense odds with a leader who is worth all the risks and all the chances ...'.[50]

There was at work a mythopœic process: the stress on Parnell's human qualities is a feature of the posthumous myth of the Parnell of the fall. Arthur Lynch later wrote: 'I never admired Parnell so much as after the "split". He came down from his pedestal there, but it was all human and understandable ...'.[51] Canon Sheehan, twenty years after Parnell's death, detecting in the Parnell of Committee Room 15 and of Boulogne 'an absence of sincerity', perceptively surmised that 'it was only afterwards when he found his power over the Irish mind threatened and the ground, which he deemed so sure, slipping from beneath his feet, that he rose to heroic stature'.[52] The young J. L. Garvin, covering Parnell's funeral, wrote that the grief of his colleagues attested to the lovable side of his nature that Parnell occasionally revealed. An Irish journalist told him: 'There is not a man in Dublin who ever spoke half an hour with him that could refrain from tears when his death was announced'.[53]

Parnell in April, the vote of the Irish party and two by-elections down, combatively asserted: 'I am very well satisfied with the results of the last three months'.[54] This professed optimism, unconvincing at the time, became yet more so as the split wore on. The *Daily Express* wrote in late July that probably the Carlow election 'coming as it did immediately after the announcement of the marriage represents the lowest point to which the tide of Parnellism can ebb ...'.[55] In one sense this is likely to be correct: Parnell's electoral decline had probably bottomed out. Yet the sequence of adversity had not exhausted itself: in the train of the Carlow result came the declaration against him of Dillon and O'Brien, and the related defection of Gray's *Freeman's Journal*.

In contemporary perception of Parnell's fortunes in the split's latter phase two distinct, though related, propositions merged. The first was that of a supposed continuing loss of support, which was almost certainly exaggerated: allegiances in the split tended to set hard, early, and immutably. The second was that the course of events continued to go unremittingly against Parnell. The pattern of cumulative adversity surprised many who expected at least a partial Parnellite rally. Reversal followed reversal in grim succession, leaving Parnell still responding to events, deprived of the opportunity to regain the initiative and display his old mastery. Parnell had indeed encountered staggering reversals. Harrington later wrote: 'The stars in their courses fought against him'.[56] In the clash of will and contingency, Parnell was up to the time of his death severely worsted. He seemed pinioned by adversity. Surveying his treble by-election defeat, he declared inscrutably:

> Luck has been against us up to the present, and in the constituencies that have been tried we have not had the fortune which is necessary, according to Napoleon, for the co-operation of providence — we have not had the fortune of the big battalions on our side.[57]

Henry Harrison, perfervidly Parnellite, wrote on the basis of conversations with Parnell during and immediately after his Carlow defeat: 'He was as conscious of present defeat as he was confident of ultimate victory. He was calm and detached as ever, assured in his opinion and neither dismayed nor exasperated nor embittered'.[58] Labouchere's *Truth* quoted Parnell as saying to a friend a week before his death: 'It will take me several years to reconstitute my Party, but I shall do it'.[59]

Yet the immensity of his reversals, and the massiveness of the opposition to his restoration, must have weighed heavily on Parnell's mind, and oppressed his will. Declaring at Dublin in September that 'we must fight on', he hollowly argued, 'it is sometimes good to be beaten at the commencement of a struggle', and unconvincingly asserted: 'During my sixteen years in public life my mind has never been so free from care; my heart has never been so confident of the future, as it has been during the last ten months'.[60] Rather more characteristically, asked what he would do if he was the only person returned of his party, Parnell was supposed to have replied: 'Then I shall be sure of having a party whose integrity will not be sapped'.[61]

Yet it would be wrong to underestimate the resilience of Parnell or the suppleness of his statescraft. According to T. P. O'Connor, Parnell had as early as the debate in Committee Room 15 confided to an adherent that he had no prospect of winning the ensuing election, but that his time would come at the election after the introduction of an inadequate measure of home rule by Gladstone. Joseph Chamberlain shared this perception of Parnell's prospects. Parnell would have been severely worsted at the general election:

> If Parnell ever possessed a chance of restoring himself to the leadership of a united Irish party it lay in the future, after the introduction of Mr. Gladstone's Home Rule Bill. He might have deemed such a measure insufficient and unsatisfactory,and raised a national agitation which would, for the moment, have conquered priestly influence.[62]

If Chamberlain's hypothesis polemically imputed to Parnell a cynically destructive purpose, it correctly situated Parnell's opportunity to restore his fortunes after the general election, in the next parliament and in the election on its dissolution. After a year of unparalleled adversity, Parnell could reasonably have felt as the opening of the parliamentary session approached, that he had passed through the worst of his ordeal. He looked to the parliamentary arena to assert his mastery, to outmarshall an anti-Parnellite party bereft of any tactic or strategy save that of clinging to the Liberal alliance, and expected to benefit from a damaging, and even grimly comical, war for supremacy within the anti-Parnellite ranks.

The immediate question which his death left unanswered was the prospects for the leaner, minimalist Parnell, shorn of the incubus as well as the advantage of leadership, reverting — in what were admittedly utterly altered circumstances — to the role of parliamentary *frondeur* which he had played at the outset of his career to such devastating effect.

Parnell's death coincided with the nadir of his political fortune. The precipitateness of his decline had by the time of his death led to what were almost certainly exaggerated predictions of electoral decimation. T. P. O'Connor estimated that Parnell would win between one and six seats at the general election, and anticipated a waning of support in what he considered Parnell's areas of strength: Dublin, Meath and Wicklow.[63] Davitt declared that Parnell could not be re-elected in Cork, but speculated somewhat offensively that he would contest East Wicklow as a 'popular landlord'.[64] Healy did not depart from his shrewd public prediction in March that Parnell could possibly return eight of his thirty-three followers at the general election, and would not return more than twelve.[65] On the assumption that Parnell's death led to no change in the Parnellite vote at the 1892 election, and that accordingly the number of seats won at that election are the number which the party would have obtained with Parnell at its head, predictions of Parnell's electoral annihilation were unfounded. The Parnellites in fact carried nine seats (as against seventy-one anti-Parnellites). On the 1892 result Parnell himself would have narrowly scraped home as the second MP for Cork, had he run as the sole Parnellite candidate. While sustaining a very heavy defeat, he would have achieved his redefined objective in the split of averting a total rout and maintaining a small, but not trivial, Parnellite representation at Westminster.

Parnell's minority support in the country at large was mirrored by his ominous isolation from the body of his own parliamentary supporters. Theirs was the Parnellism of Committee Room 15, of the insistence that the Irish party was obliged to stand by Parnell in the face of Gladstone's *diktat*. Beyond that they had little appetite for Parnell's political course in the split. Their support endured through a stoicism of personal allegiance, fortified by a deep sense of the unfairness of the attacks upon Parnell. Dismayed, they remained loyal. Parnell had in any event taken care to bind them to him with iron bonds lest their sympathy waned, and conducted himself with immense shrewdness and tenacity in his dealings with Dillon and O'Brien to close off any possibility of defections from his own parliamentary ranks.

It was to the Parnellite parliamentary party that Dillon was referring, when thirty years later, his habitual mournfulness admittedly exacerbated by the final eclipse of the Irish party under his leadership, he observed of Parnell to Lady Gregory that 'if he had lived a little longer he would have had no follower left'.[66] Michael MacDonagh, a perceptive journalist who enjoyed a privileged engagement with the events of the split, wrote that Parnell towards the end found it difficult to bear 'the cold fit which had come over his parliamentary colleagues', who were unnerved by the rapid succession of blows which continued to rain on their leader, culminating in the defection of the *Freeman's Journal*. Parnell repudiated their advice to hold back and await developments, rather than obtrude on public attention.[67]

The absence of Parnellite MPs other than Luke Hayden from Parnell's meeting at Creggs elicited bitter comment after his death. Sophie O'Brien wrote: 'The inner history of the last meeting ... was piteous. He could find no man of importance in his party to accompany him. Many gave different pretexts, others evaded replying'.[68]

John Redmond in particular was accused of waning in his commitment to Parnell. In the ugly controversies which followed Parnell's death, especially in the by-election for Parnell's Cork seat which Redmond contested, the charge levelled against him of bad faith in the Boulogne negotiations was confounded with the contradictory allegation of a readiness to desert Parnell. It was a charge which was later to be exploited by enemies of the Irish Parliamentary Party under Redmond's leadership. Arthur Griffith, advertising what he considered to be his own superior credentials as a Parnellite, wrote of Parnell going to Creggs 'deserted by his Parliamentary followers' after the three by-election defeats, and that 'Mr. John Redmond found pressing engagements after the smashing defeat of Parnellism in Carlow to keep him from standing by Mr. Parnell's side on public platforms'.[69]

In the opinion of that most ardent of Parnellites, the leader's wife, Redmond faltered towards the end in his support of Parnell.[70] Redmond was conspicuously economical in his professions of allegiance to Parnell in the split's latter phase. Unhappy with Parnell's refusal to moderate the pace and tenor of his campaign, he sought to constrain Parnell towards the adoption of more moderate courses in anticipation of the general election. Yet there was nothing to suggest a wavering in his commitment to Parnell. The interpretation of Redmond's ostentatious reserve in terms of inchoate treachery was unfounded. Yet the suspicion, sedulously cultivated by the detractors of Redmond and the Irish party, damagingly endured, and helped to ensure that the election of Redmond as the leader of a reunited Irish party in 1900 did little to strengthen the party's claim to the legacy of Parnell, or to allay the hostility of its critics.

The odds against Parnell eventually prevailing inspired the wry comment of Joyce's Leopold Bloom on the myth that Parnell had not died, and that his coffin had been filled with stones: 'Highly unlikely of course there was even a shadow of truth in the stones and, even supposing, he thought a return highly inadvisable, all things considered'.[71] Parnell's prospects, if not utterly hopeless, in the period prior to his death appeared exceedingly bleak. There was little to suggest that the verdict of the split's three by-elections was unrepresentative, or reflected a temporary aberration of nationalist political preference. The split revealed a high constancy of allegiance on both sides: if this permitted Parnell to avoid complete elimination from the equation of nationalist power, it suggested equally that he would face a high degree of resistance in the re-conversion of anti-Parnellite voters. After his death nationalist Ireland was to remain divided for almost ten years into two non-communicating, indeed stagnating, sectors with remarkably little fluctuation of voters.

The *Kilkenny Moderator*, whose unionism was tempered by a deep susceptibility to Parnell, provided one of the most perspicacious commentaries on the split. On Parnell's death, the paper presented the most optimistic political scenario for Parnell had he lived. Conceding that 'his fortunes were not only fallen low, but were daily and hourly continuing to fall', it continued:

> But we believe also that had Mr. Parnell lived for a few years longer he would have reasserted his dominant position with even greater power and authority than before, for he stood, and would have continued to stand, before the eye and mind of the country as the incarnated representative of the only form of Constitutional action which by any possibility could have achieved results ... Very soon, at all events within the compass of a few years, the Nationalists of Ireland would have clearly perceived that between Mr. Parnell's leadership and the Irish Parliamentary Party on the one hand and physical methods on the other there would be really no *via media*. Constitutionally, Nationalism could only succeed by maintaining the independence of the Irish Parliamentary Party, an independence which on this occasion was accidently wrapped up in the person of Mr. Parnell.[72]

It is not without irony that a unionist paper should, without cynical purpose, have consistently provided the most reasoned optimistic assessment of Parnell's prospects in the split. In an editorial in April 1891, when Parnell was two by-elections down, it had professed itself confident that he would yet carry constituencies 'and that though he may be worsted he will certainly not be driven from the field'. In a memorable evocation of Parnell's strength of purpose in recommencing the construction of a shattered edifice of his power, the editorial continued:

> Then too we must remember that there is in that singular man a power of tenacity and resolution which will make him formidable under any circumstances. On his return from the struggles in No. 15 Committee Room he said publicly that he was young enough and strong enough to begin again at the beginning and tread the old path once more. The meaning of this threat was not quite generally appreciated at the time. What Mr. Parnell meant was that he was prepared, if necessary, to obstruct once more, even though he stood alone, and by Obstruction, as he did formerly, build up another Irish party pledged to sit on the Opposition benches till what he conceived to be the rights of Ireland should be conceded. A man who entertains such thoughts and such a resolution can never be brushed aside as long as he can find a constituency willing to return him to Parliament. One cannot but entertain a certain feeling of awe at the contemplation of such a phenomenon as that of a middle-aged man calmly promising to begin again, if necessary, at exactly the same point where he began thirteen years ago, in the freshness of youth. It may be supposed that this is a mere threat. We do not regard it as only such. If a threat, certainly it has frightened no one as a threat should. Then too everything that we know of Mr. Parnell supports the belief that he really is capable of buckling again to that extraordinary task. If he does, the second edition of that portentous labour will be greater than the first. When he and Mr. Biggar began Obstruction in 1878 they had only Great Britain against them, for Ireland was at the time neutral. When next he takes up the policy of obstruction he will have against him not only Great Britain but Ireland also, for the McCarthyite party will in that event hold the representation of Ireland.[73]

What this argument overlooked was the extent of the transformation of Irish society and politics, against which it is unlikely that either Parnell's extraordinary personal resolve or the classicism of his political technique could have prevailed. The Ireland of the split was no longer the Ireland in which Parnell had embarked on his career.

Two years after Parnell's death, Harrington wrote that 'the fortuitous combination, at a critical moment, of influences — which neither before nor since could ever be so concentrated — caused his defeat'.[74] Unfortunately for Parnell, that combination of influences was neither ephemeral nor truly fortuitous. Parnell faced a formidable coalition, socio-economic as well as political, within which the values of a political Catholicism and of the pursuit of peasant proprietorship were fused. There was for the first time open opposition to him from the Catholic Church in Ireland and from a powerful phalanx of conservative nationalists, which together not merely opposed but anathematised him. After the devastating collision between the imposing but fragile barque of Parnellism and the rock of Catholic proprietorial nationalism, it is difficult to see how his authority could have been reconstituted.

To ask whether he believed that he could eventually prevail is not an altogether appropriate enquiry in relation to a politician of Parnell's tenacity and professionalism. By the time of his death he had reformulated the immediate objectives of his campaign. He was committed to a long-term struggle for ascendancy, dependent upon the demonstrated excellence of his leadership of a minoritarian nationalist cohort in parliament; and on the majority against him splitting in turn, as indeed it did almost immediately after his death. He proposed to reassert his dominance in the parliamentary arena, through sheer force of personality and political skill, and then to re-project his restored allure on Ireland as he had done at the outset of his career.

Yet even Parnell's reformulated objectives were hardly modest. He deferred, rather than abandoned, his own pretensions of leadership. He not merely pursued his own ascendancy, but upheld the principle of strong governance within nationalism. His refusal to compromise his pretensions derived from an exacting sense of professionalism as a politician. He declined to sever the two objectives — the restoration of his leadership, and the maintenance of what he insisted were the preconditions for the exercise of effective authority within nationalism. Indeed his axiomatic assertion of their identity defined his political purpose in the split. In this, rather than the monomaniacal pursuit of personal power with which Healy charged him, lay his hubris.

Inevitably his prospects were cruelly measured against the scale and type of authority he had formerly enjoyed. If predictions of his political effacement were groundless, it is difficult to envisage Parnell recouping anything like his former status as the leader of a united nationalist movement. That particular lost eminence — based on an almost absolute nationalist consensus — was in any event gone for ever, an irretrievable product of historical circumstance.

The prospect of a return to substantial influence within nationalism, short of full leadership, at the head of an influential minority, cannot be discounted. Such an outcome in the case of a politician of Parnell's capacity and strength of purpose, pursuing respect over affection, remained a possibility. What is more doubtful is Parnell's reaction. It is true that he would not have been pleased with such an outcome, yet it might have sufficed to fulfil his exacting sense of his 'responsibilities', in terms of which it was less important that he should succeed to the full extent of his maximalist aims than that he should have refused to compromise them. If Parnell's cold fury in the split showed no sign of abating, it should not be unquestioningly assumed that he was incapable of achieving a new equilibrium in defeat, or that he would have conformed ever more closely to the restless spectre of unquiet ambition so devastatingly caricatured by Healy. This must remain an open question. At the time of his death, Parnell had still not recovered his political poise, or fully retrieved his sense of direction. He appeared unreconciled to defeat, poised uneasily between an uncompromising quest to restore his lost authority and a more realistic minoritarian role.

It remains central to the elucidation of the posthumous myth of Parnell to appreciate that his death coincided with his political nadir. To most contemporary observers, death broke a plummeting fall. Exaggerated perceptions of an accelerating decline crystallised on Parnell's death and compounded the misunderstanding of his campaign in the split. Perceptions of Parnell were arrested in death, as he struggled with unremitting purpose against odds considered insuperable. What was widely perceived as the deepening futility of his campaign at the end gave to the image of Parnell in the split to some its romantic élan, to others its sinister dementia.

The *Kilkenny Moderator*, while continuing to believe that Parnell would eventually prevail, faithfully reflected the prevalent contemporary perception of Parnell's political fortunes at the time of his death. It wrote that 'since the great split last November his cause has been a falling one': 'At the time of his death, the tendency was still downwards, ever downwards, with a momentarily accelerated degree of speed. To what point exactly his fortunes would have fallen had not the awful figure of Death stepped upon the scene it would be, perhaps, idle to enquire'.[75]

To many contemporaries Parnell's fall indeed seemed as precipitate as Vulcan's:

> ... from morn
> To noon he fell, from noon to dewy eve ...[76]

That death froze Parnell in a posture of Miltonic perdition did much to distort perceptions of his political purpose. Later extremist nationalist ideologues were not alone in imputing to Parnell a mystically heroic purpose. In unionist perceptions of Parnell on his death there was an intimation of unnatural defiance in Parnell's indomitable purpose against the grain of political fortune as well as of fate, which complemented the later nationalist myths of Parnell. Irish Unionists, if politically unswayed, felt personal ambivalence towards the Anglo-Irish prince of the nationalist darkness. Few, wrote the *Daily Express*, were able to withstand 'a certain admiration for the man who fought so strenuously against great odds'.[77] Edward Dowden, Trinity Professor and Unionist publicist, set his comparison of Parnell to Milton's Satan in a grimly exultant celebration of the débâcle of nationalism after Parnell's death:

> It is not in human nature, certainly it is not in Irish human nature, to feel no sense of stern satisfaction at the sight of the divided forces of the Separatists — Separatists now indeed — tilting furiously at each other's breasts over the new made grave of one who, compared with the pigmy forces whom he has left behind, seems hardly less in stature than the Archangel ruined *(cheers)*
>
> > Care
> > Sat on his faded cheek, but under brows
> > Of dauntless courage and considerate pride
> > Waiting revenge:
>
> waiting revenge which never came to him *(hear)*.[78]

In similar vein John Morley wrote to Gladstone on Parnell's death: 'You could not but be moved by the disappearance of that singular and sinister man who has played so eventful a part for the last dozen years'.[79] Others likewise discerned something disquieting, even macabre, in Parnell's tenacity. Lord Randolph Churchill, the fractured rhythm of whose career coincided closely with Parnell's, writing to his wife some six weeks after Parnell's death, gave vent to his sense of political fatigue: 'I am quite tired and dead sick of it all, and will not continue political life any longer. I have not Parnell's dogged, but at the same time sinister, resolution'.[80]

This sense of 'sinister resolution' informed also Harold Frederic's superb obituary of 'the most strange, weird, and tragic figure of his time', whose behaviour through the split always had 'an eerie side':

> But public attention was fastened upon the tireless, fearless, and indomitable determination with which he fought on in what every one could see had been from the start a hopeless struggle. It was like the fight of Richard II on Bosworth Field — an unhorsed King struggling one against a hundred till literally overwhelmed.
>
> In all there has been such wild disregard of what other men think and do, such frantic chasing here and there, now doubling on his track, now passionately leaping barriers and racing over new courses, such ferocity of purpose, such measureless disdain for all about him, followers and foes alike, that men may well stand amazed and bewildered in contemplation of his clay. There has been no other like him anywhere.[81]

The Miltonic Parnell of unionist perception had arguably a greater fidelity to his persona than the shattered desperado of Healy's rhetoric, or the
expiring martyr of later nationalist myth. The latter was formulated immediately on his death by the spuriously imputed last words 'Give my love
to the Irish people', and by the invention by Parnell's poetically excitable
mother of a letter, in which he declared himself, in the accents of a
neurasthenic altruist, 'weary unto death but ... all in a good cause'.[82] Yet
it is surely more convincing to see in the Parnell of the closing weeks of
his life a figure of constant purpose, unyielding in his belief in the correctness of his own course, waiting for the tide of fortune to reverse itself:
a figure whose perseverance reflected his professionalism as a politician
as much as heroic fortitude.

The *National Press* of 24 September again proclaimed Parnell defeated:
the National Federation should thenceforth address itself to the defeat of
landlordism, 'liberated from the burden of Mr. Parnell's stained personality'. In the *Weekly National Press* cartoon of 26 September 1891, Parnell
was depicted as a shattered and deranged Humpty Dumpty, whom his colleagues struggled ineffectually to restore to the top of the wall, under the
confidently mocking eye of an anti-Parnellite tenant farmer. In the suicide
of General Boulanger in Paris over the grave of his mistress — 'his guilty
passion was stronger than his ambition' — the *National Press* professed
to discern a moral allegory of wider application.[83]

Healy's disquietingly mortal idiom persisted to the end. A week previously he had committed himself at Belfast 'to fight Parnellism to the death'.[84]
On the eve of Parnell's death the *National Press* declared, 'His power for
evil must be near the point of exhaustion now'.[85] On the morning of the
day Parnell died, Healy, his grammar fracturing under the brutality of utterance, declared in Thurles that 'we were engaged in this battle before
ever Mr. Parnell was heard of, and we will fight this battle when there is
an end put to him'. At the convention later in the day Healy developed
this unhappy theme:

> I decline to turn Irish politics into a bloody puddle, and let me add this:
> I would rather that Mr. Parnell was triumphant in this contest, and it would
> be better for Ireland that Mr. Parnell should wipe us out than have a distracted
> Ireland in the House of Commons. So it is better that we should wipe him
> out *(cheers and a cry 'He is wiped out already')*, and wipe him out we shall,
> for in this business I have neither ruth nor pity. When a charge is ordered
> in warfare how many times has the charging force to make their way over
> the bodies of their wounded comrades? How often has the artillery to fur-
> row the very limbs of those who have fought by their side? We cannot in
> this struggle play fast and loose with the interests of Ireland.[86]

Parnell's death was neither the object nor the consequence of Healy's
rhetoric. Yet there was a terrible apparent consistency between Healy's idiom
and Parnell's death, as the culmination of the mortal imagery of his vicious

attack on Parnell. Parnell's death would fix Healy within the compass of his own rhetoric of desire, guilt, betrayal and mortality. With Parnell's death Healy was hopelessly embroiled in the pseudo-moralistic scheme of his attack on Parnell. The trap of his own rhetoric snapped shut about him.

The jolting rhythm of Parnell's punishing railway odyssey was drawing to a close. Reaching Dublin on Saturday 26 September, he sent a note to Joseph Kenny stating he was unwell. He asked him to call, but warned him to say nothing lest any suggestion of ill health should reach the newspapers. He subsequently disregarded Kenny's advice not to attend the meeting scheduled for the next day at Creggs, on the borders of Roscommon and Galway.[87]

So it was that Parnell departed for his last political meeting, his final encounter with the atrocious weather of the Irish autumn of 1891, which had already devastated the harvest. J. P. Quinn, a National League organiser, was alarmed at the physical appearance of Parnell, whom he met at Westland Row, complaining of rheumatism in his wrist and shoulder joints.[88] A crowd of fifty Parnellites waited in the cold of the night at the terminus of the Great Western Railway at Broadstone for the night mail. Among them was the twenty-year-old Arthur Griffith, who would later set his own presence against the absence of Redmond and other Parnellite members. Griffith wrote an account of Parnell's appearance at Broadstone some twenty years later, which is a set piece of the sentimental myth of Parnell. The leader looked 'wretchedly ill':

> His face was livid and haggard, one of his arms bandaged, and the hand I shook had no longer the firm grip I had felt previously. His eyes were still keen, and his mouth firm, but it was evident that it was a case of Parnell using his iron will to surmount his physical pain. As he descended from the car a woman beside me stretched out her hand to him, saying 'God bless you, Mr. Parnell — don't go tonight'. He turned towards her, smiled and shook his head. That was the last we saw of Parnell alive.[89]

Against his intentions, Parnell was prevailed on to speak at Broadstone, and again at Athlone. Before he spoke at Athlone it was arranged that no one could shake his hand.[90] As the train pulled out of Athlone, an elderly Parnellite in the crowd fell under the wheels of the train and was killed. On learning what had happened, Parnell became deeply agitated and walked up and down the carriage for some time. He had, as Quinn recalled, a dread of railway accidents (Quinn had seen him more than once avert his eyes from men clinging to the footboards of trains). The tragedy elicited the culminating viciousness of Healy's attack on Parnell, in a purported account of the incident in the *National Press*, which with sectarian ferocity played on the superstitious dread of death which Healy believed to fill the void of Parnell's religious faith:

> Yet utterly unmoved by the calamity the Only Possible Leader calmly addressed the survivors as if nothing had happened. This is certainly worthy

of the gentleman who insulted the corpse at the Kilkenny election by shrieking out an unfeeling parallel above a coffin as a funeral went by his hotel window. When his trains became a juggernaut he might surely spare his victims a word of compassion, if he cannot remain silent in the presence of death. With the corpse of poor Fallon probably resting only a few feet away in the adjoining waiting room, Mr. Parnell entertained those who remained on the platform after the calamity with 'a few words on the new paper'. It is not so long since an Irish crowd so situated would have engaged themselves in saying the *De Profundis* when a sudden and terrible death overtook one of their number.[91]

Reaching Roscommon after midnight, Parnell obtained supplies from a chemist and put his arm in a sling. Loath to be alone he sat up by the fire into the small hours with Quinn. He talked of rheumatism, and of the men of his party, whom he discussed in turn. He spoke affectionately of the people of Dublin, and of the Dublin women who had supported him. The following morning he set out on the seven miles journey to Creggs. With a rug around him in the carriage he was still cold, and allowed Quinn to put a top coat about his legs. He had mislaid his change of clothes, and cabled Katharine from Creggs before he spoke that the weather was terrible. It rained as he spoke, but he refused to have an umbrella held above him.[92]

It was a laboured speech. At the outset Parnell sought to account for his debilitated appearance:

Physically I am not in a good condition to address you today. Nothing but a desire not to disappoint the men that I see around me overcame the orders of my doctor that I was to go to bed last night when I arrived in Dublin. However, I do not think that any very material damage will come to me from this meeting. If I was to allow the suggestion of such a thought we should have our enemies throwing up their hats and announcing that I was buried before I was dead *(laughter)*, and although a man on the other side of forty cannot do things that he used to do in the days of his youth, still I intend to bury a good many of these men *(cheers)*. I have to tell you that you must not take me today as I always am, and I hope when I see you again at the next general election, and to ask for your votes, that you will find a very considerable improvement physically *(cheers)*.[93]

The *Daily Express* wrote with more prescience than it knew that 'Mr. Parnell would have made better use of his Sunday, if he had stayed at home and nursed his rheumatism as his physician advised him to do instead of rushing off to make a speech at Creggs', a village whose location was 'known only to minute students of Irish topography'.[94] Police reports stated that the attendance at Parnell's meeting had been less than at O'Brien's recent meeting at Westport, but that the crowd 'had showed more zeal':[95] it was the story of the split.

Parnell travelled back to Dublin in the company of a journalist, Russell. He was ill and in pain. He talked all the way and would not let Russell sleep.[96]

He remained in Dublin from Monday 28 September to Wednesday 30 September, attending to the establishment of the *Independent*. He looked poorly, and suffered from what he believed to be rheumatic pains in his hand and arm. At a meeting of the promoters of the new paper on the Wednesday, he arrived pale and unwell. At one point he felt so ill that he was given brandy. He refused a proffered chair, addressed the meeting standing, and at the end leant wearily against the wall. On the Tuesday evening, Parnell's carriage drew up alongside Quinn on Sackville Street. He said that he wanted his meetings arranged fortnightly rather than weekly, adding, 'These Sunday meetings are killing me'.[97] On the Wednesday evening, Parnell again defied Kenny's advice and set out to cross to London. At Westland Row station two Parnellite activists, John Clancy and John Kelly, met Parnell by chance and accompanied him to Kingstown. Parnell remarked that the pain had left his arm, but he feared that it had got into his body. Ill and nervous, he asked them to book his berth. As the ship's whistle blew, Parnell left Kelly, assuring him he would be back on the following Saturday week for a meeting set for Macroom.[98]

So, what the *National Press* described as 'Brighton's weekly emigrant' set out on the journey home. He reached Brighton dangerously ill. Katharine prevailed on him to see a doctor. He wrote to Sir Henry Thompson, but would not agree to his being sent for, and saw instead a local doctor.[99] On Saturday 3 October, he felt somewhat improved, and sat up in bed after breakfast and smoked a cigar, writing notes for a speech.[100] On the Sunday night he did not sleep, a fact which according to Katharine disquieted him 'as he had a superstitious belief that if he did not sleep for two consecutive nights he would die'. The next day he was in great pain, and again passed a sleepless night. On the Tuesday, 6 October, he was feverish, his face lividly pale. He died that evening. 'Something,' he had told Healy, 'happens to me always in October.'

His death, at the age of forty-five, occurred eight days before the tenth anniversary of his incarceration in Kilmainham Jail. He died, in the words of the Dublin *Daily Express* 'too soon and too late'. 'England', wrote the *Spectator*, 'survives all foes ... and she has survived Mr. Parnell.'[101]

While Parnell had appeared manifestly ill in the course of the split, his death was completely unexpected. Alfred Robbins wrote that while over the preceding months those who met him felt certain he was on the point of collapse, 'the suddenness of the end has come as a shock'. T. P. O'Connor's comment best captured the stunned incredulousness which Parnell's death elicited: '... nobody ever thought it would end so disastrously. There was infinite faith in Mr. Parnell's luck for one thing'.[102]

Up to the time of Parnell's death there hung about the split a strange air of unreality. Nationalists had not yet come to terms with the wreck of their world. With Parnell's death the split achieved a terrible finality, beyond the assuaging flux and reflux of electoral preference. The sense of a violent abridgement, of business unfinished, was to give Parnell's memory its powerful and troubling resonance in Irish politics. As Joyce's Leopold Bloom was to muse, 'looking back now in a retrospective kind of arrangement all seemed a dream'.[103]

Parnell's funeral, the baroque nationalist obsequies of a Protestant leader, took place in Dublin on Sunday 11 October. The turbulence of the weather provided the final touch of exaltation to the myth. The steamer containing his coffin, accompanied by most of the Parnellite members, ploughed heavily from Holyhead through rough sea in a cold and beating rain, as the wind moaned and whistled through the rigging. The wildness of the night called to mind Davis' 'The Burial', as if Parnell's death had been foretold in nationalist psalm. Katharine Tynan, awoken by the storm in Dublin, later wrote: 'The elements were mourning Ireland's Dead, and the ghosts of dead heroes were going by'.[104] Parnell's remains reached a city swept by wind and rain. His cortège lasted from the grey dawn at Kingstown to dusk at Glasnevin.

Through the morning, Parnell's remains lay in state in the City Hall, outside which a great crowd gathered. The young J.L. Garvin, graphically described the scene:

> When the coffin at last appeared above the balustrades in front of the portico the scene was a strange one, and never to be forgotten. Every head was at once bared, the eyes of strong men filled with tears, which they vainly bit their lips to restrain, and a shadow of pallor seemed to flit distinctly over the sea of upturned faces.

The cortège traversed the city to Glasnevin through massed crowds, whose silent grief disappointed the expectations of hostile commentators. At Glasnevin in the still, clear evening which followed the storm, after the great crowd, overwhelmingly Catholic, had heard the unfamiliar words of the Protestant funeral rite, Parnell was buried. Nature seemed to spare no effect. As the service commenced, a shooting star, which would become a stock image in the cult of Parnell, appeared overhead.[105]

> Under the Great Comedian's tomb the crowd.
> A bundle of tempestuous cloud is blown
> About the sky; where that is clear of cloud
> Brightness remains; a brighter star shoots down;
> What shudders run through all that animal blood?
> What is this sacrifice? Can someone there
> Recall the Cretan barb that pierced a star?[106]

References

1 Wilde, *De Profundis* (3rd ed., London, 1905), p. 139.

2 Joyce, *Ulysses*, p. 530.

3 C. S. Parnell to Harrington, 11 Sept. 1891, Harrington Papers (2). After the 1885 general election Parnell had written to Harrington directing him to have election costs taxed widely wherever they were the maximum: 'Apart from other considerations I am convinced if a candidate pays a returning officer a penny more than he can prove he has properly spent on the elections, he violates the law' (Parnell to Harrington, 3 Jan. 1886, Harrington Papers [2]). Parnellite tightfistedness in expenditure on the Sligo election was amusingly derided in a piece of local doggerel directed at the taxation of election costs by the Parnellite candidate: 'Is it hillside work for heroes, who are to free us all with sabres,/ Colloguing with attorneys to reduce their honest neighbours?' (*N.P.*, 29 May 1891).

4 *F.J.*, 24 Sept. and 29 Aug. 1891, Commercial Branch, NL.

5 *F.J.*, 20 Sept. 1891.

6 Katharine O'Shea, *Parnell*, ii. pp. 262-3; Parnell to Katharine Parnell, 7 Sept. 1891; Leamy, *Parnell's Faithful Few*, p. 146; *N.P.*, 14 Oct. 1891. On the establishment of the *Irish Daily Independent*, generally see Harrington Papers, NLI MS 8314; in relation to the dispute between shareholders see in particular T. Moore to T. Baker, 7 Sept. 1891, J. Shanks to T. Baker, 7 Sept. 1891.

7 Parnell circular dated 22 Aug. 1891, Harrington Papers, NLI MS 8581; *Sunday Sun*, 15 Nov. 1891; see also *I.N.*, 10 Sept. 1891.

8 R. B. O'Brien, *Parnell*, ii. p. 332.

9 McCarthy, 'My Relations with Parnell', proofs of article, Davitt Papers.

10 *Roscommon Herald*, 4 Apr. 1891.

11 *W.N.P.*, 3 Oct. 1891. The 'Impossible' was a Healyite rejoinder to the Parnellite assertion that Parnell was the 'only possible leader'. The cartoons are the work of Thomas Fitzpatrick, for whom see L. P. Curtis, *Apes and Angels* (London, 1971) pp. 72-81. The anti-Parnellite depiction of Parnell drew much of its inspiration from hostile unionist depictions of Parnell before the split, most notably from what Katherine Tynan termed 'the haggard desperado invented by Sir F. Carruthers Gould' (Tynan, *Twenty-Five Years*, p. 234).

12 *N.P.*, 22 Sept. 1891.

13 *Wicklow People*, 3 Oct. 1891.

14 *F.J.*, 28 Feb. 1891.

15 O'Connor, *Parnell*, p. 206; *Weekly Sun*, 14 June 1896, 'Reminiscences of My Public Life'.

16 *Black and White*, 17 Oct. 1891.

17 'My Relations with Parnell After the Split', First article, Proof, Davitt Papers, TCD. McCarthy himself is almost certainly the parliamentary colleague on whom Parnell called some three weeks before his death, and with whom he discussed affairs until after three in the morning. The colleague 'strongly advised him not to rack himself out with incessant travelling and speech-making. Mr. Parnell smiled blandly, and said that the travelling and speech-making did him good'. The incident is recounted in an article which appeared in the *Daily News*, for which McCarthy wrote in the split, entitled 'Recollections of Parnell by One of His Colleagues' (quoted *N.P.*, 9 Oct. 1891). The same incident appears in McCarthy's *History of Our Own Times* (London, 1905 ed., 5 vols., v. p. 383)

18 *B.D.P.*, 8 Oct. 1891.

19   H. W. Lucy, *A Salisbury Parliament*, p. 444, 9 Oct. 1891.
20   R.B. O'Brien, *Parnell*, ii. pp. 321, 341. On one occasion recalled by Patrick
     O'Brien, Parnell uncharacteristically accompanied him to an opera in the Gaiety
     Theatre, and at 2.00 in the morning after supper, a strange ritual was enacted.
     When O'Brien escorted Parnell to Morrison's Hotel on Dawson Street where
     he was staying, Parnell then insisted on walking across the city with O'Brien
     to the National Club in Rutland (now Parnell) Square. When they reached the
     National Club, O'Brien walked Parnell back to Morrison's, where he had to
     dissuade Parnell from not escorting him back to the National Club (ibid, pp.
     343-44).
21   Katharine O'Shea, *Parnell*, ii. p. 260.
22   Robbins, *Parnell*, p. 189.
23   R. B. O'Brien, *Parnell*, ii. p. 330.
24   O'Connor, *Memoirs*, ii. p. 323.
25   Tynan, *Twenty-Five Years*, p. 337.
26   Sophie O'Brien, *Recollections*, p. 194.
27   *Leinster Leader*, 10 Oct. 1891, 'Personal Recollections of the Chief, by "A
     Nationalist Member"'.
28   *F.J.*, 22 Dec. 1890, Johnswell.
29   *F.J.*, 11 May 1891, Mullingar.
30   *F.J.*, 14 June 1891, 28, 29 Jan. 1892.
31   Healy to Maurice Healy, 12 Jan. 1892, *Letters and Leaders*, Proofs, B 159;
     deleted *Letters and Leaders*, i. p. 373.
32   Healy, 'A Great Man's Fancies'.
33   Thomas Parnell, 'A Night Piece', in *The Collected Poems of Thomas Parnell*,
     ed. Claude Pearson and F. P. Lock (Delaware, 1989).
34   *B.D.P.*, 8 Oct. 1891; see also O'Connor, *Parnell*, p. 210.
35   Katharine O'Shea, *Parnell*, i. pp. 127-8.
36   *Contemporary Review*, Harold Rylett, 'Parnell' (Apr. 1926), p. 481.
37   W. O'Brien, *Parnell*, p. 142. Henry Harrison observed of Parnell: 'His decisions
     frequently preceded his reasons . . . His superstitions were largely foibles to
     which he did not attach any great *real* importance' (William Robert Fearon,
     Parnell of Avondale [Dublin, 1937], p. xi).
38   Katharine O'Shea, *Parnell*, i. pp. 138, 258
39   Lucy, *Salisbury Parliament*, p. 358 (11 Mar. 1891).
40   *I.W.I.*, 8 Oct. 1898, 'As Caesar Fell — Sidelights on Parnell's Career'.
41   Harrison, *Parnell Vindicated*, p. 91.
42   MacDonagh, *Home Rule Movement*, p. 236.
43   *Daily Sketch*, 18 May 1914, interview with Katharine Parnell.
44   Maev Sullivan, *No Man's Man*, Sequel.
45   R. B. O'Brien, *Parnell*, ii. pp. 331, 341.
46   Justin McCarthy, 'My relations with Parnell after the Split, First Article', proofs,
     Davitt Papers, TCD; Sophie O'Brien, 'Recollections', p. 194. This incident is
     likely to have occurred on 11 Sept.; see Parnell and McCarthy to Harrington,
     11 Sept. 1891, enclosing cheques (Harrington Papers, NLI MS 8581[I]).
47   *I.W.I.*, 7 Oct. 1893, 'Parnell's Resolution'.
48   *F.J.*, 2 Oct. 1911.
49   *I.W.I.*, 'Parnell: A Retrospect', 6 Oct. 1894; see also Tynan, *Twenty-Five Years*,
     pp. 326-26.
50   *U.I.*, 5 Oct. 1895; Tynan, *Twenty-Five Years*, p. 336.
51   *I.W.I.*, 8 Oct. 1898; Arthur Lynch, 'Parnell'.
52   *Cork Free Press*, 3 Dec. 1910, review of William O'Brien, *An Olive Branch
     in Ireland*.

53 *Newcastle Weekly Chronicle*, 17 Oct. 1891.
54 *F.J.*, 28 Apr. 1891, Tipperary Banquet.
55 *D.E.*, 24 July 1891.
56 *I.W.I.*, 7 Oct. 1893.
57 *F.J.*, 24 July 1891, National Convention.
58 Henry Harrison, *Parnell, Chamberlain, Garvin*, p. 218.
59 *Truth*, 15 Oct. 1891, 'Scrutator'.
60 *F.J.*, 21 Sept. 1891.
61 Katharine Tynan, *Twenty-Five Years*, p. 336.
62 *Sunday Sun*, 15 Nov. 1891; *B.D.P.*, 8 Oct. 1891.
63 *Wicklow People*, 3 Oct. 1891.
64 *San Francisco Examiner*, 17 June 1891.
65 *New Review*, 'The Rise and Fall of Mr. Parnell', 194 at p. 202.
66 Lady Gregory, *Journals* (2 vols., London, 1978), p. 344 (entry for Easter Sunday, 1922).
67 MacDonagh, *Home Rule Movement*, p. 237.
68 Sophie O'Brien, 'Recollections', p. 198; see also *Sunday Sun*, 15 Nov. 1891 (T. P. O'Connor). The poster for the meeting ('The people are asked by their presence to show their gratitude for the great services rendered to Ireland in the past by Mr. Parnell and their confidence in his Leadership for the future') promised the attendance of Col. Nolan and other members of the Irish party. *I.W.I.*, 6 Oct. 1895.
69 *Sinn Féin*, 7 Oct. 1911.
70 Harrison, *Parnell Vindicated*, p. 28.
71 Joyce, *Ulysses*, p. 530.
72 *K.M.*, 14 Oct. 1891.
73 *K.M.*, 8 Apr. 1891. The authorship of these articles is unknown. Standish O'Grady was to become editor of the paper, but very much later, 1898-1901; see Hugh O'Grady and others: *Standish James O'Grady, The Man and the Writer* (Dublin, 1929).
74 *I.W.I.*, 7 Oct. 1893
75 *K.M.*, 14 Oct. 1891.
76 Milton, *Paradise Lost*, Book 1, lines 742-43.
77 *D.E.*, 12 Oct. 1891.
78 *D.N.*, 17 Oct. 1891, City of Dublin Unionist Registration Association.
79 Morley to Gladstone, 8 Oct. 1891, Gladstone Papers, BM Add. MS 44256, f.163.
80 W. S. Churchill, *Lord Randolph Churchill* (London, 1906, 2 vols), ii. p. 452, letter dated 23 Nov. 1891.
81 *New York Times*, 11 Oct. 1891.
82 Katharine O'Shea, *Parnell*, ii. p. 275; R. F. Foster, *Parnell*, p. 239.
83 *N.P.*, 1 Oct. 1891.
84 *N.P.*, 1 Oct. 1981..
85 *N.P.*, 5 Oct. 1891.
86 *N.P.*, 7 Oct. 1891
87 R. B. O'Brien, *Parnell*, ii. p. 349; *F.J.*, 27 Sept. 1891; *D.E.*, 28 Sept. 1891.
88 *U.I.*, 7 Oct. 1893, 'Creggs and the Final Departure'. This article comprises interviews with Quinn and another Parnellite activist, John Kelly, and is drawn on in the account which follows.
89 *Sinn Féin*, 7 Oct. 1911. The article, entitled 'Parnell' is unsigned but is evidently by Griffith and is attributed to him by Seán O'Luing, in his *Art O'Gríofa* (Dublin, 1953) at p. 27. Griffith professed that the coterie of Parnellites at Broadstone knew that Parnell was dying, but not how imminent his death, while Parnell knew Creggs would seal his fate.

90 *U.I.*, 7 Oct. 1893.

91 *N.P.*, 28 Sept. 1891.

92 *U.I.*, 7 Oct. 1893; Katharine O'Shea, *Parnell*, ii. pp. 265-66; R. B. O'Brien, *Parnell*, ii. p. 350.

93 *F.J.*, 28 Sept. 1891.

94 *D.E.*, 28 Sept. 1891.

95 Divisional Commissioner's Report for Sept. 1891, Western Division, CBS 520 S 3974, PRO.

96 R. B. O'Brien, *Parnell*, p. 350; Sophie O'Brien, 'Recollections', p. 198.

97 *U.I.*, 7 Oct. 1893.

98 R. B. O'Brien, *Parnell*, ii. 351; *U.I.*, 7 Oct. 1891.

99 *N.P.*, 28 Sept. 1891; Katharine O'Shea, *Parnell*, ii. pp. 265-71.

100 Katharine O'Shea, *Parnell*, ii. p. 268; *U.I.*, 5 Oct. 1891. Some doubt must surround the report of an interview with Parnell that morning with the London Correspondent of *U.I.*, dealing with Gladstone's speech at the National Liberal Federation at Newcastle. It is possible that the 'interview' was made up from Parnell's notes given to a reporter before his death.

101 Katharine O'Shea, *Parnell*, ii. pp. 270-75; Healy, *A Great Man's Fancies; D.E.*, 8 Oct. 1891; *Spectator*, 10 Oct. 1991. F. S. L. Lyons cites the view to which Professor J. S. McCormick inclined, that Parnell's death was due to lobar pneumonia complicating kidney failure of unknown cause (F. S. L. Lyons, *Parnell*, pp. 601-02). Professor J. B. Lyons has argued at greater length, taking account of what is known of Parnell's medical history and that of his family, that the probable cause of death was coronory thrombosis: J. B. Lyons, *'What did I die of?' The Deaths of Parnell, Wilde, Synge and other Literary Pathologies* (Dublin, 1991), pp. 92-102. See also his 'Charles Stewart Parnell and his Doctors' in Donal McCartney (ed.), *Parnell, The Politics of Power* (Dublin, 1991), pp. 183-91.

102 *B.D.P.*, 8 Oct. 1891; *Sunday Sun*, 11 Oct. 1891.

103 Joyce, *Ulysses*, p. 532.

104 *I.T.*, 12 Oct. 1891; *D.E.*, 12 Oct. 1891; *Newcastle Chronicle*, 17 Oct. 1891; Leamy, *Parnell's Faithful Few*, p. 97; Tynan, *Twenty-Five Years*, p. 347.

105 *I.T.*, 12 Oct. 1891; *Newcastle Chronicle*, 17 Oct. 1891; *N.Y.T.*, 11 Oct. 1891; Tynan, *Twenty-Five Years*, pp. 349-50. Harold Frederic had virulently predicted that the burial of Parnell by this 'excited and scatterbrained element' would be attended as a matter of course by 'violent and disgraceful scenes'. Of the funeral, the *Irish Ecclesiastical Gazette* wrote, with involuntary pride: 'It goes without saying that no Roman Catholic clergymen were visible at Sunday's demonstration. On the other hand, it was noticed that some of the bands, especially those from Cork, played Protestant hymn tunes' (16 Oct., 1891).

106 From 'Parnell's Funeral', in W. B. Yeats' *A Full Moon in March* (London, 1935); see also Katherine Tynan, 'A Wandering Star', *U.I.*, 17 Oct. 1891. The shooting star is not a poetic fiction and is noted in the contemporary account of the *Daily Express*, (12 Oct. 1891). The 'Great Comedian' is Daniel O'Connell, whose grave lay close by.

8

'A PROVED BRITISH PROSTITUTE'

Mr. Parnell had only in the Providence of God at the time he was deposed but nine months to live. Had he been sustained his day and hour were appointed whether he remained leader or he did not. The dispositions of Providence are eternal and we for the sake of preserving his leadership for nine months would have driven Gladstone into retirement and would have split the Liberal party and would have reduced Ireland practically to blank confusion and chaos.

T. M. Healy, 17 June 1892[1]

Healy's virulence did not abate with Parnell's death. Incensed by the blocking of the release of the Paris Funds by the Parnellites and Parnell's widow, less than a month after Parnell's death he made his most atrocious attack on Katharine Parnell in a speech to his Longford constituents:

I thought to myself how shamed and disgraced must be the men — the Harringtons, Kennys and Redmonds who would resort to the instrumentality of this abandoned woman ... I say no more shocking incident has been heard of than this alliance between so-called Irish patriots and a proved British prostitute. I mince no words in dealing with this matter *(cries of 'Bravo Tim')*.

Upholding Healy's attack, the *National Press* asserted that the Parnellites misunderstood the Irish people if they believed that 'on this topic any spurious and sickly sentimentality can be excited. This woman darkened the brightest page of Irish history, she wrecked the career of the most successful of Irish leaders and plunged a united country into dissension'. 'Her dark and ominous personality' lay at the root of the trouble.[2]

Two days after the speech, Healy was called out of the Law Library of the Four Courts by Tudor MacDermott, Parnell's nephew, the son of his sister Sophia. He called on Healy to apologise and undertake never to

187

mention Katharine Parnell, 'or I would thrash him as long as I could'. Healy replied he would not be intimidated, whereupon MacDermott took him by the collar and, in the account of *The Times*, 'proceeded to castigate him with great vigour' with a horsewhip until a policeman came to the rescue. Healy sought to make light of the attack by suggesting MacDermott was drunk.[3] Undeterred, Healy proceeded the following night at the National Federation to repeat verbatim the terms of his reference to Katharine O'Shea as 'a proved British prostitute'.[4]

Healy had run amok, and was no longer amenable to restraint by any of his political colleagues. What ensued was a highly revealing sequel to Gladstone's intervention on the issue of the Irish leadership. Henry Labouchere, evidently with a view to constituting himself the peacemaker between the warring factions of the majority, had taken himself to Ireland, whence he wrote to Gladstone. He found the moderate anti-Parnellites deeply concerned as to the effects of Healy's rhetoric. Healy would neither hear of the extinction of the *National Press* in favour of the *Freeman's Journal*, nor would he moderate his language. Dillon believed Healy's reference to Katharine Parnell had cost thousands of supporters. What those whom Labouchere referred to as 'our friends' wanted was, without making any concessions to the Parnellites, 'to pour oil on the waters, and to let Parnellism die out by leaving it alone. This will probably happen, for whilst the Parnellites are numerous, they have no man of commanding personality amongst them to lead them'.

The difficulty lay with Healy: 'The Irish leaders can do nothing with Healy, and they say that it is useless to argue with him'. Labouchere had been asked to prevail on him, but 'I doubt if I could, for he is a person more easy to egg on than to restrain'. Labouchere thereby laid the ground for soliciting Gladstone's intervention, emphasising Healy's susceptibility to the Liberal leader, of which he gave a striking instance:

> But it has occurred to me that, if you were to write me a letter expressing your views, this would probably exercise an influence upon him. He has a great respect for you; indeed you are the only person for whom he has any respect. He has been greatly flattered by your approval of his former action and by your notice of him. He once told me, with tears in his eyes, that he never saw you in the House of Commons without an impulse to lie down before you, and to ask you to trample on him, because he used to attack you in the Parliament of 1880.[5]

Morley, who had met Labouchere at the Reform Club, urged Gladstone to do as he was urged, adding of Healy 'I confess that I have always regarded his ferocities of the last twelve months with utter aversion and — what is more to the point — with the conviction that such brutalities really served the turn of Parnell's faction'.[6]

Gladstone's reply to Labouchere survives in draft. He stressed the necessity of achieving the largest possible home rule majority, and the danger of set-backs at the general election in Ireland not by a high Parnellite poll 'but lest a residue of animosities should break into narrow local majorities, and hand over seats to the adversary'. There was not so far as he was aware a shadow of difference between 'the Nationalists and the so-called Parnellites, or between either of them and the British Liberals' as to home rule, and it was accordingly discreditable to Ireland that 'there should be anything like broken ranks when the day of battle comes'. Any action, Gladstone continued, by Morley or himself would only elicit the cry of English dictation. This objection did not arise in the case of Labouchere, 'as an independent friend of the Irish cause', 'and I urge you to kindly consider whether you can prudently make any effort *motos componere fluctus*'. Observing that 'everything respecting Mr. Parnell himself seems now to be in the past tense', he proceeded, in a classic study in Gladstonian moral utterance, to touch upon Healy's attacks on Katharine Parnell:

> I understood much complaint is made of Mr. Healy's references to the unhappy woman who has been, I cannot help thinking, at the very root of *all* the mischief.
> It is difficult to rein in a gallant horse at the exact moment when his work is done, nor can I for one blame allusions made early in the day to denounce a particular mischief. But the Almighty has smitten the woman heavily. Nor will her social punishment be slight. In his present position nothing can react on her behalf, unless it be displeasure and resentment at anything thought to be like hitting her when she is down. I cannot help hoping Mr. Healy may now feel he has done enough in this matter.
> I say this the more freely because I have a genuine and deep respect for him, with implicit faith in his honour and his unselfish patriotism, as well as a lively admiration for his abilities and courage.[7]

Gladstone's letter, which Labouchere read to Healy, had the desired effect: 'He promises not again to allude to Mrs. Parnell'. Healy's moralistic vituperation and political purpose were as ever intricately linked. He sought to justify to Labouchere his attack on Katharine Parnell as an attempt to forestall any reconciliation with the Parnellites: 'He wishes me to explain to you that they would be ruined in Ireland were they to make it up with the Parnellites, who are endeavouring to stir up the old Fenians and Secret Societies'.[8]

Healy never again after Gladstone's intervention referred so vituperatively to Katharine Parnell, in spite of a muttered threat at the end of the year:

> I am neither ashamed or afraid of anything I have said in the course of this controversy *(applause)* ... I will argue this question out as I have argued it before, whenever the occasion arises *(hear hear)*: and to my mind the whole question of what was the beginning of the struggle will remain a living question and a necessary question to touch upon for many a long day to come. Politicians will have to deal with it and although for a moment the unfortunate and ill-timed death of Mr. Parnell has given a tinge of melancholy deeper than before to the entire incident, and has strengthened his party by

enabling them to heap up every kind of adulation on his head, while depriving us out of respect for the dead, of most of the weapons which we formerly employed to put the truth in its proper light.[9]

His later muted references to the issue were largely confined to the suggestion that the Parnellites were 'in confederacy with Mrs. O'Shea in the matter of the Paris Funds'.[10]

So closed the 'proved British prostitute' incident. Both the virulence of the attack, and the fact that Gladstone's intervention was necessary to restrain Healy, epitomised the abject condition to which the once-great Irish party, deprived of its unity and of Parnell's mastery, had been reduced within twelve months of the schism in Committee Room 15.

Gladstone did not cease to be fascinated by Parnell, whom he described in 1897 as the most remarkable man he had ever met, and 'an intellectual phenomenon'. Of Healy, in what J. L. Garvin described as a 'cut of the most subtle unkindness', Gladstone commented: 'Well, Healy was very clever; he made very clever speeches. I do not know what has become of him now, but under Parnell he was admirable'.[11] Even the mercurial Labouchere, confronted with Parnell's successors, discovered for the first time the virtues of the Irish leader: '... there is a great deal of "the beggar on horseback" in them ... Parnell, with all his faults, was the only practical man amongst them'.[12]

References

1 *F.J.*, 18 June 1892, (Kilkenny Convention)
2 *N.P.*, 2 Nov. 1891.
3 *The Times*, 4, 9 Nov. 1891; *N.P.*, 4 Nov. 1891; *D.E.*, 4, 5 Nov. 1891. A correspondent wrote to the *Daily Express*: 'If the Bar will have us continue to believe it is composed of Irish gentlemen, it will take measures to check Mr. Healy's obscene delirium' (*Daily Express*, 5 Nov. 1891, T. P. Manning to the editor).
4 *N.P.*, 5 Nov. 1891.
5 Labouchere to Gladstone, 18 Nov. (1891) enclosing memorandum, Gladstone Papers, BM Add. MS 56449, ff. 238 and 240. Healy in two letters to Dillon concerning the Paris funds referred with calculated provocativeness to Katharine Parnell as 'Kitty' (Healy to Dillon, 23 Oct. and 30 Nov., 1891, Dillon Papers, TCD MS 6755, ff. 697, 701).
6 Morley to Gladstone, 18 Nov. 1891, Gladstone Papers, BM Add. MS 44256, ff. 175-77.
7 Gladstone to Labouchere, draft, 24 Nov. 1891, marked 'secret', Gladstone Papers, BM Add. MS 56449, f. 243.
8 Labouchere to Gladstone, 4 Dec. 1891, Gladstone Papers, BM Add. MS 56449, f. 246.
9 *N.P.*, 30 Dec. 1891, Glasgow.

10 *N.P.*, 22 Jan. 1892, Westmeath Convention; see also speeches of Healy reported in *N.P.*, 3 Mar. 1892, *F.J.*, 17, 21 Oct. 1892. Healy asserted that Katharine Parnell's intervention was prompted by a telegram from the National League. He may have been influenced by, and drawn the wrong conclusion from, the fact that he believed the notice served on the French bank on Katharine Parnell's behalf to be the handwriting of Henry Harrison (Labouchere to Gladstone, 4 Dec. 1891, Gladstone Papers, BM Add. MS 56449, f. 246).

11 Interview with R. B. O'Brien, 28 Jan. 1897 in R. B. O'Brien, *Parnell*, ii. pp. 357, 364; J. L. Garvin, 'Parnell and his Power', *Fortnightly Review*, vol. 64, p. 880 (1 Dec. 1898). Gladstone's verdict had been anticipated by Dillon, responding to the taunt of 'bossism' levelled by Healy against Dillon's leadership of the Irish party: 'I am sometimes inclined to think that what Mr. Healy very badly wants is to be bossed. He was bossed in the old days by Mr. Parnell and he did some good work for Ireland' (*F.J.*, 2 Nov. 1895, Draperstown). Redmond recorded an exchange with Morley a year after Parnell's death. Redmond had asserted that reunion had been made impossible by the insults and blackguardism of Healy and others:

'Morley: Yes. The misfortune of the thing is that the man with the best brains among the anti-Parnellites is — what shall I say? — without character.

Redmond: "A political savage" '. (Redmond, memorandum of interview, 17 Oct. 1892, Redmond Papers, NLI MS 15207 [I]).

12 Labouchere to Herbert Gladstone, 27 Aug. (1892), Viscount Gladstone Papers BM Add. MS 46016, f. 157.

II PARNELL'S LAST CAMPAIGN

UNDER WHICH KING.
THE DESPERADO OR THE DRIVELLER?

Figure 5   'Under which King, the Desperado or the Driveller?',
(*St. Stephen's Review*, 31 Jan. 1891)

9

PARNELL'S DEFENCE

Never indeed was the commanding power, the inflexible tenacity, the indomitable courage of the Irish leader more conspicuously shown than in that fierce struggle against overwhelming odds which was prematurely terminated by his death.

W. E. H. Lecky [1]

A good deal has been said of the falling off in Mr. Parnell's speeches at and after the Kilkenny election of last year, and a falling off there certainly was. But the difficulties were enormous ... Every speech had to be improvised under circumstances as wearying and uninspiring for a man of Mr. Parnell's temperament as can well be imagined. But whatever other impression they left, the first was that of absolute, indeed of fanatical, sincerity and earnestness. It was not possible to think of him as one trying to retain power for the pleasures of it, but only as one intensely and disinterestedly convinced of the absolute necessity of his own services to a cause in which he was intensely interested. Such a statement lends itself to burlesque, but it is the only way in which to describe the extraordinary mingling of deep impersonal feeling with imperious self-assertion which was to be seen in all the acts and speeches of the Irish campaign.

Manchester Guardian, 8 October 1891 [2]

Some people say I am prompted by insane ambition *(no no)* and others say that I have cast on one side an honourable position, and that I now intend to throw in my lot with the enemies of my country *(no no)*.

Parnell, 11 January 1891 [3]

Parnell's treatment of what Healy insisted was the central issue of the split, the O'Shea divorce, was distinguished by its astuteness, its dignity, and its brevity. His references to the divorce question were inhibited by the fear of prompting the intervention of the Queen's Proctor to challenge the making absolute of the divorce decree nisi. He confined himself to the laconic, and rhetorically effective, assertion that his side of the case had not been heard. The opposition to him was

> ... a movement which depends for its strength upon invincible ignorance. It is a movement which depends on testimony of which only one side has been heard; and do you not think there is no other side? *(cries of 'we do').* But I will not dwell upon this portion of my defence. I need not *(cries of 'no necessity' and cheers).* My defence will be known some day *(loud and continued cheers)*, and I could not come amongst you and look you in the face as I look you in the face to-night, did I not know that there is another side to this question, as to every other question, and if you will wait to hear that other side *(cheers)* before you decide that, unworthy as I am *(cries of 'no')*, I am too unworthy to walk with you within the sight of this promised land which, please God, I will enter with you *(loud cheers).*[4]

At Kilkenny Parnell in the same vein described the clergy opposed to him as 'men who have not the opportunity of knowing what is in my inmost heart'.[5] It was a line of argument which had been foreshadowed by his celebrated statement on being re-elected leader of the party on 25 November, in lifting 'a corner of the curtain' to appeal for a moratorium on discussion of the circumstances of the O'Shea divorce until the decree was made absolute: 'I would rather appear to be dishonourable than be so'.[6]

Parnell subtly contrived to maintain an adamantly defiant attitude while presenting the split itself as an embattled atonement. He declared to the mob in Castlecomer: 'I am not afraid to meet my countrymen face to face, I have been amongst you before now, and I can lay my heart bare to you, and defy any man to say that I have been false to my trust. What is brought against me? The mud of the stream'.[7] He later asserted at Johnswell that until every constituency had pronounced 'I shall regard myself as still your light, still your champion, still the upholder of our flag, still a man who can look you in the face without flinching and can ask you what fault have you to find in me'.[8] *United Ireland* asserted that through the divorce proceedings Parnell had 'atoned for his sin by what, to a man of his proud spirit, must have indeed been a bitter humiliation'.[9]

In the Carlow election, as the 'moral issue' flared into prominence with his marriage, and his campaign faltered further, his treatment of the divorce question became less assured. He asserted, with considerable audacity, that if guilt attached to him, 'a far deeper shade of dishonour and guilt' attached to those who had connived at it.[10] At Carlow he made a desperate and uncharacteristic boast on which Healy mercilessly fastened:

> If the men who are traducing me had gone through the same fiery ordeal that I have gone through, if they had been submitted to the same examination of their private lives and actions, I know that there are many of them who would have come out far worse, and I believe that there are few who have led purer private lives than I have *(prolonged cheers).*[11]

Parnell's most moving plea was an appeal to loyalty in consideration of the services he had rendered the country. Hence his entreaty that he should be permitted to come within sight of the promised land, and his description in a speech at Newcastle-upon-Tyne of his supporters in Ireland as men 'who, with hearts of steel, withstood every influence, clerical and otherwise, and were not afraid to testify to their faith in Irish Nationality, and to stand by the man in his hour of trouble who had stood by them in theirs'.[12] The affecting reference to reciprocal sustainment in the 'hour of trouble' marked a momentary dropping of his severe mask of emotional restraint.

Parnell's substantive defence was confined to the insistence that no fault had been, or could be, alleged against him in his public life. At Limerick, in January, he asserted 'my fault, if it has been a fault, has not been a fault against Ireland,and I can look you in the face and say with a clear brow, heart, and conscience, that never have I willingly deviated from the course which I believe to be ultimately for the best interest of the Irish race ...'.[13] This assertion provoked the vehement denunciation of the more excitably moralistic anti-Parnellites. Healy responded with a salvo of comic derision, and a reiteration of the anti-Parnellite case that Parnell's fault was indeed a fault against Ireland, because it had threatened to wreck the home rule alliance.

This claim permitted Parnell with some dignity to recast the charge against him so as to permit him to declare: 'I don't pretend to be immaculate. I don't pretend that I have not had my moments of trial and temptation but I do claim that never in thought, in word, or in deed have I been false to the trust that Irishmen have confided in me'.[14] He asserted that history did not present a single example of a leader 'either in the camp or the senate' being deposed for 'the fault alleged against him'.[15] He was a leader 'against whom no dereliction of public duty has ever been proved, and scarcely even alleged'.[16]

Of the charges levelled against him, he contended that only the charge of absenteeism came close to being a 'crime against Ireland', and to this he responded with frequently emotional invocations of the state of his health from late 1886. While they were shrewdly calculated to underscore the pitilessness of Healy's rhetoric, Parnell seemed genuinely stung by the unfairness of the charge of neglecting his public duties in a period through which he was often seriously ill. Thus at Cork, he declared:

After eleven years of hard labour by night and by day, I fell sick at the beginning of 1887, and I was not able to go to the House of Commons to move the rejection of the motion of the second reading of the Coercion Bill. That is the most conspicuous fault that they have been able to find against me in public life.[17]

Parnell sought to identify his opponents in the split with the 'Whiggish' opponents he had confronted at the outset of his career. He harked back to the heroic inception of the parliamentary and agrarian struggles to equate the embattled circumstances of the split with his isolation at the outset of his career. He exploited the mystique of the solitary hero to assert the constancy of his nationalism, declaring at Westport: 'I stand here in integrity and strength of purpose and strength of will the same man that I came to you twelve years ago'.[18] At Limehouse in May, he exaggerated and stylised his solitude at the commencement of the struggle, when the main support on which he, aided by Biggar, could draw, was that of the Irish in England:

> I commenced this struggle with only one faithful friend by my side in the House of Commons *(hear hear)*. For many years we had both the great English political parties arrayed against us, hating us with a virulence that was extraordinary *(hear hear)*. We had not even the Irish people at home at our backs in those days. We had to obtain their confidence painfully, laboriously, and by degrees.[19]

'I am as willing as I was then', Parnell declared at Waterford, 'to go into the lobby as one Irishman against 650 Englishmen'.[20] It was a theme to which he reverted in March, when, anticipating 'a severe and bitter struggle' in the ensuing months, he asserted, 'I have walked through the lobby of the House of Commons one man against six hundred'. However seemingly extravagant, Parnell's statement in the same speech that 'if I had not a colleague in No. 15 Committee Room I would have gone back to the Irish people to get their verdict' expressed his sense of grim perseverance and solitariness even within the post-split Parnellite party, and should not be discounted as idle bombast.[21]

Parnell at Galway in March engaged in a sustained piece of self-dramatisation, which coupled an evocation of his resistance to the corrupting ambience of British politics with the assertion that his health had been broken in the service of his country:

> I have never been one to mix among the English members of the House of Commons, to be 'hail fellow well met' with them, or to go to their clubs or dinner parties *(hear hear)*. During the whole of my sixteen years in public life I have never been inside an English club six times; during that period of service I have never dined out in London half a dozen times *(hear hear)*. I have spent my days and my nights until my health broke down, when I had nobody to help me but honest Joe Biggar *(applause)*; and it was not until 1887 — the beginning of 1887 — when my strength left me, and I was not able to put one foot before the other, that I ever failed in my duty to your interests by night or by day in that Imperial assembly *(cheers)*, and it is monstrous for these raw recruits who came in at the general election of 1886, who have never been under fire ... to throw in my teeth that I, who have lost my strength and my health in the service of Ireland, should ever be taunted by them who have never lost anything, but who have gained much *(hear hear)* — should be taunted by these mushrooms of yesterday *(applause)* because on some half-dozen occasions sickness prevented me from taking my post on the floor of the House of Commons *(hear hear)*.[22]

His most remarkable self-heroisation came in a speech at Navan in March:

> I have lived in the fierce light of public opinion for sixteen long years. During many of those years the informer has been on my track. The agents of the police have beset my footsteps during day and night for the purpose of inveigling me, if possible, into some conspiracy, so that some false evidence might destroy me, or send me to penal servitude or the gallows *(cheers)*.[23]

While it would be unwise to attach too much significance to an isolated utterance, this strangely melodramatic assertion from a man notorious for his eschewal of grandiloquence remains disquieting. Insofar as it reflects calculated dramatisation, it discloses the price the split exacted in compromising his mystique of reticence and froideur; to the extent that it is an involuntary lapse, it reflects the toll which the split was taking of Parnell's equanimity.

Parnell sought, without obvious success, to turn to his advantage the virulence of Healy's attacks. His extravagant protest at Kilkenny against the excesses of Healy and Tanner — 'could these men have left aside for one moment, for one short hour, the assassin's argument and the liar's stab'[24] — is at least as suggestive of calculated self-dramatisation as of wounded personal sensitivity. At Tralee in January, he declared that 'it has been a bitter blow to me to see the Irish people divided upon this question, to be loaded myself with every contumely and insult that the vile and malignant ingenuity that my chief opponents can suggest *(voices: 'Healy') (prolonged hissing)'*.[25] At Tipperary in April, he declared 'I have almost turned for them the other cheek to smite':

> I have perhaps gone too far in that direction; but I am perfectly satisfied and perfectly willing that Mr. Healy *(groans)* and his friends should come within striking distance, and should level their best blows against me. I despise these blows *(loud cheers)*; I feel them not — and certainly I should be a contemptible antagonist if I could not submit to any number of blows from such contemptible antagonists.[26]

The language is again of calculated self-dramatisation rather than anguish, as he relentlessly sought to extract some compensating political advantage for being compelled to run the gauntlet of Healyite moral vituperation.

Parnell chafed at the remonstrances of his supporters, and expected allowance to be made for the circumstances in which he found himself. At Johnswell, during the Kilkenny election, he said 'Mr. Harrington is at my elbow and says I am not to be bitter. I don't want to be bitter'.[27] As he struggled to moderate his tone in the split's latter phase, he recalled at Carlow his pledge to O'Brien at Boulogne not to use degrading language:

> ... and I hope and trust, though at times sorely tempted and sometimes carried away by momentary passion, I may have gone beyond the line I marked out for myself, yet that on the whole, during these six months, my language has been creditable to Ireland and to the cause we all have at heart.[28]

References

1 *Spectator*, 26 Nov. 1898; for Lecky's authorship, see *A Memoir of the rt. hon. W. E. H. Lecky, by his wife* (2nd ed., London 1910), p. 321.

2 The correspondent of the *Manchester Guardian* covered Parnell's campaigns in Kilkenny and Carlow.

3 *F.J.*, 12 Jan. 1891, Limerick.

4 *F.J.*, 11 Dec. 1890, Rotunda.

5 *F.J.*, 20 Dec. 1890, Kilkenny.

6 Sullivan, *Room 15*, p. 5. The quotation provides the epigraph — and argument — of Henry Harrison's *Parnell Vindicated*.

7 *F.J.*, 17 Dec. 1890.

8 *D.N.*, 22 Dec. 1890.

9 *U.I.*, 22 Nov. 1891.

10 *F.J.*, 30 June 1891, Borris.

11 *F.J.*, 6 July 1891, Carlow.

12 *F.J.*, 18 July 1891.

13 *F.J.*, 12 Jan. 1891.

14 *F.J.*, 11 Dec. 1890, Rotunda.

15 *F.J.*, 18 Mar. 1891, Cork.

16 *F.J.*, 30 Mar. 1891, Sligo; see also *F.J.*, 30 June 1891, Borris.

17 *F.J.*, 18 Mar. 1891, Cork.

18 *F.J.*, 7 Sept. 1891.

19 *F.J.*, 14 May 1891.

20 *F.J.*, 24 Jan. 1891.

21 *F.J.*, 2 Mar. 1891, Navan.

22 *F.J.*, 16 Mar. 1891, Galway. The opening part of the passage elicited a predictable retort from T. D. Sullivan: 'What a well-conducted and virtuous gentleman! What an ascetic, self-sacrificing man ... Would that he had been no worse employed' (*N.P.*, 16 May 1891, NF).

23 *F.J.*, 2 Mar. 1891.

24 *K.M.*, 20 Dec. 1890, Kilkenny, 18 Dec.

25 *F.J.*, 10 Jan. 1891.

26 *F.J.*, 28 Apr. 1891, Tipperary.

27 *F.J.*, 22 Dec. 1890.

28 *F.J.*, 6 July 1891.

10

INDEPENDENCE

I will allow no combination, however strong, however influential,
however apparently respectable to drive me from my duty to Ireland
(prolonged cheering). While I have life I will go from one constituency
to another, from one county to another, from one city to another, from
one town and village and parish to another, to put which I know is
the truth before the people *(renewed cheering)*. I know that I must win
(cheers). So let nobody think that I am made of mud *(renewed cheering)* ... To the voice of Ireland alone I will bow *(cheers)*. I will not yield
to English dictation.

Parnell at Kilkenny, 20 December 1891[1]

Mr. Dillon says now that he is in favour of unity, and that it was by
unity and strict discipline that we attained our successes in the past.
I will tell you, fellow countrymen, it was by something greater and
stronger than unity that we obtained this success. It was because we
were independent *(loud cheers)*. It was because we were independent,
that our members were independent of both the great English parties,
that we won; and much as I value unity I say that the greatest force
and the greatest strength which has ever existed in Irish public life,
without which the breath of our best orators and speakers would be
valueless and of no avail, has been the spirit of independence, the love
of nationality ...

Parnell at Thurles, 2 August 1891[2]

Parnell's concept of 'independence' is central to his politics and rhetoric
in the split. The term did not signify an overreaching of the objective of
home rule by the pursuit of complete legislative independence. Parnell
used the term rather as an abbreviated synonym for 'independent opposition', as a watch-word to designate the fundamental strategic premise of
Parnellism; and in a broader usage, in opposition to 'dictation', to signify

resistance to the political pretensions of both the Liberal party and of the Catholic Church in Irish politics.

His espousal of the concept of 'independence' does not evidence what has been described as 'an instinctive recoil towards independence, in the sense of a struggle to re-establish a movement independent of all British connections'.[3] Still less does it represent a foreshadowing of the mystical ideology of later cultural nationalism, or of Irish republicanism in the twentieth century.

Parnell's doctrine of 'independence' asserted that there was no such neutral pragmatic choice as Healy's rhetoric posited. The political legitimacy of a legislative solution to the Irish question required the underpinning of a strict ethic of independence, which he insisted was incompatible with nationalist acquiescence in Liberal, and latterly in clerical, 'dictation'. His rhetoric proclaimed the split itself a prelude to statehood, an essay in the politics of independent opposition, and an habituation to the responsibilities of power. What he referred to as 'my responsibility as the Irish leader'[4] mirrored his belief in the conduct of nationalist politics under the discipline of 'independent opposition'.

A conception of the Parnellite notion of 'independence' is necessary to an understanding of both the emotional strength and the political vulnerability of Parnellism. The reflex of personal allegiance was integral to the Parnellite sensibility and to the concept of 'independence'. The term retained some of its eighteenth-century savour, of a patriotic independence of character and conduct, which had lingered long in Irish politics. The rhetoric of 'independence' in the split attested the rootedness of Parnellite loyalism in independence of political judgement. 'Independence' was the unifying cry of Parnellism in which considerations of patriotism, loyalty and honour commingled. It expressed a code of fealty as well as a political creed.

The connotations of 'independence' were neither fixed nor static. As the split progressed, and anti-Parnellism became entrenched as the nationalist orthodoxy, the term came to acquire a sense of standing aloof from the concerted mass homogeneities of Catholicism and peasant proprietorship which Healy's rhetoric so intimidatingly championed. Parnellite 'independence' was increasingly an inchoate critique of the values espoused in Healy's rhetoric, with its synthesis of considerations of race, class, land and Catholicism, and its tight and symmetrical alignment of nationalist sentiment and proprietorial aspiration.

The romantic individualism of Parnellite allegiance could hardly compete in political strength with the Catholic agrarian consensus on which anti-Parnellism could draw. The relative weakness of Parnellism was manifest in the split's competing rhetorics: the shrill accents of the Parnellite rhetoric of independence, of allegiance to Parnell in the face of Liberal and ecclesiastical 'dictation', was no match for the vigorously chauvinistic populism of Healy's attacks on Parnell. The governing irony of the rhetoric of the split was that, though Parnell sought nakedly to outflank his opponents by laying claim to a more advanced nationalism within the confines of home rule, Parnellism was of a less comprehensively ideological character than the dominant, Healyite, strain of anti-Parnellism.

This consideration gives force to Parnell's astute depreciation of his own rhetorical aptitude. He declared in April 'it is not my fault if I cannot charm the multitude to the gifts of oratory. I have endeavoured during my period in politics to speak words of common sense and truth to the people, and so long as I live in public life I shall stick to my text'. He avowed in the Carlow election: 'I have never pretended in my public life to any eloquence or what is called oratorical power. I have always endeavoured to be a practical man and a practical statesman'.[5]

Healy's savage parody of Parnell as a posturing representative of the eighteenth century Protestant patriot tradition merits consideration. Parnell had a strong sense of his family tradition, though one he refrained from expressing publicly. His sister Anna commented laconically on his death 'he was not a man who thought much of creeds, but he did think a good deal of his ancestors'.[6] The late eighteenth century marked the heroic phase of Parnell's ancestry, and the epoch of Grattan, the precursor with whom he felt the greatest affinity. At the Parnell Commission, the Attorney-General confronted Parnell with a passage from his speech at Cincinatti, to suggest that it was consistent with the spirit of the celebrated reference to breaking 'the last link' with the Crown ascribed to Parnell but which he denied making; Parnell calmly replied 'Well, I see a good deal of difference in it, and Mr. Henry Grattan also saw a good deal of difference'.[7]

Parnell's rhetorical excesses were frequently in the high eighteenth-century mode. In 1879, extolling a resolution of the land question which would permit the Irish landlords to throw in their lot with nationalists, Parnell misappropriated the idiom of Burke to declare, 'let them see, as in 1782, a hundred thousand swords — both Catholic and Protestant — leaping from their scabbards'. At the Special Commission, Parnell, lamely assenting to a leading question put to him on re-examination by Sir Charles Russell, said that 'the reference was evidently to the swords of the volunteers which remained in their scabbards'.[8]

Parnell's sense of ancestry and pride of caste brought with it a consciousness of fragility and precariousness within his class and tradition. It may be more plausible to see a heightened sense of historical frailty, rather than the crude and atavistic allegiance of caste with which Healy charged him, as central to his political sensibility, and as giving him that cold intimation of historical irony in which his opponents were conspicuously lacking.

Parnell's rhetoric and purpose in the split has frequently been wilfully misinterpreted as an anticipation of later extreme variants of nationalism, while the eighteenth-century influence on Parnell's rhetoric and thinking has been neglected. The latter contributed something to his occasionally shrill and extravagant idiom of personal honour, while his political argument was marked by a clarity, rationality and scepticism which owed more to the discourse of eighteenth-century politics in Ireland than to nineteenth-century nationalist ideology. His nationalism was a technique of power rather than an ideology. He brought what might be characterised as an eighteenth-century clarity of purpose to bear on the mass social aggregates and hardening popular ideologies of late-nineteenth-century Ireland.

Independent Opposition

Parnell in the split contrasted independent opposition with the policy of parliamentary beggary — 'dependent opposition'[9] which he imputed to the majority: 'Once Ireland cringes to England and proclaims to England her helplessness without English help, the future of our nation is undone'.[10] The achievements of the national movement under his leadership were won because 'we were independent of both political parties, because we owned no Englishman our master'.[11] Campaigning in Carlow, he treated as axiomatic the proposition 'that no English party and no English leader really loves Ireland. They will respect you, they will respect your power, so long as you keep together'. History demonstrated that progress was not made 'on account of the love and affection of any Englishmen or English party for us'.[12] 'Legitimate liberty ... will never be gained if the Irish people forget their independence of character and allow the Irish representatives to forget theirs.'[13] Parnell was quoted, in a passage attributed to him at the conclusion of his last speech, as saying:

> Sir William Harcourt says his idea of the future of Ireland is leaning on the strong arm of the Liberal Party. That is not our idea. We believe in the principles and means which paralysed the strong arm of the Liberal Party from 1880 to 1885 until we hurled them from office.[14]

He asserted that his overthrow by the Irish party was a gesture of sentimental obeisance to Gladstone, an ill-judged act of faith in the objective capacity, if not the subjective will, of the Liberal leader to deliver a sufficient measure of home rule. He insisted that to defer to the Liberals in the split was an irreversible act. He warned against the folly of folding the nationalist tent in an access of sentimental gratitude to Gladstone.

The imprudence of succumbing to dependence on the Liberal party prior to securing an adequate home rule legislature was a recurrent theme of Parnell's rhetoric, habitually presented in terms of an extravagant analogy with the acquiescence in the disbanding of the Irish Volunteers

of Henry Grattan, the historical figure with whom Parnell identified himself most closely in his pronouncements of the split. Thus he declared, in the course of his speech at Johnstown in the Kilkenny election:

> That great Irishman, Grattan, who was born in 1746, just a hundred years before the date of my birth, almost won Irish legislative independence; but in the moment of his victory and of ours he forgot that he had a wily and a treacherous foe to deal with — a foe who knows how to use the dagger and the poisoned bowl of diplomacy with just as much skill as the more ponderous ninety-ton gun *(hear hear)*. He forgot that in dealing with English statescraft it was his duty as an Irishman to surrender no vantage ground whatever, and in the hour of his victory the cup was dashed from our lips and the disbandment of the Volunteers in 1792 lost for Ireland the freedom which was well within her grasp *(hear hear)*. We shall be warned today by the lessons which were taught to them.[15]

Speaking at a convention of Gaelic clubs in Dublin, Parnell invoked the Grattan precedent, declaring that until a satisfactory measure of home rule was conceded 'we will refuse to surrender one particle of our power'.[16]

Parnell, in a speech at the Historical Society of the Catholic University on 13 December 1877, had regretted he was one of 'those unfortunate beings ... who only acquired a knowledge of Irish history at a very late period of his life', explaining that he had been educated at a place where Irish history had not been taught, and that 'anything learned late in life was learned imperfectly' (he was then thirty-one).[17] He thereby quickened what became the powerful but deceptive myth of his own ignorance of Irish history. Yet if Parnell fell short of the elaborate standards of his more pedantic nationalist contemporaries, his rhetoric was informed by a powerful sense of history, directed to his own purpose. While Grattan was the figure to whom Parnell most frequently referred, at Navan he invoked Frederick Lucas, John Mitchel and John Martin: the first time he had been in the House of Commons he had heard the ailing Martin defend Mitchel against an attack by their fellow-countryman David Plunkett.[18]

He drew a common moral from the Treaty of Limerick, the disbanding of the Volunteers and the parliamentary debacle of 1852, as demonstrating 'what became of our country, her interests, and her future, whenever in our history she was beguiled into ceasing to trust in herself, her own strength, and her own courage'.[19]

When Dillon unguardedly declared that he would be the first to oppose an inadequate Home Rule Bill and declare against the Liberal party, Parnell responded vehemently that Dillon would have by then already permitted the irreversible disbanding of the nationalist movement, and the ebbing of the impetus of nationalist politics:

> Who are the forces by whose help he is going to fight the Liberal party in case of necessity in twelve months time? Where are they? ... He does all he can in the interval to crush and destroy the national sentiments of Ireland.

He does, perhaps unconsciously, probably unconsciously, all he can during the interval to destroy the spirit, the courage, the forces of the great army of Nationalists upon whom he has always depended for his strength and support *(hear hear)*, and it will not be for him when that time comes, as it most assuredly will come, then to appeal to the men by whose help in years gone by he mounted to power and achieved his fame and his position of strength as an Irishman and to fall back upon those forces which in the meanwhile he will have done his best to discredit and destroy *(cheers)* ... I ask Mr. Dillon not to throw away his sword, not to disband his army, not to give up any force or strength which he now possesses, which Ireland now possesses, until we have tested the promises of these English liberals by their performances *(cheers)*.[20]

This passage exemplifies Parnell's enduring ability to advance an impeccably constitutionalist argument in terms with which Fenians and advanced nationalists could feel an affinity, and which made a veiled and ambiguous acknowledgement of their contribution to the success of a movement to which they were — in terms of their formal dogma — opposed.

He insisted that he was doing no more than restating the necessary basis of any political collaboration with the Liberal party, and that the anti-Parnellites' failure to understand the nature of the Liberal alliance was destroying the work of sixteen years. In the concluding peroration of his speech at Newcastle-upon-Tyne in July, he defended 'independent opposition' in terms of the stylised lessons of Irish history, asserting that the cohort of support he had marshalled in the split would prevail against the unwitting dismantlement of the nationalist movement by his opponents:

... looking back upon these sixteen years I ask you when has Ireland in her history so progressed or obtained great force for the attainment of her liberty *(applause)*, when has she been able ever to hold her head more proudly and defiantly against her foes *(hear, hear)*; when has she ever before compelled, as she has done in this interval, both the great English parties to come to her and ask her what her terms of peace are? *(loud cheers)*. We have declared those terms of peace in no uncertain sound. We have repeated them on this platform tonight, and as Irishmen, when these terms are granted to us, when we hold them in our hands, and when we hold power to make them, we will make a treaty of peace *(loud cheers)*. But until then, guided by the lessons which the disbanding of the Volunteers taught Grattan in the last century, when too late *(hear, hear)*, guided and taught by the lessons which Sarsfield and the people of Ireland learned at Limerick, when too late *(cheers)*, we stand here tonight with everything that is sound amongst our countrymen at our back *(hear, hear)*, determined to maintain the independence of the cause of our country and her representatives *(cheers)*; taught by the lessons of the past and the experience of history, determined to consolidate our strength, undismayed by temporary defeats, knowing that we have great forces behind us in Ireland, the 1,500 brave men and independent men of Carlow *(cheers)*, the 2,500 men of North Sligo *(cheers)*, and the 1,400 men of North Kilkenny, who with hearts of steel withstood every influence, clerical and otherwise *(cheers)*, and were not afraid to testify to their faith in Irish Nationality, and to stand by the man in his hour of trouble who stood by them in theirs *(loud and prolonged cheering)*.[21]

Parnell's stance was conceived as a retaliation to Gladstone's abrogation of the necessary formalism of the Liberal-Nationalist alliance. 'Independent Opposition' was in part reality, in part necessary myth. If the Parnellite home rule demand, as expressed in the manifesto in response to Gladstone's intervention in the matter of the Irish leadership, was more a matter of form than substance, Parnell asserted it to be integral to the logic of political action, and to the legitimacy and finally the viability of constitutional politics in Ireland.

However damaging Parnell's rhetoric was in practice to the prospects for any future collaboration between him and Gladstone or any future Liberal leader, he insisted throughout that his campaign was not directed against the principle of a Liberal-Nationalist alliance. He asserted that he was doing no more in the split than re-articulating the necessary premises for collaboration between the Irish party and the Liberal party. His rhetoric stressed the absoluteness of the distinction between an alliance and a fusion of parties. He cast the opposition in terms of the difference between a coalition of parties and a treaty of nations.

He thereby doggedly and insistently confronted Gladstone with the avowed logic of home rule. As Gladstone had in his own rhetoric sought to justify the home rule alliance in terms of a high entente between nations, so Parnell strove to constrain him by reference to that rhetoric. He struggled to hold Gladstone to the principle of non-intervention in Irish affairs to which his espousal of home rule had bound him. Gladstone, he insisted, had done exactly what he had committed himself not to do: he had intervened in Irish affairs on an issue which fell uniquely within the province of the Irish party, that of its leadership. Having treated with Parnell as the leader of a nation, Gladstone had then intermeddled to procure his dismissal as the leader of a party. 'We are willing to have him as a friend,' Parnell declared, 'but we will not own him as a leader'.[22] He sought to demonstrate that Gladstone's intervention in the issue of the Irish leadership exposed the contradictoriness of Gladstone's pretensions, as the leader of an English party, to the status of the honest broker of a home rule settlement.

Parnell charged that the attacks on his leadership emanated from England, from men

> ... who mistake the relative position of England and Ireland in the alliance which we have entered into with them. We entered into an honourable alliance — an alliance, if you will, of a weaker nation with a stronger nation, but still a nation with a nation ... These Englishmen have mistaken, as I have said, the relative position of the two nations'.[23]

The policy of the majority had, he asserted, eventuated 'not even in a fusion of nations', but merely in the surrender of the majority of the Irish party to Gladstone and the Liberals.[24]

At Maryborough in May Parnell delivered the most trenchant statement of the tenets of his parliamentary strategy, in distinguishing between an alliance and what he termed a fusion of parties:

> We are actually now told that without an alliance with the Liberal party we could do nothing. I say that such teachings show that men have to learn the very alphabet of Irish politics, and if they truly mean what they say they don't know the 'ABC' of Irish politics *(cheers)* ... We came into our present position of power and unity by fighting both English political parties, and it was not until we had fought them that they both came round to say they had recognised the principle of Irish nationality *(cheers)* ... I don't say that we should not ally ourselves with the English Liberal party *(interruptions)*. I am perfectly willing to ally myself with any English party from time to time, but I decline to sell either myself or my country for an English alliance *(cheers)*. But there is all the difference in the world between an alliance and a fusion. An alliance between a smaller party and a larger party is always a dangerous thing, and an attempt to treat has always been more dangerous to Ireland than a battle pitched. Ireland has always lost more on the field of negotiation and of treaty making than she has in the camp or in pitched battle. The Liberal alliance which was watched by me most carefully has now degenerated into a fusion, by turning an honourable and self-respecting alliance into a dishonourable blending and fusion *(hear hear)*.[25]

This distinction ran like a seam of ore through his rhetoric in the split. He declared at Westport in September that the Irish party was willing to make an alliance with an English party but not to fuse with them, to which he added the characteristic observation, derived from his metallurgical pursuits, that 'fusing means burning'.[26]

Parnell thus asserted that the Liberal alliance should not compromise the independence of the Irish party. He insisted on the maintaining intact of the necessary myth of independent opposition. If this argument obviously subserved the immediate purposes of his campaign to regain his leadership, it remained a lucid and compelling statement of the principles which had avowedly governed the parliamentary relation of the Nationalist party with the Liberal party up to the split. Contrary to the premise underlying the anti-Parnellite stance, the battle was not yet won. As Anna Parnell wrote in her only political intervention in the split, 'the whole position of the Irish party rests on a claim to prophetic powers'.[27]

Parnell in his attacks on the anti-Parnellites frequently cast this argument in cruder polemical form. In deferring to Gladstone's *fiat*, the anti-Parnellite party had become 'an appendage and tail of the Liberal party'.[28] He discerned an 'Anglo-Irish conspiracy', and denounced this 'Anglo-Irish party'.[29] The *Weekly Freeman's Journal* characterised the split in terms of 'the Secession of the West Britons'.[30] Invoking the discredited shades of Sadlier and Keogh, who had venally and feebly espoused the principles which Parnell had rendered politically actual, and of the episcopacy which had sustained them, the *Freeman's Journal* deprecated 'the revival of Whiggery and the place hunting of a new Brass

Band'.[31] Andrew Kettle warned of a reversion to 'the days of Whiggery and beggary'.[32] *United Ireland* ridiculed 'the Anglo-Irish Liberals' and 'the new Gladstonian Irishmen'.[33] Joseph Kenny's suggestion that the anti-Parnellite National Federation should be called 'the White Featheration' revealingly coupled the taunt of political cowardice with a mimicking of rustic pronunciation to convey the predominantly rural composition of anti-Parnellite support.[34]

Parnell in the split invoked the precepts of the halcyon days of independent opposition 1880-86. He opportunely rediscovered the 'coercionist' past of the Liberals: 'The Tories have coerced us too, but who taught the Tories to coerce us? ... There is no lesson in coercion which the Tories have not learned from their liberal predecessors'.[35] This crude and regressive polemicising of the Liberals as a party of repression nonetheless underpinned a more subtle argument. Repression was part of the alternating sequence of British policy which independent opposition was devised to break: 'Each ministry in turn has shot down the people, and used the constabulary for the purpose of evicting people, for the purpose of destroying their homes and devastating their hearths with equal impartiality'. The Liberals, Parnell charged, had coerced before and would coerce again, should the Irish question not be resolved by a sufficient measure of home rule.[36] 'Mr. Gladstone's Home Rule policy is the creation of circumstances ... we remember perfectly well that Mr. Gladstone tried every other policy first before he tried the policy of conciliation'.[37] 'Independent opposition' was part of the learning process of British parties in office, an education in Irish realities.

Parnell in July presented the concept of independent opposition in its most simplistic form. He asserted that if the Tories found themselves once again dependent on Irish votes to take office, another Tory politician would approach the Irish party as did Lord Carnarvon in 1885 to ascertain the minimal Irish demand for home rule: 'They are all alike, the Liberals and Tories: they have coerced us alternately; and they have both offered us Parliaments alternately ...'.[38] As a principle of strategy, this was untenable. The hardening mould of British politics on the Irish question after Gladstone's sponsorship of home rule eliminated the possibility of even so equivocal an initiative as that of Carnarvon in 1885.

The reality was that 'independent opposition' was now more than ever an asymmetrical tactic, a device which relied simply on the political leverage afforded by a readiness to keep the Liberals out of office in the absence of a commitment to a sufficient measure of home rule on their part, rather than predicated on the possibility of eliciting home rule from the Conservatives. Parnell's statement that the Conservatives would offer home rule was a dramatisation of the argument for independent opposition rather than a prediction or strategic premise. His doctrine of independent opposition was, and was understood to be, reducible to the threat to keep

the Liberals out of power until they agreed to enact an adequate home
rule measure, a threat which he insisted was integral to the effectiveness
and legitimacy of the Irish party at Westminster. He at the same time
deployed a more modest, scaled-down, variant of the 'independent opposition' argument to justify his policy of constructive engagement with
the Conservative government to secure land purchase, public expenditure
and local government reform in Ireland.

Parnell asserted that the split was a re-enactment of the struggle of the
early years of his career to launch the nationalist movement in its contemporary form. The specific comparison most frequently drawn was with the
1880 election, in which he attained a narrow ascendancy over the so-called
'Whigs' and 'nominal' Home Rulers, and thereby laid the foundations for
the Parnellite landslide of 1885. One Parnellite apologist stressed the 'extraordinary resemblance between the circumstances, character, and speeches
of the present campaign and that of 1880'.[39] At Newry in March 1891,
Parnell declared, 'I stand here, unhappily, to commence a great deal of
my work over again'. While his 'army' was more numerous than in 1875,
he anticipated that after the general election 'although we may not have
as numerous a party as we had in 1885, it will be more solid, it will be
stronger, its principles will be clearer, sharper, and more independent'.[40]
He posited a symmetry with the antecedent struggle: 'We have to fight over
again the rotten Whigs who were creeping into our arms ... We have to
fight the men that we beat at the general election of 1880, whom we drove
out of public life in 1885 ...'.[41]

It is notable that throughout the split Parnell stressed the parliamentary rather than the agrarian origins of the movement he had led. When
Parnell spoke at Irishtown, County Mayo, on the twelfth anniversary of
the great meeting of 1879 which marked the inception of the land struggle, he recast the land struggle as an essay in independent opposition.[42]

Parnell's enduring tenacity of purpose, as he rediscovered his status as
the leader of a beleaguered minority, invested the comparison with the early
years of the struggle with much of its force (it drew also an artificial
plausibility from the fact that he was in many instances in the split addressing meetings in towns where he had not spoken in the intervening
decade). The equation, however, afforded a flawed premise for policy, while
his reduction of the anti-Parnellites of 1890-91 to the status of 'rotten
Whigs' seemed to many contemporaries an unpardonable excess.

Parnell pitted himself against what he asserted to be the disintegratory
effects on the nationalist movement of the Liberal alliance and of the
generally anticipated home rule settlement. The corollary of the doctrine
of independent opposition was the need to maintain a possibly protracted
struggle. He proclaimed his resolve to maintain intact the vigour of the
nationalist movement. In his manifesto, while declining to admit 'for one
moment the slightest possibility' of his continued leadership indefinitely

postponing Ireland's chances of obtaining home rule, he implicitly conceded just such a possibility in reverting to the subject in the concluding passage:

> I do not believe that any action of the Irish people in supporting me will endanger the home rule cause, or postpone the establishment of an Irish parliament; but even if the danger with which we are threatened by the Liberal party of to-day were to be realised, I believe that the Irish people throughout the world would agree with me that a postponement would be preferable to a compromise of our national rights by the acceptance of a measure which would not realise the aspirations of our race.[43]

In his platform rhetoric in the split Parnell accepted that a possible consequence of his rupture with Gladstone was the deferral of home rule. He denied however that this was necessary or inevitable, and contended that the greater danger lay in the premature acceptance of an insufficient measure of home rule.

In his most *simpliste* extension of this argument, Parnell propounded a conspiracy theory of the Liberal alliance and improbably warned that the Liberals intended to concede an inadequate measure of home rule devised to break the independence of the Irish party: 'Their design is to erect a Parliament in Ireland with maimed and crippled powers, which will have no control over any of the questions which really constitute the grit of the Irish question'.[44]

Yet the considerations which actuated Parnell were more subtle and prescient than the intermittent crudity of his rhetoric might suggest. As a tightly marshalled political force, the home rule movement was breaking fast even before the divorce crisis. Parnell in 1890-91 sought to arrest its dissolution by fighting out the issue of the split as against Gladstone in Ireland. It was not merely that he was temperamentally immune to the belief in the imminence and inevitability of an adequate Liberal home rule settlement that paralysed the faculties of so many of his contemporaries. His argument in the split stretched beyond the weakness of the Liberal commitment to home rule to deficiencies within nationalism. The danger he discerned lay less in the concession of an insufficient measure of home rule *per se*, than in its concession to a nation which had not achieved and affirmed its political maturity. This argument underlay the stylised humility of Parnell's avowal, late in the split, that '... it is no longer a question of leadership. It is a question of whether our country is worthy of being a nation. I happen only to be the humble and unworthy instrument'.[45]

Parnell asserted that it could well prove necessary to lengthen again the time-scale of nationalist aspirations, which the popular anticipation of Gladstonian home rule had drastically foreshortened. He argued against a precipitate grateful succumbing to the prospect of a Gladstonian settlement, and sought to inculcate forbearance as part of the discipline of 'independence', reflecting an acute sensitivity to the threat posed by the perceived imminence of home rule to the maintenance of political authority within the nationalist polity.

With that axiomatic fusion of personal and political purpose which marked his rhetoric in the split, Parnell equated the duration of the struggle for home rule with that required for the reconstitution of his own authority. They were, he warned, engaged in what might prove 'a long a bitter fight'.[46] Sometimes he suggested that victory might be attained in the course of a few parliamentary sessions; on other occasions he seemed to suggest that it would be over the span of two elections, thus re-enacting the course of the struggle of 1880-85. At Cork in March he declared himself confident that his position would be supported 'to the very end of my campaign, for two campaigns, and for as many as are necessary'.[47] In April he sought to reassure his audience in Ballina:

> It would not be a question of fighting for ten years or twenty years or thirty years, as it was after the act of traitorism of 1852. It would be simply a matter of three or four sessions *(cheers)*, and you would have the two English parties, coming as they did in 1885 and 1886, to ask what would be the smallest measure of Home Rule you would take *(cheers)*.[48]

Parnell set his campaign in the longer nationalist perspective: 'The Irish question cannot be settled in a moment. Legitimate liberty cannot be given to the Irish people in one year, or two years, or three years'.[49] At Westport he asked:

> What does it matter if we are beaten for a year, or for two years, or for three years? Ireland's future has depended upon a struggle which has been going on now for a great many centuries. It is not reasonable to suppose that the whole of this struggle could be ended in a few weeks or a few years.[50]

There was 'no short cut to freedom'.[51]

In an impressive piece of apologetics which yoked the principles of constitutional action to the campaign to establish his leadership, Parnell, at Westport in September, insisted on the necessary protractedness of the struggle under constitutional principles. The progress of Ireland under his leadership, while more rapid than that previously achieved was slow, but its gradualness had ensured its irreversibility:

> The slow progress has been disappointing, but at least it was sure; it cannot be recalled. No step that the Irish nation has taken can be retraced. No gain once won can be taken from you. They all constitute a stronger basis from which to advance for further progress and fresh conclusions, and although the progress of these twelve years may have been slow it was sure *(loud cheers)*. Constitutional Parliamentary effort must be slow. If we are to fight not with the weapons of the field and revolution we cannot gain liberty and freedom for Ireland in a year or in a day. Our steps must be by degrees ...
>
> We are told by some of our new guides and leaders that the whole Irish question — freedom for Ireland, restitution for the evicted tenants — is going to be gained immediately the Liberals and Mr. Gladstone come into power.

I say that the march of progress of Irish liberty must be slow and toilful, that progress must depend upon the spirit of independence of our people, and if you once forget the lessons which your forefathers taught you in '98, when they cheerfully shed their blood, with no prospect of hope or victory before the nation, if you forget the means and principles by which we have gained our progress on constitutional lines, then, and not till then, may you despair of the cause of Ireland.[52]

This was not the utterance of a man threatening to forsake constitutional action. Parnell, although accused of engaging in a facile and irresponsible appeal to extreme nationalism, argued the necessity for a hardening of nationalist discipline and purpose.

Parnell condemned his opponents' want of foresight, in grasping prematurely at the prize of home rule held out by Gladstone. The efflux of time had a personal significance for Parnell. In a disturbing mortal idiom, reflecting his pressing intimation of his own mortality, he declared with ghastly effervescence:

... I have heard Irish members to argue as if they had got one foot in the grave *(laughter)*, they were so desperately afraid that their time would come before the gaining or achievement of any great measure for Ireland, but if these men had done their duty they would have at least earned a good funeral *(cheers and laughter)*. But who will mourn them now? *(cheers and laughter)*. Who will care to follow the hearse of a deserter or seceder? *(cheers)*. These men will go down 'unwept, unhonoured, and unsung'. When their political demise comes at the next general election *(cheers)*, and whereas at one time they would have the hope of such memory and recollection from a grateful people as was due to their mediocre talent and ability, they can now only hope that the curses may be modulated because of the futility of their traitorism *(great cheering)*. So from the point of view of their own interests their bolt has fallen short of the mark *(cheers)* and they have not secured even a decent funeral for themselves *(cheers and laughter)*.[53]

'My position as a colleague of the Grand Old Man has ceased, I have regained my freedom, and I am now free to interpret the National aspiration of the Irish people',[54] he declared at Drogheda. The damaging extravagance of statements such as these, and the vehemence with which he assailed Gladstone and his former colleagues, obscured the studied moderation of Parnell's substantive commitments in the split.

Parnell did not depart from the demands made in the manifesto, in which he had sought clear provision in any home rule scheme for the resolution of the Irish land question, for control by the Irish legislature of the Irish constabulary and of judicial appointments; and, if any powers were to be withheld for a stated period from the Irish legislature, that the then existing complement of 103 Irish members at Westminster could be maintained.

These were not extreme demands, but they were rendered calculatedly provoking to the Liberal leadership by reason of their provenance in Parnell's bitterly controverted version of his colloquy with Gladstone at

Hawarden in December 1889. Notwithstanding Joseph Chamberlain's mischievously inflammatory assertion that Parnell sought to make of the constabulary a Parnellite militia, so that in the event of a dispute between Ireland and England, it would be impossible for the English parliament to sustain its authority 'without a great, serious, and it may be, a disastrous civil war',[55] Parnell's demands were not intrinsically immoderate: indeed it was precisely on their unexceptionable and moderate character that Parnell relied to bait the trap for the Liberal and anti-Parnellite leadership. However cynical and opportunistic the allegations and demands made in the manifesto, and reiterated through the split, they provided the grid within which Parnell's campaign in the split was fought, and attested an undiminished commitment to the framework of home rule.

Parnell sought 'a large and great measure of self-government' which did not trench on English or imperial matters. He warned that an inadequate settlement would end 'in disappointment, in bitterness, in renewed strife between the two nations', and added the vatic pronouncement that the more he considered the importance of a sufficient settlement 'the more I am convinced that Ireland and England will ultimately say that the leader of Ireland was right'.[56] Even in Parnell's controversial reference at Listowel to 'the legitimate independence of Ireland as a nation', the epithet does service as a limitation as much as an attribute. In the heat of the split, Parnell was not quite so fastidiously cautious in the deployment of the moderate nomenclature of home rule as theretofore (William O'Brien had advised his lawyers in the Parnell Commission that Parnell had compelled him to change a reference to 'national independence' in his election address for Mallow in January 1883 by substituting the word 'legislative' for 'national' and had observed: 'We can never go further than that ... We will get it all right if these extreme gentlemen would only give us a little more fair play').[57] Yet in his considered utterances in the split, Parnell was studiedly moderate in the parlance of home rule itself, and in his manifesto went so far as to substitute the term 'home rule' for 'legislative independence'.[58]

Parnell's espousal of 'real legislative independence'[59] was reducible in terms of policy to these modest proportions. At Bermondsey he illustrated the idea of Ireland having 'real power over her own affairs' by reference to the control of police and the appointment of judges.[60] At Newry, while declaring he would not accept 'a mock and sham settlement', he acknowledged the clear distinction between imperial and Irish affairs, and stated:

> We do insist upon this, and, we will accept no settlement as final which will not secure it, that we shall have control over our own business, and especially that power, that usurped power, which now belongs to the crown, of levying and maintaining and arming a body of constabulary shall cease by repeal of the statutes which now give that power.[61]

At Limerick, Parnell succumbed to the temptation to use the ambiguous word 'veto' with reference both to Liberal dictation (the sense in which he used the term throughout his manifesto) and to a derogation from an adequate measure of home rule by the maintenance of a legislative veto:

> We want a Parliament with full power to manage the affairs of Ireland *(cheers)*, without trenching on any Imperial prerogative or injury to any Imperial or English interest, but a Parliament we must have that will be supreme with reference to Irish questions *(cheers)*. We will have no English veto. An English veto, whether in the appointment of your leader, or on the laws that you shall make, would break down and destroy that Parliament before it was two years in existence *(hear hear)*.[62]

Morley seized on, and misconstrued, a similar remark by Parnell at Ennis on 1 February, to warn Dillon, after his return with O'Brien from Boulogne, that 'this repudiation of parliamentary supremacy is absolutely fatal to any home rule associated with Parnell'.[63] Parnell nowhere challenged the only provision in the 1886 Bill which approximated to a veto (the requirement for the Queen's assent through her lord lieutenant to legislation by the home rule parliament), and expressly provided for such a veto in the body of an amendment which he drafted to the National League constitution.[64]

His extravagantly futuristic apostrophe at Navan ('Men of Royal Meath, perhaps some day or other in the long distant future some one may arise who will have the privilege of addressing you as men of Republican Meath *(loud cheers)*. Of the future I know nothing, and shall predict nothing here'.)[65] attracted comment but was generally regarded by contemporaries as unguarded hyperbole rather than as an overreaching by Parnell of the confines of home rule.

It is difficult to detect in any of Parnell's rhetorical extravagances a superseding of constitutional action or of the concept of home rule. Home rule had deeply pervaded the contemporary nationalist consciousness, and was widely accepted as embodying the nationalist demand in its realisable form. The success of parliamentary nationalism under Parnell's leadership had itself rendered the concept of home rule sufficiently robust to contain his rhetoric in the split within its confines.

In rebuttal of the charge of violating the Irish party pledge to act with the majority, Parnell at the National Convention in July had recourse to the contention that the anti-Parnellites, in leaving Committee Room 15 before a vote on the leadership itself, had 'seceded from the party, held a hole and corner meeting of their own and constituted themselves into a fresh party'. By their action they had 'put themselves outside the pale of the constitution of the party'. They had in consequence disentitled themselves to rely on what Parnell described as 'a very technical pledge'. He insisted that he had abided by the pledge even though 'I believe I personally did not subscribe to it'.[66] From this argument derived the stilted

Parnellite practise of designating the majority 'seceders', even though the unremitting fierceness with which Parnell fought to reclaim his leadership rendered preposterous the contention that those minded to oppose him had any alternative but to quit Committee Room 15.

The sturdier Parnellite response was that the majority was not competent to depose Parnell without the consent of the constituencies. Parnell at the Kilkenny election asserted:

> ... my duty was clear. It was to hold firm to the position to which you had elected me until you deprived me of it. It was not in their power to depose me. They could not hurl me from it ... The men who [were] elected in 1885 to fill the Irish seats were men who were elected for a particular work, but they were not elected to sit in judgement on me *(cheers)*, and when they arrogated to themselves the right to depose me, I said to them show me your authority, countersigned by the voice of the Irish people, and until you show me your warrant I decline to budge one single inch *(cheers)*.[67]

J. J. Clancy put the argument bluntly: while the party went through the form of annually electing Parnell its sessional leader it did so 'because he had already been elected leader of the Irish race'.[68] Clancy further contended that the 'real meaning and object' of the pledge to sit, act and vote with the Irish party, was to preclude the virtual absorption of the Irish party by the Liberal party. This was to argue that the pledge was devised to impose a commitment to a minimum home rule demand; that it was asymmetrical and existed to constrain nationalist parliamentarians of weak convictions from attaching themselves to the Liberal party, rather than to inhibit those who espoused a nationalism more advanced than the majority.

Parnell also sought to diminish his vulnerability on the issue of the pledge by the rather transparent device of interposing a further pledge. He drafted and procured the adoption of an amendment to the constitution of the National League to provide that all parliamentary candidates would be required to pledge themselves to refrain from taking office under the imperial government, until the concession of a home rule parliament conforming to Parnellite requirements.[69] He sought thereby to highlight his contention that his opponents craved office under the crown, and to distract attention from the charge that he had failed to abide by the decision of the majority of the Irish party. He went so far as to hint that he would not himself take office even in an Irish parliament:

> Under the Crown in an English Parliament I would never accept office *(cheers)*, and under the Crown in an Irish Parliament it is extremely unlikely that I ever should accept it. It would certainly be no act of self-sacrifice on my part if, after we had gained a complete measure of Home Rule, I declined to take office under the Crown, for my genius and inclination do not lie in the direction of tying myself down to any office. And if I consult my own wishes in the future, when Ireland has a right to send her representatives to a Legislature in College Green, I shall certainly choose some other position than that of a paid Minister of the Crown, even subject to the wishes of my own countrymen.[70]

SCUTTLED!

Figure 6 'Scuttled!' (*St. Stephen's Review*, 21 Mar. 1891)

Parnell's self-denying declaration smacked too much of making a virtue of necessity.

Gladstone and the Liberal Party

> And if there exists any such fanatic who persists in telling us today, in view of the fact that we have the greatest man of the English race pledged to his utmost to grant Ireland her legitimate freedom and means of future prosperity, that we have side by side with us the great Liberal party, which has never lost any fight that it once commenced, I say that if such a person exists ... who could tell us now to turn back into the old paths of revolution and violence, the Irish race would with one accord ... tell him that he would not be their guide.
>
> Parnell at Edinburgh, July 1889 [71]

Few of Parnell's errors in the split were as grievous, or as revealing, as the misjudged aggressiveness of his assault upon Gladstone. It was of course necessary for him to attack Gladstone: it was essential that he kept to the fore the charge of Liberal dictation. Parnell could not afford to concede Healy's ceaselessly reiterated argument in the split's later phase, that he had been overthrown by the majority of the Irish, through their representatives, rather than by Gladstone. His manifesto, however, involved him in a dangerous frontal assault on Gladstone's bona fides. His later attacks, even though tartly mocking rather than virulent, gave almost equal offence to large sections of nationalist opinion.

Gladstone's espousal of home rule had placed him upon a moral eminence such that many nationalists regarded Parnell's attacks upon him as gratuitously offensive, disrespectful and ungrateful. Parnell was oblivious to the full extent of the transfiguration of public opinion in Ireland wrought by the 'union of hearts'. Through a commingling of sentimental nationalist gratitude and Gladstonian moral fervour, what had been a pragmatic political conjuncture had become a sentimental coalition. Some slackening in the tension of 'independent opposition' was inherent in the Liberal-Nationalist home rule alliance, but Parnell badly underestimated the extent to which it had already taken hold. From Parnell's point of view, what had been a contingent alliance had become a fatal embrace.

Ominously for Parnell, the pervasive sense of gratitude in nationalist Ireland was only an aspect of his deeper predicament. A profound shift of nationalist sentiment had altered perceptions not merely of Gladstone, but of the nature of politics itself. The dispassionate realism and ruthless clarity of Parnell, in which the Liberal-Nationalist alliance had originated, appeared increasingly redundant and even reprehensible. Parnell offended against the new nationalist dispensation not merely by the virulence of his attacks on Gladstone, but by what Healy brilliantly charged to be the larger cynicism and amorality of his mode of politics. Parnell's ruthlessly unsentimental practice of politics had become in the split itself a source of scandal.

Parnell, at Balbriggan in June 1891, delivered a revealingly tendentious account of his response after Morley had read to him Gladstone's letter:

> ... I said to him: 'Mr. Gladstone is just doing the very thing he has no right to do. There are many other things that he might do equally effective from his own point of view, and equally effective in regard to English public opinion but in taking the step of interfering with the election of the Irish leader he is letting loose forces in Ireland that he will not live to see the end of'.[72]

According to Morley's contemporary note of their meeting, which is to be preferred, Parnell said no such thing. On the contrary, on being advised of Gladstone's intention to publish the letter, Parnell actually commented that Gladstone was right to do so, and that it would 'put him straight with his party'.[73]

The discrepancy is suggestive. Parnell had seriously underestimated the impact which the Gladstone letter would have on Irish opinion. His own instincts seemingly confirmed by the tenor of the Leinster Hall meeting and other manifestations of support in Ireland, it is even possible that Parnell initially believed that the Gladstone letter would actually help to consolidate his own position in Ireland — that it would put him straight with his party. Parnell's version of events at Balbriggan stands both as an involuntary gesture of self-rebuke for his initial complacency, and as a revelation of the cold and furious resentment of Gladstone's intervention which he had magisterially dissembled in his response to Morley.

Parnell persisted, as if compulsively, in attacking Gladstone's bona fides long after it was apparent that this was counterproductive. If his persistence owed something to his personal resentment of Gladstone, it reflected also his abiding inability to acquiesce in the prevailing readiness of nationalists to repose implicit trust in Gladstone and his party, in the face of what he considered to be the elementary and self-evident dictates of prudence.

The irrepressible instinctuality of Parnell's attacks on Gladstone was palpable in his great speech at the Rotunda on his first return to Ireland. Parnell spoke impressively in praise of the solitary endeavour of Gladstone, to whom he referred as 'this Grand Old Man, for he is a grand old man'. In epitomising him as 'this unrivalled leader of his own people but not of Ireland', Parnell was asserting the necessity of maintaining intact the independence of the Irish party. The effect of this temperateness was, however, largely undone when he proved unable to restrain himself from a jocular reference to 'grand old spiders'.[74] It was a mild enough joke, but one which he could ill afford in the solemn ambience of the union of hearts. Similar ventures in what Parnell appears to have intended as light-hearted raillery — such as a reference to Gladstone as 'a very good old strategist'[75] — were ill received by many moderate nationalists.

Having to a dangerous degree cast the issue of the split in terms of Gladstone's personal trustworthiness, Parnell failed to avoid gratuitous excesses, and to treat the argument with the rigid economy which it required. On the contrary, he recklessly broadened his attack on Gladstone. Thus he asserted that Gladstone, being advised of the terms of the manifesto by Justin McCarthy, had not raised any objection to it.[76] The nadir of Parnell's judgement came with the wild and bizarre allegation, made as late as April, that Gladstone had received at Hawarden sympathisers of the extreme Irish-American dynamitards, effortlessly dismissed by Gladstone as 'absolutely false from beginning to end'.[77]

Parnell's own dispassionate, placidly ironic, disposition led him to underestimate the devastating impact of his attack on Gladstone on public opinion in Ireland. He never came to terms with the popular reverence accorded Gladstone. With grim jocularity, he rebuked himself for having been excessively indulgent towards Gladstone — 'perhaps I was a little too amiable with the Grand Old Man', and undertook not to be so in the future. He declared himself glad that negotiations with Gladstone were broken off, that Ireland never gained from negotiations, and more characteristically that Gladstone and the Liberals were fully aware of the Irish demand.[78] His critique of Gladstone vaunted his own watchful statescraft in dealing with English party leaders, his 'knowledge of English statesmen', of their peculiarities and of their sophistry'.[79]

Parnell's attacks on Gladstone excited acute unease among at least his Parliamentary supporters, and provoked in March the unique spectacle of a public dissent by a member of his party, Pierce Mahony, lamely endorsed by the *Freeman's Journal*. For Mahony, the break with Gladstone had been particularly distressing. He had written to Gladstone's wife Catherine, from the House of Commons library on 8 December, expressing 'the great sorrow it gives me to appear even for a time to be acting in opposition to Mr. Gladstone. In the course of the last ten days expressions have been used in moments of great excitement and passion, regarding Mr. Gladstone, which have given me great pain'.[80]

As the split progressed, the pressure on Parnell from his own side to moderate his attacks on Gladstone increased. There was a growing consensus in the country that the appropriate (bipartisan) nationalist policy was of 'fair play' for the Liberals. This would facilitate the introduction of a Home Rule Bill in the event of a Liberal-Nationalist victory at the general election, and provide the basis for a limited parliamentary accommodation between the two nationalist factions. Parnell adopted the 'fair play' policy in bitterly ironic terms, as affording an opportunity to expose the shallowness of the Liberal commitment to home rule:

> I have been accused of trying to keep the Liberal party out of power, and
> to keep Mr. Balfour in power. Now, that is a most untruthful accusation.
> If I could bring Mr. Gladstone into power tomorrow by lifting up my little
> finger I would do it. Why? Because I want the Irish people to see as quickly
> as possible the truth of the question, as I know and see it.[81]

Parnell thus, belatedly and sardonically, subscribed to the watchword
of 'fair play' for the Liberals, in terms of the opportunity which it afforded to expose the hollowness of the Liberal commitment to home rule, which
represented at least as deep an affront to Liberal professions of good intention towards Ireland as his fiercest attacks on Gladstone.

To his provoking embrace of the watchword of 'fair play' for the Liberals,
Parnell towards the end added the claim that his campaign had secured
a better settlement, and that the course of the split had itself demonstrated
that home rule was not in danger.

> You remember the threats that were held out to you some six months ago
> that unless you fell into line and obeyed the whip of Mr. Gladstone that the
> chance of Home Rule would be lost to our country. Such counsels were the
> counsels of cowardice, of intimidation, and of ignorance *(cheers)*. Ireland
> has today as good a chance of Home Rule as she ever had *(cheers)*. She has
> lost no ground on account of the creation of this great and independent party
> throughout the country ... On the contrary, she has gained respect for herself
> by this movement, and unquestionably she will continue to gain respect for
> herself from the English nation and from the peoples of the world *(cheers)*.
> The settlement of Home Rule when it does come, the Parliament which you
> will gain will be all the better, all the stronger, and all the more powerful,
> because there are some men, many men in Ireland still left of independent
> spirit and courage who were determined above all things and before all things
> to create Ireland's right of independence and of nationhood *(cheers)*.[82]

The argument, if it smacked somewhat of desperation, demonstrated
how determinedly Parnell was retrenching his position, and how formidable
an opponent he was likely to prove at the head of a minoritarian nationalist
party at Westminster. The notion of Parnellism as a stiffening force and
of Parnell maintaining a vigilant eye over any home rule settlement was
peculiarly troubling for the Liberals, and reminded them of the limited
extent to which Parnell's defeats, in Committee Room 15 and in Ireland,
had rid them of their most skilful adversary.

In the split, Parnell's smouldering dislike of Gladstone flared into open
loathing. Quite apart from the troubled history of their political relations,
Parnell harboured a professional disdain for the patronising grandiloquence
of Gladstone's political manner. He bridled at what he regarded as
Gladstone's cloying profession of disinterested benevolence towards Ireland,
which rendered Ireland a sentimental province of Liberal altruism, when
Gladstone was, as he believed. merely responding to a political necessity
sharpened by Parnellite strategy. This disdain had informed his celebrated

attack on Gladstone in October 1881 as 'this masquerading knight errant, this pretended champion of the liberties of every nation, except the Irish nation', which immediately preceded his arrest at the direction of Gladstone's government.[83]

Notwithstanding his unwonted lauding of Gladstone after their Hawarden meeting, Parnell's judgement of the Liberal leader was not greatly softened by Gladstone's espousal of home rule. He seemed to adhere to the view expressed by Joseph Biggar of Gladstone in his 'coercionist' phase, as 'a vain old gentleman'.[84] Parnell found Gladstone's prolixity particularly grating. After their Hawarden interview, Parnell declined to tell the journalist Edward Byrne the substance of what had passed, while adding 'but I will tell you this, the old gentleman did most of the talking!' Even in the fury of the manifesto, Parnell took the trouble to insert that sarcastic aside that at the Hawarden meeting the conversation was 'mainly monopolised by Mr. Gladstone'.[85] For Gladstone, wrote Byrne, Parnell appeared to have 'no genuine respect'. Parnell was much amused by a Tory comparison of the Irish treatment of Gladstone to that accorded by certain savage tribes to their idols who when they did not grant their prayers 'give them a good sound drubbing'.[86]

If any single consideration accounted for Parnell's cold rage in the split, it was the depth of his personal resentment of Gladstone's intervention. A note of furious Anglo-Irish hauteur is audible in his declaration that Gladstone 'could not have given such short notice to the meanest servant in his employment'.[87] Parnell's anger at his imprisonment by Gladstone in 1881-82 never abated. After the 1885 election, but before Gladstone's acceptance of home rule, Parnell observed to T. P. O'Connor 'with a smile, but in earnest all the time — that he meant to pay back that six months imprisonment'.[88] It was inevitable that he should have equated his imprisonment by Gladstone with the latter's intervention in the matter of the Irish leadership in 1890.

At Balbriggan in June 1891, in a vein of bitter irony, Parnell catalogued his grievances against Gladstone culminating in a ruthless reference to Gladstone's age, so as to suggest that retirement or death would supervene before Gladstone could crown his public career with the enactment of home rule:

> There are three things which Mr. Gladstone did in times past to myself which were fatal mistakes and which he will always have to regret. The first of them was putting me into Kilmainham Jail in the autumn of 1881 *(cheers)*. The second was letting me out of Kilmainham Jail in the spring of 1882 *(laughter)*; and the third was in interfering with the question of the leadership of the Irish party *(cheers)*; and I consider that the last step having been taken at a time when recovery is impossible, at all events for him, will prove to be so fatal a one that it will prevent the measure of usefulness which Ireland and Great Britain in common with Ireland, ought otherwise to have obtained from his services.[89]

Parnellite attacks on Gladstone were interspersed with references of vary-
ing degrees of brutality to Gladstone's age. Indeed Healy rationalised the
violence of his own attacks on Parnell in part as a retaliation for Parnell's
shameless playing on the fact that Gladstone was approaching his mortal
span. Parnell, however, was suggesting less death or failing powers than
that Gladstone, in the vanity of his old age, was frantic to consummate
his *mission civilisatrice* in Ireland, and that the urgency of his self-regard
had determined his course of action in the split.

He said of Gladstone to Barry O'Brien: 'He is an old man, and he cannot wait. I am a young man, and I can afford to wait'.[90] He implied that
Gladstone's improper intervention in the split was undertaken in the frenzied and unseemly haste brought on by intimations of mortality, which
belied the selfless dedication to Irish interests which Gladstone professed.
Parnell's attacks on Gladstone in this respect disclose his peculiar hubris,
which lay not in the megalomaniac craving of which he was commonly
accused, but in the uncompromising professionalism of his own temper
and judgement, sharpened by the split's adversity.

Parnell's anger was rooted in his sense that in intervening Gladstone had
committed a manifest error. He never wavered in his conviction that
Gladstone's intervention was in political terms wholly misconceived. His
attack was devised as an exactly proportioned retaliation for what he considered to be the Liberal leader's abrogation of the basis of their political
collaboration. He sought to confront Gladstone with what he insisted was
the havoc wreaked on the Liberal-Nationalist alliance by his incursion into the domain of the Irish leadership.

He fiercely asserted that it was Gladstone's intervention which had
precipitated the crisis within the Liberal-Nationalist alliance, that it was
Gladstone who had brought into play the underlying conflict of interest
between Nationalists and Liberals, and stripped bare the rhetoric which
had swathed the 'Union of Hearts'. He contended that Gladstone, by pro-
pounding a distortion of what the Liberal-Nationalist alliance entailed to
attack his leadership, had cut at the foundations of the alliance. Parnell
retaliated by a forceful restatement of the premise, or at least the necessary
myth, of Parnellism, that the home rule initiative was engendered by Irish
pressure rather than Liberal magnanimity.

Parnell charged that Gladstone in intervening on the question of the
Irish leadership had breached the protocol which underlay the Liberal-
Nationalist collaboration. Gladstone he insisted had made a grave and
elementary error, which had destroyed the equilibrium of the alliance. In
his Rotunda speech, he insisted that Gladstone had underestimated his own
authority, and with persuasive irony asked: 'Does he appear to be a nominal
leader — does he appear to be a thing of the past when he is able to bring
about a climax in Irish affairs we see today?' While acknowledging the
stature of Gladstone as the Liberal leader, Parnell declared: 'We decline

to fuse with you, we decline to surrender to you'. In a superb inversion, Parnell called on Gladstone to resume his rightful position, expressing his insistence that he had lost his own position only because Gladstone had exceeded his. He calmly asserted that the issue in the split was that Gladstone had compromised his leadership of the Liberal party, rather than that he himself had forfeited the leadership of the Irish party:

> ... the message that Ireland sends back to the Grand Old Man tonight is this: 'Resume your place as leader of your party; take up your legitimate authority, and when you have put yourself in the position of an independent leader such as ours, then, and not till then, will we allow our leaders to treat with you upon those equal terms which alone can assure a lasting, a peaceable, and a permanent settlement *(cheers)*.[91]

Parnell, whose policy from 1886 to 1890 had been increasingly bent towards procuring Conservative acquiescence in a Liberal measure of home rule, and to shaping Irish society in anticipation of home rule by means of land legislation, now found himself rudely wrenched back to the preceding phase, of fighting Gladstone over again. Contempt and considerations of policy fused in Parnell's wrath at what he derided as the anti-Parnellites' sentimental deference to an aged English opposition leader whose career was drawing to its close. At Boulogne, Parnell characterised Gladstone to O'Brien as personally senescent and politically superannuated: 'Parnell no longer looks upon Gladstone as the leader of the Liberal party. Gladstone, he thinks, is a helpless old man casting about left and right for hints. He says that Gladstone may have the will to help Ireland but he has not the power'.[92] If this prognosis was to prove in part correct, Parnell badly underestimated Gladstone's immediate resilience, and the allure of his name in Ireland.

Parnell charged that Gladstone had shown deficient judgement and political capacity by panicking in the face of the divorce court verdict. Not merely had Gladstone by his precipitate intervention breached the central principle of the Liberal-Nationalist alliance, he had thereby also committed a domestic political error and rendered himself powerless to resist the pressure of his own nonconformist wing. Parnell had declared at Kilkenny that 'the old women and humbugs of England are taking this opportunity of airing their virtue. They need not talk to Ireland about virtue.'[93] If Parnell had not Gladstone directly in contemplation as one of the 'old women and humbugs' of the nonconformist conscience, he certainly blamed him for having failed to withstand their predictable clamouring, thereby putting in jeopardy the prospects for a durable Irish settlement.

Gladstone, Parnell charged, had failed to realise the strength of his leadership of the Liberal party, the transience of the divorce outcry, and the buoyancy of the Liberal vote. He even seized on Liberal by-election victories after an initial reverse at Bassetlaw in December as evidencing the irrationality of Gladstone's pessimism. The Liberal party was, he insisted, on a course for victory from which it had not been deflected by the divorce crisis. The Liberal win at Hartlepool in late January demonstrated that his deposition was brought as the result of a false alarm, to which the majority had succumbed. The Hartlepool result demonstrated that 'it was not a case of Home Rule or no Home Rule, but a question about Home Rule and a miserable substitute', and 'scatters to the wind the talk of home rule being in danger, and the cause of Ireland being lost, because Ireland was never in danger'.[94]

Parnell now reiterated the principles of 1880-85. He insisted that the true position was that the Liberals were dependent on the Irish, and not vice versa: 'The Liberal party have a much greater interest in the settlement of this question than you have; they must settle it or they cannot return to power'.[95] Parnell later in the campaign reverted to the refrain of the 1885 election, the danger of a Liberal majority so large as to be independent of Irish support: 'If there is one thing more certain than another it is that the Liberal party will come into office at the next election, and the only question is whether they would not perhaps be a little too big and too powerful for poor little Ireland, as they were in 1880'.[96]

Parnell's attacks on the likely future composition of the programme and personnel of the Liberal leadership after Gladstone were better judged than his attacks on Gladstone himself. As he declared, ungrammatically but concisely, of Gladstone at the Rotunda, 'he is one man, and his party is another'.[97]

Parnell assailed the unfolding, cautious endeavour of the Liberal Party to recast its domestic programme in popular and progressive terms. The so-called 'Reserve Programme' of the Liberal party adopted by the National Liberal Federation at its annual meeting, at Newcastle, shortly before his death broadened the Liberal commitment to popular social reform. It was seized on by Parnell, as well as by Unionist critics, as effecting a dilution of the Liberal commitment to home rule. In thus warning of the conflict of priorities between home rule and British social reform, which was to prove a central political theme in the ensuing quarter century, Parnell in his last public statement showed himself ruthlessly prescient.[98]

Parnell had voiced his suspicions earlier in the split in relation to the contemplated Liberal commitment to universal manhood suffrage. Speaking in the House of Commons in April he said:

> We do not exactly know what the Liberal Programme is ... We have heard that it may be Home Rule, or rather 'one man one vote'. In recent times the balance seems rather inclining to 'one man one vote' as the *pièce de resistance*, at all events, for the first year'.[99]

While he endorsed the inclusion of a commitment to 'one man one vote' in the National League programme, he warned that it was 'a rather ambiguous expression, which will be of more importance to the English Liberal party than it will be to us'.[100] He argued that the franchise reform contemplated by the Liberals, while not extending the franchise in Ireland, would increase the franchise in England to the benefit of the Liberals, and would possibly be linked to a redistribution of the constituencies to lessen the Irish representation in the House of Commons. The effect would be to reduce the leverage of the Irish party at Westminster.[101]

Parnell attacked the shallowness of the commitment of the Liberal party at large to home rule. While shortly before the split Parnell had privately expressed his belief that the bulk of the Liberal party was dedicated to home rule, he claimed in July 1891 that the rank and file of the Liberal party in the House of Commons were unsound on the question of home rule, and that only one-third were in favour of home rule, while a majority 'would be satisfied with some form of ambiguous scheme of local government'.[102]

He repeatedly denounced the Radicals within the Liberal party as hostile to Irish interests as well as instrumental in procuring his defeat in Committee Room 15. He warned that reliance by Ireland on the Radicals would prove 'a broken reed which would pierce her hand'.[103] In suggesting that the dominant progressive ideology within the Liberal party was Radical rather than Gladstonian, Parnell was playing adroitly on the deep-rooted nationalist mistrust of radical ideology, of utilitarianism, and political economy. In an attack which astutely evoked the political landscape of Chamberlain's Birmingham, Parnell imputed the constricted historical sensibility of the Radicals to the Liberal party at large: 'They have acted without the knowledge which a study of our history would have given them ... They have shown their judgement — the judgement of the short-sighted English factory-owner and of the English caucus-monger without a knowledge of the glorious history of Ireland'.[104]

Parnell also trained his fire on Harcourt as the likely successor to Gladstone. He warned that Harcourt, rather than the more sympathetic and stalwartly pro-home rule Morley, would succeed to the Liberal leadership (which in the event passed in 1894 to Rosebery), and assailed Harcourt's coercionist record.[105] Parnell taunted Dillon and O'Brien on their release by referring to 'their new leader, Sir William Harcourt ... 'their taskmaster ... the future leader, the present leader of the seceders'.[106]

Parnell only once alluded to the mechanism by which the second Home Rule Bill was actually to be defeated in 1893. Replying to an interjection at Bermondsey he declared: 'You will never send the House of Lords about their business on an Irish question — you may on an English question. The people of England do not love the people of Ireland so much as to send the House of Lords about their business upon an Irish question'.[107]

The Anti-Parnellites

Leaving on one side 'the crocodile emotions' of Mr. Tim Healy, we may feel sure that with many of the party it was a real sense of patriotism that influenced their conduct. But it was 'a movement to the rear', rapid, and I think, undignified, in the truer sense of the word, as the world has hardly ever seen. Never did men 'execute themselves' with fewer searchings of heart or less compunction ... Are we to feel wholly amazed at the bitter scorn which has burst forth from Mr. Parnell? ... Mr. Parnell's nature has many black depths in it; but the stirring and the bringing of these depths to the surface has been the work of the light heart with which he was flung overboard, and the pettiness of the feelings which bubbled up so readily against him.

Auberon Herbert [108]

'The policy of the Tim Healyites' Parnell categorised as 'the policy of cowardice'.[109] His treatment of this charge was too often wildly vituperative. He linked the 'traitor's dart' to the 'coward's sneer'.[110] At Navan he declared: 'I thank God I never trusted some of my Parliamentary colleagues, who, within the last few weeks, have shown that they are endowed with the worst spirit of the informer.'[111] He referred at Wicklow to 'rats of secession'[112] and at Listowel to 'traitorous and cowardly seceders'.[113]

Yet, when he eschewed abusiveness, Parnell tellingly charged his parliamentary opponents with a serious failure of nerve, brought about by a debilitating deference towards the Liberal leader. In a characteristic martial image, he taunted the majority with succumbing to panic in the face of the Gladstone letter:

It was like a whisper through the ranks of an army going into battle that their enemies were about to overpower them; but the veteran soldiers, instead of being dispirited, closed up their ranks and put down these cowards and this poltroonery.[114]

This cowardice underlay the inconstancy of 'men who on the afternoon of one day elected their leader, and before the sun had set were flying, panic-stricken, from that leader before the voice of an English statesman'.[115] Having made up their minds on the Irish leadership, they 'because an English political leader and party tells them, unmake their minds ... some of them changed four times over, backwards and forwards, see-saw, until the public got giddy looking at them'.[116] In attacking the lack of competence of his opponents, Parnell asserted his own indispensability. He denounced 'the incapables' who sought to replace him, and declared 'none of these men is fit to lead the Irish party for twelve hours'.[117]

Parnell charged that the majority had disrupted the natural structure of command of the Irish party. Through his discernment of the talents and limitations of his lieutenants, he had put in place an objective hierarchy of aptitude and merit which their secession had broken up. He had shaped and honed the collective leadership of the party. He had taken the measure of his lieutenants: 'I know every one of them, and their weaknesses public and private. I know best what can be made of them and position they can best fill, and I have in my time made good use of them'.[118]

During the Carlow election Parnell convincingly characterised his own mode of leadership, and warned prophetically of an anarchic struggle for supremacy among the lieutenants he had selected.

> I have always endeavoured to find out as many eloquent Irishmen as possible to supply my own deficiencies in that respect, because my view of every man is that he is capable of some good if you keep him to the work for which he is best qualified. That was my view with reference to Tim Healy when I first brought him out. Every general's duty is to select the men best fitted for the different branches of the service. Some men are good for cavalry, some for artillery, and some good skirmishers, and so we got together a fine Irish army at Westminster until the time came when two or three or four of the skirmishers thought that they ought to become generals *(groans and laughter)*. And now we have eight of these skirmishers competing amongst each other as to who is going to be the general *(cheers for Parnell)*. I know them well enough to know this, that if' I was gone tomorrow, if they were not bound by the instinct of mutual self-preservation to hold together in order to try and overcome me, every one of these eight men would be at each other's throats *(cheers)* with just as much bitterness as they are at my throat now *(cheers)*.[119]

Parnell seized on the establishment of a Parliamentary Committee by the anti-Parnellites after Committee Room 15 to draw a contrast between his own decisive leadership and the ineffectuality of a directionless collective leadership riven by individual jealousies: '... I may almost be proud of this that it took nine men of the Irish party to fill the chair when they succeeded in dragging me out of it ... I don't believe in this dividend system of leadership'. He declared, 'It would have been a cowardly part to leave Ireland to be torn asunder by twenty factions who would have contended for the power and the place which they had deprived me of'.[120]

When Dillon gauchely described Parnell's strategy in Committee Room 15 as a 'rat trap' to split the majority, Parnell retorted with open mockery and dry wit:

> I am almost accused of having led the Irish Party into what? A rat trap *(laughter)*. I think Mr. Dillon might have spared his forty-four followers of Number Fifteen Committee Room the application of that suggestive word 'rat' *(loud laughter and cheers)*. I led these poor rats, according to Mr. Dillon, these innocent and confiding rats into a rat trap *(renewed laughter and cheers)*. I brought them into that room with a piece of toasted cheese *(laughter)*.[121]

In the Sligo election, he characterised his leading opponents with a brutal perceptiveness which the polemical context did not entirely obscure:

> ... I say that, knowing these forty-five seceders well and intimately for a long number of years, I say that there is not one of them fit to represent the national aspirations of the country or to save her from humiliation and death *(cheers)*. Can you make of any one of them a leader *(cries of 'No')* who would unite with him any section of the country or any section of his colleagues? Can you select the foul-mouthed Tim Healy *(groans and cries of 'no')*. Can you trust in uncertain and wobbling Tom Sexton? *(No)*. And can you follow hysterical Davitt, who never belongs to any party for twenty-four hours together? You cannot.[122]

Parnell cunningly intimated that his proper successor, after home rule had been achieved, would come from outside the ranks of the majority, and indeed from outside the ranks of the Irish party as a whole (a less than flattering reflection on his own supporters). At Bagenalstown he declared:

> I have not been able to see amongst the ranks of the Irish party any man of them that I could select as leader or to whom I could bequeath my place. I do not know that there are many hundreds of Irishmen capable of filling my place *(cries of 'no')*. But they have not had the chance of showing what is in them, and I claim the right and I ask you to permit me, having led you so far through the wilderness, until we are in sight of the promised land, until we are almost entering within the gates, not to thrust me back but to allow me to enter those gates with you *(cheers)*. And when we have obtained for Ireland the right to make her own laws on Irish soil ... then, fellow countrymen, if you like, you will be able to select a man in my place.[123]

At Sligo Parnell announced that, once Ireland had control of her destiny, he would retire and yield to the man chosen, from outside the ranks of the majority and by implication of the Irish party generally. Home rule would provide the opportunity 'of bringing to the front all that bright genius and intellect which so distinguished our country'.[124] This rhetorical undertaking to retire in favour of a leader coming from outside the ranks of the Irish party as then constituted, after the achievement of home rule, if crudely self-serving, permitted him to reply to Healy's charge of unfathomable arrogance in claiming to be, in the words of his supporters, 'the only possible leader', by means of a shrewdly ingratiating appeal to a new political generation.

The fact that he had selected and brought to prominence many of those who now opposed him prompted Parnell to reflect ironically on the charge of 'dictatorship' levelled against him. He asserted against the taunt that many of his opponents, in particular Healy and Arthur O'Connor, owed their presence in Parliament to his 'dictation',[125] and attributed his failure to keep one anti-Parnellite in line to 'the fact that I spared the rod and spoiled the child'.[126]

At his nadir, in Dublin in August, Parnell responded characteristically to the criticisms of his leadership: ' ... the only fault that I can charge myself with was of having been too lax, having been too amiable to many of my colleagues'.[127] The plaint was understandable, and reflected his private convictions. In conversation with R. Barry O'Brien, he observed that his greatest mistake had lain in affording an excessive discretion to his parliamentary lieutenants, particularly in the nomination of prospective members of parliament: 'They call me a dictator. I was not dictator enough ... It is called my party. It is everybody's party more than mine ... I did not build up a party of personal adherents. I took the nominees of others'.[128]

He pledged himself to 'lay bare the history of this movement'.[129] The split's controversy encompassed a bitter political retrospect, which marred the achievements of the Irish party in the preceding decade. Each side sought to arrogate to itself the credit for legislative achievements and deny the contribution of the other. While Parnell's polemical revisionism was less audacious than that of Healy, he demeaned himself in seeking to deprive those opposed to him of any of the credit theretofore accorded them for specific legislative achievements under his leadership. Thus Parnell sought to deny T. P. O'Connor the credit for what he referred to as 'my' Labourers' Act of 1883, which he claimed had been drafted by himself with the assistance of a London barrister he had personally retained for 'a draft of a measure which not even the genius of the great Timothy Healy was equal to'.[130] Parnell likewise sought unjustly to deprive Maurice Healy of any credit for the Arrears Act of 1882, which he described as 'my own Bill drawn up by me in Kilmainham, immediately after my release from Kilmainham', reducing Healy's role to that of a porter of law books.[131]

At Listowel in September Parnell again adverted to the disloyalty and want of political capacity of his opponents. From the moment the majority in Committee Room 15 showed 'the cloven hoof', he declared, 'I decided that nothing would ever induce me to lead such a pack again ... A general cannot be expected to take his place in front of men who will take the first opportunity of shooting him in the back'. He would not 'go under the leadership of men who have shown themselves so utterly incapable of political judgement, so utterly inconsistent in their actions, and so entirely ignorant of the springs and motions which actuate the purposes of the people with whom they have to deal'.[132] Thus Parnell gave his contention that the split in its latter phase was 'no longer a question of leadership' a final ironic twist: he could no longer bring himself to lead such men as the anti-Parnellite party was composed of.

He treated Justin McCarthy, chairman of the anti-Parnellite party, with private grace and affection, and open public contempt. He dismissed him as 'without an ounce of steel in his whole body', 'an amiable man, a quiet good-hearted soul ... the sort of a man who would be an ornament to a quiet and early tea party'.[133] He warned that the country would continue to experience political ineptitude 'until the kindly extinguisher of a general election and the voice of the City of Derry deprives our great leader *(roars of laughter)* of his place in Parliament'.[134] Parnell's indelicate electoral prophesy was ruthlessly accurate: McCarthy would indeed lose his marginal Derry seat to a unionist challenger at the 1892 election.

In the Kilkenny by-election Parnell retaliated against Davitt's charge of appealing to 'the hillside men' by impugning the constancy of his accuser.

> I haven't been a member of many parties like the jackdaw Davitt. I was not a physical force man in 1880, and did not desert in 1881. I did not become a member of the Land League in 1879 and leave it in 1883 *(cheers)*. I did not join Patrick Ford and his nationalisation of the land in 1885 and desert him in 1886. I did not then leave Patrick Ford and the *Irish World* in 1886 and join William Ewart Gladstone in 1887 *(cheers)*. I did not leave Gladstone and constitutional Home Rule in 1887 and attempt to upset it and undermine it by the formation of a so-called labour party in 1889 and 1890 *(cheers)*.[135]

Parnell's principal target, at least until the release of Dillon and O'Brien, was Healy rather than McCarthy or Davitt. If McCarthy epitomised 'the ignorance and the incapacity of the party', and Sexton its cowardice, Healy embodied its treachery.[136] It was in Parnell's clear interest to stress Healy's ascendancy within the majority: 'They might elect Mr. McCarthy one hundred times to the chair, but they did not make him their leader. Mr. Healy was their leader. It was from Mr. Healy they had taken their policy. It was his language that voiced their sentiments'.[137] In the Carlow election he referred to the majority as 'Tim Healyites', and mocked 'the new saviour of the Irish people, Timothy Healy'.[138] He sought thereby to taint the anti-Parnellites comprehensively with what he described as 'the immeasurable filth and blackguardism which issues from the lips of Tim Healy and Dr. Tanner'.[139] When he distinguished the bulk of his Parliamentary opponents, 'the inexperienced men and the faint-hearted men', from the few who had 'hearts of black malevolence towards their comrades and myself, only bursting to vent and give expression to it' who, he charged, had brought about the schism in the party, the name uppermost in the mind of his audience among the latter category was Healy's.[140] Parnell and his apologists built up a composite portrait of Healy as an Irish Iago, the lieutenant turned traducer, whose treachery was aggravated by ingratitude.

Healy was the principal object of Parnell's charge that his most envenomed opponents in the split had once been distinguished by their sycophancy towards him. In relating their virulence to their former praise, he astutely contrived to fix them with responsibility for the excesses of his cult.

> The men who are trying to hound me to death and to get me thrown in the common fosse of the camp were the men who were loading me with praise.

Figure 7 'The National Disgrace' (*Weekly Freeman's Journal*, 23 May 1891)

They were the very men, who when they expected anything from me, loaded me with fulsome adulation *(hear, hear)* ... I say that they were liars and always so *(cheers)*. But they were just as much unworthy of credit in the years gone by when they exaggerated my good services to Ireland as they are today, when they seek to defame and destroy me *(cheers)*.[141]

Healy's career was a study in betrayal:

I never knew the people of a nation who came to greatness or who obtained anything under the guidance of cowardly liars and slanderers like Tim Healy and his friends *(groans)*. The man has thriven at every stage of his career by slanders and lies. He has left every party that he ever belonged to, and he has always bitten every hand that cherished him ... I have not been false to any party, or to any political principle that I ever advocated *(cheers)*. I did not join the Fenian organisation at Newcastle on Tyne, and take an oath to be true to the Fenian Brotherhood, in order that I might have the opportunity in another two years of getting into Parliament and taking another oath to be true to the Queen of Great Britain and Ireland.[142]

The significance of the unfounded taunt of Fenian membership was as a charge of the culminating betrayal, in swearing conflicting oaths of allegiance.

Parnell pointed to the irony that he had placed Healy on the eminence from which he was now assailed. He asserted that in the absence of the 'dictation' with which he was charged '... it would have been a long time ... before the men of Wexford would have taken Mr. Timothy Healy from behind the counter'.[143] In Carlow he delivered his most comprehensive formulation of the charge of gross ingratitude against Healy, whom he alleged had received from him favours, preferment, and money:

I have always endeavoured to bring him to the front. I have always endeavoured to give him any chance of showing the ability and the talent which he undoubtedly possesses, while I never thought he was plotting behind my back and seeking to destroy me. I have served him, I have brought him forward. I have endeavoured to enable him to use his talents for his own interests as well as for that of the benefit of the country. I have filled his pockets with money and I have done everything for him that his very best friend could have done for him strenuously from the first to the last *(cheers)*. From the first moment then, in '79, I recognised his talent and capacity, from the moment that I brought him out of obscurity and gave him the power that he is using against me today, I befriended him and placed him in the position which he now occupies and utilises for purposes of slandering me.[144]

The specific allegations were largely either incorrect or misleading. Parnell had no direct involvement in procuring Healy's election for Wexford in November 1880, although Healy would not have been nominated but for his close association with Parnell. Any money paid to Healy was in respect of work for the Land League or National League. Yet the inaccuracies did not substantially detract from the cogency of Parnell's depiction of Healy as a soured apprentice.

Parnell woundingly charged that Healy had, after the Galway by-election of February 1886, sought to re-ingratiate himself with Parnell. He proceeded audaciously from the argument that Healy was disentitled by his post-Galway acquiescence in Parnell's leadership now to oppose him in the split:

> ... all I can say is that if he is actuated by patriotic motives in opposing my leadership he should have taken action many years ago, because in '85, six years ago, he accused me publicly and openly of the conduct and of the guilt which he is accusing me of today and recently in this town of Carlow, and after having accused me of that conduct he crept back to me and asked my forgiveness and my pardon. Nay more, after having accused me of that conduct he gave me his lip service. He acknowledged me as his leader *(cheers)*, and he took money from me *(cheers)*.[145]

Parnell dismissed Healy's accusation that he concluded the Kilmainham treaty to pursue his affair with Katharine O'Shea, as emanating from a man who had been in treaty with Joseph Chamberlain 'to sell me behind my back',

> ... and the origin of whose spite and malevolence was because I then checked his intriguing, as I have continued to from that day to this, when they have often been repeated, and when he taunts me with the mistrustful statement that I concluded a treaty with Joseph Chamberlain, I know well, and he cannot deny it, that he wished to conclude a treaty at that time, while I was in jail, with Joseph Chamberlain, behind my back and the backs of his party, and sell the cause of Ireland for nothing.[146]

If Parnell exaggerated the extent of Healy's dealings with Chamberlain, the charge at least accurately conveyed the suspicion he had formed at the time. Parnell remained ignorant to the end of Healy's much more incriminating attempts in 1885-86 to negotiate pre-emptively a home rule settlement with Gladstone, through Herbert Gladstone and Henry Labouchere,[147] the extent of which surpassed his wildest suspicions.

To Healy's attack on him as an Anglo-Irish landlord, Parnell retorted by denouncing Healy as a venal and ambitious barrister, and castigating the majority as a consortium of lawyers presided over by him. Parnell numbered sixteen lawyers among the majority, who were 'the salt and aristocracy of this great movement of secession'. Healy was the principal target of Parnell's observation on the patriotic decline and fall of the post-Union Irish bar: '... the bar of Ireland was at one time a patriotic body, but it unhappily ceased to be a patriotic body when we lost our Parliament, and it will never again become a patriotic body until a self-governed nation shows these gentlemen that the only way to preferment is through the hearts of their fellow countrymen'.[148] Parnell derided Healy as an aspiring Lord Chancellor.[149] He would not see constitutional action 'perverted ... and put into the hands of designing lawyers'.[150] He developed the allegation of his manifesto that Morley had suggested that one of the Irish law offices be filled by a member of the Irish party by charging that the Liberals would concede an insufficient measure of home rule, and, having broken the independence of the Irish party, would proceed to distribute places among its lawyers.[151]

Parnell struggled to retaliate against the 'Stop Thief' allegations by condemning Healy for avariciously hoarding his resources rather than applying them in Ireland: 'from first to last he has kept the interests of his own pocket steadily in view'. He alleged that Healy had invested £16,000 of the £20,000 to £30,000 he had received 'for his valuable services during the past ten years', in a floor-cloth factory in Kirkcaldy, Scotland — a reference to John Barry's linoleum business.[152]

Parnell attacked the Sullivans, Healy's kinsmen, as 'timid men'. He recalled his moment of disillusionment with one member of the family, presumably A. M. Sullivan, in the course of his endeavours to form an independent Irish party at the outset of his career, in the House of Commons: '... I went home with tears in my eyes, regretting that [my] idol had been shattered, and recognising for the first time that although genius and eloquence might be great things, courage and determination were greater still'. He also invoked the wavering of T. D. Sullivan in the face of clerical pressure in the Ennis by-election of 1879, 'shivering and shaking as he is now', and drawing the moral that 'the battle is not to be fought by timid or shivering men'.[153]

Parnell's attack on Healy was shrewdly pitched. Cumulatively the charge of disloyalty and ingratitude, the depiction of Healy as an unscrupulous opportunist in his relations with his former leader, ingratiating as circumstances required and treacherous when they permitted, represented a rhetorically effective dramatisation of the history of their relations and a telling characterisation of Healy. They conformed to the perception, widespread among both nationalists and unionists, of Healy as an uncouthly ambitious nationalist politician. *The Economist* characterised Healy as a real leader of the majority and as 'an ambitious and bitter man of the country attorney kind of mind', while the *Spectator* memorably observed that 'Mr. Healy, shrewdest of the faction, belongs to a class of men whom Irishmen have, with a sort of instinct equivalent to unconscious culture, throughout their history rejected as their leaders'.[154] Parnell's attack cut in granite the contemporary mistrust of Healy, and shaped hostile perceptions of Healy by anti-Parnellites as well as Parnellites for the duration of his long career in Irish politics.

Parnell's supporters followed his lead, seizing on Healy as the anti-Parnellite prototype. In Healy was discerned the profile of the most reviled stock character of nationalist politics, the socially aspiring Catholic who entered parliament in furtherance of an unscrupled desire to better himself and to slough off the traces of his origins. He was assailed in the intricate class discourse of nationalism as the uprooted clerk, lacking even the ancestry of decent agrarian destitution, who had through nationalist politics attained to the lucrative respectability of the bar, only to succumb finally to the corrupting ambience of Westminster.[155] The *Freeman's Journal*, in referring to 'Timothy Tappertit Healy', denounced him as a caricatural Dickensian *arriviste*, and asked: 'Where would Tim Healy be now if he had not got politics to get astride of? Would he not still be ticket-nipping on the railway at Newcastle-on-Tyne?'[156] The laboured snobbery of the Parnellite attacks on Healy ironically corresponded closely to the English social disdain which greeted Healy's early parliamentary career.

Healy featured in Parnellite speeches and cartoons generally as a Castle barrister, and aspirant to the Lord Chancellorship, and was falsely accused of having taken crown bribes while acting for the defence in the course of the Maryborough trials in 1889.[157]

Most tellingly, Healy's relations with Parnell were presented as a progression from insinuation to betrayal. He was reviled in Parnellite rhetoric as an insidiously disloyal former acolyte, whose adulation of Parnell conduced, through the mimesis of corrupted ambition, to attempted usurpation. He was characterised by the *Freeman's Journal* as Parnell's 'ingrate and rebellious ex-private secretary'.[158]

The Parnellites charged that Healy had been seduced by the atmosphere of Westminster and by his social relations with the Liberals. Years before Healy had boasted of his refusal to 'civilize himself', and observed that 'so far as the House of Commons was concerned the great force of civilization was the dinner napkin'. The *Freeman's Journal* now taunted Healy with having succumbed to the 'dinner napkin'.[159] Andrew Kettle charged that Healy had 'a standing invitation to Gladstone's table or Chamberlain's table'.[160]

Inevitably the 'Bantry Gang' (or 'Band')* featured prominently in Parnellite attacks as a sinister parvenu dynasty which had systematically aspired to usurp Parnell's leadership. Harrington asserted that the split was precipitated by 'a few individuals in Dublin, a small family party'.[161] The *Freeman's Journal* gave extravagant expression to its metropolitan disdain for what it derided as an aspiring provincial dynasty, 'a gang from a remote corner of the island whose inordinate grasping and self-seeking have already pressed the patience of Irishmen'.[162] Writing in 1895, James

---

* The term 'Bantry Band' originally referred to the numerous members of the Irish party who hailed from Bantry or its environs. There were ten members from Bantry or close by over the decade 1882-92: T. M. Healy, Maurice Healy, Thomas J. Healy; A. M. Sullivan, T. D. Sullivan, and Donal Sullivan; Timothy Harrington and Edward Harrington; William Martin Murphy; James Gilhooly. T. D. Sullivan later defended the undefiled purity of Bantry by observing that the Harrington brothers, who were Parnellite in the split, were from Berehaven (T. D. Sullivan, *Bantry, Berehaven, and the O'Sullivan Sept* [Dublin, 1908], p. 89). The later and most common use of the term was as a pejorative designation of the Healy-Sullivan connection in nationalist politics.

O'Kelly saw in Committee Room 15 'the culmination of a long premeditated effort to drive Mr. Parnell from the leadership of the Irish nation' and commented that the 'Bantry gang' had been permitted to pack the party 'until there seemed to be a danger that there would soon be no room for anyone in Parliament who did not happen to be at least a son-in-law of one of the numerous Sullivans or Healys'.

The correspondent of the *Manchester Guardian*, who had covered the Kilkenny and Carlow elections, wrote on Parnell's death of 'the extraordinary mingling of deep impersonal feelings with imperious self-assertion which was seen in all the acts and speeches of the Irish campaign'.[163] What gives Parnell's speeches in the split their fusion of abstract considerations of policy with fierce personal intensity is his sense of his own proficiency in the techniques of power. His dogged combativeness in the split was rooted in his sense of the unsoundness of Gladstone's intervention against him, and the deficient capacity demonstrated by the Irish party and by the hierarchy in upholding that intervention. His insistence on the correctness of his own judgement against that of his opponents provided the justification for his course in the split, culminating in the supreme derision of his designation of the controllers of the Plan of Campaign as 'a parcel of idiots', and his fastening upon Dillon's description of Committee Room 15 as 'a rat-trap'. Even when Parnell purported to deny at Listowel in September 1891 that what was involved was a question of leadership, his argument made clear that that was precisely what was at issue:

> Now, it has always appeared to me that the question of leadership has only come into the subject because it so happened that it was on the question of the leadership that the majority of the elected representatives of Ireland had the first chance of showing their weakness and their incapacity *(applause)*. They would have done so sooner or later on some other question. Our enemies try to make out that this is all a question of leadership *(hear hear)* ...[164]

Parnell's furious sense of affronted professionalism is perhaps the consideration most neglected in interpreting his last campaign. His exacting sense of professional competence affords a preferable explanatory hypothesis for his political course in the split than those conventionally advanced of thwarted megalomania, or of a mystical identification with a pseudo-fenianesque conception of the nation.

Parnell's professional anger informed his strategy in Committee Room 15 and again at Boulogne, finely poised between on the one hand alleviating the difficulty of majority brought about by what he believed to be their misjudgement, and on the other contriving to hold them to the consequences of their expressed choice, and almost obsessively condemning them repeatedly to rehearse their initial error. The same exasperated professionalism helped inspire his angry perseverance in defeat, and accounts for his isolation from his parliamentary colleagues. His frustration at the failure of his friends and allies to comprehend the thrust of his campaign was aggravated by an unforgiving self-reproach for his persisting failure to turn the course of events in his own favour.

The fanaticism imputed to Parnell in the split, such as it was, owed much to this exacting sense of political excellence. What he repeatedly described as his 'responsibility' was instinct with impersonal pride in the technique of power.[165] His campaign, which Healy so devastatingly reduced to the acting out of an overweening personal ambition, derived to a neglected degree from the unremitting classicism of his political technique. In the split he passionately asserted the coldness of his political logic. Under the vehemence and intermittent excess of his rhetoric lay the hard and unyielding lineaments of the Parnellian conception of power.

The 'Appeal to the Hillsides': Parnell and the Fenians

> 'I know', said Charles Stewart Parnell in private conversation in 1881, to a Fenian leader who doubted his power to deal effectively with English parties by Parliamentary action. 'I know I can bring English parties to their knees over this Home Rule question without risking anything like an insurrectionary movement. I cannot tell you how I will do it. Perhaps, I do not know exactly myself. But I am convinced that I can do it and that I will do it'.[166]

The attractive, but inhistorical, interpretation of the split as a climactic chapter in a fixed and constant struggle for ascendancy between parliamentary nationalism and a unitary and historically invariant 'physical force' tradition (habitually linked to the thesis that the Irish party succumbed belatedly to the death-wound of the split some twenty-five years after its infliction) continues to distort perceptions of Parnell's campaign in the split.

Perhaps the central criticism of Parnell in the split was that he embarked upon an 'appeal to the hillsides' which compromised his standing as a constitutional nationalist. Yet, while he made an overt pitch for Fenian support, he did so in terms which neither derogated from his commitment to parliamentary action, nor marked a break from the classic politics of Parnellism. The definitive articulation of the 'appeal to the hillsides' came in a celebrated passage in Parnell's speech in the Rotunda on his return to Ireland immediately after his defeat in Committee Room 15:

I have not promised you success, but I have said, and I repeat tonight, with all the force and energy that my poor words can give to the declaration — that if Ireland cannot win upon this line within the constitution she can win upon no other line within the constitution *(cheers)*, and that if our constitutional movement today is broken down, sundered, separated, discredited, and forgotten, England will be face to face with that imperishable force which tonight gives me my vitality and power *(loud and prolonged cheers)*, and without which we are broken reeds, bending and blown about by every puff of wind. And if Ireland leaves this path upon which she has trodden until she is almost in sight of victory, I will not for my part say that I will not accompany her further *(cheers)*; but I shall claim for myself the right which each one of you has to consider the future, to be warned by the mistakes of the past, and to shape his course as the side lights and the guide lights and head lights may best direct for the future success and prosperity of Ireland *(cheers)*. You may ask what I mean? Whether I intend to cross the Rubicon and burn my boats? I cross no Rubicon *(cheers)*. I have no boats to burn *(cheers)*; but my position is the position of 1880; and I say to you, and to all Irishmen — beware while you have time and while the power is still in your hands before you surrender for ever a force which you cannot control, the illimitable power of our race which has shown itself on these streets of Dublin tonight, without which I should be worthless and useless, with which I am strong *(cheers)*, and with which at my side I pledge myself to push forward until we have either reached the goal, or until the majority of the Irish people tell me that the goal is not there, and that I must try some other method.[167]

It is surely more convincing to interpret this passage as a demonstration of Parnell's consummate mastery of Irish democratic politics, rather than as an equivocation in the pursuit of constitutional methods. In an arabesque of double negatives, Parnell affirmed the dependence of parliamentary action on continued popular support and demonstrated effectiveness, a contention with which every contemporary constitutional nationalist would have been constrained to agree. The reference to 'that imperishable force which tonight gives me my vitality and power', with its hint of insurgency, has a calculated Fenian resonance. Yet what gives the argument its rhetorical force is Parnell's recasting of the commonplace argument that if parliamentary nationalism failed physical force would take its place, to invest constitutional politics with renewed vigour and urgency. With masterly elusiveness Parnell cheated Fenian ideologues of any substantive concession. He made the quintessentially Parnellian point that he alone was capable of leading the constitutional movement while constraining, and directing into constitutional channels, Fenian energies and sentiment. In the dancing syntax, he affirmed a constitutional purpose.

Rather than a rupture with his past, his speech was an avowal of constancy, an electrifying restatement of the premises of parliamentary action and an assertion that the Liberal alliance had not compromised the essential character of Parnellism. In response to the slackening of nationalist discipline and purpose wrought by the Liberal alliance, Parnell sought to achieve a sharpening of the inner logic of Parnellism, a tautening of those tensions which provided its political dynamic. His 'appeal to the hillsides', such as it was, drew its force from the assertion that his overthrow could portend a Fenian resurgence. Throughout his career Parnell systematically exaggerated the Fenian threat to his authority, to reinforce his indispensability as a leader, and to force the pace of constitutional reform. This had always been part of the armoury of his tactics: once deployed against the British government and party system, it was now directed within Ireland in furtherance of his quest to reconstitute his leadership.

Parnell's 'appeal to the hillsides' lay principally in the contention that constitutional action required to be justified in terms of its effectiveness. His most seemingly extravagant rhetoric was reducible to the unexceptionable commitment that he would desist from parliamentary politics when it became in his judgement ineffectual: that he would in that event so advise the Irish people, withdraw from politics and not impede the adoption by the country of other political courses. His pledge was of intellectual honesty: 'I have not misled you ... I have never said that this constitutional movement must succeed'. He promised that should parliamentary politics become demonstrably barren he would admit this candidly rather than seek to deceive the country by lending his authority to a perseverance in futile courses. It was a daring and masterly argument. Without compromising his constitutional purpose, Parnell sought to turn his weakness to strength. With unflinching suppleness he threw his full weight upon the paradox that he was at once the only constitutional leader who commanded a degree of confidence among Fenians, and the parliamentary leader who could most capably thwart and defeat Fenianism. Through this dynamic counterbalancing Parnell sought to recreate the matrix of his power.

At Kilkenny, in rejecting Davitt's taunt that he was engaged in an appeal to the 'hillside men' and was leading young men into insurrectionary courses, Parnell restated the argument of the Rotunda speech:

> I have not promised to lead them against the armed might of England. I have told them, so long as I can maintain an independent Irish Party in the English Parliament, there is hope of winning our legislature by constitutional means ... So long as we can keep our Irish Party pure and undefiled from any contact or fusion with any English Parliamentary party, independent and upright, there is good reason for us to hope that we shall win legislative independence for Ireland by constitutional means *(cheers)*. So long as such a party exists I will remain at its head *(loud cheers)*. But when it appears to me that it is impossible to obtain Home Rule for Ireland by constitutional means — and this is the extent and limit of my pledge *(cheers)*, that is the pledge which has been accepted by the young men of Ireland whom Michael Davitt in his derision calls the hillside men — I have said that when it is clear to me that I can no longer hope to obtain our constitution by constitutional and Parliamentary means I will in a moment so declare it to the people of Ireland, and returning at the head of my party I will take counsel with you as to the next step *(loud cheers)* ... if the young men of Ireland

have trusted me it is because they know that I am not a mere Parliamentarian; that I can be trusted to keep my word to them to go as far as a brave and honest heart can go on this Parliamentary alliance, and test it to the uttermost, and that when and if I find it useless and unavailing to persevere further, they can depend upon me to tell them so *(cheers).*[168]

While one might demur at the use of the term 'mere parliamentarian', by which Parnell intended to recommend himself to advanced nationalists, it hardly amounted to a detraction from his constitutional purpose. The phrase occurred elsewhere in Parnell's rhetoric in the split. 'Although we may be mere Parliamentarians, we do not recognise, and we never admitted that we were permanent Parliamentarians', he declared to cheers at the banquet in Cork in March.[169] This represented little more than the assertion that constitutionalism was not an end in itself, but the most effective means to an end. It was further an avowal of patriotic integrity, of incorruptibility in the face of parliamentary pomps and forms: 'I did not go to Westminster as a placehunter or to become an English party man'.[170] At Newry in March Parnell reverted to this theme:

The Irish people accepted my declaration sixteen years ago that there was a fair hope and possibility of regaining our national rights by means of an independent Irish party *(hear, hear)*. I did not pretend to you then that it was possible always or for ever to maintain independent members at Westminster. I told you often of the great dangers, the insidious influences which are always at work to sap the independence and integrity of Irish members there *(hear, hear)*. I told you to beware of those influences. I told you that without an independent party I would take no part in Parliamentary action ... I stand here today, unhappily, to commence a great deal of my work over again ... I cheerfully look, and with confidence, for the decision to be given by the Irish people, and I will submit to no other decision *(applause)*. And if that decision should be in favour of the slavery of our race, and the dependence of our people upon any English political party or statesman, I shall bow to it, and I shall retire from constitutional agitation *(loud cries of 'Never')* and from public life. I shall admit my failure, while regretting it *(never)*, but I will never be a party to misleading the men who have stood by me, the men who have given me the position which I hold today *(hear hear)*, and I will never ask them to trust in a weapon which has proved to be blunted and corrupt *(applause)*. But fellow countrymen, I am confident that that time will not come, and that the decision of Ireland when she is given the opportunity will be clear and decisive, and although we may not have as numerous a party as we had in 1885, it will be more solid, it will be stronger, its principles will be clearer, and more independent *(hear, hear)*.[171]

What rendered even this limited commitment somewhat academic, was that Parnell reserved to himself the judgement as to whether parliamentary methods in fact no longer held out any realistic hope of success, and so constituted himself the sole arbiter of the effectiveness of constitutional politics. He was sedulously evasive as to when the point at which constitutional politics could be considered to have failed might be reached. He pointedly declined to equate a Parnellite defeat at the ensuing general election with the failure of constitutional politics. At worst his rhetoric contained an implicit threat to desist from constitutional politics in the event of a defeat so annihilating as to eliminate entirely the Parnellite representation at Westminster — an exceedingly remote prospect — and he did not commit himself even to this.

What appears initially to be a pledge to withdraw from politics, once he adjudged perseverence futile, was rather an affirmation of his resolve to fight on so long as there was a Parnellite party in Parliament. Similarly, when he declared at Balbriggan that if it ever became too evident to him that the struggle at Westminster was hopeless, 'I shall come back to the Irish people and I shall tell them that constitutional effort by parliamentary action has failed', he was careful to add that he had no more fear of that contingency arising than at any time in the preceding sixteen years 'although our discouragement at the moment may be great and heavy'.[172]

Parnell in the split thus contrived to couple a rhetorical play for Fenian support with a fierce and intense affirmation of his constitutional purpose:

> I shall stand upon this constitutional platform until they have torn away the last plank from under our feet. I desire to say here tonight that we can win on the constitutional platform. But if we cannot win upon it, well, I shall be prepared to give way to better and stronger men, and it can never be said of us that we have prevented better or abler men than ourselves from dealing with the future of our race.[173]

The dramatic opening image is hardly that of a man despairing of constitutional politics, or seeking to subvert public belief in parliamentary action.

Parnell throughout the split celebrated the establishment of the primacy of constitutional methods as an achievement of his own leadership. He declared that 'the Parliamentary weapon has now been more brought within the grasp of the humblest peasant', and lauded 'this great constitutional weapon'.[174] Parnell's references to the ascendancy of parliamentarianism and the eclipse of physical force nationalism were, it is true, on occasion imbued with a vague hint of menace, as at Tipperary in April:

> Tipperary has had to fight its own battles in the days gone by outside the constitution *(cheers)*. Perhaps there is no other county in Ireland so little indebted to the constitution as the county of Tipperary ... However these are reminiscences of the past which will never come again. As an apostle of constitutional methods I should be ashamed of myself if it were necessary for those bygone times to return.

Yet he proceeded to develop his argument with impressive temperateness:

> We can contend for the first time in history upon an equal footing within the constitution for our rights ... Permit not then, fellow countrymen, these forces, these weapons of precision, sharpened as they have been by years

of exertion, to be directed against yourselves, and the men proved to be good in your cause.[175]

Parnell was not departing from the path marked out from the outset. As Elizabeth Bowen later wrote, he had 'set out to concentrate Irish will and to break down the Irish mistrust of constitutionalism'.[176] He did not resort to the cynically despondent evocation of the woes of Irish history commonplace among jaded nationalist rhetoricians, but vibrantly asserted the possibility of prevailing against the odds, and by disciplined constitutional action breaking the cycle of defeat. Parnell's characteristic technique was to induce Fenian sympathisers to impute to him a deeper affinity with their views than he actually possessed. He achieved this by conveying a sense of heightened understanding of Fenian sensitivities, and an intimation that his practise of parliamentary politics was not hidebound by that bourgeois Catholic nationalist constitutionalism which excited particular Fenian mistrust. Accusations of Fenianism levelled against him served Parnell's purpose particularly well. In response to Davitt at Kilkenny, he declared 'when anybody has the audacity to taunt me with being a hillside man I say to him that I am what I am because I am known to be an honest and unchanging Irishman'.[177]

To Harcourt's taunt that he was espousing 'Fenian Home Rule' Parnell retorted: '... I tell Sir William Harcourt, who derides Irish nationality and terms it Fenianism, that unless he and the English Liberal party recognise this spirit they may bid goodbye to the attempt to reconcile Irish public opinion or to settle the Irish question'.[178] The concluding portion of Parnell's last speech on an Irish platform was addressed to this subject:

> ... we do not subscribe to Sir William Harcourt's doctrine that the legitimate independence of Ireland means a recourse to the resources of Fenianism, of outrage, and of dynamite. We tell Sir William Harcourt that in using those words he is a liar. Ireland has a right to her legitimate freedom, and when Sir William Harcourt defines our platform according to that fashion we see his measure of sympathy for Ireland, and the desire of the new leader of the Liberal Party to give Ireland her legitimate freedom.[179]

Parnell's rhetoric in the split was not without precedent in his career. His assertion in the manifesto that the integrity and independence of a section of Irish members had been 'apparently sapped and destroyed'[180] had been prefigured in pronouncements at the outset of his career. Then he used the time-hallowed theme of the deleterious effect wrought by sustained presence at Westminster on the patriotic fibre of Irish members to invest parliamentary politics with a sense of purpose that it had previously lacked, so as to render the constitutional struggle 'short, sharp and decisive like a bayonet charge'.[181] From the outset he had warned against 'contaminating influences in the House of Commons' and declared he was not one of those who believed in the permanence of an Irish party in the

House of Commons', because of his conviction that 'sooner or later the influence which every English government has at its command ... will sap the best party you can return to the House of Commons'.[182] At Tralee, in January 1891, he cited a remark he had made in the town some twelve years earlier to the effect that the air of London was 'very contaminating'.[183]

Parnell had dramatically restated this caveat in a speech at his zenith in May 1889, when he stated he would not remain in the House of Commons once it had become very clear that parliamentary nationalist efforts to achieve self-government were unavailing:

> ... the most advanced section of Irishmen, as well as the least advanced, have always thoroughly understood that the parliamentary policy was to be a trial and that we did not ourselves believe in the possibility of maintaining for all time, or for any lengthened period, an incorrupt and independent Irish representation at Westminster.[184]

This speech has been rightly interpreted as a corrective adjustment necessitated by his dismissal of Fenianism as an historical force in his evidence to the special Commission.[185] He sought thereby to renew his strange rapport with Fenianism, conveyed in allusive hints of imaginative affinity and historical sympathy, which rendered his firm and unyielding containment of Fenianism endurable to its adherents. He sought to convey then, as he would again in the split, that he alone of parliamentarians had an innate understanding of the predicament of the Fenian sensibility. What might be called Parnell's affective compact with Fenianism was that he would pursue a constitutional solution in a manner which would not gratuitously wound Fenian susceptibilities, and would ensure that the values and politics of the home rule state were not those of a supremacist conservative Catholic nationalism.

On Parnell's death the perceptive correspondent of the Gladstonian Liberal *Manchester Guardian* who covered the Kilkenny and Carlow elections attested his abiding reserve:

> As one heard him speaking to an Irish audience in Carlow, or even in Kilkenny, one seemed to find the secret of his power over Irishmen in the high degree in which he possessed two or three distinctly un-Irish qualities. In his best speeches he never followed his audience. He always led them. Complaisance to their hearers is nearly always a vice of Irish speakers. Mr. Parnell was constantly pulling his audience back, constantly moderating a sweeping sentence that had been uproariously cheered with some exception or statement that brought a dead silence upon everybody. As one heard him, for instance, in the fine speech — scarcely reported in England — that he made at Bagenalstown on the day before the polling at Carlow, one felt that the standard of value for Irish public assertion was rising ... But even the written speech gives little idea of the high reserve of Mr. Parnell's delivery ... When he spoke thus he was the embodied corrective of Irish national faults, and the complement that the national character needs before it can attain completeness and efficiency.[186]

This commentary serves as a corrective to Healy's caricature of Parnell as the ruthless saboteur of constitutional politics, and to the complementary extreme nationalist myth of Parnell.

It is true that Parnell's assertions of the contingent nature of constitutional action acquired in the split an emphasis and occasionally a crudity which disconcerted many contemporary nationalists. Yet Parnell could validly, and did fiercely, assert the unity of his career and the constancy of his political principles. His campaign in the split constituted a furious challenge to the anti-Parnellite contention that the success of the movement under his tutelage had rendered redundant the principles he had laid down at the commencement of the struggle.

After the Kilkenny election, Parnell brought to prominence the issue of amnesty for 'political' prisoners convicted for treason felony arising out of the dynamite campaign of 1883-84 in England. The advocacy of amnesty, based on humanitarian considerations and on juridical doubt as to the correctness of the convictions, was common to Parnellites and anti-Parnellites. Parnell, while invariably coupling his references to the subject with a deprecation of physical force, contrived to transform the amnesty question into a bridge between Parnellism and Fenianism.

He sought to identify himself closely with the amnesty issue in speeches at Limerick and Waterford in January 1891, in the latter of which he proclaimed extravagantly asserted that 'the question with which my mind, heart and soul has been identified from the first moment of my entry into politics has been the question of amnesty which founded the home rule movement, which brought myself and others to Irish life'.[187] In late February he agreed to attend an amnesty rally, and expressed his desire to enrol as a member of the Amnesty Association of the National Club.[188] At the rally, in the Phoenix Park in April, he determinedly sought to appropriate the amnesty issue for his own political purposes. He exploited the opportunity it presented for an attack on the Liberal party, alluding to 'the remarkable coincidence ... that the Liberals have always been distinguished for making political prisoners and the Tories for letting them out again'. Parnell, notorious for his habitual eschewal of poetic allusion, was in unwontedly lyrical mood, and it is difficult not to discern some trace of cynicism in the maladroit sentimentalism of his declaration, prompted by a downpour, that 'the quality of mercy is not strained, it falleth like the gentle rain from heaven'. He asserted that 'I have always thought that the most beautiful prayer in the English language is that which asks the Almighty to have mercy upon all prisoners and captives'. Rather more characteristically, he added, 'I know the language of petition and of supplication is not what is asked of us by those men if they could speak to us'. He declared that 'mere politicians, mere Members of Parliament, should feel a sense of shame in standing to plead the case of the political prisoners'.[189] This denigration of parliamentarians *vis-à-vis* Fenian prisoners was Parnell's most abjectly ingratiating deployment in the split of the term 'mere parliamentarians', and could only tend to validate the exclusionary rhetoric which Healy directed against him in the split.

In the House of Commons in July, Parnell moved a reduction in the prisons vote to advocate the granting of political status to the prisoners, and a measure of amnesty, canvassing the possibility that they had been convicted 'owing to a most disgraceful plot on the part of the Irish police and Home Office of that day' — the latter being a reference to Harcourt's home secretaryship. He warned: 'You will always have political prisoners so long as the Irish question remains unsettled'.[190] Supporting a clemency resolution of John Redmond a week later, he argued from the demonstrated obsoleteness of the dynamitard strategy: 'These conspiracies, even in America, have now been abandoned for many years, and nobody now wishes to blow up the British Empire with dynamite — an idea which has passed out of the view of the most extreme Irishmen'.[191] So it was that Parnell's last three speeches in the House of Commons were concerned with the issue of amnesty and the plight of political prisoners.[192]

The anti-Parnellites denounced Parnell's ostentatious espousal of the amnesty issue as wholly cynical, and warned that Parnell's advocacy of their cause was likely to militate against the interests of the prisoners themselves. The *National Press* accused Parnell of neglecting the three Phoenix Park prisoners, the 'hapless remnant of a terrible conspiracy', in favour of the dynamitards whom he believed to have 'friends in Ireland', and warned that his opportunistic adoption of their cause would hinder their release, which could only be urged 'on grounds of clemency and expediency'.[193] It charged that a fatal mistake had been made in permitting amnesty to be identified with 'the failing and degraded cause of Parnellism': 'The result of the alliance of Amnesty with Parnellism ... tends to double-bolt the doors of those prisoners'.[194] William O'Brien alleged that Parnell had failed to respond to representations made on behalf of the prisoners prior to the split, which he denied.[195]

Parnell's evidence to the Special Commission had placed his relations with Fenians under severe strain. His writing of Fenianism out of contemporary Irish history had approached the patriotic recantation which Fenian diehards believed to be the ineluctable nemesis of the parliamentary politician.[196] His treatment of the amnesty question in the formation of the home rule movement permitted him to atone for his affront to Fenian susceptibilities. The issue of amnesty had acted as a catalyst in the emergence of the home rule party under Isaac Butt: in the split Parnell sought, by enlarging the significance of this circumstantial role, to acknowledge the involvement of Fenians in the shaping of the home rule movement.

At Waterford in January, he declared that the home rule movement owed

its existence to 'the upheaval of feeling on behalf of those imprisoned suf-
ferers in 1870 ... they are the men whose sufferings led to the foundation
of our movement and without whom we should be nought'. At Listowel
in September, he went so far as to assert 'it would be no exaggeration of
me to say that to the question of amnesty belongs most of the success which
has attended the constitutional movement of later years'. This a flagging
Parnell, in limp and hackneyed vein, attributed to the patriotic inspiration given by Fenian prisoners at a time when parliamentary politics were
sunk in disfavour.

> It was the sacrifices and the sufferings of the men of '65 which kept alive
> during many long years the spirit of Nationality in the heart of the Irish
> people. If the betrayal of Keogh and Sadlier in 1852 had caused the hottest
> Irishmen to despair of the future of the country, these men in those days
> did not despair, and the national spirit of Irishmen burned with renewed
> vigour as a consequence of their enterprise and their sufferings *(cheers)*. For
> them there were no honours and rewards; for them there was no applause
> of crowded public meetings; for them there was no seat in Parliament, which
> many of your latter-day Nationalists think the crown of the Irish patriot's
> ambition.[197]

Parnell at Limehouse in May similarly contrived to pay historic tribute
to Fenianism, in adumbrating a 'history of Irish reform'. The achievement
of reform in Irish history was due to 'the courage and union of the Irish
people alone':

> ... no English statesman, from Gladstone to Balfour, has ever done anything
> for Ireland until he had first tried by imprisonment, persecutions, by penal
> servitude — aye, and by executions — to destroy the unity of our race and
> the independence of our people *(applause)*. That is the history of Irish reform,
> and the English friends who come here tonight to instruct us in Irish politics
> [*a reference to hecklers*] do not know the history of Catholic Emancipation.
> Early in the century, when it would not be conceded by England to Ireland
> until the English Ministry told the Sovereign and the Parliament that unless
> it was conceded Ireland would be lost to England *(applause)*. They forget
> the history of the passage of the Irish Church Act, and of the Land Acts
> of 1867 and 1870, when these measures were yielded to the intensity of
> Fenianism which were denied to the considerations of justice *(applause)*. It
> was not until — to use Mr. Gladstone's own words — 'the explosion at
> Clerkenwell had tolled the chapel bell', that even his conscience was awakened
> to the terrible injustice and crime of supporting an alien Church of Ireland
> out of the pockets of the masses of the Catholic people *(applause)*.[198]

Parnell's dubious 'history of Irish reform' promiscuously linked
Parnellism with O'Connell and with Butt, and pointedly if obliquely with
Fenianism, availing of the admitted effect of the Clerkenwell explosion in
arousing Gladstone's conscience to an awareness of injustice in Ireland.

Parnell's veiled tribute to Fenianism, archly couched in the form of a
historical acknowledgement, arguably went further than his political purposes rendered strictly necessary or desirable. Yet it presented also the

creative obverse of Parnell's so-called 'appeal to the hillsides', whereby he
sought as he had throughout his career to embrace Fenianism within an
ambitiously conceived constitutional movement. It was a renewal of one
of the classic motions of Parnellism, the implicating gesture, the drawing
inward of Fenianism to within a unitary nationalist movement. In according to Fenianism a deliberately exaggerated measure of credit for the success of nationalism under his leadership, he was seeking once again to
encompass Fenianism within a quintessentially Parnellian synthesis.

To assess adequately the rapprochement between Parnell and Fenianism
it is necessary to consider the nature of the Fenian allegiance which Parnell
attracted, and in particular the position of John O'Leary, James Stephens,
and other Fenians in the split: in this aspect the split is an essay in the
renewal of the complex equivocality with which Parnell was regarded within
the Fenian movement. This in turn requires a reconsideration of the nature
of contemporary Fenianism. Twentieth-century nationalist and republican
ideologues have obscured the complex and diverse character of late-
nineteenth-century Fenianism, and the sharp discontinuities which demar-
cate Fenianism in the era of Parnell from its professed successor movements,
discontinuities so sharp as to render problematic and tendentious the concept of a 'Fenian tradition'. This calculated ideological misrepresentation
has influenced *à rebours* modern liberal historiography, and issued in the
tendency to project anachronistically on to the Parnell era the malaise of
twentieth-century Irish republicanism.

What united Fenians of the old school was a commitment to Irish independence, in the attainment of which they were willing to countenance
a resort to physical force. Their conception of legitimate physical force
was however so severely circumscribed ethically, and so militarily obsolete,
as to render it somewhat platonic. Old Fenians such as John O'Leary
adhered to a severely chivalric code of martial honour. Even James
Stephens, the most intransigent keeper of the physical force flame outside
the United States, discountenanced atrocities and was wedded to the engag-
ingly archaic concept of open military engagement He remained unswerv-
ingly faithful to the single strategy of the 'battle on Irish soil'. 'I have never
believed', he declared quixotically, 'in anything but a stand-up fight'.[199]
The first stirrings of a dynamite strategy, prefiguring modern terrorism,
elicited the sharp disapprobation and disdain of the old guard. Irish-
American extremists such as O'Donovan Rossa had no fiercer critic than
John O'Leary.

The high Fenianism of O'Leary and others was not confined to the
espousal of national independence, but extended to a deep hostility to the
political influence of the Catholic clergy (as well as latterly of the substantial
tenant farmers), to the point where one dispassionate contemporary looked to Fenianism as 'the bulwark of the civil rights of the Irish laity',[200]

a prophesy of which the split can be considered a partial fulfilment. This pertains to the neglected, and subsequently betrayed, radical aspect of Fenianism.

Fenianism in 1890-91 was in decline and disarray, a condition brought about by the objective predicament of a movement which lacked any discernible strategy with which to confront the changing prospect of Irish politics. That predicament had been excruciatingly sharpened by Parnell himself, whose masterly pursuit of a parliamentary strategy consummated the eclipse of Fenianism. In the words of one of the most perceptive chroniclers of Fenianism: 'Parnell had crowded the I.R.B. out of public life, and out of the public mind in Ireland'.[201]

Parnell in the split commanded extensive Fenian support. A substantial minority of the Dublin Parnell Leadership Committee were members of the Irish Republican Brotherhood, while others were sympathisers. This pattern was reproduced across the country. While not formally sanctioned by the Supreme Council of the Irish Republican Brotherhood, the support of Parnell by individual Fenians was openly connived at. Influential members of the Supreme Council such as O'Leary, John Wyse-Power and P. N. Fitzgerald were themselves active Parnellites.[202]

Fenian support for Parnell represented a much-needed accretion of campaigning strength, partly compensating for the atrophied condition of the post-split National League, and the active opposition of the clergy. The principal purpose of the establishment of a network of Parnell Leadership Committees, standing outside the formal structure of the National League, was presumably to accommodate Fenian scruples, by permitting Fenians to adhere to the Parnellite organisation without being obliged actually to join the National League.

Parnell in the split enjoyed the support of men who had in the past been strongly opposed to him. P. N. Fitzgerald, for example, was described by Davitt in evidence to the Special Commission as 'a very extreme man ... a bitter opponent of the Land League and Mr. Parnell's policy'.[203] Yet while Fitzgerald was an opponent of Parnell, he was one of the 'advanced' men with whom Parnell had throughout his career remained on speaking terms. Parnell told the Special Commission that Fitzgerald was one of his Cork constituents, and 'an advanced man who is very much opposed to my policy and to the Land League from first to last ... He considers that we are demoralising the Irish people and drawing them away from the true path'. Parnell was on personally friendly terms with Fitzgerald and they conversed whenever they met: 'He always tries to reason me out of the errors of my ways and I try to reason with him and neither of us has any success'.[204] Parnell's evidence illumines the nature of the Parnellite-Fenian axis in the split: rather than an abrupt volte-face, a sharp resiling from constitutional purposes, Parnell in the split sought to turn to political advantage those relations which he had always taken care to maintain with influential Fenians and 'advanced' men individually.

Parnell, wrote the *Spectator* close to the end, had 'nothing respectable left him, except Mr. O'Leary and the old-fashioned Fenians — a body of men not numerous but composed in part of really high-minded men'.[205] Underlying John O'Leary's adherence to Parnell's cause in the split was a deep and complex affinity between the two men masked in the prior history of their relations. O'Leary had resisted overtures from Parnell at the outset of his political career to endorse his parliamentary policy, then in its early obstructionist phase, and had held aloof from the New Departure, proclaiming that the Fenians were not 'a transacting party'.[206]

The split rejuvenated the sixty-year-old O'Leary, and liberated him from the dogmatic aloofness he had previously felt obliged to maintain from Parnell: 'I condemned many things he said and did in the past, and I condemn them still, but I have ever held that in him, and in him alone, rested all our hopes from constitutional action'[207]. O'Leary returned from London, where he had been living. to campaign for Parnell. He became an active Parnellite, joining the Parnell Leadership Committee and becoming a member of the working executive of its fund. He collaborated with Parnell: significantly he was reported as engaged in a lengthy consultation with Parnell at Westminster, after Dillon and O'Brien had on their release declared against Parnell. He was to be, with James Stephens, a prominent mourner at Parnell's funeral.[208]

O'Leary was prompted to rally to Parnell's defence in the first instance by the Gladstone letter. He wrote that Parnell 'is not now other than he was because Mr. Gladstone and the whole howling voice of prurient British hypocrisy has been heard'.[209] The support of O'Leary and other Fenians owed much to Parnell's abiding capacity, in the fierce strength of his resolve, to engage Fenian respect. Their support reflected a romantic predilection for Parnell's independent strength of character as against the conformism of the anti-Parnellite 'combination'. Thus O'Leary wrote of the Parnell manifesto that 'there was a man — whether a good or a bad one was beside the point — behind it': 'But what is behind the manifesto of the now notorious forty-five? Simply an old woman, or possibly several, for a more nerveless, boneless, sapless production I never remember to have read.'[210] This response was shared by W. H. Mitchel, brother of John Mitchel, who prior to his death in January 1891 twice endorsed Parnell in the split.[211] Mitchel declared that Ireland would be slow 'to replace his strong affirmative personality by a committee of negatives'. While Parnell was not blameless, his virtues outweighed his vices: 'Moreover his faults are common, while his virtues are rare'. Parnell was to be preferred to his opponents: 'Against him are all the big wigs, all the political wiseacres, all the specious reasoners, all the high-collared respectabilities'.[212] In like vein, Arthur Griffith twenty years later condemned the replacement of Parnell by a committee, which substituted for his judgement 'the conglomerate wisdom of the Irish party'.[213] The most dramatic, almost Carlylean, statement of Parnell's faculty to enlist support on the strength of his human qualities, which elicited the allegiance of many Fenians, came ironically from a Parnellite priest, Nicholas Murphy, in 1895: 'Parnell may have had many sins but one sin he had not, that of cant. With all his dross he was a man, fiery, real, from the great fire-bosom of nature itself'.[214]

There is an important and neglected second dimension to the rapprochement of Parnell and O'Leary in the split. O'Leary was and remained the most trenchant adversary of agrarian nationalism, of which his critique strikingly complemented Parnell's policy on land purchase in the split. He forcefully articulated the distaste of the Fenians of the old guard for agrarian agitation — the commingling of nationalism and the drive for proprietorship which they believed to detract from the integrity of Irish nationalism. He had in 1883 condemned Parnellite agrarian publicists as 'a set of loose principled agitators as have ever disgraced Irish politics'.[215] With the Plan of Campaign his distaste intensified. He forswore sympathy for 'these pets of the agitators — the strong farmers', and morally disapproved of the withholding of rents.[216] He carried his attack on the Plan of Campaign and its progenitors into the split. He denounced the débâcle of the Smith Barry tenants in Tipperary as the result of 'a piece of cowardly cruelty on the part of Mr. William O'Brien with no intellectual reason behind it save that of lying to England' — which was to say, misrepresenting the agrarian condition of Ireland for the supposed benefit of the Liberal-Nationalist alliance.[217]

O'Leary in March 1891 openly challenged Parnell publicly to justify his continued support of the 'New Tipperary' project, the most self-evidently disastrous initiative of the Plan of Campaign, which he described as 'this tragic farce'.[218] He thus prefigured and helped inspire the increasing vehemence of Parnell's condemnation of the Plan of Campaign. Parnell's position on the Plan of Campaign, and the implicit critique of the excesses of agrarianism which underlay his rhetoric in the split, conformed increasingly to that of O'Leary and other Fenian critics of agrarian nationalism. Behind Parnell and O'Leary's opposition to the Plan of Campaign lay a common concern with the disposition of social power in Ireland, and a shared apprehension of the predominance of a Catholic nationalist proprietorial order.

O'Leary's support for Parnell was not uncritical. As if somewhat defensively asserting the doctrinal soundness of Fenian support for Parnell, he declared in mid-September 1891:

> ... if Mr. Parnell were dead tomorrow, I and men like me, who are above and before all things Irish nationalists, should never dream of following the party of clerical dictation and compromise with England. We go with Mr. Parnell so far as he goes, and insofar as he goes, for Irish freedom.

This argument strikingly complemented Parnell's almost contemporaneous declaration at Listowel on 13 September ('if I were dead and gone tomorrow, the men who are fighting against English influence in Irish public life would fight on still'). He thereby insisted that his endorsement of Parnell was not purely a matter of personal allegiance, but involved an issue of principle, which the nature of the forces arrayed against Parnell threw into high relief.[219]

Parnell's ally of old, John Devoy, in the United States, rallied to his defence. He cabled at the outset: 'Retirement means chaos, leaving Ireland at mercy of English whims and Irish cranks. Retention involves temporary hurt but ensures final victory'. Devoy, however, proved unable to fulfil his promise of increased financial support from Irish Americans, reflecting Parnell's general failure to attract the financial assistance he had hoped for from American nationalists. His endorsement of Parnell proved unavailing, as did his peace initiative of August-September 1891.[220]

In September 1891 the old Fenian leader, James Stephens, returned to Ireland from Paris, like a phantom from the picaresque *demi-monde* of Fenian exiles, but one whose legendary intransigence had sanctified his name among extreme and sentimental nationalists alike. Stephens had declared for Parnell at the outset of the split, and his return to Ireland was sponsored by Parnellite sympathisers. *United Ireland* established a fund to purchase a cottage for him in Ireland, to which, if the paper is to be believed, Parnell very shortly before his death telegraphed an endorsement and forwarded a subscription. The Parnellites ostentatiously fêted 'the old rebel chief' on his return. *United Ireland* archly declared that Stephens would be consoled to learn that 'though Fenian methods are not the methods of our times, at least Fenian courage and Fenian spirit, and Fenian nationality are not dead today'.[221]

Stephens returned to Ireland on 28 September on the ship on which Parnell was making his last crossing to Ireland. While according to *United Ireland* they had 'long been anxious to meet each other', each was unaware of the other's presence. Three days later, Parnell was at his request privately introduced by a Parnellite MP, Patrick O'Brien, to Stephens at a cottage in Sandycove, outside Dublin. The fact of this meeting was only disclosed by O'Brien on the third anniversary of Parnell's death. He recalled a rather flat exchange:

> 'I am indeed proud to know you, Parnell, and I am sorry we did not meet sooner in life, as we might have done something for the freedom of Ireland,' was the salutation of the venerable rebel as he grasped the hand of Parnell, who replied, 'Yes Mr. Stephens, and I am sorry too, for I believe we could have done much together'.[222]

There is no reason to doubt O'Brien's assertion, published in Stephens' lifetime, that the encounter took place. It accounts for Stephens's otherwise inexplicable references to Parnell as his friend: he cabled to the

National Club the day after the death of 'my revered personal friend and the noblest Roman of them all', and later, weeping over the death of 'the noblest Irishman of our time', laid a wreath on Parnell's grave inscribed to the memory of 'my sincere friend'.[223]

The assignation recalled the 'New Departure' (to which, however, Stephens had not himself been a party). It was above all a demonstration of Parnell's unremitting tenacity, less than two weeks before his death, in his declared purpose of starting over again from the beginning his work of creating an independent Irish party. The meeting was not, in the phrase the Dublin *Daily Express* applied to Parnell's visit to Tralee in January, a revisiting of 'the glimpses of the moon'.[224] It did not represent the affirmation of a mystical nexus with Fenianism. Rather Parnell, without derogating from his constitutional purpose, was reworking his old formula and mechanically amid the ruins of his leadership re-laying the foundations of his power.

Turning away from the 'old guard', Frederick J. Allan was a prominent young Fenian and radical activist in Dublin, and rationalised Fenian allegiance to Parnell in more progressive terms. He wrote that even the sympathy for Parnell created by the Gladstone letter could not have assured him of active Fenian support, which was elicited rather by the intervention of the Irish Catholic hierarchy of the 'English' side. Extreme nationalists had for generations struggled to break the alliance of the Catholic Church and English power: 'When therefore, the real fight in Parnellism burst upon us, it found many of us only too ready to carry out into the open a battle which for so long had been kept beneath the surface, and in which the clergy had hitherto all the advantage of position, and every opportunity of choosing their ground'. Allan considered that Parnell's Rotunda speech had 'contained nothing that really would carry the support of Irish Revolutionists', but that the domestic struggle against ecclesiastical influence took precedence and determined Fenian allegiance:

> ... those men, whose vision was quickened by bitter experience, knew as they stood beside Parnell that night that the real issue in the Parnellite fight was to be fought out in Ireland, and would not be with England, but with that power in Ireland which had thrown in its lot with the British Government in every great crisis of our national life.[225]

Allan's views, while more representative of radical nationalist opinion in Dublin than mainstream Fenian sentiment, convey the significance of opposition to the political pretensions of the Catholic Church in determining Fenian support of Parnell in the split.

More representatively, an unnamed 'physical force man' and acquaintance of Parnell's sought, on Parnell's death, to account for what he lucidly described as the phenomenon of Fenians rallying to Parnell 'even while it seemed to bring them deeper and deeper into courses that they would never have taken but for him'. The cause of this seemingly perverse allegiance lay he suggested in Parnell's 'thinly veiled hatred of England', and in the treachery of the anti-Parnellites. Perhaps, the writer surmised, 'it was because he never degraded the deep national feelings of Ireland'.[226] The candid concession of this Fenian obituarist that their support for Parnell compromised Fenians rather than Parnell, is to be contrasted with a markedly cruder assessment of Parnell written six years later, which reveals the emergence of the extreme nationalist myth of Parnell: '... the farther we recede from his epoch the clearer becomes his personality, and the higher he towers above his contemporaries ... Instead of growing timid, like some other constitutional leaders, he developed bolder national views as he advanced'.[227] Such were the perspectival tricks of nationalist historical retrospect: the further nationalist ideologues receded from the era of Parnell the more readily could his political purpose be misconstrued in terms of their own agenda.

Fenian allegiance to Parnell is better understood in terms of instinct, than of any belief that Parnell was making any substantive concession to Fenianism. The many Fenians who espoused the Parnellite cause in the split, were prompted by a respect for Parnell personally, and for the fierce resolve which marked his style of constitutional politics, which did not exhibit the demeaning political beggary and social deference towards English politicians which Fenians regarded as the endemic vices of parliamentary nationalism. Fenian support for the Parnell of the split cannot be adequately accounted for in terms of what would have been, in Fenian terms, an ideologically highly dubious gamble on Parnell forsaking constitutional action. The most cursory consideration of the earlier course of Parnell's career could have left few illusions about his tenacity of purpose as a constitutional politician. He had ruthlessly subordinated Fenianism as a political force before, and there was little reason to believe he would not do so again. Dillon, years later, wrote admiringly of 'the steely fibre of Parnell, who did not fear or hesitate to fight the Fenians at the election of 1880, altho' it was they who created his movement'.[228]

It is true that Fenianism stood to gain from the sundering of the Irish party, and in the event of Parnell's final defeat, from the bitterness and disillusionment of his followers. If such considerations cannot have failed to influence Fenians in the split, there is little in the ardour of Fenian support for Parnell in the split to suggest that such cold revolutionary calculation was uppermost in their minds. Fenian support for Parnell in the split was more gratuitous than might appear. The objective circumstances of the split, a contest which pitted Parnell against Gladstone, the Church and the forces of conservative Catholic nationalism represented by Healy and the Sullivans, sufficed to ensure Parnell of a high degree of Fenian support.

What occurred was a reprise of the tactics which Parnell had adopted at the outset of his career, strikingly conveyed in Davitt's description of

Parnell's relations with Fenians at the time of the New Departure: 'Parnell *shut his eyes* and held out his hand for money and help'.[229] What was termed Parnell's 'appeal to the hillsides' was largely by way of a guarded reciprocating gesture. Fenian backing for Parnell was inspired by respect for Parnell as a politician whose integrity as a nationalist they believed uncompromised by parliamentary action, as evidenced by his break with Gladstone. That backing was moulded by common enmities and antagonisms, and sealed in the split's deepening controversy.

A later generation of more doctrinaire nationalist ideologues would seek to divert the Parnell myth to their own purpose, and lay claim to his political legacy. Yet the wilful impreciseness of their treatment of his historical persona suggests an inhibiting awareness of how close Parnell had come to success by parliamentary methods, and an intimation of the awkward implications which a consideration of his career raised for their political project. 'The pale and angry ghost of Parnell' was narrowly edged out of the curious nationalist pantheon instituted by Patrick Pearse, the inner sanctum of which comprised Wolfe Tone, Thomas Davis, James Fintan Lalor, and John Mitchel. Parnell was situated ambiguously on its threshold. Slipping elusively from argument into imagery, Pearse described Parnell as 'less a political thinker than an embodied conviction; a flame that seared, a sword that stabbed'. Parnell's instinct was, he asserted, 'a Separatist instinct'.[230]

P. S. O'Hegarty, obliged to concede that Parnell was a constitutional leader, and kept strictly within the constitutional framework, added that he was a constitutional leader with what he described as 'the root of Nationalism firmly within him, who used constitutional language in the tone and temper and with the intellect of a Separatist'.[231] More straightforwardly, using Parnell as a stick with which to beat his successors in the leadership of the Irish party, Arthur Griffith laid down what became an axiomatic proposition of Sinn Féin: 'the era of constitutional possibilities for Irish Nationality ended on the day Charles Stewart Parnell died'.[232]

Parnell's rhetoric was misconstrued, originally in the polemical onslaught of Healy and Davitt, devised to marginalise Parnell in the split, and in a curious collusive dialectic thereafter magnified in the myth of Parnell fostered after his death by extreme nationalist ideologues. This served in turn to provoke the excessive acerbity of the assessment of the Parnell of the split in modern liberal historiography. There was an 'appeal to the hillsides' in the sense of a play by Parnell for Fenian support. However the term, insofar as it is used to suggest a resiling by Parnell from constitutional purposes, is profoundly misleading. Parnell struggled desperately to turn to his advantage what had been perceived as his unique strength as a nationalist leader, what William O'Brien had termed 'Mr. Parnell's peculiar quality, that he exercised a spell over extreme and moderate men alike'.[233] He was not in the split engaged in undoing what was his greatest achievement, vaunted in his observation to Alfred Robbins that while he was depicted as a dangerous revolutionary, he had ensured that the Irish people espoused constitutional courses: 'If it had not been for our movement most of them would have become Fenians long before this'.[234] Parnell's rhetoric in the split, however ruthless or vehement, remained squarely within the grid of parliamentary politics, and subordinated to his purpose of reconstituting his authority of the leader of a constitutional nationalist movement. Throughout the split, he did not cease to speak as the prospective premier of a home rule Ireland.

If Parnell stopped short of compromising his constitutional purpose, there remains a measure of reckless cynicism in the rhetoric by which he endeavoured to outflank the majority. His rhetoric was less sternly proportioned to the ends of his campaign than the circumstances of the split required or permitted. His excesses cost him dear, and increased his vulnerability to Healy's counter-attack which mocked the demeaning spectacle of a once great constitutional leader conceding the possible futility of the struggle on which he had been engaged, and paltering to those who had opposed or stood aloof from it. His intermittent vehemence marred what was otherwise a classic and trenchant statement of the premises of constitutional action.

Allied to the complex rapprochement between Parnell and Fenianism was the endeavour to harness to the Parnellite cause the nationalism of a younger generation of intellectuals, which was to be of particular significance for the later shaping of the Parnell myth. There was an attempt to re-animate and marshal in the Parnellite interest the network of largely moribund nationalist literary societies. The Literary Society of the National Club (which had passed under Parnellite control) called for a convention of Young Ireland societies and of other associations which upheld 'the independence of Irish politics and opposed all English and other dictation', obvious Parnellite code-words.[235] This appeal led to the establishment of the Young Ireland League, of which John O'Leary and the eager young poet and man of letters, W. B. Yeats, were the moving spirits. The defeat at the inaugural convention of the League of a resolution to delete from its rules a transparently Parnellite reference to 'the principle of independence in Irish politics' revealed the disingenuousness of the League's affectation of neutrality in the split. Yeats' exhortation to heroic conduct was couched in unmistakably Parnellite accents:

> The ideal which they put before them was to see that there grew up in this nation a heroic people; to never do anything that should make these people feel that their manhood had been lowered; to never lower the national flag of Ireland to England, or to any power within the country, even though that power were a power that in the long process of ages had often been true to them.

The last was a veiled but obvious reference to the Catholic Church.[236]

Anti-Parnellite commentators were undeceived: the *Irish News* warned against 'the new O'Leary-Parnellite party'.[237] Yet in one respect, which pertains to the ambitiousness of his cultural politics, Yeats' professions of impartiality are to be taken very seriously indeed. Yeats astutely discerned in the split an opportunity to aggrandise the influence of a nationalist literary movement. In his assertion that the recalcitrantly anti-Parnellite Young Ireland Societies of Belfast and Cork would join when they saw that the League was genuinely neutral, 'and that, perhaps, in ours alone of nationalist organisations may they find the peace that comes for working for distant purposes',[238] Yeats was constructing a larger argument. The poet could transcend the acrimony of political discord. Literature might prevail where politics could not. It was an early articulation of a disquieting tendency to prefer the pretensions of cultural nationalism over the necessary mundanities of conventional democratic politics.

One of the most active of the Parnellite literary societies was the Leinster Literary Society, of which the young Arthur Griffith was president, and his friend and collaborator William Rooney a member.[239] Griffith never ceased to think of himself as a Parnellite, and the assertion of his own greater fidelity to Parnell in the split and in its political aftermath informed his later onslaughts on the Irish Parliamentary Party under John Redmond's leadership.

Yeats and Griffith were to be the most influential interpreters of the Parnell myth in the rising generation, in their respective spheres of literature and politics. The brushing of generations — Griffith shaking hands with Parnell at Broadstone station before the Creggs meeting, Yeats standing on Dun Laoghaire pier as the ship bearing the dead leader's body came in — would critically influence the shaping of the Parnell myth, and with it the course of Irish politics and literature.

Around Yeats and Griffith were the dark stirrings of a younger nationalism, marked by a deepened mistrust of conventional politics, of which they partook. Yet while they would both seek to turn the myth of Parnell to their own purposes, they were to maintain a degree of fidelity to the actual persona and politics of Parnell, bred of the experience of a felt allegiance in the split. Their direct involvement set them apart from those of their generation who, unconstrained by participation in its events, would reinterpret the split.

The split coincided with, and quickened, a shift in the nationalist sensibility which originated independently of the split. It arose from the ideological contraction within nationalism precipitated by the achievements of parliamentary nationalism under Parnell's leadership. Nationalists struggled to accommodate themselves to what was correctly perceived as the inevitability of a settlement of the land question by land purchase, and what was mistakenly believed to be the assured and imminent concession of home rule by a Gladstone government. The prospect of success was peculiarly unsettling to a nationalism habituated to an adversarial role, unburdened by the responsibilities and disciplines of power, whose evasion of central issues of policy was superficially validated by the romantically transcendental pretensions of its ideology. The perceived imminence of political victory sharpened the contradictions within nationalism and precipitated an unravelling of the nationalist movement. Even prior to the split, the movement was breaking fast on its cultural axis.

Cultural nationalism had its origins in the romantic writings of Young Ireland, and in particular in Thomas Davis' beguilingly naive essays in the edification of Irish taste. By the late nineteenth century it was undergoing a transformation into the pursuit of an elusively mystical conception of nationalist identity, which came to preoccupy many of the rising generation of nationalist intellectuals. In its late nineteenth and early twentieth century form, it reflected a disillusionment before the fact with home rule, a sullen critique predicated on a complacent anticipation of the concession of legislative independence. It involved a dangerously illiberal querying of the capability of conventional modes of politics and governance — including home rule — truly to reflect and to translate into actuality the peculiar genius of nationalism. It posited a conflict between the dictates of conventional liberal democratic rationality and nationalist values. The quest for a culturally authentic nationalist society marked a regressive flight from the challenges of self-governance: it created the treacherous undertow of the nationalist tide, the troubling rhythm of premonitory nationalist disaffection and disillusion.

For the future of the home rule movement this had the gravest implications. With the failure of Gladstone's second Home Rule Bill in 1893 the party created by Parnell confronted a double dilemma: not merely had it failed to achieve home rule, but it faced a deepening questioning of the sufficiency of home rule itself as a vehicle of nationalist self-realisation. This inchoate disillusionment, while it owed nothing to Parnell, came later to distort perceptions of the split, and to shape an unhistorical myth of the Irish leader.

At the most superficial level, the crisis manifested itself as a problem of style in nationalist rhetoric. The grandiloquence of traditional nationalist rhetoric and patriotic declamation had been cropped in the more brutally realistic idiom of agrarianism. A critique, published ironically in the Dublin Unionist *Daily Express*, elicited widespread comment and approbation in the nationalist press. It argued that agrarian satiety had impaired the legendary Irish faculty of patriotic versifying. The article, attributed to Standish O'Grady, addressed itself to the question, 'Are the Irish growing a prosy race?', and deplored the fallen state of a poetic people: 'Six years of agrarianism has not added one song to Anglo-Irish literature', excepting possibly one poem by Parnell's sister Fanny. Agrarianism had garrotted the patriotic muse: 'Patriotism, since it got stuck in the land question, has grown of the earth, earthy ... Ireland has never been so well fed, so well clothed, and so well housed as now, and never less literary? Can it be that material comfort tends to make the spirit coarse?'.[240] The fatuousness of the proposition should not distract from its ideological significance. Its concern with the quality of the contemporary Irish patriotic literature touched on the larger crisis of nationalist rhetoric, brought about by the rift between the conspicuously materialistic orientation of agrarian nationalism and the supposedly transcendental spirituality of nationalist values, skilfully but superficially masked in Healy's rhetoric.

The clearest assertion that the achievement of home rule could not of itself fulfil the deepest aspirations of nationalism was in an article in *United Ireland* of February 1891. A notably early articulation of modern Irish cultural nationalism in an expressly political context, it rehearsed those arguments which would become tediously familiar and were oppressively to mould the politics of Sinn Féin and of the independent Ireland. Entitled 'Irish Nationality', it posed the disquieting question: 'Is a mere Parliament the end of Ireland's aspirations?' What followed extended to a cultural nationalist critique of the Parnellite programme itself:

> Let us not forget that the sentiment of nationality has only a very remote connection with the science of political economy; nor that Ireland, with a powerful and capable Parliament to which Mr. Parnell's four points had been fully conceded, might yet be as much a province of England as she was during her whole history ... To attain our legislative independence is not to attain our nationhood'.

'Nationhood' was a condition suffused and defined by supposedly authentic nationalist values, from which were excluded those professed nationalists 'who are English from top to toe, from the soul into the skin out, who have no Irish ideas in their heads ... and who in their heart of hearts consider all this talk of making Ireland a nation, either in art or war, as the merest feather-brained Celtic balderdash':[241] the bombastic equation of culture and insurrection is noteworthy. The article is an early revelation of the coalescing around Parnell in the split, as more systematically around his posthumous image, of a school of nationalist thought with which he could have had little affinity or even comprehension, but which would in the years after the split lay claim to his myth.

Culturally as well as socio-economically, nationalism was developing in a direction which rendered it less amenable to rational leadership. Nationalist Ireland had greater need than ever of Parnell's severe and restraining purpose. Even without the split, the longer term evolution of nationalism would have severely tested his capacity to direct and contain its excesses.

'Clerical Dictation': Parnell and the Catholic Church

> Parnell has had a real *facer* at Carlow. It was one of the few seats
> which it was thought he might hold ... It looks now as if he were real-
> ly done, and as if there would be a united Irish party again. It is
> marvellous certainly how the Irishmen have managed to close their
> ranks after the fearful split last November. The change in the aspect
> of affairs is no doubt mainly due to the attitude assumed by the priests;
> and in connection with their increased power over the people, a fresh
> Irish difficulty may quite possibly arise; for the idea of extensive 'priest-
> ridden-ness' will jar terribly on the nonconformist mind. Moreover,
> Ulstermen will conjure up religious as well as political terrors, the dif-
> ficulty of dealing with Ireland will become tenfold enhanced, if
> religious troubles are to be combined with national and agrarian ones.
>   E. W. Hamilton, 9 July 1891 [242]

Parnell was obliged in the split to confront the the intervention of the Irish
Catholic Church within nationalist politics. It was an issue which through
the 1880s he had taken care to delegate to his Catholic co-adjutors. He
now faced the dilemma of addressing the issue without further exacer-
ting the confessional animosities brought into play against him in the
split.

Although he regarded the encroachment of the Irish Church on the
political domain with a jealous professional eye, he was free from the sectarian prejudices which Healy so freely imputed to him. While he took
up the gauntlet which as he asserted the hierarchy had flung down by intervening in the split, he repudiated the taunt of bigoted opposition to the
clergy. Privately he enjoined his followers: 'The priests have been our very
good friends in the past. They will be very good friends in the future. Do
not say a word against them'. [243]

Parnell's guarded attitude to clergymen was not confined to Catholic
priests. 'Towards clerics of all persuasions Mr. Parnell presented a stiff
front', wrote Edward Byrne. With superb coldness he rebuffed a Protestant
clergyman who had called on him during the Carlow by-election to urge
him to withdraw his candidate: he informed him that he denied his right
to intervene, while not blaming the Catholic clergy for the part they had
taken: 'A Catholic clergyman has to undergo a most severe and searching
course of discipline. He has to take a vow of celibacy, and deny himself
gratifications that are freely indulged in by Protestant clergymen'. [244]

Parnell's professional mistrust of the political capacity of the Irish
Catholic hierarchy and clergy owed much to the deficient patriotic record
of the Irish Church in the nineteenth century, commencing with episcopal
support for the Act of Union. This historically engrained suspicion, commonplace among Fenians, was heightened in Parnell's case by pride in his

patriotic ancestry and an identification with the eighteenth century Protestant patriotic tradition. Edward Byrne recorded that Parnell was fond of citing an observation made by a Catholic prelate to his forbear Sir John Parnell, Chancellor of the pre-union Irish Exchequer, 'to the effect that he would rather have a union with the Beys and Mamelukes of Egypt than be under the iron rod of the Mamelukes of Ireland'[245] (by which the bishop meant that he preferred the Act of Union to the maintenance of a Dublin Parliament under Ascendancy control).

Parnell charged in the split that in the years between the Act of Union and his own emergence the country had been under the direction of the Church, and that the political barrenness of the era of Church hegemony spoke for itself.

> Since the passing of the Act of Union Ireland was under the charge of the Irish bishops and clergy. The history of those 75 years is before you, and you know how many concessions were gained for Ireland. You know how many hundreds of thousands of the Irish people were evicted and exterminated, and you know how utterly the affairs of Ireland were mismanaged. During the sixteen years of my public life you know what has been done.[246]

Parnell's sceptical attitude to the Catholic hierarchy derived from his sharp demarcation of the spheres of professional competence of politicians and churchmen. In response to the attacks on him by the Archbishop of Cashel, Parnell retorted that some of the bishops were getting 'somewhat muddled as to the border line between religion and politics':

> I will only say to his Grace that while I believe his Grace to be a most excellent archbishop, I don't believe him to be a good political leader. If you want a pair of boots you go to a shoemaker; if you want a cart built you go to a carpenter, and if you want a ship constructed you go to a shipwright; and if you want a steam engine you go to an engineer, and if you want to confess your sins or get absolution you go to a priest *(hear, hear)*; and if you want advice about politics or political service I advise you to go to men who have served their time at it, and who understand it *(loud cheers)*.[247]

It is difficult to conceive a more tart rebuke to the political pretensions of the Irish hierarchy and clergy than Parnell's circumscription of their role to that of purveyors of absolution. His precisely drawn distinction could not however prevail against the heavy smudging of the frontiers of Church and nation in Irish nationalist politics.

Parnell did not hesitate to attack the hierarchy as fiercely as he had assailed the majority of the Irish party, for having failed to express their opposition to him until after after Gladstone and the voluble exponents of the 'non-conformist conscience' had done so:

> The Bishops waited a whole fortnight before they expressed their opposition *(cheers)*; they waited until Gladstone *(hisses and groans)*, until Stead, and every miserable old woman in England desirous of airing his virtue had interfered and expressed his opposition before they expressed theirs.[248]

In his most developed formulation of this charge, at Belfast on 22 May, Parnell audaciously deployed the Catholic vocabulary of sin to formulate his case against the hierarchy in terms of acts of omission and of commission:

> I submit that the highest teachers of morality in the Catholic Church ought not to have watched 117 of their priests at five important conventions, ought not to have watched hundreds of thousands of the Catholic laity and Irish Catholic members of Parliament declare themselves on my side, without having hastened to express their opinion as to the moral question.[249]

The hierarchy had trespassed on the terrain of secular politics. He retaliated remorselessly. He fastened on the temporising strategy which the hierarchy had adopted under Walsh's inspiration at the outset of the split, which left it in the first instance for Parnell to retire or for the party to remove him, as demonstrating that bishops' opposition to him was political rather than moral.

The 'acts of commission' Parnell alleged were those of Nulty, Bishop of Meath (whom Healy told Harrington had initially expressed himself in favour of Parnell's retention), and of Archbishop Walsh. When Walsh inadvisedly made public allusion to his letter to Joseph Kenny of 24 November 1890, Parnell immediately called on him to authorise publication of the letter, and charged that the letter came seven days after the decree of the divorce court and urged his retirement on grounds of expediency rather than morality. He returned to the attack a week later, insisting that the letter could reveal 'whether his Grace's mind, which became a semi-political one after the publication of Mr. Gladstone's letter, was of the same character before its publication'. 'I fear,' he taunted, 'that we find his Grace in this matter taking his politics from England — if he does not take his morality'.[250]

Parnell had always regarded Walsh as a politically inept and meddlesome prelate. His estimate of Walsh's political capacity was shared by John Morley, who, sending a communication from Walsh to Gladstone in 1886 commented, 'He does not show much strength of political judgement, and I can understand why Parnell never takes him into counsel'. Parnell furiously resented Walsh's attack in June 1890 on the slack parliamentary attendances of the Irish party, which he improbably atributed to the archbishop's jealousy at a flattering reference he had made to Croke at William O'Brien's wedding.[251]

Parnell's attack on Walsh was a pitilessly exact reprisal for Walsh's political intervention in the split. He thereby sought to confront Walsh with the full consequences of the overreaching of his episcopal function. Yet in moving from the high ground of his abstract demarcation of the spheres of Church and nation to assail the indulgent, if self-serving, temporising of the hierarchy under Walsh's tutelage, he appeared gratuitously ruthless. It revealed his predicament in the split: compelled to pare his political technique to the bone, he risked appearing merciless and fanatical.

Parnell in defeat levelled the charge of 'dictation' increasingly at the Church as much as at the Liberal party. In the split's deepening controversy, resistance to clerical dictation became in its own right an issue of Parnellite principle. Parnell declared in April:

> This struggle has been changed, and materially changed, in its character since its commencement. Influences have been used, intimidation has been exercised against the due exercise of the constitutional right of Irishmen, which will have to be met and defeated *(cheers and cries of 'No Dictation')*, and this battle will have to be fought out, and the Irish people will show that they know how to make up their minds without the dictation of anybody *(cheers).*[252]

At Newcastle West in May he asserted that

> ... the area of this struggle has been widened in such a fashion by our opponents, the forces and influences which they have been compelled to bring forward in their own support have been of such a character as to leave us no choice but to fight it out.

He committed himself to fight 'on behalf of independent Ireland, of freedom of action and thought for my fellow countrymen'.[253] He thus elegantly and obliquely rendered the issue of intervention by the Catholic Church in nationalist politics, seeking to avoid where possible directly naming the Catholic Church, in an attempt to avoid further exciting the sectarian Catholic animosities against him on which Healy's rhetoric skilfully played.

On his return to Dublin after his defeat in Carlow, Parnell sought to rationalise his by-election reversals. He declared that while substantial bodies of independent thought and opinion existed in the three constituencies, it was difficult for Dublin nationalists to realise

> ... the tremendous meaning and import of the intimidation which was practised in each of these elections ... You must remember that the people in these constituencies are mainly isolated, living apart from each other, not in daily consultation with each other, not cheered and supported by each other's presence, and therefore it is possible for an organised system of intimidation to prevail in such constituencies where it would not be possible of success in a large city.

At each of the elections, 'a section of the most ignorant and uninstructed of the Irish electors' had been led astray by new guides and new doctrines.

> ... it is our duty to maintain our independent attitude and to stand together, to organise our strength throughout the country, and form solid rallying squares in every Irish constituency, behind which the foolish sheep who are now being led into the paths of destruction may have an opportunity of retreating when they find out their mistake.[254]

This presentation of the different circumstances under which politics was practised in urban and rural Ireland was his most compelling evocation of the clerical influence deployed against him in the split.

That influence was deep and pervasive. The episcopacy publicly condemned Parnell. Irish priests denounced and campaigned actively against him: more discreetly, and probably more decisively, they deployed the social influence their office brought them in opposition to him. Yet, without discounting the role of the Church as an independent agency, it is more plausible to interpret the power of priestly suasion as an effect as much as a cause of the weakness of Parnell's support in rural Ireland, and to regard the Church as an element, albeit a peculiarly influential one, in a larger conservative nationalist coalition against him. It was necessary for Parnell and his adherents to overstate the degree, and the independent significance, of clerical opposition for his persisting reversals, much as they also exaggerated that of Gladstonian Liberalism. Parnell understandably fastened upon the theme of 'clerical dictation' to contend that his defeat had been procured by means which were neither legitimate nor fair. Yet it may be doubted that the Church, however gross its incursions into nationalist politics in the split, bore so high a degree of responsibility for Parnell's defeats as he charged.[255]

In support of his resistance to 'clerical dictation', Parnell warned of the dangers of entrenching unionist perceptions of Irish nationalism as a sectarian force.[256] Thus at Tralee in January he declared that the obstacles to home rule were twofold. The first was the land settlement: 'The other great difficulty is not English political opinion, it is Irish Protestant opinion ... it is of the utmost importance that we should do everything to assuage the alarm of these men'.[257] Elsewhere he rhetorically asserted that the Irish people would resist dictation and show

> ... that our country — our Ireland — is to be the Ireland of our whole people, and that it is not to be the Ireland of any section or any sect, no matter how numerous ... that Ireland is large enough for all; that we cannot spare — and will not spare — one single Irishman; and that we insist on having equal rights for all.[258]

It was of course necessary for Parnell to avoid the taunt of bigotry by asserting that he did not himself believe that a sectarian nationalism would prevail:

> I have always had full confidence in my fellow Catholic countrymen. If I did not know their boundless capacity for tolerance, their absolute freedom from every sort of religious prejudice and bias, I, as a Protestant, never could have thrown myself into this struggle as I have ... I am sure that the Catholics of Ireland, the great majority of them, will leave no stone unturned, will exhaust every method for the purpose of tranquillising the alarm of the Protestants of Ireland.[259]

He argued that without the conciliation of Protestant opinion, 'the work of building up a free and independent Ireland would have upon it a fatal clog'. He warned of the dangers of alienating Protestant opinion in the split's contest, and of the need of the combatants 'to avoid doing anything which would attach to the struggle more than was legitimate of a sectarian or religious aspect'.[260] After O'Brien's adherence to the majority, Parnell astutely lamented that O'Brien might have assisted him 'in securing for our people the independent expression of their opinions, in tranquillising the fears of the Protestant section of our fellow-countrymen, and in showing the nations that, while she desires freedom above all things, Ireland also desires to use that freedom with toleration to all'.[261]

Other Parnellite spokesmen followed suit. Redmond warned that if the priesthood became the 'ruling power', home rule would be forfeit for a generation.[262] *United Ireland* less convincingly claimed that before the split Parnell's policy of religious conciliation had been bearing fruit: 'Slowly but surely, it was turning the hearts of the liberal-minded Presbyterians and Protestants of the northern province towards their fellow-countrymen'. That evolution was now imperilled, and the paper warned the bishops: 'There is no use in having an Irish Catholic parliament'.[263] It asserted that the anti-Parnellite triumph in nationalist Ulster had been procured in a manner which represented 'the most absolute vindication of the Unionist position': 'How do the priests of Ulster imagine that the bigoted and prejudiced Protestants and Presbyterians of the North will ever join us in the making of a nation whose public opinion can be made from the altar steps?'[264]

Those 'bigoted and prejudiced Protestants and Presbyterians of the North' were unpersuaded. The *Belfast Evening Telegraph* rudely rebuffed Parnell's professions of solicitude at Belfast. He had spoken in 'a tone of specious sincerity', professedly as a Protestant: 'He is of course a Protestant in so far as he is not a Roman Catholic, and in this connection he thought fit to refer to Wolfe Tone. Wolfe Tone was as much a Protestant as the late Mahdi of the Soudan'. There were two things Ulster did not want: one was priests; the other was Parnell.[265]

The response of Irish unionism outside Ulster was more subtly opportunistic. Southern-unionist opinion, initially opposed to Parnell in the split, discovered his virtues in defeat. If the southern-Unionist response was determined primarily by an understandable desire to ensure that the split divided and discredited nationalism to the greatest extent possible, it also reflected an awareness that the contest had profound implications for their future under home rule, as well as in some quarters an involuntary sympathy for Parnell. The Dublin *Daily Express* discerned in the conflict between Parnell and the Irish hierarchy 'a contest of the greatest magnitude ... by the issue must be marked out the channel in which Irish politics will for a long time flow';[266] while the organ of the Church of Ireland, the *Irish Ecclesiastical Gazette*, declared, admittedly only on the death of Parnell, that

'"Parnellism" has lately come to mean a "Home Rule" which is not "Rome Rule"'.[267] However indifferent southern Protestants professed to be to the issue of the split, they could not be insensible to the overthrow of Parnell by a movement in opposition to him which had disquieting overtones of Catholic nationalist supremacism.

Parnell's invocation of the theme of religious toleration was not without precedent in his career. Most famously, in the more tranquil circumstances of the debate on the address of Gladstone's 1886 administration, Parnell had declared:

> ... I myself was born a Protestant; I have always lived a Protestant, and I hope to die a Protestant; and if in the future, after the concession of the Irish claims, any danger were to arise to my Protestant fellow-countrymen, I would be the first to stand up for liberty of speech, liberty of conscience, and liberty to live and thrive for every section of the community, whether they be Protestants or whether they be Catholics.

He added drily, and characteristically, that he might prove a more effectual aid in times of real danger than those opposed to home rule who vaunted their concern for the rights of the minority.[268]

The *Spectator* charged Parnell with exploiting the fear of a sectarian Catholic domination within nationalism 'with sinister adroitness'.[269] Yet his pretensions in the split to champion a pluralistic nationalism, whether conceived objectively or subjectively, cannot be lightly discounted. His espousal of the issue owed less to the recidivist allegiance of caste with which Healy's rhetoric so remorselessly taunted him, than to his long-standing purpose of avoiding the entrenchment of Catholic ascendancy within a stagnant nationalist state.

While Parnell's playing of the 'Protestant card' appeared opportunistic, his dilemma in the split, which compelled him to engage in a vulgarisation of his politics, and crudely to articulate, in what appeared the furtherance of an obvious self-interest, considerations which had theretofore subtly and discreetly inflected his political course. The containment of the destabilising preponderance of Catholic nationalist power was integral both to his strategy in the split and to the larger architecture of his statescraft. Parnell's fate was in this respect indeed subtly bound up with that of his class and co-religionists, as if in ironic affirmation of the crude reductionism of Healy's rhetoric.

The split was the first, and in some respects the definitive, confrontation between church and nation in modern Irish politics. If the precipitating event of the divorce was in some sense fortuitous, the same could not be said of the forces which it called forth against Parnell. Faithful to his strategy of facing down the opposition, he protested vigorously against the menace of a confessional nationalism. For this he was denounced as a cynical and amoral schismatic. Not for the last time in such encounters, the furiously protesting victim was condemned as the aggressor.

His uncompromising delineation of the proper limits of ecclesiastical influence and secular nationalist politics was not reducible merely to a desire to reconcile his estranged co-religionists, or to assuage English apprehensions. He insisted that it was a question of state. The pluralistic treatment of the Protestant minority was a defining criterion of the Parnellian conception of the nation-state. The supremacist Catholic Home Rule Ireland, which he charged his Healyite opponents with seeking to bring about, he dismissed as a travesty: a confessional pseudo-nation, a negation of the pretension to statehood.

The criticism made of Parnell in modern historiography, of an insensitivity to the predicament of Irish Protestantism in general and of Ulster Protestantism in particular,[270] is anachronistically conceived. Parnell did not address, because he did not concede, the inevitability of the subsequent conformation of the Irish question into a partitionist mould which would shape both the island's dominant ideologies. The accusation moreover detracts from the supple integrity of Parnell's statescraft which treated the minority question not statically as a discrete issue, but dynamically within his larger political strategy. The charge of a want of prescience, of a failure of historical sympathy in his attitude to Irish Protestantism, fails to recognise his sustained if fragile endeavour to shape a pluralistic framework of state, and to conserve through the country a tensile web of Protestant proprietorship and economic involvement to turn the tensions of the Union to liberal purpose within the Irish nation.

References

1 *W.F.J.*, 27 Dec. 1891.
2 *F.J.*, 3 Aug. 1891.
3 Lyons, 'Political Ideas of Parnell', p. 772.
4 *F.J.*, 13 Dec. 1890, Cork.
5 *F.J.*, 28 Apr. 1891, Parnell banquet, Tipperary; and *F.J.*, 6 June 1891, Bagenalstown.
6 *I.T.*, 20 Oct. 1891, Anna Parnell to *I.T.*
7 *S.C.P.*, vol. 7, p. 111 (1 May 1889). The invocation of Grattan was striking, as was his reference to him as ' "Mr." Henry Grattan', reminiscent of Gladstone's famous allusions to ' "Mr." Pitt'. For the Cincinnati speech, see Lyons, *Parnell*, pp. 111-2.
8 *S.C.P.*, vol. 7, pp. 365, 369 (8 May 1889).
9 *F.J.*, 1 July 1891, Carlow.
10 *F.J.*, 23 Mar. 1891, Drogheda; see also *F.J.*, 20 Dec. 1890.
11 *F.J.*, 30 June 1891, Borris.
12 *F.J.*, 6 July 1891, Tullow.
13 *F.J.*, 20 July 1891, Newcastle upon Tyne.
14 *St. James's Gazette*, 7 Oct. 1895, quoted *I.W.I.*, 12 Oct. 1895.
15 *F.J.*, 22 Dec. 1890
16 *F.J.*, 25 Feb. 1891.

17 *Nation*, 22 Dec. 1877.
18 *F.J.*, 2 Mar. 1891.
19 *F.J.*, 23 Mar. 1891, Drogheda.
20 *F.J.*, 3 Aug. 1891.
21 *F.J.*, 20 Jul. 1891, Newcastle upon Tyne. The voting figures are accurate approximations.
22 *F.J.*, 30 June 1891, Bagenalstown.
23 *F.J.*, 12 Jan. 1891, Limerick.
24 *F.J.*, 30 Mar. 1891, Sligo.
25 *F.J.*, 18 May 1891.
26 *F.J.*, 7 Sept. 1891, Westport.
27 *F.J.*, 9 Jan. 1891, Anna Parnell to *Freeman's Journal*, d. 6 Jan.
28 *F.J.*, 23 Feb. 1891, Roscommon.
29 *F.J.*, 20 Apr. 1891, Irishtown; 29 June 1891, Carlow.
30 *W.R.J.*, 13 Dec. 1890.
31 *F.J.*, 23 June 1891.
32 *F.J.*, 26 June 1891, Leighlinbridge.
33 *U.I.*, 28 Feb., 6 Aug. 1891.
34 *F.J.*, 22 Apr. 1891, National League.
35 *F.J.*, 20 July 1891, Newcastle upon Tyne, 18 July.
36 *F.J.*, 25 Feb. 1891, meeting of Gaelic Clubs.
37 *F.J.*, 1 June 1891, Wicklow.
38 *F.J.*, 20 July 1891, Newcastle upon Tyne, 18 July.
39 *F.J.*, 24 Mar. 1891, 'The Parnell Campaign of 1880'.
40 *F.J.*, 9 Mar. 1891.
41 *F.J.*, 16 Mar. 1891, Galway.
42 *F.J.*, 20 Apr. 1891.
43 Parnell manifesto, *F.J.*, 29 Nov. 1890, quoted Lyons, *Fall*, pp. 320-6.
44 *F.J.*, 7 Sept. 1891, Westport.
45 *F.J.*, 3 Aug. 1891, Thurles railway station.
46 *F.J.*, 4 May 1891.
47 *F.J.*, 18 Mar. 1891; see also R. B. O'Brien, *Parnell*, ii. p. 337.
48 *F.J.*, 22 Apr. 1891.
49 *F.J.*, 20 July 1891, Newcastle upon Tyne.
50 *F.J.*, 7 Sept. 1891.
51 *F.J.*, 3 Aug. 1891, National Club, Dublin.
52 *F.J.*, 7 Sept. 1891, Westport.
53 *F.J.*, 22 Apr. 1891, Ballina.
54 *F.J.*, 9 Mar. 1891.
55 *The Times*, 1 Jan. 1891, Birmingham.
56 *F.J.*, 26 Jan. 1891, Waterford.
57 Special Commission Brief, O'Brien proofs, p. 20.
58 Manuscript draft of the Parnell manifesto (incomplete) NLI MS 21,933.
59 *F.J.*, 23 Feb. 1891, Roscommon.
60 *F.J.*, 18 June 1891, Bermondsey; see also *F.J.*, 2 Mar. 1891, Navan, *F.J.*, 22 June 1891, National League Convention, Dublin.
61 *F.J.*, 9 Mar. 1891.
62 *F.J.*, 12 Jan. 1891.
63 *F.J.*, 2 Feb. 1891; Morley, *Recollections*, ii. p. 264.
64 Parnell to Harrington, 20 July 1891, Harrington Papers, NLI MS 8581 (1).
65 *F.J.*, 2 Mar. 1891.
66 *F.J.*, 24 July 1891, National Convention.
67 *F.J.*, 22 Dec. 1890, Johnswell.

68 *F.J.*, 1 May 1891, J. J. Clancy, MP, 'The Irish Party Pledge'.

69 20 July 1891, Parnell to T. Harrington, Harrington Papers, NLI MS 8581 (1); see also *F.J.*, 24 July 1891.

70 *F.J.*, 23 Mar. 1891, Drogheda.

71 *Nation*, 27 July 1889.

72 *F.J.*, 22 June 1891.

73 Morley, *Gladstone*, ii. pp. 440-1, Morley note dated 25 Nov. 1890.

74 *F.J.*, 11 Dec. 1890.

75 *F.J.*, 4 May. 1891.

76 *F.J.*, 12 Jan. 1891, Limerick. The allegation, denied by Gladstone, was repeated by Parnell (*F.J.*, 13, 14 Jan. 1891). Curiously, Parnell thereby imputed to Gladstone a response to the manifesto remarkably similar to his own insouciant reaction on learning of Gladstone's intention to publish his letter.

77 *F.J.*, 6 Apr. 1891; *Nation*, 11 Apr. 1891.

78 *F.J.*, 26 Jan. 1891, Waterford.

79 *F.J.*, 12 Jan. 1891, Limerick.

80 *F.J.*, 6 Mar. 1891; Mary Drew, *Catherine Gladstone* (London, 1919), p. 189. Years later Mahony wrote to Gladstone's daughter of her mother, 'I felt the unfortunate separation from her and Mr. Gladstone very deeply' (see Mahony to Mary Drew, 6 July 1925, Gladstone Papers, BM, Add. MS 46253).

81 *F.J.*, 7 Sept. 1891, Westport.

82 *F.J.*, 21 Sept. 1891, Co. Dublin.

83 *F.J.*, 10 Oct. 1881, Wexford. Francis Hackett wrote that Parnell 'judged the moral hospitality of Gladstone as a general would judge terrain' (Francis Hackett, *Ireland, A Study in Nationalism* [New York, 1918, p. 245; see also p. 331]).

84 H. W. Lucy, *A Diary of the Home Rule Parliament 1892-95* (London, 1896, pp. 43-44). Rosebery's memorable evocation of Gladstone at a cabinet meeting in late 1892 as a 'pale old croupier' (quoted Robert Rhodes James, *Rosebery*, London, 1963) would have elicited Parnell's approval.

85 Byrne, *Parnell*, p. 14; *F.J.*, 29 Nov. 1890; Lyons, *Fall*, p. 322. Gladstone was in the habit of engaging in correspondence with members of the public by postcard, which he frequently published. Following a particularly effusive missive by Gladstone, Parnell commented to Byrne: 'Mr. Gladstone's supply of postcards ought to be cut off'. Parnell's distaste for Gladstone's portentous prolixity was shared by Oscar Wilde, who consigned Gladstone to the ranks of the great Victorian bores, in writing of W. S. Blunt, 'it is impossible not to feel a strong prejudice against a man who might have poisoned Lord Tennyson, or Mr. Gladstone, or the Master of Balliol' (*P.M.G.*, 3 Jan. 1889; quoted Owen Dudley Edwards, *The Fireworks of Oscar Wilde* [London, 1989], p. 110).

86 Byrne, *Parnell*, p. 29.

87 *F.J.*, 23 Feb. 1891, Roscommon. Parnell protested at Drogheda: 'He is actually arrogating to himself the prerogatives of the Sovereign' (*F.J.*, 23 Mar. 1891).

88 *Weekly Sun*, 2 Aug. 1896; see also a remark in the same vein, but of more doubtful authority, ascribed in James Bryce, *Studies in Contemporary Biography* (London, 1903), at p. 239, n.1.

89 *F.J.*, 22 June 1891.

90 R. B. O'Brien, *Parnell*, ii. p. 337.

91 *F.J.*, 10 Dec. 1890.

92 Labouchere to Healy, 3 Jan. 1891, memorandum of conversation with O'Brien at Boulogne, *Letters and Leaders*, Proofs, B 147.

93 *K.M.*, 24 Dec. 1890, Kilkenny, 20 Dec. 1890.

94 *F.J.*, 26 Jan. 1891, Limerick Junction, 24 June 1891; Waterford, 25 Jan. 1891.

95 *F.J.*, 26 Jan. 1891, Waterford.

96 *F.J.*, 3 Aug. 1891, Thurles.
97 *F.J.*, 11 Dec. 1890.
98 *The Speeches of the Rt. Hon. W. E. Gladstone*, ed. A. W. Hutton and H. J. Cohen (2 vols., London, 1902), pp. 375-96; *U.I.*, 10 Oct. 1891.
99 *Hansard*, vol. 352, col. 771 (16 Apr. 1891).
100 *F.J.*, 24 July 1891.
101 *F.J.*, 21 Sept. 1891, Co. Dublin.
102 Byrne, *Parnell*, pp. 28-9; *F.J.* 20 July 1891, Newcastle upon Tyne; see also *F.J.* 24 July 1891, National Convention, NL.
103 *F.J.*, 23 Feb. 1891, Strokestown; see also *F.J.*, 20 Jan., Athlone, *F.J.*, 20 Apr. 1891, Enfield.
104 *F.J.*, 20 Jan. 1891, Athlone.
105 *F.J.*, 19 Jan. 1891, Tralee; *F.J.*, 20 July 1891, Newcastle upon Tyne. See also *St. James's Gazette*, 7 Oct. 1895, quoted *I.W.I.*, 12 Oct. 1895, for what is alleged to be the unreported conclusion of Parnell's Creggs speech.
106 *F.J.*, 14 Sept. 1891, Listowel.
107 *F.J.*, 18 June 1891.
108 Auberon Herbert, ' "The Rake's Progress" in Irish Politics', *Fortnightly Review*, 1 Jan. 1891, n.s. vol. 49, pp. 134-35.
109 *F.J.*, 6 July 1891, Nurney.
110 *F.J.*, 9 Mar. 1891, Newry.
111 *F.J.*, 7 Mar. 1891.
112 *F.J.*, 1 June 1891; see also *F.J.*, 3 Aug. 1891.
113 *F.J.*, 14 Sept. 1891.
114 *F.J.*, 26 Jan. 1891, Limerick Junction, 24 Jan.
115 *F.J.*, 3 Aug. 1891.
116 *F.J.*, 7 Sept. 1891, Thurles; see also Parnell at Listowel where he characterised the conduct of the majority as 'the most disgraceful episode which has ever occurred in the history of Ireland'.
117 *F.J.*, 22 Dec. 1890, Johnswell; *F.J.*, 18 Mar. 1891, Cork.
118 *F.J.*, 18 Mar. 1891, Cork.
119 *F.J.*, 6 July 1891, Bagenalstown; 4 July.
120 *F.J.*, 22 Dec., Johnswell.
121 *F.J.*, 11 Aug. 1891, Kells.
122 *F.J.*, 30 Mar. 1891, Sligo.
123 *F.J.*, 6 July, Bagenalstown.
124 *F.J.*, 30 Mar. 1891.
125 *F.J.*, 18 May 1891, Maryborough.
126 *F.J.*, 30 June 1891, Bagenalstown (of John Deasy).
127 *F.J.*, 3 Aug. 1891.
128 O'Brien, *Parnell*, ii. pp. 333-34.
129 *W.F.J.*, 27 Dec. 1890, Kildare, 23 Dec.
130 *F.J.*, 14 Sept. 1891, Listowel.
131 *F.J.*, 23 Mar. 1891, Drogheda; see also *F.J.*, 7 July 1891, Bagenalstown and 25 Mar. 1891, Sligo.
132 *F.J.*, 23 Mar. 1891, Drogheda; see also *F.J.*, 2 July 1891, Bagenalstown.
133 *W.F.J.*, 27 Dec. 1890, Kilkenny 20 Dec; *F.J.*, 22 Dec. 1890, Johnswell.
134 *F.J.*, 28 Apr. 1891, Clonmel.
135 *F.J.*, 22 Dec. 1890, Johnswell; for Parnell's attitude to Davitt see Byrne, *Parnell*, p. 21.
136 *U.I.*, 2 May 1891, Parnell at Clonmel, 26 Apr. 1891.
137 *F.J.*, 22 Mar. 1891, Navan.
138 *F.J.*, 6 July 1891, Nurney, 4 July, and 6 July 1891, Tullow.

139 *F.J.*, 30 June 1891, Carlow.
140 *F.J.*, 24 Mar. 1891, Ballina.
141 *F.J.*, 30 Mar. 1891, Sligo.
142 *F.J.*, 1 July 1891, Glynn.
143 *F.J.*, 18 May 1891, Maryborough.
144 *F.J.*, 4 July 1891, Carlow.
145 *F.J.*, 4 July 1891, Carlow.
146 *F.J.*, 19 Jan. 1891, Tralee.
147 Algar Thorold Labouchere, *The Life of Henry Labouchere* (London, 1913), pp. 227-86; Viscount Gladstone Papers, BM Add. MS 46015-6, *passim;* Labouchere correspondence, Chamberlain Papers, University of Birmingham, *passim.*
148 *F.J.*, 24 Dec. 1890, National Club.
149 *F.J.*, 30 June 1891, Leighlinbridge; see also *F.J.*, 18 June 1891, Bermondsey.
150 *F.J.*, 1 July 1891, Glynn.
151 *F.J.*, 7 Sept. 1891, Westport; see also *F.J.*, 2 Feb. 1891, Athenry.
152 *F.J.*, 1 July 1891, Carlow; *F.J.*, 30 June 1891, Leighlinbridge; see also *F.J.*, 6 July 1891, Tullow.
153 *F.J.*, 7 July 1891, Bagenalstown.
154 *The Economist*, 13 Dec. 1890; *Spectator*, 14 Feb. 1891; see also *P.M.G.*, 16 Jan. 1891, Lord Derby; *The Times*, 23 Mar. 1891.
155 For a compendium of Parnellite attacks on Healy see *N.P.*, 2 July, 11 Aug. 1891, *W.N.P.*, 22 Aug. 1891.
156 *F.J.*, 12 Jan. 1891, quoted *N.P.*, 2 July 1891; see also *F.J.*, 23 Jun. 1891, *N.P.*, 24 June 1891 for an attack on 'the Tappertit traitor'.
157 See also *W.F.J.*, 18 July, Horgan to *F.J.*, n.d.; *F.J.*, 3 June, Harrington's speech at NLI; *F.J.*, 24 Apr., Redmond speech at Arran Quay Ward of NL.
158 *F.J.*, 19 Jan. 1891.
159 *F.J.*, 24 Apr. 1891.
160 *F.J.*, 29 May 1891, Wood Quay Br NLI.
161 *F.J.*, 28 Jan. 1891 NL.
162 *F.J.*, 18 Dec. 1890; see also *F.J.*, 23 June 1891; *I.W.I.*, 4 Oct. 1895, James O'Kelly, 'A Dark Chapter, The Story of the Great Betrayal'.
163 *M.G.*, 8 Oct. 1891
164 *F.J.*, 14 Sept. 1891.
165 Conor Cruise O'Brien has written finely of the Parnell of the split as, rather than an exhausted woman-driven politician, 'a man exalted to combat, delighting in his craft and in a sense — an exaggerated sense — of personal power': *Parnell and his Party*, p. 348.
166 *Westminster Gazette*, 30 Sept. 1893, Letters from Ireland, iii, Avondale, Part II (R. Barry O'Brien?).
167 *F.J.*, 17 Dec. 1890.
168 *F.J.*, 22 Dec. 1891, Kilkenny.
169 *F.J.*, 18 Mar. 1891.
170 *F.J.*, 22 June 1891, Balbriggan.
171 *F.J.*, 9 Mar. 1891.
172 *F.J.*, 22 June 1891.
173 *F.J.*, 23 Feb. 1891, Longford.
174 *F.J.*, 23 May. 1891, Belfast; 22 June 1891, Balbriggan.
175 *F.J.*, 28 Apr. 1891, Tipperary banquet.
176 Elizabeth Bowen, *Bowen's Court* (London, 1942), p. 264.
177 *D.E.*, 22 Dec. 1890, Kilkenny.
178 *F.J.*, 21 Apr. 1891, Ballina.

179 *St. James's Gazette*, 7 Oct. 1895, quoted *U.I.*, 12 Oct. 1894. The article is unfortunately anonymous, but purports to be an account of the latter part of Parnell's Creggs speech omitted when the evening ran late and the reporters left for Dublin.

180 *F.J.*, 29 Nov. 1890.

181 Quoted Henry Harrison, 'Memories of an Irish Hero', *Listener*, 22 Mar. 1951, vol. 45, pp. 445-46.

182 *Nation*, 30 June 1877, 6 Nov. 1880, quoted Lyons, 'Political Ideas of Parnell', p. 754.

183 *F.J.*, 19 Jan. 1891, quoting speech of 9 Nov. 1878. Parnell at Kildare warned against 'the very powerful engines of contamination which the English parties have ready at hand' (*F.J.*, 24 Dec. 1890).

184 *F.J.*, 24 May 1889.

185 Lyons, *Parnell*, pp. 444-45; see also C. C. O'Brien, *Parnell*, p. 234, n.I.

186 *M.G.*, 8 Oct. 1891.

187 *F.J.*, 12 Jan. 1891, Limerick; *F.J.*, 26 Jan. 1891, Waterford.

188 *F.J.*, 27 Feb. 1891.

189 *F.J.*, 6 Apr. 1891, Phoenix Park.

190 *Hansard*, vol. 356, cols. 443-49 (27 July 1891).

191 *Hansard*, vol. 356, cols. 1171-74 (3 Aug. 1891).

192 *Hansard*, vol. 356, cols. 363-70 (24 July 1891); cols. 443-49 (27 July 1891); cols. 1170-4 (3 Aug. 1891). See also *I.W.I.*, 10 Oct. 1896, Frank McDonagh, 'Parnell in Parliament ... Maiden Speech and Last Words'. Even after Parnell's death, amnesty endured as a Parnellite theme: Redmond charged in 1894 that Parnell would have succeeded in prevailing upon the Conservative Home Secretary to grant amnesty were it not for the opposition of Harcourt, the Parnellite *bête noire* (*I.W.I.*, 6 Oct. 1894, J. E. Redmond, 'Mr. Parnell and Amnesty').

193 *N.P.*, 12 Aug. 1891.

194 *N.P.*, 28 Aug. 1891.

195 *N.P.*, 2 Sept. 1891, O'Brien to *N.P.* d. 1 Sept.; *F.J.*, 3 Sept. 1891, Parnell to *F.J.*, d. 2 Sept.

196 See *I.W.I.*, 6 Oct. 1894, F. J. Allan, 'Parnell's Legacy'.

197 *F.J.*, 14 Sept. 1891.

198 *F.J.*, 14 May 1891.

199 *F.J.*, 21 Feb. 1881, interview.

200 T. W. Rolleston, 'The Archbishop in Politics', *Dublin University Review*, Feb. 1886, p. 103; noted C. C. O'Brien, *Parnell and his Party*, p. 130 n.I.

201 O'Hegarty, *Ireland under the Union*, p. 633.

202 Marcus Bourke, *John O'Leary* (Tralee, 1967), pp. 204-5.

203 *S.C.P.*, vol. 9, pp. 440-49, 8708, 3 July 1889.

204 *S.C.P.*, vol. 7, p. 276, q.61, 670-5, 7 May 1889.

205 *Spectator*, 26 Sept. 1891.

206 O'Connor, *Parnell*, p. 52; Tynan, *Twenty-Five Years*, p. 77.

207 *F.J.*, 10 Mar. 1891, O'Leary to the honorary secretaries of the Parnell Leadership Committee, d. 7 Mar. 1891.

208 Marcus Bourke, *John O'Leary* (Tralee, 1967), pp. 202-03; Tynan, *Middle Years*, p. 25; *F.J.*, 10 Mar. 1891; *F.J.*, 6 Aug. 1891.

209 *F.J.*, 1 Dec. 1890, O'Leary to *F.J.*, d. 30 Nov. O'Leary is almost certainly the 'old Fenian leader' referred to by R. Barry O'Brien who attributed his action in supporting Parnell to the Gladstone letter: R. B. O'Brien, *Parnell*, ii. pp. 252-57.

210 *F.J.*, 13 Dec. 1891, O'Leary to *Freeman's Journal* d. 12 Dec.

211 *F.J.*, 23 Jan. 1891.

212 *F.J.*, 16 Dec. 1891, Mitchel to *Freeman's Journal*, d. 12 Dec.
213 *Sinn Féin*, 7 Oct. 1911.
214 *I.W.I.*, 28 Sept. 1895, Nicholas Murphy to *I.W.I.*
215 John O'Leary to John Devoy, d. 9 Nov. 1882, in William O'Brien and Desmond Ryan (eds.), *Devoy's Post Bag* (Dublin, 1948, 1953), 2 vols, ii. p. 222.
216 *Nation*, 27 Sept. 1890; see Marcus Bourke, *John O'Leary* (Tralee, 1967), pp. 195-9.
217 *F.J.*, 8 Jan. 1891, O'Leary to *F.J.*, 7 Jan. 1891.
218 *F.J.*, 19 Mar. 1891.
219 *F.J.*, 15 Sept. 1891, O'Leary to *Freeman's Journal*, 14 Sept. 1891; quoted *The Times*, 16 Sept. 1891. Marcus Bourke is surely wrong to interpret this avowal as an expression of waning enthusiasm for Parnellism on O'Leary's part and a reversion to old certitudes (Bourke, *John O'Leary*, p. 206).
220 O'Brien and Ryan, *Devoy's Post Bag*, ii. pp. 316-29; T. D. Williams, 'John Devoy and Jeremiah O'Donovan Rossa' in T. W. Moody (ed.), *The Fenian Movement*, Dublin, 1978, p. 96.
221 *U.I.*, 3, 10 Oct. 1891; *F.J.*, 27 Apr. 1891.
222 *I.W.I.*, 7 Oct. 1892, Patrick O'Brien, 'Two Irish Chieftains : The Old Guard and the New'.
223 *D.E.*, 8 Oct. 1891; *U.I.*, 31 Oct. 1891; *F.J.*, 26 Oct. 1891. The meeting provides the missing link in Owen Dudley Edwards's account of the interrelationship of the careers of Parnell and Stephens in his postscript, 'Stephens and Parnell', to Desmond Ryan's *The Fenian Chief* (Dublin, 1967). Parnell in 1880 had briefly met Jeremiah O'Donovan Rossa, the most extreme of physical-force nationalists. He disclosed to the Special Commission that he had met O'Donovan Rossa in the breakfast room of the Philadelphia hotel where he was staying and had 'a few minutes conversation' with him. Parnell, surprisingly, was not pressed further. He instructed his own counsel that the introduction had been effected by his rampantly Anglophobic American mother: 'I came down to breakfast and saw him talking to my mother who introduced him to me' (*S.C.P.*, vol. 7, p. 58, q. 58, 992 [1 May, 1889]); Special Commission Brief, Parnell Proofs, p. 57.
224 *D.E.*, 17 Jan. 1891.
225 *I.W.I.*, 6 Oct. 1894, F. J. Allan, 'Parnell's Legacy'.
226 *U.I.*, 10 Oct. 1891, 'Mr. Parnell as I knew him' by 'A Physical Force Man'.
227 *U.I.*, 9 Oct. 1891, 'The Chief's Tactics'.
228 11 Dec. 19(24) Dillon to O'Connor, Dillon Papers, TCD MS 6744, f. 970. The context was an unfavourable contrast of Ramsay MacDonald with Parnell.
229 Davitt to R. Barry O'Brien, 6 Dec. 1893, Davitt Papers, TCD MS 9377.
230 Patrick Pearse, 'Ghosts' (Dec. 1915), in *Collected Works of Padraic H. Pearse, Political Writings and Speeches* (Dublin and London, 1922, p. 241).
231 P. S. O'Hegarty, *A History of Ireland Under the Union* (London, 1952, p. 597).
232 *United Irishman*, 8 Apr. 1899.
233 Special Commission Brief, O'Brien Proofs, p. 27.
234 *B.D.P.*, 8 Oct. 1891.
235 *U.I.*, 23 May 1891.
236 *F.J.*, 18 Sept. 1891, Inaugural Convention of Young Ireland League.
237 *I.N.*, 21 Sept. 1891; for unionist comment see *D.E.*, 18 Sept. 1891.
238 *U.I.*, 3 Oct. 1891.
239 *F.J.*, 17 Dec., 3 Aug. 1891. See also *F.J.*, 20 June 1891 for Rooney's rather innocuous verses, 'Hurray for the Hillside Men'.
240 *D.E.*, 11 Sept. 1891; *U.I.*, 10 Oct. 1891. The argument had been anticipated by Richard Pigott in his essay, 'The Political Poetry and Street Ballads of Ireland', in the *Gentleman's Magazine*, vol. 258, p. 584 (June 1885).

241 *U.I.*, 7 Feb. 1891; for Unionist comments see *The Times*, 6 Feb. 1891, *P.M.G.*, 7 Feb. 1891. See also articles in similar format, *U.I.*, 17 Jan. 1891, 'The Hillside Men', 8 Aug. 1891, 'Peace and Nationhood'.

242 E. W. Hamilton, Diary entry for 9 July 1891, Hamilton Papers, BM Add. MS 48656, f.23.

243 Tynan, *Twenty-Five Years*, p. 331; *Memories*, p. 19.

244 Byrne, *Parnell*, p. 26; Kettle, *Materials for Victory*, p. 96. Parnell, according to Kettle, considered Catholicism 'the only spiritual religion in the world, (*ibid*, p. 55). Parnell's aversion to religiosity took shape early in life. John Howard Parnell recalled that whenever the Rev. Henry Galbraith visited Avondale to give bible lessons to the Parnell children, his brother habitually bolted and hid (*U.I.*, 5 Oct. 1895, 'Some Untold Reminiscences of Parnell').

245 Byrne, *Parnell*, p. 26.

246 *F.J.*, 17 Aug. 1891, Drogheda.

247 *F.J.*, 1 June 1891, Wicklow.

248 *F.J.*, 12 Jan. 1891, Limerick.

249 *F.J.*, 23 May 1891.

250 *F.J.*, 12 Jan. 1891, Limerick, 10 Jan; *F.J.*, 23 May 1891, Belfast; *F.J.*, 1 June 1891, Wicklow. For Walsh's indignant, indeed enraged, apologetics see *D.E.*, 24 Feb. 1891, Walsh to *D.E.*, d. 24 Feb; *N.P.*, 25 May 1891, Walsh to *The Times*, d. 23 May; *N.P.*, 27 May 1891, Walsh to *The Times* d. 26 May; *N.P.*, 4 June 1891. The allegation against Nulty originated in a speech of T. C. Harrington in which he alleged that Healy, while drafting the Leinster Hall resolutions, had said that he had dined with Nulty the previous night, who 'said there was nothing for us to do but stick to Mr. Parnell'(*F.J.*, 10 May 1891; see also *F.J.*, 28 May 1891, Harrington to *F.J.*, d. 27 May). While the allegation was denied by Nulty, and by his administrator, Nulty added that he had been aware of Parnell's letter to O'Brien at Glengariff asserting his moral innocence, and had felt 'disposed to discredit and disbelieve the reality and truth of Mr. Parnell's guilt' (*N.P.*, 27 May 1891, Nulty to *N.P.*, d. 24 May; *N.P.*, 25 May 1891, Michael Woods to *N.P.*, d. 23 May). Kenny had written to Walsh on 19 Nov.: 'Healy tells me he was conversing yesterday with Dr. Nulty and that the tenor of his Lordship's remarks was in this direction', namely that of endorsing Parnell (Kenny to Walsh, 19 Nov. 1890, Walsh Papers, DDA).

251 Morley to Gladstone, 19 July 1886, Gladstone Papers, BM Add. MS, 44255, f. 80 (Walsh's identity is concealed in the published version: Morley, *Gladstone*, iii. p. 347); Robbins, *Parnell*, pp. 30-1.

252 *F.J.*, 20 Apr. 1891, Athlone

253 *F.J.*, 25 May 1891, Newcastle West.

254 *F.J.*, 9 July 1891, Dublin.

255 See Frank Callanan, ' "Clerical Dictation" ': reflections on the Catholic Church and the Parnell split', *Archivium Hibernicum*, XLV, 1990, pp. 64-75.

256 *Spectator*, 24 Jan. 1891.

257 *F.J.*, 19 Jan. 1891.

258 *F.J.*, 20 Apr. 1891, Athlone. See also speeches at Castlerea and Irishtown, ibid.

259 *F.J.*, 2 Mar. 1891, Navan; see also *F.J.*, 23 May, 1891, Belfast; 2 July 1891, Carlow.

260 *F.J.*, 23 May 1891, Belfast.

261 *F.J.*, 3 Aug. 1891, National Club, Dublin.

262 *F.J.*, 7 Apr. 1891, Naas, 5 Apr.

263 *U.I.*, 28 Mar. 1891.

264 *U.I.*, 22 Aug. 1891.

265 *Belfast Evening Telegraph*, 23 May 1891; see also ibid, 12 Feb, 22 May 1891.

266 *D.E.*, 18 Feb. 1891; see also *D.E.*, 27 Jan. 1891.

267 *Irish Ecclesiastical Gazette*, 9 Oct. 1891.

268 *Hansard*, vol. 302, cols. 153-4 (21 Jan. 1886). Parnell in March of that year discouraged the holding of open air nationalist meetings 'in all the localities where such may occasion ill-feeling and excitement, and I refer specifically to Belfast and Derry'. It was he explained 'at all times desirable that we should do nothing to excite the irritation of the Orange section of our fellow countrymen. This is of vital importance now' (*F.J.*, 14 Mar. 1886). While serving an obvious nationalist interest in the prelude to the introduction of Gladstone's Home Rule Bill, it marked at least an attempt to break the turbulent cycle of demonstration and counter-demonstration which had gripped Ulster politics in the preceding three years.

269 *Spectator*, 24 Jan. 1891.

270 See in particular Lyons, 'Political Ideas of Parnell', pp. 768-9; Lyons, *Parnell*, pp. 349-55. At the opposite extreme of misinterpretation stands Katharine Parnell's fatuous, but intriguing, observation in the throes of the Ulster crisis almost a quarter century after her husband's death: 'Parnell was always the enemy of England. I really think Sir Edward Carson's little army would have appealed strongly to him, only he would have tipped the Ulster rebellion into the Home Rule cauldron and have directed the resulting explosion at England' (*Daily Sketch*, 18 May 1914, interview).

11

THE POLITICAL ECONOMY
OF PARNELLISM

The last or almost the last words that my lamented friend ... Mr. Biggar
said to me were 'I wonder what are Mr. Parnell's real politics'.
> T. M. Healy, 15 March 1891[1]

One night before the debates in Committee Room 15 had concluded,
Parnell sat in the Smoking-room of the House of Commons having
a cup of tea with one of the Irish members. For some moments he
remained quite silent, and then suddenly, as if thinking aloud, said:
'Yes, I always felt it would end in this way'. His companion said
nothing. His first thought was that Parnell might be going to talk about
the Divorce court.
'Yes', repeated the Chief, 'I always said it would end badly.'
'What', at length said his companion, 'what did you say would end
badly?'
'The Plan of Campaign', answered Parnell.
> R. Barry O'Brien, *Parnell*[2]

A deepened appreciation of Parnell's economic politics in 1890-91 — then
and since commonly dismissed as crudely opportunistic to the point of
incoherence — is essential to an understanding of his political purpose.
The *Spectator* discerned in his early speeches in the split evidence of 'the
sterility of brain often found in aristocrats who can govern'.[3] His leading
modern biographer wrote that Parnell's public and private pronouncements
were devoid of any coherent doctrine, and marked only by bitterness,
repetitiveness, 'and by an intellectual crudity which caused even sympathetic
observers to wonder if his tragedy had mentally unhinged him'.[4]
Parnell's views require less cursory consideration. The discounting of
his politics in the split, as intellectually vacuous and politically self-serving,
misinterprets the intemperance of Parnell's utterances and demeanour in

276

terms of a deeper incoherence of policy. The crude lurches of his policy
in programmatic terms obscured the subtlety of the perception of the
nationalist dilemma by which they were informed. His pronouncements
on land purchase critically illumine his political purpose in the split, as
well as his antecedent career. His views on other, more narrowly economic
issues, combined the hackneyed with the perceptive, the opportunistic with
the visionary, and were an integral feature of his last campaign.

Parnell's immediate purpose was to rally a radical coalition without abdication of his pretensions to the leadership of the entire nation. 'I have
appealed to no section of my country', he declared at Kilkenny. 'My appeal has been to the whole Irish race'. His commitment was to 'a nation
of the whole of the people'.[5] He marked out his strategy clearly in his
Rotunda speech, of which the *Kilkenny Moderator* in a perceptive analysis
wrote that 'he plainly intimated that he was about to bring up his reserves'.
They comprised those who espoused the Fenian tradition, the labouring
classes, and the boys and young men of the country. The paper shrewdly
noted that the class whose allegiance Parnell implicitly mistrusted was the
tenant farmers:

> He perceived that it was quite within the range of possibility that the farmers
> would go with the Bishops. He perceived too that they were the class who
> would be most likely to attach disgrace to the O'Shea story; and, in the third
> place, that as men who now had a valuable interest in the soil they might
> be inclined to lean upon some great Imperial Party able and willing to preserve
> order, and might be disinclined to follow him much further into the morass
> in chase of wild geese or will-o'-the-wisps.[6]

Parnell would accordingly play off against the farmers the labourers, 'a
class of men to whom if we add the western cottiers — labourers as they
really are — quite outnumber the farmers proper', whom he intended to
divert from their traditional allegiance to Michael Davitt by a promise 'to
organise them; to marshal their forces and be their general for the future'.

Defiant at Kilkenny, Parnell declared: 'I will allow no combination, however
strong, however influential, however apparently respectable to drive me
from my duty to Ireland'.[7] In designating the alignment against him,
Parnell used the term 'combination', as well as 'conspiracy', to embrace
both personal antagonism to him and larger sociological configurations
of opposition. The attack on the 'apparent respectability' of the opposition to him, with its muted class connotations, recurred through his rhetoric.
Of the anti-Parnellite candidate in Sligo, Parnell asked:

> Where was Alderman Collery in 1879 ...? Ah! But Irish Nationality was not
> respectable in those days *(hear hear)*. Of course it was not respectable, it
> did not become respectable until the new-born professors of Irish Nationality
> saw their way to line their pockets with English gold and to appreciate English
> places *(cheers)*.[8]

When he declared after the poll in Carlow that his future task was 'to consolidate the gallant and the independent men of every Irish country and city',[9] the archaic mode of his rhetoric conceded the degree to which his campaign was against the grain of power in nationalist Ireland, and afforded a striking contrast to Healy's assured evocation of the support of a Catholic peasant people.

Taunted with his minoritarian status, Parnell retorted that the support he retained comprised a coalition of the progressive forces within nationalism. He pointed to his high level of support in the cities and towns of Ireland. Speaking in the Dublin working class district of Inchicore (mockingly designated by the *National Press* 'the Mecca of Parnellism'), he asserted that his opponents were contending against 'the elite of the intelligence of the working class, artisans, traders, merchants of Ireland and of Dublin. They are contending against the voices of the great cities like Cork, Limerick, Waterford, Tralee, and the Nationalists of Belfast'.[10] To this urban support, he added that of the rising generation of nationalists: 'I am glad to find that the young men who have grown up with the movement have not forgotten me'.[11]

Parnell further boasted that he retained the allegiance of the veterans of nationalism, the men who had supported him from the outset and sustained the New Departure. He claimed that 'our army is the Old Guard', comprised of 'the same materials that Napoleon called upon at Waterloo'. The opposition to him was 'composed of men who did practically nothing in support of the old Land League movement and came into the movement of the National League — some of them came in at the close of the year 1885, when victory had been practically won'.[12] In spite of the extravagantly martial idiom, Parnell's assertion was justified to the extent that he enjoyed proportionately higher support from politically active nationalists than among the population at large, and shrewdly played on the fact that, after the Land League, the nationalist movement in Ireland had acquired a more conservative aspect, socially as well as politically.

With considerable skilfulness, Parnell at once exploited and controlled the degree to which the split was an inchoate social schism within nationalism as well as a political divide. He remained careful to avert an overtly sociological polarisation which might compromise his pretensions to the leadership in the future of a unitary nationalist movement.

Parnell's claim to have rallied a cohesive and purposeful minority had, notwithstanding his bombastic rhetoric on the subject, considerable substance. He had assembled a formidable minoritarian coalition which was less fractious and disparate than anti-Parnellite rhetoricians could afford to concede. If Parnellism was by the time of the later split distinctly a minority allegiance, and likely to remain so indefinitely, it possessed a sociological as well as a political coherence which posed a serious challenge to the pretensions of anti-Parnellite nationalism. The furious insecurity of the anti-Parnellites in victory unwittingly attested to the strength of Parnellism as a minoritarian nationalist movement. Parnellism was a more coherent and sociologically compact political force than has been appreciated, although it became much less so when deprived by Parnell's death of its political direction. It is in this respect that the posthumous literary myth of Parnell is most misleading: Parnellite allegiance in the split was not reducible to a confederacy of exasperated romantic nationalists, heroically defiant Catholics, and thwarted literary intellectuals.

Just as Parnell's challenge cut deeper than the hasty and cynical campaigning improvisations to which his opponents sought to reduce it, his economic policies possessed a coherence which surpassed their more blatantly opportunistic aspects. He mounted a characteristically ambitious challenge to the configuration of power within Irish society, the significance of which lay as much in its calculated violation of the virtual proprietorial consensus within nationalism as in any of its specific programmatic commitments.

Alone of nationalist leaders, Parnell had a deep awareness of the potential impasse of a home rule state, in which policy would be reduced to the working through of the politics of peasant proprietorship. He was determined to avoid the unconstrained predominance of a Catholic nationalist proprietorial order within an Irish state. It was no part of his purpose to replace a Protestant with a Catholic Ascendancy. He did not intend to permit conservative nationalist values to delimit the ambit of nationalist politics under home rule. He refused to acquiesce in the definition of the national question in terms of the land or to allow land purchase to crowd out other policy commitments.

Parnell remained a sceptical observer of the disposition of socio-economic power in Ireland, and had intimations of the dilemma of nationalist policy more acute than those of his supposedly more intellectual former collaborators. He was profoundly aware of the need for a social structure which achieved a dispersal of political and economic power. An apprehension of socio-economic immobility, as well as political enfeeblement, within nationalism underlay his pronouncements in the split. His response was to seek to couple a guarded heightening of the socio-economic tensions within nationalist society with an insistence on the need for strong political direction. He sought to achieve a controlled, scrupled, social cleavage which would at once facilitate his own restoration and permit the exercise of effective political authority within nationalism: the pestle and mortar of his power.

With that dramatic, even hubristic, fusion of purpose which marked his campaign in the split, Parnell addressed himself simultaneously to his own predicament and what he perceived to be the malaise of nationalism. He fiercely insisted that the forces arrayed against him were the same forces which would threaten the effectiveness of a home rule state. This hegemonical equation of his own interests with those of the nation was integral to his campaign. What unites his programme in the split, on land purchase as on other economic issues, is the attempt to constrain the social and political predominance of the middle and larger tenantry, and to delimit the extent to which it was rendered independent either of his leadership or of a prospective home rule government. To this end, he sought to divide the smaller from the larger tenants, and to withhold proprietorship, at least provisionally, from the larger tenants. He sought to constrain their predominance from above by the retention of a residual class of residential landlords, and from below by constituting a more coherent and powerful nationalist underclass comprised of the smaller tenants and the labouring classes.

He championed a powerful and economically interventionist role for a home rule state in promoting industry and rural development, to counter the economic predominance of agriculture. Implicit in this programme was the premise that without countervailing state economic power, a home rule government would find its freedom of action lastingly curtailed by the predominance of an indivisible class of peasant proprietors. The undertaking of so ambitious a political endeavour when he was politically *in extremis*, while it astonished contemporary observers and severely taxed the endurance of his parliamentary supporters, was characteristic of the audaciousness of Parnell's statescraft in the split as he applied himself to sculpting, if he could not fragment, the monolith of peasant proprietorship.

Historiographical consideration of Parnell's position on the land question has tended to stop at his controversial speeches on the second reading of the Land Purchase Bill in April 1890, and on the Chief Secretary's vote in July of the same year; and even those speeches have been regarded as curious parliamentary aberrations rather than as of intrinsic significance. Yet the politics of land purchase are central to the controversy of the split. There is a striking complementarity between Healy and Davitt, a conservative and a radical nationalist respectively, in their response to Parnell's support of Balfour's Land Purchase Bill in the split. Healy's brilliant and devastating attack on 'Mr. Landlord Parnell' marked the public ebullition of suspicions long harboured and criticisms privately expressed. Likewise, Davitt wrote to a correspondent in 1886 that 'Parnell is most anxious to retain the landlords as such, even under a home rule constitution, and I fear that if he succeeds in this policy, he will be wrecking that constitution within 12 months after it is conceded'.[13] Davitt, like Healy, construed Parnell's views in terms of a recidivism of caste.

Characterisations of Parnell's views on the land question as the product by his own class provenance are echoed in the *marxisant* modern historiography of the land war and of Parnellism, which analytically replicates Davitt's contemporary failure of political perception. To assess

Parnell's policy on the land question primarily in terms of 'an Anglo-Irish squire' seeking to reconcile his 'own people' to nationalism so as to enable them to assume their proper place as leaders of the home rule movement is to perpetuate a chauvinistic reductionism of Parnell's politics in the split. To write of Parnell's 'essential social conservatism', without sharply differentiating Parnell's 'conservatism' from that of the proprietorial Catholic nationalism championed by Healy, obscures a distinction without which Parnell's career cannot be comprehended.[14] Conversely the concept of 'Parnell's ideal of a rural bourgeois Utopia', for which F. S. L. Lyons argued, misconceives the thrust of Parnell's politics, identifying as his aim what he struggled most determinedly to avoid.[15]

Class reductionism affords limited assistance in elucidating Parnell's political purpose, and neglects the subtle perception of the complex interrelationship between the land question and the politics of home rule which informed his statescraft. Parnell was neither a prisoner of his caste nor the incorrigible agrarian reactionary of Healy's rhetoric. His object, as well as the immediate restoration of his own leadership, was the establishment of a viable, economically pluralistic, Irish state: the conservation of a residential Anglo-Irish landlord class was instrumental, rather than prompted by an atavistic allegiance of class.

Parnell's policy on the land question remained integral to his statescraft at the close of his career, as it had been at its outset. Not least, it afforded a means of addressing the difficulty posed by the opposition of unionists in Ulster to home rule. None of the landlords need go, and most of them would stay, he sanguinely advised Lord Ribblesdale in 1887: 'Ulster', he said, 'would have accepted the Home Rule Bill had it passed, as she would not have deserted her co-religionists disseminated over the rest of Ireland'.[16] Likewise at Portsmouth in June 1886 he could not accept as credible the idea of partition, declaring in an unhappily forceful image: 'It would be like the garrison of a city, who finding themselves beleagured, sought refuge within the citadel, and left the rest of the population to be massacred'.[17] If Parnell underestimated the intensity of the opposition within Ulster to home rule, what distinguished his policy from that of his nationalist contemporaries was his determination to retain a residual grid of landlord power throughout the country to mitigate, if it could not overcome, unionist apprehensions on the advent of home rule. His policy on land purchase was intended to strengthen the rational self-interest of Irish Protestants in the avoidance of partition. It was through the land question that he sought to contain what was (even though the concept of partition, mooted in the parliamentary debates on the Home Rule Bill, was subjectively abhorred) the objectively partitionist tendency within nationalism itself.

Writing in 1898, J. L. Garvin wrote that 'to bring the Irish gentry and Unionist Ulster into the new system in support of an Irish Parliament one

thing was necessary' — the cessation of the land agitation. He argued that
Parnell intended to do just this, as his opposition to the Plan of Campaign attested. 'Under a Home Rule Parliament he would have dropped
the land agitation. Within six months he would have shifted his base, and
Belfast and the landlords would have been the support of his power. Ireland
would have become a whole.'[18] Garvin neglected the subtlety of Parnell's
policy, and, in exaggerating the prospects of his strategy successfully overcoming unionist opposition to home rule, strayed from analysis into myth.
Yet he grasped the essential thrust of Parnell's strategy. It was a strategy
that revealed an alertness to the dilemma posed by unionist resistance to
home rule which, though imperfect, far surpassed that of his nationalist
contemporaries.

From the outset of the divorce crisis, Parnell moved to shift his position
on Balfour's Land Purchase Bill from exceedingly — even suspiciously —
qualified opposition to open support. He actively promoted the idea, thrice
mooted by him in 1890 before the divorce crisis[19] and adopted by Balfour
in the course of the split, of discriminating in favour of the smaller tenants.
Parnell's distinction between two broad classes of tenants was highly significant, emanating as it did from a nationalist source. It signalled his determination to divide — so as better to rule — the preponderant class of
nationalist tenant farmers. His policy was dualistic. He at once insisted
that he was the true champion of land purchase, and sought to confine
land purchase under Balfour's bill to the smallholders who made up the
majority of the Irish tenants. Even in Parnell's professed terms, of treating
Balfour's bill as an interim measure, and availing of the immediately
available funds for land purchase rather than as a final settlement of the
land question, it was a dramatic initiative, and marked his most ambitious
attempt to reconcile the land question and the home rule movement since
the New Departure. It would have required all of Parnell's pre-split authority to implement it; with the split he lost what power he possessed to contain, and redirect, the flowing tide towards a complete measure of land
purchase.

Moreover, compelled to present what had been the premises of his policy
in crudely programmatic terms, he rendered himself vulnerable to a
devastating counter-attack by Healy and Davitt. They accused him of a
cynical endeavour to polarise the tenants in pursuit of his own lost
hegemony, revealing that the true allegiance of the erstwhile Irish leader
was owed to his own class. Parnell, they taunted, stood exposed as a fac-
tionist and a landlord. On this issue most of all, Parnell's subtle statecraft,
necessarily vulgarised as he struggled to reconstitute his leadership, was
highly susceptible to polemical misrepresentation.

In supporting Balfour's bill, Parnell sought to present himself as the
supporter of land purchase as against the anti-Parnellites, who, he

unconvincingly charged, had no wish to see the land question settled. He sought to impute to the majority generally the view associated with John Dillon, as to the necessity of maintaining the agrarian agitation so as to avoid any diminution in the ardour of the nationalist struggle for home rule (a view to which Healy was vociferously antagonistic). He further charged the majority with deferring to the Liberal alliance and in particular to Radical opposition to the expenditure of public moneys on an Irish land settlement, in its doctrinaire opposition to Conservative legislation, even where beneficial to Ireland. 'What harm did the reduction of your rents since 1881 do to the cause of Irish nationality?', he asked at Irishtown,[20] a theme to which he frequently reverted:

> The Seceders say — 'No, don't let us settle the land question. Let us keep the tenant farmers poor and miserable, because if we make them prosperous we shall have no cry to appeal to them with' ... I protest against this doctrine which is now preached by the Tim Healyites *(groans)*, that in order to retain the forces of Irish nationhood we must keep the tenant-farmers and labourers under the hoofs of the landlords.[21]

Ironically, this was precisely the policy which Parnell was himself pursuing in relation to the larger tenants. It was moreover an unconvincing taunt. Parnell was unable to posture credibly as the true champion of land purchase, or to transform any residual gratitude to him on the land question into support on the scale he required for the restoration of his leadership.

Parnell alleged that Healy's determination to wreck Balfour's Land Bill of 1887 had led Morley to intercede to ask him to restrain Healy. Healy, he charged, did not dare to vote against the Land Purchase Bill: 'No; he comes over to Ireland, sneaks over, and calumniates me in the columns of his miserable newspaper'. Invoking Harold Frederic's cabled report to the *New York Times*, he alleged that, after his speech on the Irish estimates the previous year, Healy had cabled to America 'to consign me to a lunatic asylum'.[22] He asked abusively, 'Where would Tim Healy *(groans)* get his fees if there were not more tenants to be evicted *(groans)*'. He construed Healy's opposition to the Land Purchase Bill in terms of a dogmatic refusal to accept any measure, however beneficial, from 'Bloody Balfour'.[23]

Parnell justified his support for Balfour's bill on the grounds that the sum of £30 million provided represented the limit of the moneys available from the exchequer for land purchase for the conceivable future. However questionable this assumption, what was far more controversial — and in nationalist terms deviant — was that he came exceedingly close to suggesting that Balfour's bill, in modified form, could provide for an indefinite period an adequate resolution of the Irish land question. Parnell in May hailed the Balfour amendment, for which he declared himself 'undoubtedly responsible', as 'encompassing a very large reform' which would, 'practically settle one half — and the worst half — of the Irish land question'. That half, however, was computed by reference to the total number of tenants affected, rather than the area of farmland (which fell far short of one half). It was an ambitious, if too obvious, attempt to sunder the ranks of the Irish farmers, which had been in the main opposed to him, so as to carry the allegiance of the numerically predominant smallholders. He added an expression of regret that an additional £10 million was not forthcoming, which would have permitted the entirety of the tenants below £30 valuation to buy out their holdings (which comprised 514,000 out of a total number of holdings of 585,000).

In response to Healy's attacks on his support of the Balfour amendment, Parnell sought to mitigate its rigours in the case of 'the small class undoubtedly, but still most important class', of tenants over the valuation of £30, by advocating that they should be advanced moneys up to £30 of their valuation as a contribution to the purchase price of their holdings, or to fine down their rents. He thereby himself abrogated the £30 million financial limit which was the rationale for supporting the bill in the first place.[24] In attacking the subsequent emasculation of the Balfour amendment by the House of Lords 'aided and abetted by the seceders', he claimed that the amendment in its original form would have reduced the cost of solving the land question from £140 million to £70 million, being a sum of £30-£40 million in addition to the £40 million already advanced.[25]

In a speech at the outset of the Sligo election, Parnell enlarged his agenda on the land question in a transparently opportunistic fashion. In a variation of his policy of discriminating in favour of the smaller tenants, he advocated the application of moneys to be saved by a reduction in the numbers of the Royal Irish Constabulary (a hackneyed nationalist revenue-saving proposal) to permit the 200,000 to 250,000 Connaught smallholders, in his alarmingly anachronistic phrase, 'go rent-free in perpetuity'. 'It would be a great stroke to give these poor people their freedom, just as great as liberating the negro slaves of America'. He added somewhat defensively: 'That is not a wild scheme; it is one that I have thought over for many years'.

In the same speech, made before Balfour had unveiled his amendment, Parnell afforded a dramatic glimpse of what was in agrarian nationalist terms the profoundly heretical tendency of his thinking on the land question. While acknowledging the eventual necessity of providing for land purchase facilities for the tenants of large- and medium-sized holdings, he made a highly revealing proposal for the legislative alleviation of their position, avowedly as an interim measure. He suggested that the rents fixed under the Land Acts be reduced by 30 per cent, in return for the advance from public funds of a loan to the landlords at a favourable rate of interest of a sum equal to seven to ten years purchase, for the purpose, remarkably, of enabling them to discharge the encumbrances of their estates.[26] It is difficult to interpret this proposal as other than an attempt to stabilise, at least in the medium term, the relationship of landlord and tenant in the middling to large holdings by eliminating, if not the

necessity, at least the urgency of the need, to extend the scope of land purchase to those holdings. Moreover the effect of enabling landlords to
discharge encumbrances of their estates was to enroot them more deeply
in the tenurial landscape: there was little point in discharging their secured
liabilities if the estates were shortly to be sold or expropriated under land
purchase legislation.

Rather than clearly qualifying his support for the measure as simply
an instalment in the unfolding settlement, Parnell appeared to contemplate
(as he almost certainly did) the possibility of Balfour's bill in amplified
form affording a practical approximation to a resolution of the Irish land
question. It was a perilous equivocation, for which he was remorselessly
assailed by Healy. In subsequent controversy with John Dillon, Parnell
insisted that he never contended that Balfour's bill might have settled the
Irish land question, merely that had the Balfour amendment remained intact, 'it would have settled about four-ninths of the land question, and
would have brought the rest of the land question within measurable distance
of solution'.[27] By that time the damage had been done.

The declared premise of Parnell's strategy was in any case unconvincing. His contention that the Balfour bill represented the final offer for the
indefinite future of a British government to solve the Irish land question
did not command credence among a tenantry which sensed an inexorable
legislative trend towards a resolution of the land question by a broad
measure of land-purchase. Most nationalist farmers correctly believed that
it was premature to close with a British government to achieve a final settlement of the land question: the purchase price of holdings was not yet
acceptable, nor were the land-purchase facilities deemed adequate. The
shrewdness of Healy's response to the Land Bill commended itself to tenant
farmers. They did not believe Healy's position to entail the ideological antipathy to land purchase to which Parnell sought desperately to reduce it.
They understood and approved his stance in terms of a 'bearish' agrarian
strategy, the creation of a purchasers' market in land. Parnell moreover
was out of step, not merely with the aspirations of the tenants, but with
the expectations of the landlords. Irish landlords and tenants were already
embarked on that long course of collusive engagement which would mould
the legislative politics of the land question. Irish unionist opinion looked
with disfavour on the Balfour amendment, and the Irish Landowners' Convention was instrumental in procuring its emasculation in the House of
Lords.[28] In the event, the Balfour Land Purchase Act was to prove a
failure, complicated and unpopular with landlords and tenants alike, and
the moneys drawn down were only moderately in excess of those advanced
under earlier and more restrictive land-purchase provisions.[29]

Parnell's ambitious attempt to use his policy on the Land Purchase Act
to effect a far-reaching modification of the balance of power in Ireland
was misconceived. It came too late, and was in his political circumstances

in the split quite unrealistic. The moment of equipoise in the power of landlord and tenant, on which his strategy was predicated, had already passed; moreover, in the face of Healy's marshalling of Catholic nationalist power, such delicate equilibration of social forces had become impossible. Yet Parnell continued to conduct himself as if he were the leader of an unbroken movement. He boldly maintained his advocacy of a limitation on eligibility for land-purchase facilities, rather than leaving it to the government to assume the responsibility. It was characteristic of Parnell that, while he was aware that he would at best emerge after the general election as the leader of a minoritarian nationalist party, he adamantly declined to conduct himself as the leader of a defeated minority. He refused to cease to behave as the Irish leader.

Parnell in July sought to counterbalance his support for the Balfour Land Purchase Act by the advocacy of compulsory purchase. He added to the constitution of the National League a commitment to an extension of the legislation provisions to all occupying tenants and to the compulsory expropriation of all lands remaining unsold after five years.[30] This was stronger ground politically, but the initiative was too belated and unconvincing to undo the damage of his support for the Balfour act.

Parnell further damaged the credibility of his policy on land purchase by his confused espousal of the principle of land nationalisation at the labour conference held under Parnellite auspices in March. While disassociating himself, in a clear reference to Davitt, from 'crude theories which have been put forward by certain persons for the purpose of carrying out that principle', he professed himself to have been always in favour of land nationalisation. He immediately rendered this surprising avowal virtually meaningless by defining land nationalisation in terms of what he declared to be its intended object, the transfer of taxation from food and other items to land. He went on to urge purchasing tenants to 'leave a very wide margin' in settling a price with their landlords:

> ... they ought to remember that the taxation of land for the purposes of education, for the purposes of promoting the industrial resources of Ireland, and for the benefit of the working classes, is bound to be materially increased in the future, and that they should leave a very wide margin for themselves in the making of those bargains, so that they may be able to do their duty to the landless masses of their fellow-countrymen who have stood so gallantly and valiantly by them in the struggle for their hearths and homes *(applause)*.[31]

By this wilful misdefinition of land nationalisation, Parnell sought to reconcile his dual claim, as the champion of land purchase and the special protector of the interests of those who held no land. His spurious embrace of land nationalisation was impossible to reconcile with his complete repudiation of the idea, as espoused by Davitt, in 1884.[32] Healy effortlessly derided the pronouncement: 'Why, the idea of this man who only six months ago proposed in the House of Commons that landlordism should be maintained, and that the farmers should not be bought out, but that rents should be fined down, now being so extreme that nothing will satisfy him but the nationalisation of the land!'[33]

Through the split a bitter controversy raged on the issue of the evicted tenants of the Plan of Campaign. This was inextricably linked to the question of the so-called Paris Funds, American moneys subscribed to the Irish party and lodged in an account in Paris of which Parnell, Justin McCarthy and Patrick Egan were trustees. Parnell at Boulogne succeeded in procuring the release of £8,000, thereby deepening Healyite mistrust of William O'Brien's bona fides and of McCarthy's ability to deal with Parnell.[34] Thereafter he continued to conduct himself with unyielding determination. In insisting that he would consent to the release of the funds only if they were to be administered by McCarthy and himself, a proposal he knew to be unacceptable to the anti-Parnellites, he sought to exploit anti-Parnellite doubts as to McCarthy's capacity: 'They would not allow him to go into a room alone with me. I suppose they were afraid I was going to eat him up. They would not allow him to meet me unless the whole of them were at his back'.[35] In one of a series of public letters to McCarthy, he astutely dismissed the implication that McCarthy could not be trusted to administer the fund: 'However natural it may be that your colleagues should thus reiterate their declaration of my unworthiness for the duty, it is remarkable that they should extend the same condemnation to you, their newly chosen leader'.[36]

At the outset Parnell had pledged himself in extravagant terms to protect the evicted tenants. He promised 'that no evicted tenant shall suffer — that the last shilling of the National coffer shall be expended to save and protect them'.[37] As the controversy turned against him, and the evicted tenants of the Plan of Campaign aligned themselves with the majority and fell under Healy's sway, his attitude hardened. He now insistently urged the course of action he had pressed on William O'Brien at Boulogne, the parallel pursuit of 'fair and honourable settlements' and of legislative redress, while 'reserving sufficient funds to cover the retreat of the remaining wounded soldiers who cannot be protected by settlements of fair legislative protection', which he advocated as a reprise of the strategy he had adopted in relation to the evicted tenants in 1882.[38]

At Clonmel in April, he emphasised his own opposition to the Plan of Campaign at the time of its inception, and accused the majority of improvidently squandering scarce nationalist resources. He drew the distinction he had expressly declined to countenance in January, between the evicted tenants of the Land League and those of the Plan of Campaign. His main responsibility was to the former, larger group ('I suppose there are five or six evicted tenants from the old Land League tenants evicted by Gladstone for the one Plan of Campaign tenant evicted by Balfour'). He charged the anti-Parnellites with discriminating against the Land League evicted tenants, and weakly argued that 'they can make more readily political capital and create a clamour against me out of the Plan of Campaign tenants'. Parnell codified his policy on the Plan in terms of four principles: no discrimination between categories of evicted tenants, the careful husbanding and application of nationalist financial resources, the pursuit of fair settlements, and of legislative redress.[39]

Parnell's vulnerability on the evicted tenants' issue, set against the background of the near-breakdown of the Plan of Campaign, and the drying up of financial support in Ireland and the United States, was manifest in the triumphant cry his Clonmel speech elicited from the Dublin unionist *Daily Express:* 'The Plan of Campaign has collapsed. Mr. Parnell now advises a *sauve qui peut.* The tenants are to take what terms they can get, one and all. The Campaign is broken and the army of paid patriots is routed ... Patriotism at a pound a week proves to be more than the resources of the party can bear'.[40]

At Wicklow in June, Parnell proclaimed his determination not to have the Paris moneys 'lavished and wasted' by nominees of the majority other than McCarthy. He declared that 'since the Plan of Campaign tenants have been taken under the special protection of the Seceders, and I regret that it should be so, we can say of ourselves that the Land League tenants are under our special protection'.[41] Yet in August Harrington was obliged to announce the suspension of grants from the National League to the evicted tenants, blaming the diversion of funds to the National Federation, an open admission of the increasingly parlous financial state of Parnell's organisation. The National League, exulted the *National Press*, had 'completed its treason by throwing to the wolves the evicted tenants'.[42]

Parnell increasingly emphasised the responsibility to the evicted tenants of those who had initiated the Plan of Campaign — namely Dillon and O'Brien — and of the anti-Parnellite party which had assumed responsibility for its direction. With Dillon's and O'Brien's adherence to the anti-Parnellite cause, the controversy surrounding the Plan of Campaign entered its most embittered phase. Parnell disavowed with increasing vehemence any responsibility for the Plan. Using the same justification for his non-intervention against the Plan of Campaign on which he had relied in his Eighty Club speech of May 1888, he explained that, having recovered from the illness which had afflicted him at the time of the Plan's inception, he had been preparing to stop the Plan when forestalled by the government's prosecution of Dillon: 'I felt I could not with any sort of chivalry raise any opposition to Mr. Dillon ... I am here to admit, today, in all humbleness and humility, that it was one of the political mistakes which I have made'.[43]

Parnell's final reference to the subject was a blistering attack at Listowel on the launching and conduct of the Plan of Campaign, in particular the fiasco of the construction of the 'town' of New Tipperary. His speech proclaimed his disdain for Dillon, and the completeness of his breach with O'Brien. Insisting that the tenants should never have been urged to leave their holdings, he declared 'I am not responsible for the eviction of a single one of the Plan of Campaign tenants', and charged that the Plan of Campaign was initiated not in response to agrarian exigencies, but to the requirements of the Liberal party:

> This struggle of the Plan of Campaign was commenced not for the benefit of the tenant farmers, but for the benefit of an English political party ... These men should not have been urged to leave their holdings because certain English members said it was necessary to show that the Irish people were fighting Balfour.

Most woundingly, Parnell declared that he had made the Fund increase and grow, 'and I am not going to have it squandered and wasted without my knowledge by a parcel of idiots', who had expended substantial sums on New Tipperary to find they had no title to the ground on which it was built. Had Dillon and O'Brien not succumbed to English dictation, and continued collecting money in America, the evicted tenants could have been supported indefinitely.[44]

The evicted tenants' issue told heavily against Parnell. He was charged with preferring his pretensions to the Irish leadership over their plight. The *National Press* wrote that Parnell 'means to keep a firm grip on the Paris fund. He shifts and shuffles and tricks and dodges while the tenants starve'. 'For the perils of the evicted', it wrote, 'he displays that cold-hearted indifference which is part of his character.'[45] 'His cynical desertion of these poor devils', wrote Harold Frederic, 'was perhaps the most despicable action in his whole behaviour since the divorce court exposure'.[46]

In January Healy took the attack on the floor of the House of Commons and with shrewd polemical instinct linked Parnell's treatment of the evicted tenants of the Plan of Campaign with his policy of constructive engagement with Balfour:

> I did expect that the hon. Member for Cork [Parnell] would have enabled us, through the great influence he now possesses with her Majesty's Ministers, to hear of some great scheme, whether by means of a secret understanding or otherwise — some scheme put forward by him, or by, as his mouthpiece, one of her Majesty's Ministers.
>
> J. O'Connor (Tipperary South): Have some decency.
>
> Mr. Speaker: Order, order!
>
> Mr. T. M. Healy: Some scheme with regard to evicted tenants, who, we are informed, are the Honourable Member's special care ...[47]

Healy's savage mockery was not purely an attack on what he presented as the Parnell–Balfour entente: it was also a pre-emptive strike against any government-sponsored initiative on the evicted tenants' issue for which Parnell might have claimed the credit.

However ruthless, Parnell's indictment of the Plan of Campaign as ill conceived and ineptly directed was well founded, and reflected misgivings felt by him from its inception. While he had distanced himself from the Plan of Campaign in his Eighty Club speech in May 1888, he had not actually disavowed it, and his attack in the split came too late to avoid the taunts of opportunism and of callous indifference to the fate of its evicted tenants.[48] In the matter of the evicted tenants, as on other questions in the split, Parnell's determination to reduce the issue to one of raw competency made no concessions to the sentimentality of Irish public opinion. As in Committee Room 15, he effortlessly demonstrated his strategic mastery, yet it little commended him to an electorate which in large part believed the achievement of home rule and land purchase to be virtually assured, and to whom Parnell's displays of political proficiency appeared cynically and divisively self-advertising.

While Parnell's declaration at Ballina in April 1891 that 'my mind has always been given to the development of the industrial resources of Ireland'[49] appeared in the circumstances of the split a desperate boast, his pronouncements on economic issues in and before the split, and his entrepreneurial activities in Wicklow, revealed a commitment to economic development and industrialisation uncommon in nationalist politics.

He saw Ireland not as a pre-industrial society, but as one whose industrial development had been disrupted. This powerful intimation reflected the influence of his Wicklow background on his formation. Parnell's Wicklow as well as being the Wicklow of late-eighteenth-century politics, of Grattan and of rebellion, was the Wicklow of stalled industrial revolution. In his evidence to the Select Committee on Colonisation in July 1890, he improbably attributed the lack of industry in Ireland to the 1798 rebellion, or rather, as he awkwardly corrected himself, to its repression, 'which cut the industrial development of the country into two', and to the famine of 1845-49 which arrested the recovery.[50] If the argument was untenable, it revealed Parnell's deep sense of the aborted industrialisation in Ireland. His economic ventures in Wicklow were conceived by him as the reconstituting of a broken industrial tradition.

He sought in the split to appropriate the issue of industrialisation as a distinctly Parnellite theme, elevating trade and industry into defining criteria of statehood: '... Ireland without trade, without industry, but merely as an agricultural country, never can be a nation'. A nation without trade and industry would be 'maimed and incomplete'.[51] He looked to 'those great works of industrial improvement which were so wanting now, which were so much required, and which were the sign and type of all great nations and communities'.[52] He declared it to have been one of his most ardent hopes 'that we might at some time or other under the fostering care of an Irish legislature develop the struggling industries of Ireland ...'.[53]

In his evidence to the Select Committee, Parnell had categorised the resources of Ireland as 'underdeveloped, more underdeveloped than those of any country I know ... absolutely underdeveloped as regards her industrial resources', and urged the development of Irish resources instead of emigration.[54] At Ballina in April 1891, advocating an ambitious programme of public works to develop the west of Ireland, he assimilated the province of Connaught to South Africa: 'Connaught is like an unsettled country. It is like a desert land. It is like that great territory of South Africa which is now being opened up ...'.[55] In economic terms the comparison was perverse: the west of Ireland was notoriously considered to be over-populated. Yet if his designation of the west as a great hinterland comparable to southern Africa suggests a markedly superficial assimilation of the economics of the imperial frontier, the image of great unexploited resources was not without force. It moreover illumines a neglected vein in Parnell's thought, and suggests that the affinity between Parnell and Cecil Rhodes owed something to a common economic vision as well as to a coincidence of political interest.[56]

Parnell's economic views reflect a fusion of a strain of Anglo-Irish thinking on the development of Irish economic resources dating from the early eighteenth century, deriving from Berkeley, Molyneux and Swift, with nineteenth-century romantic entrepreneurship. Parnell was touched by the spirit of late-nineteenth-century capitalism to a degree unique among nationalist leaders. His actual proposals for the expenditure of public moneys to achieve economic development, while sketchy and fragmentary, and all too easily dismissed as improvisations to meet the needs of the political moment, nevertheless suggest an imaginative engagement with the concept of economic development conspicuously lacking in anti-Parnellite nationalism. Interviewed in the course of of the Kilkenny election, Parnell declared that 'amongst the projects which I have been considering and planning for the future development of Ireland, when I have the power to act upon a large scale, is the connection by railway of the Kilkenny coalfields with the iron ores of the Wicklow mountains'. He proposed other railway arcs of an ambitious industrial web in the south-east, as well as the linkage of the coalfields of Tyrone and the iron ores of Antrim.[57] While the proposal in the context of the Kilkenny election seemed blatantly opportunistic, he had in 1887 privately advocated a Wicklow–Kilkenny railway link.[58] At Liverpool in December 1889, speaking of Irish industrial retardation, he said: 'Our coal was inland, our iron was separated from our coal, and we were not able to bring the two into juxtaposition'.[59] He reverted to his advocacy of an Antrim–Tyrone railway in his evidence to the Royal Commission on Mining Royalties in March 1891.[60]

Parnell did not repeat his advocacy of protectionism, which he had briefly espoused for tactical purposes in 1885, but he advocated the expenditure

of public moneys to lay the foundations of Irish economic development.
He argued with some justice that the Liberals, under the influence of
Radical economic doctrines, were averse to public expenditure on land purchase and on public works in Ireland, for which he accordingly looked
to the Conservatives. This postulate was central to Parnell's espousal and
practice of 'independent opposition' in the split. It provided the political
underpinning for his *rapprochement* with Balfour's Irish administration,
from which he hoped to obtain ameliorative economic measures. He thus
seized on the promise of a Conservative Irish Local Government Bill to
urge that county boards should have 'very extreme industrial powers',
backed by power to borrow from the Treasury.[61]

The premise of Liberal frugality and Conservative bounteousness led
to two of Parnell's most ill-adjudged utterances in the split. Most damagingly, at Ballina, in the course of denouncing 'the English Radical
economical classes who tell me we are not to receive what is really Irish
money to be spent in Ireland on the alleviation of the sufferings of so many
of the people', he went on to commend, in all too memorable a phrase,
Balfour's programme of public works: 'I say "more power to his elbow",
so long as he is giving employment to the people of Ireland ... and I hope
we may be able to keep him to the work'.[62] The remark was immediately
seized upon by Healy as evidencing Parnell's landlord affiliations and his
cynical entente with the Chief Secretary.

Parnell's antipathy to doctrinaire Radical economics prompted also his
extravagant declaration at the Labour conference in March:

> I would throw what is called 'political economy' to the wind. You may de-
> pend upon it that when you have obtained universal suffrage — and even
> if you do not obtain it — the text books of political economy will be very
> materially altered within the next few years. The men who write these books
> write them for their market. They write them for the people who are able
> to pay them, and when the electoral classes by their increased educational
> knowledge and by their increased political power are able to get [the men]
> who write these books to devote their brains and their talents to their ser-
> vice you may depend upon it that these notions which now possess currency
> as full of accurate maxims of political economy will be very materially
> changed and altered.[63]

If these remarks strikingly elucidate Parnell's penetrating mistrust of
ideology, they were an extravagance he could ill afford in the political circumstances of the split, and were damagingly fastened upon by Healy as
indicative of the opportunism and incoherence of his economic pronouncements.

Parnell in 1886 had privately expressed his dissatisfaction to William
O'Brien as to the financial provisions of Gladstone's Home Rule Bill. He
was disappointed not to have secured customs and excise for a home rule
state, and concerned at the high level of the Irish contribution to the

imperial government from Irish revenues to the imperial government. While he believed that Gladstone had been ready to concede customs and excise, but had been overborne in cabinet, he complained to O'Brien that 'the old gentleman, when it comes to be a question of cash, is as hard as a moneylender'.[64] The negotiations over, Parnell had nonetheless staunchly supported the bill.

It was a card he resolved to play in the split. At Ballina he put in issue the financial scheme of the 1886 bill, a measure which 'although good in principle, almost perfect in principle, was very defective in detail'. Its financial provisions he condemned as 'simply a scheme of robbery by England of Ireland', leaving an annual deficiency of £750,000. He proclaimed his refusal to permit the perpetuation of 'the robbery which has been going on since the Union', and insisted that England should lose rather than gain financially. He estimated the development of Irish resources required an annual expenditure of £3 million on public works and the like, for which the Home Rule Bill had made no provision. He then touched on the delicate issue of taxation under home rule:

> I think you all agree with me that it would be a very unfortunate position of affairs if, after we came back to College Green with a great flourish of trumpets, we should find when we had to settle down to work that it would be necessary to send to Ballina and to the West of Ireland and Ireland generally, a message to the effect that we would require an additional rate of a shilling in the pound to pay the expenses of our Government *(hear hear)* ... I would rather think the people of Ballina and the other parts of the country have somewhat different expectations *(hear hear)*. Instead of sending down here to Ballina to levy a rate of a shilling in the pound to carry on a Home Rule Government, I rather think you would be expecting that Government to send you down a grant for the purpose, say, of deepening your river, your route to the sea, or for the purpose of doing some other useful work for your district *(cheers)*.[65]

Parnell thus staked out the ground for an attack on the financial provisions of a future Liberal Home Rule Bill, and pressed home the actuality of the problems which would confront a home rule government.

Parnell's sudden emergence as the champion of labour was central to his strategy in the split. His appeal to labour, characterised by his habitual substantive elusiveness, and tightly subordinated to his political purpose, affords an illuminating study in the guarded radicalisation of Irish politics he tried to achieve. He sought to rally labour to his cause, to incorporate it within his struggle for nationalist hegemony. What he offered labour was an enlarged role within the nationalist movement, underwritten by his personal commitment to marshal the labour interest, so as to further social justice and economic progress within a disciplined nationalist movement, and eventually under a strong home rule administration.

At the Rotunda he eschewed specific commitments and offered a pledge of sponsorship to the Irish labour movement, to vindicate the interests of labour within the nationalist consensus:

> ... above all things we can help the Irish working men to consolidate their movement, to organise it in such a fashion as will be further conducive to the best interests of the National cause *(loud cheers)*. We can show them how far they may go with regard to the due interests of the National question. We can help them to attain that limit. We can insist that they shall attain it *(cheers)* ... Taking this question at first sight as a question before Home Rule, before you can have the power of settling it for yourselves and of regulating it as you wish best, I say that I shall do my utmost to reconcile all prejudice upon this question, so that this great labour movement upon which we all depend, and which must be all powerful by its right governance and direction upon the future of Ireland, may be educated, may be guided into courses in consonance and in aid with the legislative independence of Ireland.[66]

If Parnell's speech fell short of any substantive concession, it nonetheless represented a challenging and innovative treatment of the labour question within nationalism, at a time when land purchase had eclipsed other objects of nationalist economic policy, and when the Irish nationalist movement was developing in a markedly conservative direction, away from its ostensibly radical origins. Parnell's commitment was to throw the weight of his authority into the scales to redress the balance, so as to protect and foster the interests of labour in what was an increasingly inimical political environment.

As he now looked to the Irish labouring classes 'for the recruits to the grand army of Irish nationality which I hope to lead in the near future', so they were entitled to look to him.[67] In a calculated challenge to the nationalist orthodoxy, Parnell decried the neglect of the interests of the labourers by the movement over which he had presided for a decade, which he confessed 'has been able to do very little but harm for the Irish trades'.[68] At Listowel in September 1891, he surveyed the condition of the Irish labourers, and conceded the betrayed radical promise of the Land League:

> Their lot has been the hardest lot of any class in Ireland. While the tenant farmers have had some material improvement in their condition and have been made more independent, the Irish labourers as a mass and as a whole have had nothing at all done for them. On the contrary, so far as the Land League movement has had any effect upon their conditions it has injured them.[69]

While arrogating to himself the credit for the Labourers' Act of 1883, which he claimed to have drafted, he discounted it as 'a very small measure of relief for those poor people'.[70]

Parnell's purpose was to bind up the interests of labour with those of the Parnellite movement. To labour he offered an enhanced role within nationalism rather than an independent status. If he was to secure 'for labour and for the dignity of labour her rightful and proper and overwhelming position in the councils of the nation',[71] there were reciprocal constraints on labour which he emphasised throughout his campaign. He was obliged to have regard to 'my position towards larger interests even than the interests of labour'.[72] He expressed himself confident that 'the workingmen of Ireland will remember that their fealty is first, and above all things, due to Ireland as a nation'.[73]

Parnell's espousal of the labour cause was constrained by his alertness to the different economic circumstances of Ireland and England. The labour issue in Ireland was 'a subordinate question, owing to the want of manufacturers in our country'.[74] He was concerned to maintain Ireland's existing industries,[75] and to avoid Irish economic backwardness becoming copperfastened by unrealistic wage expectations derived from English levels of economic development. Confronted with a strike at his Arklow quarries, and politically attacked in his capacity as a private employer, he affirmed his determination to run the works on commercial principles rather than prejudice the prospects for the establishment of what he believed could become a substantial industry.[76]

Even while embarked on an appeal to labour, Parnell preserved his habitual caution on the labour questions of the day. At the Labour Conference, convened under Parnellite auspices in March, he confined himself to endorsing the general tenor of the economic programme adopted, reserving his policy in relation to specific policies.[77] His policy on the leading contemporary labour question, that of statutory provision for an eight hour day was elaborately qualified and economically rigorous. This did not prevent it from being scurrilously lampooned by an infuriated Davitt, who at a meeting in the Sligo election chanted:

> Eight hours work and eight hours play
> Eight hours in company of Kitty O'Shea.[78]

At Newcastle-upon-Tyne in July, he displayed that economy of commitment so often obscured in the sound and fury of the split. He pledged the best efforts of Ireland in support of 'every well-considered attempt on the part of the English workingmen to improve their position', but was unable to see his way to supporting the general eight hours bill promoted by R. B. Cunninghame Graham then before parliament. He insisted that conditions of employment were subject to international competition, and could only be resolved by international negotiation. He confined his support for the statutory limitation of working hours to the cases of miners, government employees, employees in monopoly industries and those in dangerous or unhealthy employments. That commitment was substantially embodied in an amendment accepted by him to the constitution of the National League. His only immediate commitment was to vote for an eight hour mining bill then before Parliament.[79]

On the second topical labour issue, whether improvements in working conditions and terms of employment were to be brought about by statutory regulation or by recourse to strikes, Parnell favoured the former, and attacked the Liberals who 'objected to invoking the aid of the legislature to assist the working man in his unequal struggle against capital and against his employer'. He had always held that it was destructive of the interests of a trading and manufacturing community 'to invoke the rude agency of strike and combination for the purpose of obtaining what the Legislature ought to grant you by a stroke of the pen'.[80] During the Sligo election he told a deputation of labouring men that, while he had always favoured unions, he was not in favour of the strike mechanism, declaring it 'absurd that the working people should be driven into strikes when they can settle upon fair terms with their employers'. In what was intended as a reference to Davitt, he observed that 'in Ireland a number of persons have encouraged and organised strikes and then left the men to their fate in the most heartless and shameless manner'.[81]

If Parnell's stance would nowadays be regarded as suspiciously authoritarian, it was in its time the progressive view, conceived in opposition to the ravages of *laissez-faire* on the condition of the working class. In the early part of 1890, he had an interview with Davitt in relation to the likely outcome of the divorce proceedings. From the outset he counter-attacked by condemning Davitt's attempt to set up a labour organisation in the south of Ireland. He asked him whether what the labourers and artisans wanted could not be better obtained through the National League. According to Davitt, he declared trade-unionism to be 'but a landlordism of labour, opposed to individual liberty', and that were he at the head of a government he would keep them down as Bismarck did in Germany: 'Whatever has to be done for the protection of the working classes in the state is the duty of the government, and not the work of men like John Burns and others who will, by-and-by, unless prevented, organize the working classes into a power that may be too strong for the government to deal with'. Davitt was taken aback by the harshness of Parnell's comments, which were contrary to many of the views he had formerly expressed. He attributed Parnell's severity to anger at being questioned on the matter of the divorce, and regarded his comments as a piece of inspired bluff directed against him. The reference to Bismarck was probably of a piece with Parnell's celebrated semi-jocular threat to lock Davitt up on the concession of home rule.[82] Yet the thrust of his comments to Davitt, like his labour programme in the split, reflected his conviction that the amelioration of the condition of the working class was a responsibility of government rather than of trade unions.

Labour had, Parnell declared, 'before her a great parliamentary and constitutional future',[83] with which he sought to ally himself. He looked to the aggrandisement of the power of the labouring classes in Britain and

Ireland under an enlarged franchise:

> And in these days of extended suffrage, almost of universal suffrage, un-
> questionably the power of these classes has increased. I am sure that the
> progress of the improvement of the labouring and artisan classes will be
> gradual, and will be increasing and incessant ... I shall attempt every way
> that I can and assist all well-considered means for the purpose of bettering
> the condition of these long-suffering classes *(cheers)*... Great movements now
> going on in England and in Scotland will react in this country, and the legisla-
> tion obtained for the labouring classes of Great Britain and Ireland will also
> be shared by those in Ireland. I am confident that the poorer people of this
> country will benefit by the results of this labour movement in Great Britain;
> and that in the new Parliament labour will have a greater share and a larger
> representation, and that from the English legislature will come measures of
> amelioration for the working men and the labourers *(cheers)*.[84]

Parnell's deployment of the labour issue was not confined to the Irish
theatre of policy, but was aimed deep within British politics, as he sought
to contrive a vice within which to fix Gladstone and the Liberal party. From
the outset he conceived his appeal to labour in part as a reciprocal challenge
to Gladstone on English terrain. At the Rotunda, Parnell declared his party
could assist English radicals on the labour issue, 'to strengthen the back
of the Grand Old Man, and remove any unwillingness on his part to face
this question'.[85] Alive to the vulnerability of Gladstone and the Liberal
party on the labour issue, he struck hard at Gladstone's left flank. He
vehemently attacked the Liberals' treatment of the labour question, and
ostentatiously cultivated his relations with the nascent British labour party. To a labour deputation in Newcastle upon Tyne he declared: 'The labour
question will be after the Irish question, the great question of the future
and to the men who work with their hands will belong, if they intelligent-
ly use the constitutional power which is now theirs, the direction of the
political future of this country'.[86]

Parnell proclaimed himself free to address the labour question 'since
Mr. Gladstone has dismissed me with less than twenty-fours hours notice
from my position as leader of the Irish Parliamentary Party'. Up to that
time, 'it was not for me to interfere in a British question which belonged
solely, well not entirely solely to Great Britain, in which unfortunately the
Irish people, owing to the absence of trade, manufactures and industries
in that country, had a very much smaller concern than the English
people'.[87]

Parnell responded to the taunt of inconsistency on the labour question
by attributing his earlier stance to the constraints of the Liberal alliance.
Only his acquiescence in Gladstone's wishes had restrained him from championing the Labour movement prior to the split. In English constituencies
he had been obliged to abide by the wishes of the Liberal party. Specifically
Parnell repented of his action in the Mid-Lanarkshire by-election in throwing the Irish vote against Keir Hardie, in deference to the wishes of

Gladstone and against the advice of his 'very dear friend', Cunninghame Graham.[88] He declared, 'my hands are free now once more, and I shall give all the aid I can to the labour movement'.

Parnell attracted the endorsement in the split of labour leaders Keir Hardie and the maverick socialist parliamentarian R. B. Cunninghame Graham. Hardie recalled with gratitude Parnell's sympathetic reception of a Scottish Miners' Federation deputation on an eight hour bill for Scottish miners in 1887, when Parnell took the unprecedented and farsighted step of introducing Hardie and an associate to a meeting of the Irish party to state their case.[89]

Parnell's treatment of the labour question was not always assured. The *Belfast Evening Telegraph* astutely observed that 'he is proficient in all the claptrap of the agrarian agitation, but has not yet acquired the correct lingo of Socialism. He, therefore, speaks on that subject with a stammering tongue'.[90] At the engineering workshops in Inchicore he expressed himself in an inaptly extravagant idiom, though one infused by that personal intensity which set him apart as one of the rare visionaries of industrialisation in the Irish nationalist tradition:

> I have, by nature and inclination, always been irresistibly drawn towards those classes who, following the example of the great god Vulcan have transformed from the metals those beautiful works of strength and duration which so distinguish this locality, and I shall never be wanting in securing, so far as I can to the artisans, to the engineers, and to the mechanics of Ireland, every opportunity of advancing their interest through the constitution, through Parliament, through combination, and by every other legitimate means.[91]

His sudden conversion to the cause of labour excited the bitter contempt of his opponents. 'What has he done to merit being called a friend of labour?', enquired William Martin Murphy.[92] Healy charged that Biggar had twice written to Parnell urging a subscription to the strike fund of the London dockers, and had not received the courtesy of a reply. Michael Davitt, who had most cause to feel aggrieved, mocked Parnell's 'political death-bed repentance'. Parnell had formerly cast himself in the role of 'the restraining influence' on the national movement; now 'this whilom Conservative' had espoused a progressive labour programme plagiarised from Davitt's *Labour World*.[93]

Parnell's labour programme was ruthlessly subordinated to his political purpose, as part of his strategy to redress the increasingly conservative configuration of power within nationalism. For all the derision — and fear — his appeal on labour excited among his opponents, it was marked by an eschewal of facile commitments. Unbending and unyielding, he refused to engage in a sectional appeal which compromised or diminished his pretensions to power in Ireland at the head of a united nationalist movement. Far from being reckless or extravagant, Parnell's treatment of the labour issue attests to the deceptive toughness of his politics in the split, and the instinctive frugality of his substantive commitments.

His economic politics differed significantly from those of his conservative nationalist opposition in the split. What distinguished Parnell's views was the coupling of *laissez-faire* economic views with a belief in assertive governance. A cautious and conservative disposition was counterpoised by a belief in strong *dirigiste* political authority. His pledge to act as the special protector of labour, while subserving an obvious political self-interest, should not be dismissed as an entirely cynical or insubstantial commitment. Set in the context of his wider strategy in the split, in particular his treatment of land purchase and his commitment to industrialisation, Parnell offered a critique of a conservative nationalist home rule state moulded by the politics of peasant proprietorship. He proffered what was in reality the only alternative to acquiescence in the consolidation of a conservative nationalist order.

It was very much a personal commitment, and contingent on his restoration to authoritative influence within nationalism. His death supervened, and in the event, Parnell's influence on the Irish labour movement was arguably adverse.[94] He retained in death a potent allure for the Dublin working class, less as a consequence of his appeal to labour than of the intensity of the allegiance which he had attracted in Dublin. In the split he was the undisputed leader only of Dublin, and became on his death truly the capital's lost leader. His enduring myth permitted the Parnellite party to exploit electorally the labour interest in the capital at the expense of a distinct Irish labour movement. Yet the very failure of that movement to deflect the course of conservative nationalism serves to deepen the riddle of Parnell's lost promise in Irish politics.

In the split, Parnell played the Avondale card, and strove to turn to political advantage his status as a regional entrepreneur. He pointed to Avondale and its environs as a kind of experimental microcosm of Parnellite political economy.[95] He was belauded by the *Freeman's Journal* as 'the beau idéal of Davis' Irishman who knew Ireland from its history to its minerals', and excruciatingly hailed as 'an Irishman of the right metal'.[96]

He vaunted his links with Wicklow, 'the county where my interests, so to speak, lie ... and the county ... where I hope to spend the remaining years of my life'. He pointed to his involvement with the project to deepen the harbour of Arklow, expressing his hope that Arklow might take the lead amongst fishing ports and 'eventually become one of those model towns which go so much in these days to make up the strength and greatness of a nation'.[97] An Arklow curate was driven to protest at Parnell's attempts to exploit his associations with the town, observing it was 'very bad taste of Mr. Parnell's friends to try and make political capital out of his business visits to the town'.[98]

Parnell's profligate expenditure of his energies in the split was not confined to politics. He pursued with undiminished vigour his metallurgical
ventures in Wicklow, which provided him with solace and refuge. He passed
the Christmas Eve of 1890 on a visit to his iron mines, making no allusion
whatever to political events in his conversation with the *Freeman's Journal* reporter who passed the day with him.[99] In his evidence to the Royal
Commission on Mining Royalties in March 1891, Parnell made his only
unforced concession of defeat in the split. It related to his lifelong quest
for gold:

> ... I never could find any gold in Wicklow, except for the gravel; you can
> find it in the streams; if you pan gravel you can find traces of gold, but never
> gold to pay, and although I have assayed about a hundred samples from the
> county Wicklow, I have not found more than a trace of gold in any one of
> them. I fear the quantity of gold in Wicklow is very limited'.[100]

Undismayed, Parnell had already embarked on a major alternative enterprise. He acquired a lease to work iron mines lying in the district of
Ballycappell and Ballard some five miles from Avondale, and was committed to working 'the great lode of magnetic iron ore which was last
worked about two hundred years ago', and contemplated, if the lode proved
of sufficient depth, re-establishing blast furnaces in Wicklow.[101]

Attacked for having spent selfishly the moneys given him in the Parnell
testimonial of 1883, he retorted that he had spent the moneys in Ireland
among the working men of Wicklow, to some 250 of whom he had given
employment at his mines and quarries. In the Carlow election he struck
back at anti-Parnellite accusations of misappropriation of nationalist funds,
and attempts to exploit a strike at his quarries at Big Rock near Arklow,
by contrasting his own role as an entrepreneur with the deficient economic
contribution of his middle-class Catholic nationalist opponents, most
notably Healy: 'The money I have received from the people of Ireland I
have given back to the people of Ireland ... I have invested my money at
home in Ireland, I have not, like Mr. Tim Healy, sent £16,000 to invest
in a Scotch floorcloth company'.[102]

Stung by the attacks of the *National Press*, Parnell invoked his economic
contribution in Wicklow in a speech in which the roles of statesmen and
entrepreneur briefly merged:

> I have been attacked as an employer of labour by the *National Press (groans)*
> and the seceders, men who never spent sixpence of the money they grabbed
> from the different National funds in giving any employment in this country.
> I should not have spoken on this subject, because I have no desire to ob-
> trude my affairs in this contest. But I will tell what I have done as I have
> been attacked. In the neighbouring town of Wicklow during the last seven
> years I have spent from £5,000 to £10,000 a year in giving employment to
> the labourers of Wicklow and the town of Arklow *(A voice: 'Practical
> patriotism')*. And I am not ashamed to say I have rescued that town from

the poverty which always afflicted it in the winter *(cheers)*. I only wish I could have given ten times as much. I am accused of having spent my testimonial from the Irish people on my own selfish wants, but I have spent it on the people who gave it to me *(cheers)*, and any of them who go to the county of Wicklow to Arklow Rock, will see a hundred men and boys given employment all the year round *(cheers)*. That is how the money is spent, and I want to know what Tim Healy has done *(groans)* — what he has done with the £20,000 or £30,000 for his valuable services during the past ten years ... No, my interests are in Ireland *(cheers)*. I wish well to the people of Ireland. I spend my money in Ireland. I believe in the industrial regeneration of Ireland ... It was on account of these works employing the labouring men of the town, instead of being compelled to go into the workhouse in the winter or to emigrate, have found work for them at their doors *(cheers)*.[103]

It was a just and affecting reply. Yet its argument revealed how readily his economic role could be reduced, in the virulent chauvinism of Healy's rhetoric, to the stilted and archaic philanthropy of the improving landlord, an exercise in the economics of condescension.

The fury of Parnell's retort was sharpened by the awareness that he was continuing to lose a great deal of money in his economic ventures in Wicklow. He stated he had expended £5,000 to £7,000 a year giving employment during the preceding six or seven years: 'I have lost heavy sums of money from it, and I have never yet received any benefit from these works'.[104] Against false Healyite taunts that he was an evicting landlord, Parnell retorted that he had never evicted or raised the rent of a tenant. His tenants held their lands at lesser rents than any other tenants in Wicklow, at 40 per cent of judicial rents, 'and their rents are so low that I think I am the only landlord in Wicklow whose tenants never went into the Land Court, but were better outside of it'.[105] There were good reasons for Parnell's amusement, noted by Edward Byrne, at a comment of Randolph Churchill's: 'He laughed heartily — and his laugh was very rare, though he had a cheery and most genial smile — at one expression of Randolph's, who said that "the only paupers in Ireland were the Irish landlords"'. As he grimly advised his brother in 1887, 'Politics is the only thing I ever got any money from'.[106]

If Parnell's economic ventures in Wicklow were commendable, they did not reflect particularly well on his financial judgement, and call into question his mother's assertion that 'he would have died a millionaire if he had minded his own business'.[107] Parnell had embarked on a solitary endeavour to revolutionise the local economy which had disastrously overstretched his resources. The improvidence of that financial commitment, which contrasted so sharply with both his personal frugality and his realism as a politician, reflected at once the seigneurial spirit of *noblesse oblige* of the Anglo-Irish patriot and improving landlord, and the strange intensity of his industrial vision. His ventures in Wicklow must engender some doubt as to the wisdom of the ambitious industrial policies he adumbrated in the split ('when I have the power to act upon a large scale'), which, if implemented, could have resulted in the economic débâcle of Avondale writ large across the country: it is perhaps significant that Parnell's disregard of the elementary principles of *laissez-faire* had got him into some logical difficulty in his argument in relation to underinvestment in Ireland before the Select Committee on Colonisation in July 1890.[108] That is not however the sole or necessarily correct criterion to apply to Parnell's economic pronouncements in the split. The roles of entrepreneur and politician, if intersecting, remained distinct. Parnell in the split did not so much articulate fragments of an industrial programme as an enabling vision.

What endures is Parnell's intense belief in the necessity to exploit neglected opportunities for industrial development, a reproach to his own class and to his Catholic nationalist critics. This determined his investment of his own resources and provided the *idée maîtrise* of his economic pronouncements in the split. The economic views he professed were shaped by his political purpose and formed by his craft of power. In refusing to define the substantive politics of home rule in terms of the working through of land purchase, he challenged the complacencies of nationalist belief. It was characteristic that he did not seek merely to mobilise a political coalition for the purpose of reconstituting his leadership. With that unremitting ambitiousness which marked his politics in the split, he sought to recast the nationalist polity. Parnell defiantly insisted that his leadership offered the only alternative to the reactionary stasis of a Catholic agrarian nationalism.

David Thornley has written: 'Every Irish leader failed, Parnell perhaps most totally'.[109] Yet the concept of failure is hardly apposite for so overwhelming an achievement. A classic practitioner of politics in the age of transition to mass democracy, Parnell left on his country the impress of statehood. The myth in this respect embodied as well as a memory an argument: he had achieved the formation of Ireland as a modern democracy. His loyal follower James O'Kelly wrote in 1894 that through Parnell 'the national will found its supreme and authoritative expression. Under his rule Ireland was a nation'.[110]

In death he remained an indomitably challenging figure, confronting those who had opposed him in the split and his unionist adversaries alike. Two decades later F. E. Smith unhistorically appropriated for unionism the credit for his fall, and in still casting Parnell as the man to beat, paid unwitting tribute to the greatness of the Irish leader:

> When they were met, as they were today, with the message of Mr. Redmond . . . 'I stand where Parnell stood', then they replied, 'if you stand where Parnell stood, we stand with the men who broke Parnell' *(cheers)*. That was the cause for which they had fought these twenty years.[111]

References

1 *N.P.*, 16 Mar. 1891.
2 *Parnell*, ii, p. 288.
3 *Spectator*, 27 Dec. 1890.
4 Lyons, *Political Ideas of Parnell*, p. 772. Lyons went on with unwonted extravagance to characterise Parnell's last phase as 'a kind of *Walpurgisnacht* in which fragmentary notions — an appeal to the farmers, an appeal to industrial labour, an appeal to the next general election — pass and repass through the doomed man's frenzied brain until death mercifully ends the dance'.

These observations reflect, as well as an assessment of Parnell's rhetoric in the split, the marked tendency to discount Parnell's intellectual powers, and the quality of his political thinking (as distinct from his political judgement). Professor Roy Foster has gone so far as to write of Parnell's 'resolute anti-intellectualism' (in 'Interpretations of Parnell', *Studies*, vol. 80, p. 350). Some at least of Parnell's contemporaries thought otherwise. Oscar Wilde wrote of him as 'a leader of political thought as he is a creator of political force' (in 'The Soul of Man under Socialism', *Fortnightly Review*, Feb. 1891). On Parnell's death, the *Irish Times*, caste-proud against its political grain, stated that Parnell enjoyed the highest heritage of his ancestry, 'that of its intellectuality' (*I.T.*, 8 Oct. 1891).
5 *F.J.*, 22 Dec. 1891; and 20 Apr. 1891, Irishtown.
6 *K.M.*, 13 Dec. 1891.
7 *W.F.J.*, 27 Dec. 1890, Kilkenny, 20 Dec.
8 *F.J.*, 30 Mar. 1891, Sligo Town Hall, 28 Mar. 1891.
9 *F.J.*, 9 July 1891, Carlow.
10 *N.P.*, 8 June 1891. Intriguingly, Parnell's designation of his urban allegiance shaded into that of his Fenian support. The town of Tralee, elevated in an unfortunate piece of Parnellian hyperbole, into a 'great city', was a Fenian stronghold. Likewise Parnell's assertion that he enjoyed the support of 'the Nationalists of Belfast' was demonstrably false, unless the term 'Nationalist' was given its former, narrower meaning, as effectively a synonym for 'Fenian'.
11 *F.J.*, 11 Dec. 1890, Rotunda.
12 *F.J.*, 9 July 1891, Carlow; and 25 May 1891, Newcastle West.
13 *N.P.*, 21 May 1891; Davitt to Richard McGhee, 26 Mar. 1886 (copy), Davitt Papers, TCD MS 9328.
14 Bew, *Parnell*, pp. 15, 28.
15 Lyons, 'Political Ideas of Parnell', p. 760.
16 Ribblesdale, 'A Railway Journey with Mr. Parnell', in the *Nineteenth Century* (Dec. 1891), p. 971.
17 *F.J.*, 25 June 1886.
18 J. L. Garvin, 'Parnell and his Power', *Fortnightly Review*, vol. 64, p. 885 (1 Dec. 1898). Irish unionist observers were far more sceptical. W. O'Connor Morris dismissed Parnell's conciliatory course towards Irish unionist opinion in the late 1880s as merely a bait to lure Gladstone deeper into the home rule trap: 'His success in Ireland with the classes he sought to conciliate was hopeless, because they knew him well; but Mr. Gladstone and those who acted with him were deceived' (W. O'Connor Morris, *Memories and Thoughts of a Life* [London, 1895], p. 290).
19 *Hansard*, vol. 343, cols. 978-94 (21 Apr. 1891); vol. 346, cols. 1516-23 (11 July 1891); C. S. Parnell, 'Mr. Balfour's Land Bill', in *North American Review*, no. 403, pp. 43-67 (June 1890).
20 *F.J.*, 20 Apr. 1891

21 *F.J.*, 6 July 1891, Tullow; see also *F.J.*, 21 Apr. 1891, Ballina, and 11 May 1891, Mullingar.
22 *F.J.*, 2 July 1891, Hackettstown; 1 July 1891, Glynn; 18 June 1891, Bermondsey. See generally Lyons, *Parnell*, pp. 437-39.
23 *F.J.*, 4 July 1891, Carlow; *N.P.*, 2 July 1891, Hackettstown.
24 *F.J.*, 11 May 1891, Mullingar.
25 *F.J.*, 24 July 1891, National Convention.
26 *F.J.*, 26 Mar. 1891, Skreen.
27 *F.J.*, 17 Aug. 1891, Kells.
28 Irish Landowners' Convention, *7th Report of Executive Committee*, to be submitted to Convention of 3 Feb. 1891 (Dublin, 1892), pp. 16-20.
29 E. Hooker, *Land Tenure in Ireland* (London, 1938), pp. 63-70.
30 *F.J.*, 24 July 1891, N. L. Convention. Parnell contrived to elicit cheers both for the revolution and constitutional principles: 'It is noteworthy that the two greatest countries on the Continent, France and Germany, were the countries which were the first to abolish the feudal system of land tenure. France abolished it by the iron hand of revolution *(cheers)*, and in some cases by the agency of the lamp-post, and Prussia abolished by purchase, constitutional and peaceful. It has always been the desire of the Irish people to abolish this system constitutionally and peacefully by purchase *(cheers)*; but it is for the landlords of Ireland to consider, and to take warning by, the history of the past twelve years.' The reference to 'the agency of the lamp post' well exemplifies Parnell's dry and somewhat menacing wit.
31 *F.J.*, 16 Mar. 1891. In relation to current taxation, Parnell, while expressing general sympathy with a proposal for the taxation of unoccupied and pasture land, preferred 'speaking as a practical agriculturalist' to exempt tilled land, and land not under grass for a longer period than five years from rates. A vague commitment in favour of the levying of a progressive tax on grass lands was contained in the amended constitution of the National League (*F.J.*, 24 July 1891).
32 *Nation*, 19 Apr. 1884; on the question of land nationalisation see also *U.I.* 24 June 1881.
33 *N.P.*, 16 Mar. 1891, Newry.
34 *F.J.*, 18 Feb. 1891; *N.P.*, 17 Aug. 1891; Healy, *Why Ireland is Not Free*, pp. 38-42.
35 *F.J.*, 18 May 1891, Maryborough.
36 *F.J.*, 8 May 1891, Parnell to McCarthy. For the course of the controversy see *F.J.*, 7 Mar, 14, 24 27 Apr., 8 May 1891; *N.P.*, 6 May 1891.
37 *F.J.*, 20 Dec. 1890, Parnell telegraph to Tipperary tenants, d. 19 Dec.
38 *F.J.*, 4 May 1891, Newbridge.
39 *F.J.*, 27 Apr. 1891, Clonmel; see also *F.J.*, 22 Apr. 1891, speech of John Redmond at the National League. Parnell duly went through the ritual of the introduction of an Evicted Tenants' (Ireland) Reinstatement Bill (*Hansard*, vol. 354, col. 301, 12 June 1891).
40 *D.E.*, 28 Apr. 1891.
41 *F.J.*, 11 June 1891.
42 *F.J.*, 11 Aug. 1891, NL; *N.P.*, 12 Aug. 1891.
43 *F.J.*, 17 Aug. 1891, Kells; *F.J.*, 9 May 1888. Parnell at Kells also controversially disclosed that the Paris Funds were the subject of 'prior claims', which taken with the payments out already made, reduced the balance of the funds to £20,000 out of an original £40,000; for Parnell's partial detailing of the 'prior claims', which Healy was to denounce, see *F.J.*, 19 Aug. 1891, Parnell to *F.J.*, d. 18 Aug.; *N.P.*, 17, 18, 20 Aug. 1891.
44 *F.J.*, Listowel, 14 Sept. 1891. As to Liberal influence in the Plan of Campaign, see Robbins, *Parnell*, p. 11.

45 *N.P.*, 18 Apr., 9 May, 1891.

46 *N.Y.T.*, 26 Apr. 1891

47 *Hansard*, 3rd ser., vol. 349, cols. 1441-2 (30 Jan. 1891).

48 *F.J.*, 9 May 1888; see C. C. O'Brien, *Parnell and his party*, pp. 218-20; Lyons, *Parnell*, p. 384.

49 *F.J.*, 21 Apr. 1891.

50 Select Committee on Colonisation, HC 1890 (354) XII.I (8 July 1890) p. 347. At Liverpool in December 1889, Parnell blamed English restrictions on Irish exports in the eighteenth century for the rupture of Irish industrial develop-ment: 'We had lost the start in our woollen and other industries owing to the penal legislation of the Imperial Parliament' (*F.J.* 20 Dec. 1889). His rhetorically deft use of the highly charged epithet 'penal', conventionally used to describe the anti-Catholic legislative code of the late seventeenth and eighteenth cen-turies, subtly merged two disparate phenomena.

51 *F.J.*, 18 Mar. 1891.

52 *F.J.*, 27 Apr. 1891, Clonmel.

53 *F.J.*, 27 Mar. 1891, Sligo; see also J. H. Parnell, *Parnell*, p. 280.

54 Select Committee on Colonisation, pp. 337-50, HC, 1890 (354), XII.I (8 July 1890).

55 *F.J.*, 22 Apr. 1891.

56 For Rhodes and Parnell's relations, see R. P. Davis, 'C. S. Parnell, Cecil Rhodes, Edmund Dwyer-Gray, and Imperial Federation', *Papers and Proceedings of Tasma-nian Historical Research Association*, vol. 21, no. 3, Sept. 1974; Donal McCracken, 'Parnell and the South African Connection', in Donal McCartney (ed.), *Parnell: The Politics of Power* (Dublin, 1991), pp. 125-36; and see W. T. Stead (ed.), *The Last Will and Testament of Cecil John Rhodes* (London, 1902), pp. 113-38.

57 *F.J.*, 18 Dec. 1891.

58 J. H. Parnell, *Parnell*, pp. 284-85.

59 *F.J.*, 20 Dec. 1889.

60 *Second Report of the Royal Commission on Mining Royalties, 1890-91* (C 6331), p. 315 (11 Mar. 1891).

61 *F.J.*, 24 July 1891, National Convention.

62 *F.J.*, 21 Apr. 1891.

63 *F.J.*, 16 Mar. 1891.

64 W. O'Brien, *Evening Memories*, pp. 107-10.

65 *F.J.*, 22 Apr. 1891, Ballina.

66 *F.J.*, 22 Apr. 1891, Ballina.

67 *F.J.*, 11 Dec. 1890, Rotunda.

68 *F.J.*, 18 Mar, 1891, speech to United Trades Council deputation, Cork.

69 *F.J.*, 14 Sept. 1891.

70 *F.J.*, 11 Dec. 1890, Rotunda.

71 *F.J.*, 11 Dec. 1891, Rotunda.

72 *F.J.*, 16 Mar. 1891, Labour Conference.

73 *F.J.*, 8 June 1891, Inchicore.

74 *F.J.*, 20 July 1891, Newcastle upon Tyne.

75 J. H. Parnell, *Parnell*, pp. ix-x (foreword by Daniel Horgan).

76 *F.J.*, 29 June 1891, Carlow.

77 *F.J.*, 16 Mar. 1891.

78 *N.P.*, 1 Apr. 1891; for what may be the unexpurgated version adopted by Healy as a party piece, see *The Diaries of Sir Robert Bruce Lockhart* (2 vols., Lon-don 1973), entry for 13 Sept. 1933.

79 *F.J.*, 20 July 1891, Newcastle upon Tyne; *F.J.*, 24 July 1891; see also *F.J.*, 27 Feb., 16 Mar. 1891.

80 *F.J.*, 5 Mar. 1891, Clerkenwell.

81 *F.J.*, 28 Mar. 1891.

82 Davitt, *Fall of Feudalism*, pp. 636-37; W. O'Brien, *Evening Memories*, p. 65; R. B. O'Brien, *Parnell*, ii, pp. 158-59.

83 *F.J.*, 20 July 1891, Newcastle upon Tyne.

84 *F.J.*, 21 Sept. 1891, Co. Dublin.

85 *F.J.*, 11 Dec. 1890.

86 *F.J.*, 20 July 1891.

87 *F.J.*, 5 Mar. 1891, Clerkenwell.

88 *F.J.*, 17 Dec. 1891, interview in the *Irish Labour Advocate*, the Parnellite labour organ, no copy of which issue is extant; *F.J.*, 16 Mar. 1891; see also *F.J.*, 16 Mar. 1891, Galway; on Mid-Lanarkshire, see Parnell to Davitt, 20 Apr. 1886, Davitt Papers, TCD MS 9378.

89 *F.J.*, 14 May 1891, Hardie to unidentified supporter in South West Ham; *F.J.*, 13 Dec. 1890, telegraph of Cunninghame Graham, d. 12 Dec.; see also *F.J.*, 18 June 1891, London Correspondent; Minutes of the Irish Party, 11 Feb. 1887. Robert Gallnigad Bontine Cunninghame Graham sat for Lanarkshire North West, describing himself in *Dod's Parliamentary Companion* as 'a Socialist, and in favour of Legislative Independence for Ireland'. Cunninghame Graham had been elected with Parnellite support. Declaring in the Commons in August 1891 that 'I was returned to Parliament solely because I was Mr. Parnell's candidate', he went on to assert with memorable ineptitude, referring to the anti-Parnellites: 'There are some members on the benches near me who seem to have drunk mandragora, and to have forgotten that they were returned to this House simply as voting machines for the Member for Cork' (*Hansard*, vol. 356, col. 1178, 3 Aug. 1891). Already under fierce attack for supposed dictatorial pretensions, Parnell could have done without this early anticipation of the tenets of democratic centralism.

90 *Belfast Evening Telegraph*, 14 Feb. 1891.

91 *F.J.*, 8 June 1891.

92 *N.P.*, 2 May 1891, Wood Quay Ward, NF.

93 *N.P.*, 16 Mar. 1891, Newry.

94 The strength of Parnell's support among the working classes raised an obvious difficulty for the emergence of an internationally aligned Irish left. Edward Aveling, speaking with his wife Eleanor Marx-Aveling at a meeting in the Phoenix Park of the National Union of Gasworkers and General Labourers, was interrupted by cheers for Parnell. (*U.I.*, 23 May 1891; *N.P.*, 18 May 1891; *F.J.*, 18, 19 May, 1891. Ironically the ultra-conservative *National Press* published an article by Aveling [*N.P.*, 23 May 1891]).

95 *F.J.*, 18 Dec. 1890, 5, 10 Jan. 1891.

96 *F.J.*, 5 Jan. 1891.

97 *F.J.*, 28 Jan. 1891.

98 *F.J.*, 15 Jan. 1891, L. J. Farrelly, CC to *F.J.*

99 *Irish Packet*, 26 Mar. 1904, 'A Day with Parnell', by 'An Old Reporter'; *F.J.*, 26 Dec. 1890.

100 *Second Report of the Royal Commission on Mining Royalties* (C 6331), 1891, p. 317 (11 Mar. 1891).

101 *F.J.*, 18 Dec. 1890, 5, 27 Jan. 1891; *Second Report of the Royal Commission on Mining Royalties*, p. 312; see also Parnell to George Crilly, 3 Dec. 1888 (facsimile), NLI MS 15, 735.

102 *F.J.*, 29 June 1891, Carlow. The reference is to Healy's involvement in John Barry's linoleum business in Kirkaldy. See generally Foster, *Parnell*, pp. 179-82.

103 *F.J.*, 30 June 1891, Leighlinbridge.

104 *F.J.*, 29 June 1891, Carlow. At the Special Commission he put the figure at £7,000: *S.C.P.* vol. 7, p. 270 (7 May 1889). His manager Kerr put the annual wage bill between £5,000 and £10,000 (*F.J.*, 26 June 1891, Kerr to *F.J.*, d. 25 June). Parnell in the course of the split was forced to agree to reduce the price of paving setts from his quarries sold to Dublin Corporation against Welsh competition, having already lost substantial sums of money: *F.J.*, 21 Jan., 10 Feb. 1891; *W.P.*, 6 June 1891; J. H. Parnell, *Parnell*, p. 284.

105 *F.J.*, 6 July 1891, Nurney, 4 July.

106 Byrne, *Parnell*, p. 25; J. H. Parnell, *Parnell*, p. 288. H. W. Lucy as if to add the final touch of gloom to Parnell's nemesis, wrote that at the time of Katharine Parnell's second marriage, 'she and her grim spouse were financially derelict' (H. W. Lucy, *Diary of a Journalist* [London, 1920] entry for 29 Apr. 1905).

107 *I.D.I.*, 18 Dec. 1891. Mrs Parnell had been abidingly mistrustful of economic conditions in Europe. Writing in 1860 in connection with the sale of shares, she wrote of the United States: 'A country with such vast resources, and so little affected by repeated European complications, soon recovers its strong and healthy action' (Delia T. Parnell to Mr Brunker, 11 Feb. 1860, letter in possession of the author). In 1891, after Parnell's death, she justified her living alone in her large family home at Bordentown, New Jersey, on sentimental grounds, and 'the belief that the property will some day be valuable to my impoverished descendants in Europe': 'Times are growing to be worse and worse in Europe, and this in after years may be their only asylum' (Robert McWade, *The Uncrowned King* [Philadelphia, 1891], p. 68).

108 *Ibid*, p. 347. For a more sceptical and realistic Parnell, however, see his letter to Michael Davitt querying the prospects for a peat charcoal business: Parnell to Davitt, 4 Mar. 1890 (Davitt Papers, TCD MS 9378).

109 David Thornley, *Isaac Butt and Home Rule* (London, 1964), p. 9.

110 *I.W.I.*, 6 Oct. 1894.

111 *The Times*, 15 Nov. 1910, Constitutional Club, London. I am indebted for the reference to John Campbell, *F. E. Smith, 1st Earl of Birkenhead* (London 1983, repr. 1991), p. 229.

APPENDIX

A Note on the Correspondence of T. M. Healy and the Composition of *Letters and Leaders of My Day*

Healy's memoirs, *Letters and Leaders of My Day*, published in 1928, drew heavily on his letters to his brother Maurice, the '*drahareen óg machree*' to whom they are dedicated. For almost half a century, from 1877 to Maurice's death on 9 November 1923, the brothers maintained a very extensive correspondence. Healy's letters to Maurice provide a running commentary on political events. Even in the edited form published, they are startlingly candid in their fierce partisanship. Healy's letters convey the sense of embattled intimacy within the Healy-Sullivan clan, which expressed itself in unremitting viciousness towards its political adversaries. They provide the main content and tone of the memoirs, described by C. P. Curran as those of 'this Bricrui of Irish politics, "poison tongue of the territories" ... the apologia of a lonely belligerent'.[1].

The letters reflect, as well as the closeness of the political relationship between the two brothers, the fluency and immediacy of the shorthand in which they were written. The brothers corresponded in Pitman's shorthand. As a young man Healy wrote to Maurice of 'the fatal facility of shorthand writing in enabling a fellow to give vent to querulousness, which he would be ashamed to shape with his tongue'.[2]

The originals of Healy's letters to Maurice are not in the Healy-Sullivan papers, which suggests that they were destroyed after Healy had written his memoirs. The fate of Maurice's letters to Healy, which were not extant when he wrote the memoirs, is uncertain: Maev Sullivan accounted for their absence on the grounds that her father was 'the most unmethodical of men', but according to John J. Horgan Healy destroyed Maurice's letters to him 'in a moment of panic' during the period of the Black and Tans.[3]

Much earlier in his career, Healy burnt his letters to his wife, lest they should be seized by police arresting him in 1883. Likewise in November 1885, after Parnell's manifesto, Healy burnt the compromising letters he had received from Labouchere, perhaps hoping vainly that Labouchere would do likewise.[4]

Healy's memoirs also draw on his letters to his father, which are in the Healy-Sullivan papers, and to his wife, which are not.

308

It will not have escaped readers of the two volumes of Healy's memoirs that the letters are almost as brutally truncated as the leaders. From papers in the Healy-Sullivan papers, in the archives of University College Dublin, and the Beaverbrook papers in the Record Office of the House of Lords, it is possible to reconstruct the mode of composition of the memoirs, and to reinstate many of the deletions from the published correspondence.

From early 1925, while still Governor-General, Healy began working on his memoirs.[5] The first stage of composition involved Healy's sister Lizzie typing up his letters to Maurice, which were to provide the centrepiece of the memoirs. Healy wrote to Maurice's widow on 4 May 1925 that 'Liz is busy typing my letters to poor Maurice, and is now as far as 1908, a most astonishing task. Some of the comments on individuals however, are too breezy to be fit for publication. They show the stingers which short-hand enables one freely to dispense!'[6]

Editing was evidently in contemplation from the outset. It is not possible to say whether there was a preliminary editing before they were typed up. In any event, the likelihood is that any highly sensitive or compromising letters had already been destroyed by Healy, on or shortly after their receipt. An extensive body of Lizzie Healy's typescripts survive, but only for the years from 1892, in the Healy-Sullivan papers.[7]

Healy availed himself of the typescripts of the correspondence for the composition of the memoirs, throughout which the correspondence is extensively but selectively quoted from. The typescript first draft of the memoirs themselves, corrected and revised in Healy's hand, are in the Beaverbrook papers, as are the galley proofs of the memoirs which incorporate Healy's corrections and revisions.[9]

The second round of cuts then took place. Some of the excisions were evidently made by Healy, of remaining material judged too sensitive. Most were made by the publishers. In February 1928 Healy wrote to his daughter, of Beaverbrook: 'Max sent my stuff to some firm, but I don't know the result. He reserves "serial rights" for his papers, but thinks excisions will be needed as over 300,000 words make three volumes. I am sick of this knapsack'. To a cable from Beaverbrook asking him to agree to a cut of one-third in the length, 'I replied leaving it in his hands as I am sick of it'.[9] In July he wrote Annie Healy: 'I have delivered my last "galley" corrected to the publishers. I feel a galley-slave! They have cut out one third of the stuff, but I am so tired of twaddle I jerked no protest'. On 7 December 1928, Healy lunched with Beaverbrook and inscribed a copy of the memoirs to him.[10]

References

1 C. P. Curran, 'The Reminiscences of Mr. Healy', *Irish Statesman*, 23 Feb. 1928. Curran observed that 'Mr. Healy is not wholly fortunate in his biographers. There was Liam O'Flaherty, who knew too little, and now there is Tim Healy, who remembers too much'.

2 Healy to Maurice Healy, 10 May 1878, *Letters and Leaders*, Proofs Twenty-Four.

3 Maev Sullivan, *Tim Healy*, p. 179; John J. Horgan, *Parnell to Pearse* (Dublin, 1948), p. 52.

4 *Letters and Leaders*, i. p. 151; Healy to Labouchere, 22 Nov. 1885, Joseph Chamberlain Papers, University of Birmingham, JC 5/50/36.

5 Healy to Annie Healy, 4 Mar. 1925, Healy–Sullivan Papers, UCD P. 6/A/116.

6 Healy to Annie Healy, 4 May 1925; see also 16 Apr. 1925; Healy–Sullivan Papers, UCD P6/A/123, 119.

7 Healy–Sullivan Papers, UCD P6/E/2.

8 The quotations in the text are from the galley proofs, which bear reference Bbk. C/167, in the House of Lords Record Office. I have retained exactly the wayward pagination of the proofs; where relevant I have indicated how the version in the proofs differs from the published version. Otherwise, where a reference is to the proofs alone, it refers to either a passage, or an entire letter, which has been deleted from the published memoirs.

9 Healy to Maev Sullivan, 20 Feb. 1928; 1 Mar 1928, Healy–Sullivan Papers, UCD P6/A/77, 79.

10 Healy to Annie Sullivan, 4 July 1928; Healy to Maev Sullivan, 7 Dec. 1928, Healy–Sullivan Papers, UCD P6/A/170, 181.

BIBLIOGRAPHY

I Unpublished Sources

(i) Politicians' Papers

A. J. Balfour Papers, British Library
Beaverbrook Papers, House of Lords Record Office
Joseph Chamberlain Papers, University of Birmingham
Davitt Papers, Trinity College Dublin
Dillon Papers, Trinity College Dublin
John J. Dunne Papers, Correspondence with M. J. Kenny,
    National Library of Ireland
T. P. Gill Papers, National Library of Ireland
Viscount Gladstone Papers, British Library
W. E. Gladstone Papers, British Library
E. W. Hamilton Papers, British Library
Harrington Papers, National Library of Ireland
Harrington Papers (2), in the possession of Mrs Nora Jordan
Healy-Sullivan Papers, University College Dublin
William Martin Murphy Papers, formerly in the possession of the late
    Thomas V. Murphy
T. D. Sullivan Papers, National Library of Ireland
Alfred Webb Papers, Historical Library of the Religious Society of Friends in
    Ireland

(ii) Miscellaneous Papers

Irish Parliamentary Party Minutes (1) 7 Apr. 1890-5 May 1885, TCD MS 9233
    (2), 11 Jan. 1886-4 Dec. 1890, Dillon Papers, TCD MS 6500 (3), 11 Dec.
    1890-24 June 1895, Dillon Papers, TCD MS 6501
Shane Leslie Collection, Kilmainham Jail (photo-copied, NLI No. 6167)
Sophie O'Brien (Mrs William O'Brien), 'Recollections of a Long Life', unpublished
    typescript, NLI MS 14,218
Justin McCarthy and R.M. Praed, Draft of *Our Book of Memories*
    (London, 1912), comprising original and typescript correspondence, NLI MS
    24958
C. S. Parnell, Autograph draft of the Parnell Manifesto incomplete (9 pp.)
    NLI MS 21,933
Royal Irish Constabulary, Records 1890-91, National Archives, Dublin
Special Commission Brief: Special Commission Act 1888. Brief on behalf
    of Mr. C. S. Parnell M.P. and other Irish M.P.s against whom
    charges and allegations may be made, Lewis and Lewis Solicitors (including
    instructions, witnesses proofs, etc.) NLI ILB 343 p. 8.

II Official Printed Papers

A bill to provide further funds for the Purchase of Land in Ireland, and to make permanent the Land Commission; and to provide for the improvement of the Congested Districts in Ireland HC 1890-1 (III) viii. 345

Hansard's Parliamentary Debates, 3rd series

Purchase of Land (Ireland) Act, 1891, 54 and 55 Vict., c. 48

Special Commission Act, 1888: Reprint of the Shorthand Note of the Speeches, Proceedings, and Evidence taken before the Commissioners appointed under the above named Act (12 vols, London, 1890)

Report of the Select Committee on Colonisation, 1890, HC (354), xiii. 336-50

Returns of the numbers of holdings in Ireland above and below valuations of £30 and £50 for the purposes of the Purchase of Land and Congested Districts (Ireland) Bill 1891, dated 13 May 1891, 29 May 1891, 17 June 1891, HC 1890-1, ixv. 233-4, 260, 285

Second Report of the Royal Commission on Mining Royalties (C-6331), 1890-91. xxiii

III Newspapers and Periodicals

(i) Irish Newspapers

Belfast Evening Telegraph
Carlow Vindicator
Daily Express
Evening Telegraph
Freeman's Journal
Insuppressible
Irish Catholic
Irish Daily Independent
Irish News
Irish Times
Irish Weekly Independent
Kilkenny Moderator
Nation
National Press
Northern Whig
'Suppressed' United Ireland
United Ireland
Weekly Freeman's Journal
Weekly National Press

(ii) English Newspapers and Periodicals

(a) Newspapers
Birmingham Daily Post
Daily News
Daily Telegraph
Manchester Guardian
Pall Mall Gazette
The Times

(b) Weeklies
The Economist
Illustrated London News
Punch
St. Stephen's Review
Saturday Review
Speaker

The Spectator
Truth
Vanity Fair

(c) Periodicals
Black and White
Blackwood's Magazine
Contemporary Review
Fortnightly Review
National Review
New Review
Nineteenth Century
Paternoster Review
Review of Reviews

(iii) Other Newspapers

L'Éclair
Le Figaro
L'Illustration

New York Times
Le Temps

IV Articles, Works and Memoirs by Contemporaries

Adams, Richard, 'Men I have met: Parnell', *Irish Packet* (12 Mar. 1904)

Anderson, David, *'Scenes' in the Commons* (London, 1884)

Anon., *Under Which Flag? Or is Mr. Parnell to be the Leader of the Irish People?* by 'A Gutter Sparrow' (Dublin, n.d.)

Bagenal, Philip H., *The Priest in Politics* (London, 1893)

Barton, Sir Dunbar Plunkett, *Timothy Healy, Memories and Anecdotes* (Dublin, Cork and London, 1933)

Birrell, Augustine, *Sir Frank Lockwood, A biographical sketch* (London, n.d.)

Bodkin, Mathias McDonnell, *Recollections of an Irish Judge* (London, 1914)

Brabourne, 'The Parnell Imbroglio', *Blackwood's Magazine* vol. 149, pp. 142-5 (Jan. 1891)

Bryce, James, *Studies in Contemporary Biography* (London, 1903)

Butler, Sir William, *The Light of the West* (Dublin, 1909)

Byrne, Edward, 'Parnelliana', *Irish Weekly Independent*, 8 Oct 1898; Republished as *Parnell: A Memoir*, ed. Frank Callanan (Dublin, 1991)

Chamberlain, Joseph, *A Political Memoir 1880-92*, ed. C. H. D. Howard (London, 1953)

Churchill, Winston, *Lord Randolph Churchill* (2 vols., London, 1906)

Clancy, J. J., *Mr. Balfour in the Recess* (Irish Press Agency, London, 1890)

——, 'The Question of the Irish Leadership', *Contemporary Review* (Mar. 1891), pp. 455-64

Clarke, Sir Edward, *The Story of My Life* (London, 1918)

Crewe, The Marquess of, *Lord Rosebery* (2 vols., London, 1931)

Curran, C. P.,, 'The Reminiscences of Mr. Healy', *Irish Statesman*, 23 Feb. 1929

Davitt, Michael, 'The Latest Midlothian Campaign', *Nineteenth Century*, vol. 28, pp. 854-60 (Nov. 1890)

——, *The Fall of Feudalism in Ireland* (London and New York, 1904)

Devoy, John, *Devoy's Post Bag 1871-1928*, ed. William O'Brien and Desmond Ryan (2 vols., Dublin, 1948, 1953, repr. 1979)

Dicey, A. V., *A Leap in the Dark* (2nd ed., London 1911)

England's case against Home Rule (London 1896, repr. 1973)

Duffy, Sir Charles Gavan, 'The Humble Remonstrance of an Irish Nationalist', *Contemporary Review* (May 1891), pp. 654-65.

——, *A Fair Constitution for Ireland* (2nd ed., London and Dublin, 1892)

Esher, Reginald Viscount, *Journals and Letters of Reginald Viscount Esher*, ed. M. V. Brett (2 vols., London, 1934)

Figgis, Darrell, *Bye-Ways of Study* (Dublin and London, 1918)

Frederic, Harold, 'The Ireland of Today' by 'X', *Fortnightly Review*, no. 323 (1 Nov. 1893), pp. 686-706

——, 'The Rhetoricians of Ireland' by 'X', *Fortnightly Review*, no. 324 (1 Dec. 1893), pp. 713-27

——, 'The Ireland of Tomorrow', *Fortnightly Review*, no. 325 (1 Jan. 1894), pp. 1-18

Fyfe, Hamilton, *T. P. O'Connor* (London, 1934)

Gardiner, A. G., *Life of Sir William Harcourt* (2 vols., London, 1923)

Gladstone, Herbert, Viscount, *After Thirty Years* (London, 1928)

Gladstone, Mary, *Diaries and Letters*, ed. Lucy Masterson (London, 1930)

Gladstone, W. E., *The Speeches of the rt. hon. W. E. Gladstone 1886-91*, ed. A. W. Hutton and H. J. Cohen (London, 1902)

Gorst, Harold E., *The Fourth Party* (London, 1906)

Gregory, Lady Augusta, *The Kiltartan History Book* (London, 1926)

Gwynn, Denis, *The O'Gorman Mahon* (London, 1934)

——, *Seventy Years*, ed. Colin Smythe (New York, 1974)

Hamilton, Sir E. W., *Mr. Gladstone, A Monograph* (London, 1898)

——, *The Diary of Sir Edward Walter Hamilton 1880-5*, ed. D. W. R. Bahlman (2 vols., Oxford 1972)

Harrison, Henry, *Parnell Vindicated: The Lifting of the Veil* (London, 1931)

——, *Parnell, Joseph Chamberlain, and Mr. Garvin* (Dublin and London, 1938)

——, 'Memories of an Irish Hero', *Listener*, vol. 45, pp. 455-6 (22 Mar. 1951)

——, *Parnell, Joseph Chamberlain and The Times* (Belfast and Dublin, 1953)

Healy, T. M., *Why there is an Irish Land Question and an Irish Land League* (Dublin, 1881)

——, *A Word for Ireland* (Dublin, 1886)

——, 'The Secret of Mr. Parnell's Power', *Pall Mall Gazette*, 28 Dec. 1883

——, 'The Position of the Patriots' (interview), *Pall Mall Gazette*, 8 Dec. 1890

——, 'The Rise and Fall of Mr. Parnell', *New Review*, iv, pp. 194-203 (Mar. 1891)

——, 'A Great Man's Fancies, Some Reminiscences of Charles Stewart Parnell', *Westminster Gazette*, 2, 3 Nov. 1893

——, *Why Ireland is Not Free. A Study of Twenty Years in Politics* (Dublin, 1898)

——, *Letters and Leaders of My Day* (2 vols., London, 1928)

Herbert, Auberon, '"The Rake's Progress" in Irish Politics', *Fortnightly Review*, n.s. vol. 49 (1 Jan. 1891), pp. 126-42

Hughes, Dorothea Price, *Hugh Price Hughes* (London, 1904)

Hurlbert, W. H., *Ireland Under Coercion, the Diary of an American* (2 vols., Edinburgh, 1888)

Kettle, Andrew J., *Material for Victory* ed. L. J. Kettle (Dublin, 1958)

Irish Catholic, The Parnell Handbook, containing handy notes and useful extracts from speeches of Mr. C. S. Parnell M.P. before and after the verdict in the case of O'Shea v O'Shea and Parnell, reprinted from the *Irish Catholic* (Dublin, c. 1890)

Irish Landowners' Convention, *Irish Landowners' Convention, 7th Report of Executive Committee*, 1891 (Dublin, 1892)

Irish Unionist Alliance, *Publications*, vol. 1, 1891-2, (Dublin, Belfast and London, 1893)

James, Sir Henry, *The Work of the Irish Leagues. The speech of the rt. hon. Sir Henry James QC MP replying in the Parnell Commission Inquiry* (London, n.d.)

Johnson, Lionel, '"The Man who Would be King"', *The Academy*, 19 Nov. 1898; republished in *Post Liminium: Essays and Critical Papers of Lionel Johnson*, ed. Thomas Whittemore (London, 1912), pp. 150-5

Joyce, James, *Ulysses*, ed. H. W. Gabler (London, 1986)

Leamy, Margaret, *Parnell's Faithful Few* (New York, 1936)

Lecky, W. E. H., *The Leaders of Public Opinion in Ireland* (London, 1871)

——, 'The Life of Parnell', *Spectator*, 19, 26 Nov. 1898; for attribution see *A Memoir of W. E. H. Lecky, by his wife* (2nd ed., London, 1910, p. 321)

Lloyd, Clifford, *Ireland under the Land League, A Narrative of Personal Experience* (Edinburgh and London, 1892)

Lockhart, Sir Robert Bruce, *Diaries of Sir Robert Bruce Lockhart, 1915-38*, ed. Kenneth Young (London, 1973)

Lucy, H. W., *A Diary of Two Parliaments 1874-85* (London, 1885)

——, *A Diary of the Salisbury Parliament 1886-92* (London, 1892)

——, *A Diary of the Home Rule Parliament 1892-5* (London, 1896)

——, *Gladstone* (London, 1898)

——, *A Diary of the Unionist Parliament 1895-1900* (London, 1901)

——, *Memories of Eight Parliaments* (London, 1908)

McCarthy, Justin, 'Charles Stewart Parnell', *Contemporary Review*, vol. ix, pp. 625-36 (Nov. 1891)
——, *The Story of Gladstone's Life* (London, 1898)
——, *British Political Leaders* (London, 1904)
——, *Reminiscences*, 2 vols. (London, 1899)
——, *The Story of an Irishman* (London, 1904)
——, and R.M. Campbell Praed, *Our Book of Memories* (London, 1912)
McCarthy, M. J. F., *Mr. Balfour's Rule in Ireland* (Dublin and London, 1891)
——, *The Irish Revolution* (one vol. published, Edinburgh and London, 1912)
Michael MacDonagh, *The Home Rule Movement* (Dublin, 1920)
——, *The Life of William O'Brien* (London, 1928)
MacDonald, John, *Diary of the Parnell Commission*, revised from the *Daily News* (London, 1890)
McWade, Robert M., *The Uncrowned King. The Life and Public Services of Hon. Charles Stewart Parnell* (Philadelphia, 1891)
Mallet, Charles, *Herbert Gladstone, A Memoir* (London, 1932)
Moran, D. P., *The Philosophy of Irish Ireland* (Dublin, n.d.)
Morley, John, *Recollections* (2 vols., New York, 1917)
——, *The Life of William Ewart Gladstone* (3 vols., London, 1903)
O'Brien, Frank Cruise, 'Contemporary Irishmen — Mr. Timothy Healy', *The Leader*, 9 Apr. 1910
O'Brien, R. Barry, 'Federal Union with Ireland', *Nineteenth Century* (Jan. 1886), p. 35
——, *The Life of Charles Stewart Parnell, 1846-91* (2 vols., London, 1898)
O'Brien, Sophie, *Golden Memories* (Dublin, 1929)
——, *My Irish Friends* (Dublin and London, c. 1937)
O'Brien, William, *Irish Ideas* (London, 1893)
——, *Recollections* (London, 1905)
——, *An Olive Branch in Ireland and its History* (London, 1910)
——, *Evening Memories* (Dublin and London, 1920)
——, *The Parnell of Real Life* (London, 1926)
O'Connor, T. P., *Gladstone's House of Commons* (London, 1885)
——, *The Parnell Movement* (2nd ed., London, 1886)
——, *Charles Stewart Parnell, A Memory* (London, 1891)
——, *Memories of an Old Parliamentarian* (2 vols., London, 1928)
O'Connor Morris, W., *Memories and Thoughts of a Life* (London, 1895)
O'Donnell, Frank Hugh, *A History of the Irish Parliamentary Party* (2 vols., London, 1910)
O'Hara, M. M., *Chief and Tribune: Parnell and Davitt* (Dublin and London, 1919)
O'Leary, John, *Recollections of Fenians and Fenianism* (2 vols., London, 1896)
O'Shea (Parnell), Katharine, *Charles Stewart Parnell: His Love Story and Political Life* (2 vols., London, 1914)
Pall Mall Gazette, The Story of the Parnell Crisis (London, Jan. 1891)
Parnell, John Howard, *Charles Stewart Parnell: A Memoir* (London, 1916)
Pearse, Patrick, *Ghosts* (Dublin, 1916), republished in *Collected Works of Padraic H. Pearse, Political Writings and Speeches* (Dublin and London, 1992)
Pigott, Richard, *Personal Recollections of an Irish National Journalist* (Dublin, 1883)
——, 'The Political Poetry and Street Ballads of Ireland', *The Gentleman's Magazine,* vol. 258, pp. 584-93 (June 1885)
Punch, The Political Life of the rt. hon. W. E. Gladstone (3 vols., London, n.d.)
Redmond, John, *Historical and Political Addresses 1883-97* (Dublin and London, 1898)

——, 'The Lesson of South Meath', *Fortnightly Review*, vol. 59, pp. 1-6

Ribblesdale, Lord, 'A Railway Journey with Mr. Parnell', *Nineteenth Century* (Dec. 1891), pp. 969-74

Robbins, Alfred, *Parnell, The Last Five Years* (London, 1926)

Russell, Sir Charles, *The Parnell Commission. The Opening Speech for the Defence* (London, 1889)

Russell, G. W. E., *Portraits of the Seventies* (London, n.d.)

Rylett, Harold, 'Parnell', *Contemporary Review*, vol. 129, pp. 473-81 (Apr. 1926)

Sherlock, Thomas, *The Life of Charles Stewart Parnell* (Boston, 1881)

——, and J.S. Mahoney, *The Life and Times of Charles Stewart Parnell* (New York, c. 1886)

Stead, W. T., *The Pope in the New Era* (London, 1890)

——, 'The Story of an Incident in the Home Rule Cause: The Fall of Mr. Parnell',

——, *Review of Reviews*, vol. ii, pp. 598-608 (Dec. 1890)

——, 'North Kilkenny and its Moral', *Pasternoster Review*, vol. 1, no. 4, pp. 332-41 (Jan. 1891)

Sullivan, A. M., *Speeches and Addresses 1859* (2nd ed., Dublin 1882)

Sullivan KC, Serjeant A. M., *Old Ireland: Reminiscences of an Irish KC* (London, 1927)

——, *The Last Serjeant* (London, 1952)

Sullivan, Donal, *The Story of Room 15* (Dublin, 1891)

Sullivan, Maev, *No Man's Man* (Dublin, 1943)

Sullivan, T. D., *Recollections of Troubled Times in Irish Politics* (Dublin, 1905)

The Times, Home Rule, A Reprint from the Times of Recent Articles and Letters (London, 1886)

——, *Parnellism and Crime, reprinted from The Times* (London, 1888)

——, *Parnellism and Crime, the Special Commission, reprinted from The Times* (35 parts, London, 1888-90)

——, *The Parnellite Split: or, the Disruption of the Irish Parliamentary Party, from The Times* (London, 1891)

Thorold, Algar Labouchere, *The Life of Henry Labouchere Thorold* (London, 1913)

Tynan, Katharine, 'William O'Brien', *Catholic World*, vol. 48, pp. 151-7 (Nov. 1888)

——, *Twenty-Five Years: Reminiscences* (London, 1913)

——, *The Middle Years* (London, 1916)

——, *Memories* (London, 1924)

Traill, H. D., 'The Abdication of Mrs. Grundy', *National Review*, vol. xvii, pp. 12-24 (Mar. 1891)

Wyse Power, Jennie, *Words of the Dead Chief: being extracts from the public speeches and other pronouncements of Charles Stewart Parnell, from the beginning to the close of his memorable life,* compiled by Jennie Wyse Power, with an introduction by Anna Parnell (Dublin, 1892)

V   Historical Articles and Works

Abels, Jules, *The Parnell Tragedy* (London, 1966)

Beckett, J. C., *The Anglo-Irish Tradition* (London, 1976, repr. Belfast 1982)

Bew, Paul, *Land and the National Question* (Dublin, 1978)

    C. S. Parnell (Dublin, 1980)

Bourke, Marcus, *John O'Leary* (Tralee, 1967)

Boyce, George D. and Alan O'Day, (eds.) *Parnell in Perspective* (London, 1991)

Callanan, Frank, ' "Clerical Dictation": Reflections on the Catholic Church and the Parnell Split', *Archivium Hibernicum*, vol. xlv (1990) pp. 64-75

——, 'After Parnell: The Political Consequences of Timothy Michael Healy', *Studies*, vol. 80, no. 320 (Winter 1991)

Clark, Samuel, *Social Origins of the Irish Land War* (Princeton, 1979)

Cooke, A. B. and John Vincent, *The Governing Passion* (Sussex, 1974)

Côté, Jane McL., *Fanny and Anna Parnell, Ireland's Patriotic Sisters* (Dublin, 1991)

Cullen, L. M., (ed.), *The Formation of the Irish Economy* (Cork, 1969)
An Economic History of Ireland since 1660 (London, 1972)

Cullingford, Elizabeth, *Yeats, Ireland and Fascism* (London, 1981)

Curtis, Jnr., L. P., *Apes and Angels: the Irishman in Victorian Caricature* (London, 1971)

——, *Coercion and Conciliation in Ireland, 1880-92: A Study in Conservative*
——, *Unionism* (Princeton, 1963)

——, 'Government Policy and the Irish Party Crisis', *I.H.S.*, vol. xiii, pp. 295-315 (Sept. 1963)

Donnelly, James S., Jnr., *The Land and People of Nineteenth-Century Cork* (London, 1975, repr. 1987)

Edwards, R. Dudley, 'The Fall of Parnell: 1890-1: Seventy Years After', *Studia Hibernica* vol. 1 (1961) pp. 199-210

Ervine, St. John, *Parnell* (London, n.d.)

Foster, R. F., *Charles Stewart Parnell. The Man and his Family* (2nd ed., London, 1979)

——, *Lord Randolph Churchill. A Political Life* (Oxford, 1981)

Glaser, John F., 'Parnell's Fall and the Nonconformist Conscience', *I.H.S.*, vol. xii, pp. 119-38 (Sept. 1960)

Goldring, Maurice, *Faith of Our Fathers, The Formation of Irish Nationalist Ideology 1890-1920,* transl., Frances de Burgh-Whyte (Dublin, 1982)

Hammond, J. L., *Gladstone and the Irish Nation* (London, 1938)

Healy, Patrick, *The Modern and the Wake* (Dublin, 1992)

Heyck, T. W., *The Dimensions of British Radicalism: The Case of Ireland 1874-95* (Chicago, 1974)

Hind, R. J., *Henry Labouchere and the Empire 1880-1905* (London, 1972)

Hogan, Daire, *The Legal Profession in Ireland 1789-1922* (Dublin, 1986)

Hurst, Michael, *Joseph Chamberlain and Liberal Re-union* (London, 1967)

——, *Parnell and Irish Nationalism* (London, 1968)

Hoppen, K. Theodore, *Elections, Politics and Society in Ireland 1832-85* (Oxford, 1984)

Jenkins, Roy, *Sir Charles Dilke* (revised ed., London, 1965)

Kissane, Noel, *Parnell, A Documentary History* (Dublin, 1991)

Koss, Stephen, *The Rise and Fall of the Political Press in Britain* (London, 1981)

Larkin, Emmet, *The Roman Catholic Church in Ireland and the Fall of Parnell 1888-91* (Liverpool, 1979)

Lyons, F.S.L., *The Irish Parliamentary Party 1890-1910* (London, 1951)

——, 'The Economic Ideas of Parnell', *Historical Studies*, ii, ed. Michael Roberts (London, 1959), pp. 60-78

——, *The Fall of Parnell* (London, 1960)

——, *Parnell* (Dundalk, published for the Dublin Historical Association, 1963)

——, *John Dillon: A Biography* (London, 1968)

——, 'The Political Ideas of Parnell', *Historical Journal*, xvi, 4(1973), pp. 749-75

——, 'Charles Stewart Parnell', in B. Farrell (ed.), *The Irish Parliamentary Tradition* (Dublin, 1973), pp. 181-94

——, *Charles Stewart Parnell* (London, 1978)
——, *Culture and Anarchy* (Oxford, 1979)
Lyons, J. B., *'What did I die of?' The Deaths of Parnell, Wilde, Synge and Other Literary Pathologies* (Dublin, 1991)
Magnus, Philip, *Gladstone* (London, 1963)
Marlow, Joyce, *The Uncrowned Queen of Ireland, The Life of 'Kitty' O'Shea* (London, 1975)
McCartney, Donal, *Democracy and its Nineteenth Century Irish Critics* (Dublin, 1979)
——, (ed.) *Parnell, The Politics of Power* (Dublin, 1991)
Moody, T. W., *Davitt and the Irish Revolution 1846-92* (Oxford, 1981
——, 'Parnell and the Galway election of 1886', *I.H.S.*, ix (Mar. 1955)
Murphy, William Michael, *The Parnell Myth and Irish Politics 1891-56* (New York, 1986)
O'Brien, Conor Cruise, 'Parnell and Tim Healy', *Irish Times*, 8 Jan. 1944 (pseud. Donat O'Donnell) 'Parnell's Monument', *The Bell* (Oct. 1945), pp. 566-73
——, *Parnell and his Party* (Oxford, 1957)
——, 'Timothy Michael Healy', in C. C. O'Brien (ed.), *The Shaping of Modern Ireland* (London, 1960); republished in C. C. O'Brien, *Writers and Politics* (London, 1965)
——, *States of Ireland* (London, 1972)
——, 'Ireland, the Shirt of Nessus', *New York Review of Books*, 29 Apr. 1982, republished in C. C. O'Brien, *Passion and Cunning* (London, 1988), pp. 213-15
O'Broin, Leon, *Parnell, Beathaisnéis* (repr. Dublin, 1955)
O'Callaghan, Margaret, 'Crime, Nationality and the Law: The politics of land in late-Victorian Ireland' (PhD thesis, University of Cambridge, 1989)
O'Day, Alan, *The English Face of Irish Nationalism* (Dublin, 1977)
——, *Parnell and the First Home Rule Episode 1884-7* (Dublin, 1986)
O'Farrell, Patrick, *Ireland's English Question* (London, 1971)
O'Flaherty, Liam, *The Life of Tim Healy* (London, 1927)
O'Hegarty, P. S., *A History of Ireland under the Union* (London, 1952)
Ó hÓgáin, Daithí, *The Hero in Irish Folk History* (Dublin, 1985)
Palmer, N. D., *The Irish Land League Crisis* (Yale, 1940, repr. 1978)
Pearson, Hesketh, *Labby: The Life and Character of Henry Labouchere* (London, 1936)
Philbin, C. H. E., *Nationalism and Popular Protest in Ireland* (Cambridge, 1987)
Ryan, Desmond, *The Fenian Chief, A Biography of James Stephens* (Dublin, 1967)
Ryan, W. D., *The Irish Labour Movement* (Dublin, n.d.)
Steinman, Michael, *Yeats' Historical Figures* (London, 1983)
Thornley, David A., *Isaac Butt and Home Rule* (London, 1964)
Townshend, Charles, *Political Violence in Ireland* (Oxford, 1983)
Walker, Brian M., *Parliamentary Election Results in Ireland 1801-1922* (Dublin, 1978)
Walsh, Patrick S., *William J. Walsh, Archbishop of Dublin* (Dublin and Cork, 1928)
Woods, C. J., 'The general election of 1892: the Catholic clergy and the defeat of the Parnellites', in F. S. L. Lyons and R. A. J. Hawkins (ed.), *Ireland under the Union: Varieties of Tension, Essays in honours of T. W. Moody* (Oxford, 1980)

INDEX

Abraham, William, MP, 51-2, 53
Adams, Richard, QC, 60
Allan, F.J., 253
Amnesty, 245-8
anti-Parnellite party, *passim*: McCarthy elected leader of, 53; parliamentary committee of, 53; establishment of national organisation, 54, 111-2; finances of, 94-5; parliamentary committee meets, 153
Arklow, 295, 299-300
Athlone, death of Parnellite at, 179-80
Atherley Jones, Llewellyn Archer, MP, 93
Aveling, Edward, 306 n.94
Avondale, 133, 167, 299, 302

Balfour, Arthur, MP, Chief Secretary, 82, 221, 282-6, 288-9, 292
Ballina, 113-5, 293
'Bantry Band', 236-7
Bar of Ireland, 190 n.3, 234
Bassetlaw, by-election, 91, 224
Barry, John, MP, 21, 38, 41, 47, 50, 61, 92
Beaverbrook, Lord, 308-9
Belfast, 278; Parnell speech at, 264-5
Belfast Evening Telegraph, 265, 298
Biggar, Joseph, MP, 174, 198, 222, 276, 298
Bismarck, Otto von, 119, 296
Bodkin, Mathias McDonnell, 64, 88
Boulanger, Georges, General, 119, 178
Boulogne, negotiations at, 62, 80-109, 140, 150, 153-4, 224

Bowen, Elizabeth, 126, 234
Brabourne, Lord, 9
Brighton, 118, 133, 181
Brighton Gazette, 79 n.68
Brownrigg, Abraham, Bishop of Ossory, 67-9
Burke, Edmund, 203
Butt, Isaac, MP, 246, 247
Byrne, Edward, 1, 55-7, 89, 222, 260, 301

Condon, T.J., MP, 46
Conway, Hugh, Bishop of Killala, 113
Corbet, W.J., MP, 29
Cork, 64-5, 115-7, 172
Cork Daily Herald, 124
Creggs, speech of Parnell at, 150, 154, 166, 172-3, 179-80, 272 n.179
Croke, T.W., Archbishop of Cashel, 57, 64 65, 83, 121-2, 261
Cruise O'Brien, Conor, 2, 3, 271 n.165
cultural nationalism, 257-9
Cunninghame Graham, Robert Gallnigad Bontine, MP, 47, 295, 298
Curran, C.P., 308

Daily Express (Dublin), 49, 125, 144, 170, 181, 253, 258, 265, 288
Daily News, 95
    see also MacDonald, John
Davis, Thomas, 185, 255, 258
Davitt, Michael, 4, 12, 66-9, 70, 75, 80, 89, 113, 172, 229, 231, 240-1, 243, 255, 277, 280, 282, 286, 295, 296, 298
Deasy, John, MP, 54

Devoy, John, 252

Dillon, John, MP: endorses Parnell, 13; Salisbury jibe about, 14-15; declares against Parnell, 25-6; elected to committee of anti-Parnellite party, 53; assessment of political prospect, 80-1; on Kilkenny election, 81; O'Brien puts proposals at Boulogne agreed with, 82; proposed chairmanship of Irish party of, 82, 108 n.56; estrangement from anti-Parnellite party over Boulogne negotiations, 89-90, 102-3; Morley on, 96-7; Gladstone on, 97; complains of pusillanimousness of Parnell's moderate supporters, 101-2; on collapse of negotiations, 102; submits to arrest, 102-3; witholds endorsement from anti-Panellites; Healy seeks to thwart, 117, 121; finds Parnell letter in defence of Katharine O'Shea 'most indecent'; seeks to sway O'Brien in Galway jail to adhere to anti-Parnellites, 140-2; on Healy, 140, 142, 188, 191 n.11; *National Press* warns against compromise with Parnellites, 142-3; declares opposition to Parnell on release, 144-6, 151; Parnell draws into political argument, 143-4; Parnell asks not to disband his army, 143-4, 201, 285-6; fails to entice moderate supporters away from Parnell, 144-6, 151; Parnell on, 147, 150, 288-9; Parnell threatens disclosure of Boulogne terms approved by, 150; speaks at National Federation, 150-1; Healy thwarts 150-2; has majority of one on anti-Parnellite parliamentary committee, 153; on Parnell's speech at Creggs, 154; prisoner of Healy's strategy, 153-5; agonises over speaking with Healy in North Longford, 154-5; fails to protest at 'Kitty' heckle, 155; damage to reputation of, 155-6; on Parnell's prospects, 172; on

Parnell's 'rat trap' in Committee Room 15, 228; on Parnell's 'steely fibre' in fighting Fenians in 1880 election, 254

Dillon, Valentine Blake, 81, 119, 145

Dowden, Prof. Edward, 177

Dublin, 60, 62-4, 112-3, 144, 161, 179, 180-1, 239, 263, 278, 299

Economist, The, 54, 235

Edwards, R.D., xiii

Egan, Patrick, 287

Eliot, George, quoted, 118

Ennis, 1879 by-election, 235

Esher, Reginald Viscount, 30

evicted tenants, *see* Plan of Campaign

Fenians, 66, 67, 78 n.41, 84, 85, 148, 168, 189, 233, 238-56, 277

Fingal, Elizabeth, Countess of, 109 n.80

Fitzgerald, J.G., MP, 24

Fitzgerald, P.N., 69, 119, 249

Four Courts, Dublin, 113, 187-8

Frederic, Harold, 25, 29, 54, 66, 109 n.78, 115, 143, 177, 283, 289

Freeman's Journal, xiii, 10, 15, 25, 54, 62, 110-1, 112, 113, 116, 120-1, 124, 127, 132, 142, 148, 153, 154, 170, 172, 188, 236, 299

Galway, by-election of Feb. 1886, 234

Garvin, J.L., 170, 182, 190, 281-2

Gilhooly, James, MP, 236

Gill, T.P., MP, 98, 100, 145, 146

Gladstone, Catherine, 234

Gladstone, Herbert, 234

Gladstone, Mary, 25

Gladstone, William Ewart, MP, *passim*: on Salisbury's divorce jibe, 14-15; considers his response to divorce proceedings, 16-18; reaches London, 18; meets McCarthy, 18-19; letter to Morley, 19; Parnell on, 19, 23-4, 38, 44, 144, 148-50, 168, 204, 207, 211, 212-3, 218-26, 222, 230, 292-3; publishes letter to Morley, 20; compares himself to Sisyphus, 21; and Hawarden meeting with

Parnell of Dec. 1889, 23-4, 26, 86; McCarthy meets in relation to points raised in Parnell's manifesto, 28-9; Harcourt harangues, 48, 97; Stansfeld reports Healy's views to, 48; prior communication with anti-Parnellites, 49; compared to 'elderly coquette', 49; responds to request of the Irish party for assurances, 49-51; and second home rule bill, 74, 143-4; Parnell at Boulogne proposes obtaining memorandum from, 82; Labouchere reports to, 83-5; avoids formally recognising anti-Parnellites as the Irish party, 90-3; and anti-Parnellite finances, 94-5; prefers Healy, 97; response to further request for assurances, arising from Boulogne negotiations, 97-8; gratified at Maurice Healy's attack on Parnell, 116-7; Parnell makes veiled allusion to role of Katharine O'Shea as intermediary with, 124-5; great age of, 141, 223; Labouchere invites to restrain Healy, 188-9; seeks to restrain Healy, 188-90; revised opinion of Healy, 190; Rosebery on, 269 n.84; Wilde on, 269 n.85; and labour, 297-8

Glasnevin, burial of Parnell at, 185
Gold, Parnell's quest for, 300
Granville, Lord, 18
Grattan, Henry, 63, 203, 205, 290
Gray, Edmund Dwyer (junior), 111, 117, 120-1, 128, 146, 161
Griffith, Arthur, 179, 250-1, 255, 257

Hamilton, E.W., 19-20, 72, 260
Harcourt, Sir William, MP, 18, 48, 94, 149, 204, 226, 243, 246
Hardie, Keir, MP, 297-8
Harrington, Edward, MP, 28, 236
Harrington, Timothy C., MP, 13, 25-6, 81, 101, 102, 142, 151, 166, 168, 170, 175, 187, 199, 236, 288
Harrington, Edward, MP, 28, 236
Harrison, Frederic, 10, 72

Harrison, Henry, MP, 168, 170, 184 n.2, 191 n.10
Hartlepool, by-election, 225
Hawarden, meeting of Parnell and Gladstone at, December 1889, 23-7, 39, 213-4, 272
Hayden, L.P., MP, 172
Healy, Elizabeth, 308-9
Healy, Erina (Mrs T.M. Healy), 41, 50, 54
Healy, Maurice, MP, 61, 113-5, 115-7, 230, 236-7, 308-9
Healy, Thomas J., MP, 236
Healy, Timothy Michael, MP, *passim*: relations with Parnell, xiii, 21-2, 29, 42, 51, 168; social realism of, 3-4; on land purchase, 4, 120, 280-7; seeks to achieve destruction of Parnell myth, 4, 38; illness of, 10, 22; drafts Leinster Hall resolutions in favour of Parnell, 10-11; speech at Leinster Hall in favour of Parnell, 11-13; on Davitt, 12-13; reaches London, 22; seeks to organise opposition to Parnell, 22-3; on Parnell manifesto, 26; lingering admiration for Parnell, 29, 41; opening attack on Parnell in Committee Room 15, 38-9; Parnell on, 39, 52, 123, 199, 229, 231-5, 283, 300-1; on Clancy amendment, 42-7, 49; meets James Stansfeld, 48-9; asks 'who is to be the mistress of the party?', 52-3; and North Kilkenny election, 65-6, 69; on Gladstone, 65; attacks Katharine O'Shea, 66, 87, 116, 124-30, 132-3, 149, 150-2, 167-8, 187-90; on Parnell's loss of composure at Kilkenny, 69-71; and the Boulogne negotiations, 80, 82-3, 87-90, 98, 102; visits O'Brien in Paris 83-5; and *Insuppressible,* 88-9; seeks Gladstone's endorsement, 90-4; describes anti-Parnellite dilemma, 92-3; begging letter of, 94-5; Gladstone on, 97, 189, 190; establishes *National Press,* 110-1; speech at inauguration of

Irish National Federation, 111-2;
assaults on, 112-3; complains of
Parnellite priests in North Sligo,
114-5; derides Parnellite reversals,
117-20; seeks to thwart conversion
of *Freeman's Journal,* 117, 120-1;
endeavours to pre-empt initiatives
of Dillon and O'Brien, 117, 121,
139-43; 'Stop Thief' articles of,
121-4; quotes *Othello,* 122, 139;
seeks to embroil Parnell in Campbell libel action, 124; on marriage
of Parnell to Katharine O'Shea,
125-30; and Carlow election
128-32; attacks Parnell on evicted
tenants issue, 132, 287-90; inspires
reports of visit to Ireland of
Katharine O'Shea, 133; top-hat of,
135 n.8; ridicules Parnell's attempt
to reconstitute his campaign, 147,
149, 151-2; seeks to implicate Dillon
and O'Brien in his campaign
against Parnell, 150, 152-6; de-
nounces Redmond, 151; begins to
lose grip on anti-Parnellite leadership, 153; last attacks on Parnell,
178-80; political consequence of
Parnell's death for, 178-9; on
Parnell's death, 187, 189-90; attacks Parnell's widow as 'a proved
British prostitute', 187-8; horse-
whipped, 187-90; Gladstone re-
strains, 188-9; urge to have
Gladstone trample upon him, 188;
described by Redmond as 'a political savage', 191 n.11; mocks
Parnell's defence on the moral
issue, 196-7; Auberon Herbert on,
227; *The Economist,* and *Spectator*
on, 235; Parnellite attacks on,
235-7; on Joseph Biggar, 276; attacks Parnell's espousal of land
nationalisation, 286-7; papers, and
composition of memoirs of,
308-9
Herbert, Auberon, 20, 158 n.70, 227
Hishon, D.J., 13, 23
Horgan, John J., 308

Inchicore, Dublin, Parnell speech at, 123,
278
Insuppressible, 86, 88-9
Ireland, Denis, xii
Irish Catholic, 10, 69, 99
Irish Ecclesiastical Gazette, 186 n.5, 265-6
Irish Independent, 161, 181
Irish Landowners Convention, 285
Irish National Federation, 111-2, 209
Irish National League, 22, 29, 111, 147,
249
Irish Parliamentary Party, *passim:* xiii-xiv,
14, 16, 21-2, 23, 29-31, 37-59, 198,
215-6
Irish party pledge, 53, 215-6
Irish Times, The, 303 n.4
Irish Volunteers, 204-5, 206
Irishtown, Co. Mayo, Parnell speech at on
twelfth anniversary of 1879 meeting,
210

Johnson, Lionel, 5
Joyce, James, 5, 75, 76 n.13, 160, 173, 182

Kelly, Fr. John, 114
Kelly, John, 181
Kenny, Dr. Joseph E., MP, 11, 50, 113,
123-4, 142, 166, 179, 181, 187, 209,
262
Kenny, M.J., MP, 59 n.37, 127
Keogh, William, QC, MP, 208, 247
Kerr, William, Parnell's agent, 133
Kettle, Andrew, 117, 130-2, 209, 236
Kilkenny election, *see* North Kilkenny,
by-election
Kilkenny Journal, 127
Kilkenny Moderator, 155, 173-5, 176, 277
Kilmainham Jail, imprisonment of
Parnell in (1881-2), 144, 222, 230
'Kilmainham treaty', 129, 304

Labour Conference, 295
Labour, Parnell and, 276, 293-9
Labour World, 10, 66, 278, 294
Labouchere, Henry, MP, 18, 25, 30, 33
n.46, 83-5, 90-1, 92, 94-5, 170,
188-90, 234, 308
Lalor, James Fintan, 255

Land League, 4, 210, 278, 294
land nationalisation, Parnell on, 286-7
Land Purchase Bill (enacted as Purchase of Land (Ire.) Act 1891), 23, 120, 278, 294
Leamy, Edmund, MP, 30, 47, 48, 64
Lecky, W.E.H., 195
Leinster Hall, Dublin, meeting at, 10-13, 249
Leinster Leader, 146
Leo XIII, Pope, 120
Lever, Charles, 73-4
Limerick, Parnell speeches at, 86-7, 148, 195; Treaty of, 205-6
Listowel, Parnell speech at, 148, 150, 153, 230, 237, 247, 251-2
Lloyd George, David, MP, 47
Logue, Michael, Archbishop of Armagh, 99
Lords, House of, 94, 226
Lucas, Frederick, 205
Lynch, Arthur, 169
Lyons, F.S.L., xii, xiii, 95, 276, 281

Macbeth, Parnell refers to, 167
McCarthy, Justin, MP: Labouchere calls on, 18; misunderstanding as to Gladstone's position on Irish leadership, 18-19; Parnell discusses circumstances of his relations with Katharine O'Shea with, 24-5; apprised of contents of manifesto, 25; attends meeting at Westminster Palace Hotel, 28; sees Gladstone in relation to manifesto, 28-9, 220; Parnell addresses as 'my dear old friend', 29; scene with Parnell and J.H. McCarthy, at Westminster Palace Hotel, 38; on Irish deputation to seek assurances from Gladstone, 47, 51; Parnell snatches Abraham's resolution from, 51-2; leads anti-Parnellites out of the committee room, 53; elected chairman of the anti-Parnellites, 53; Parnell greets, 54; Parnell refers to at Kilkenny as 'a nice old gent for a tea party', 70; and Boulogne

negotiations, 80, 90, 91, 97, 103, 105 n.20, 107 n.46; cordial relations with Parnell, 161-2, 168-9; on Parnell's health, and nervous disposition, 164; Parnell ridicules political capacity of, 230-1; and Paris Funds, 287
McCarthy, Justin Huntly, MP, 28, 54, 59 n.37
MacDermott, Tudor, 187-8
MacDonagh, Michael, 52, 58 n.33, 136 n.28, 172
MacDonald, John, *Daily News* correspondent, 60, 68, 69, 71-2
MacHale, Administrator of Killala, 115
MacNeill, J.G. Swift, MP, 30
Mahon, The O'Gorman, MP, 166
Mahony, Pierce, MP, 28, 29, 37, 69, 127, 169, 220
Manchester Guardian, Special Correspondent of, 132, 195, 237, 244
Martin, John, 105
Marx-Aveling, Eleanor, 306 n.94
Milton, quoted, 128, 176-7
Mitchel, John, 205, 250, 255
Mitchel, W.H., 250
Morley, Arnold, MP, 18, 106 n.7
Morley, John, MP, 11, 16-20, 24, 26, 83, 90, 96-7, 103, 177, 188, 219, 226, 283
Murphy, Fr. Nicholas, 68, 251
Murphy, William Martin, MP, 13, 15, 22, 27, 29, 54, 121, 298

Napoleon, Parnell refers to, 170, 278
Nation, 10, 99, 106 n.30, 115, 127
National Club, Dublin, Parnell speech at, 144; Amnesty Association of, 245; Literary Society of, 256
National Committee in Sustainment of the Irish Parliamentary Party, 54
National Liberation Federation, 17, 149-50, 225
National Press, establishment of, 54, 73, 83, 85, 110-1; 113, 114, 117-21; 'Stop Thief' series of leading articles, 121-4; 125, 127-30, 139, 141, 142-3,

147, 149, 151, 152, 153, 154, 162, 178, 187, 188, 246, 278, 288, 300

Navan, Parnell speech at, 215

'Newcastle Programme', of Liberal party, 149-50, 225

'New Departure', 250, 253

Nolan, Col. J.P., MP, 14, 38, 42, 46

nonconformists, 18, 92

North Kilkenny, by-election, 53-4, 65-76, 206, 231

North Sligo, by-election, 113-5, 162, 206

Nulty, Thomas, Bishop of Meath, 262

Nurney, Co. Carlow, villagers of cheer Parnell, 131-2

O'Brien, J.F.X., MP, 42

O'Brien, Patrick, MP, 168, 184 n.20, 252

O'Brien, R. Barry, 161, 165, 230

O'Brien, Sophie (Mrs William O'Brien), 101, 104 n.16, 109 n.74, 146, 165

O'Brien, William, MP: endorses Parnell; retrospective assessment of split, 16, 86, 156; deplores Parnell's ruthlessness, 20-1; and Boulogne negotiations, 80-103; susceptibilities played on, 81; composes ode to Parnell, 81-2; meets Parnell at Boulogne, 82; Parnell proposes he be chairman of party, 82; meets Healy and John Barry, 83-5; 92-3; meets Labouchere, 84-5; defends Parnell, 84-5; refuses chairmanship and editorship of *National Press*, 85; Parnell calls for cheers for, 87; and *Insuppressible*, 88-9; attacked in Liberal press, 95-6; Morley and Gladstone on, 96-7; anticipates breakdown of negotiations, 98; blames 'irreconcilables', 102; submits to imprisonment, 102-3; anti-Parnellite recriminations with over Boulogne negotiations, 103; Harold Frederic on, 109 n.78; John O'Leary on, 109 n.78, 251; Healy seeks to thwart, 117, 121; Parnell offers to submit balance sheet to, 123; urges against adherence to anti-Parnellite party on release from

Galway jail, 139-42; declares against Parnell on release, 143; Parnell regrets decision of to join 'seceders', 143; fails to procure conversion of moderate Parnellites, 144-6, 151; controversy with Redmond during Cork by-election of November 1891, 144-5; Parnell criticises inception of Plan of Campaign by, 147, 150, 288-9; Parnell invites to publish Boulogne proposals, 150, 153-4; Healy thwarts, 150-4; implicated in Healy's strategy, 155-6; damage to political reputation of, 155-6; on death of Parnell, 156; Parnell induces to vary election address for Mallow, January 1883, 214; on Parnell and Fenianism, 255.

O'Brien Dalton, Michael, assaults Healy, 112-3

Obstruction, 174, 198

O'Connell, Daniel, and Demonsthenes, 113, 186 n.106, 247

O'Connor, Arthur, MP, 15, 30, 38, 52, 53, 229

O'Connor, John, MP, 46, 51-3, 288

O'Connor, T.P., MP, xiii, 53, 142, 161, 162-5, 171, 181, 230

O'Donnell, Patrick, Bishop of Raphoe, 127

O'Donovan Rossa, Jeremiah, 248, 273 n.223

O'Grady, Standish, 78, 185 n.73, 258-9

O'Hara, M.M., 62-3

O'Hegarty, P.S., 249, 255

O'Leary, John, 109 n.78, 119, 248-52, 256-7

O'Shea, Katharine (later Mrs C.S. Parnell), 1, 9, 22, 24-5; with Parnell, 34 n.68, 43, 56, 66, 87, 116; Parnell defends, 124-5; marriage to Parnell, 126; reaction to marriage in Ireland, 126-33, 149, 152, 155, 165, 167-8, 173, 180, 181; attacked by Healy as 'a proved British prostitute', 187-91, 234, 275 n.270, 295, 307 n.106

O'Shea, Captain W.H., 1, 9, 14, 18, 46, 55, 130

Pall Mall Gazette, 19, 75, 95-6
Paris Funds, 187, 287, 304 n.43; *and see* Plan of Campaign
Parnell, Anna, 203, 208
Parnell, Charles Stewart, MP, *passim*: myth of, xii, 2-5, 27, 69-72, 80, 176-7, 179, 181-2, 244-6, 257, 302; relations with T.M. Healy, xiii, 21-2, 42, 51, 168; and Land League, 4, 210, 294; evidence against, in O'Shea divorce proceedings, 9; effect of proceedings on reputation of, 10; re-elected chairman of the Irish Party, 14-15; Gladstone's estimate of, 18, 21, 90-4, 190; incommunicado, 18-19; Morley reads Gladstone letter to, 19, 219; on Gladstone, 19, 23-24, 38, 44, 144, 148-50, 168, 204, 207, 211, 212-3, 218-26, 222, 230, 292-3; refuses to reconsider his position, 22; manifesto of, 23-5, 213-4; on 'independence', 24, 148, 174, 201-75; stands his ground, 28-9; on 'Liberal wire-pullers', 29-30, 95; seeks to take advantage of position as chairman in Committee Room 15, 38; on T.M. Healy, 39, 52, 123, 199, 229, 231-5, 283, 300-1; on entering the 'promised land', 41, 63, 87, 196; loses vote on Nolan amendment, 42; seeks to modify Clancy amendment, 42-7; calls on John O'Connor over William Abraham, 51-2; omits to strike Healy, 53; left presiding over minority of party as 'seceders' withdraw, 53; his 'weird figure' on patrol, 54; declines mediation of Archbishop Walsh, 55-7; predicament of, 60-1; returns to Ireland, 61; speech at Rotunda, 62-4, 101, 238-9, 294; health of, 62, 63, 162-6, 180, 181, 197; on Grattan, 63, 203, 204-5, 206, 218-26; retakes *United Ireland*, 64; journey to Cork, 64-5; conduct of North Kilkenny campaign, 66-7; struck at Castlecomer, 67, 71, 75; listens impassively to declaration of poll, 69; demeanour, and damage to reputation of, at Kilkenny, 69-72; superstitiousness, 70, 166-7, 179;' 143 suggested insanity of, 72-3, 283; meets O'Brien at Boulogne, and makes counterproposal, 82, 150; warns of 'Saxon smile', 86-7; breaks off negotiations, 98-102; complains of lack of understanding on the part of his parliamentary supporters, 101, 161-2, 171-2; loses Sligo election, 114-5, 162, 206; attacks 'souping Presbyterians', 114; retreats from resignation challenge to Maurice Healy, 115-7; 'Stop Thief' allegations against, 121-4; evades subpoena in Campbell libel action, 124; publishes letter in defence of Katherine O'Shea, 124-5; marriage to Katherine O'Shea, 126; political repercussions of marriage, 126-8; and Carlow election, 128-33; boycotted, 131-2; alleged betrayal of evicted tenants by, 132-3, 288-9; *National Press* invents accounts of visit of Katherine Parnell to Ireland, 133; responds to declaration of Dillon and O'Brien against him on their release, 143-5; on Dillon and O'Brien, 143-4, 150, 206, 228, 288; asks Dillon in speech at Thurles 'not to disband his army' 143-4, 201, 205-6; acclaimed through the streets of Dublin on return from Thurles, 144; deters defection of J.L. Carew, 146; seeks to reconstitute basis of campaign, 146-8, 152; on Harcourt, 149, 204, 226; on 'Newcastle Programme' of Liberals, 149-50, 225; Creggs meeting, 150, 154, 166, 172-3, 179-80, 272 n.179; on Plan of Campaign, 150, 276, 287-90; establishes *Irish Independent*, 160-1, 181;

physical aspect of, 162-5, 179, 181; unwonted gregariousness, 165; family medical history, 166-7; attitude to attacks on his wife, 167-8; abiding wit and grace, 168-9; love of supporters for, 169-70; resolve, 170-1, 174, 177-8; prospects, 171-2, 175-6; Harold Frederic's obituary of, 177; supporter killed at Athlone, *en route* to Creggs, 179-80; death of, 181; funeral of, 182; Labouchere changes his mind about, 190; his defence, 195-9; and Joseph Biggar, 198; and Special Commission, 203, 214, 244, 249, 273 n.223; veneration of ancestors, 203; invokes Lucas, Mitchel, Martin, 205; policy of constructive engagement with Conservatives, 209-10, 221, 280-7, 291-2; on party pledge, 215-7; on Radicals, 226, 292; on political calibre of anti-Parnellites generally, 227-8, 287; his characterisation of his mode of leadership, 228-30; on Davitt, 229, 230, 231, 234, 277, 296; on McCarthy, 230-1; on the Sullivan dynasty, 235; 'Appeal to the Hillsides', 238-259; on amnesty, 245-8; on P.N. Fitzgerald, 249-50; and John O'Leary, 250-2; meets James Stephens, 252-3; and the Catholic church in the split, 260-75; on Croke, 261; on Walsh, 262; on the threat of a sectarian nationalism, 264-7; on Ulster, 267, 281; supposed 'conservatism' of, 281; advocates compulsory purchase, 286; and land nationalisation, 286-7; on industrialisation, 290-2; sceptical assessment of the principles of political economy, 292; on home rule finance, 292-3; champions cause of labour, 293-9; strike at Arklow quarries of, 295, 300; and Bismarck, 296; Keir Hardie supports, 297-8; economic ventures in Wicklow, 299-302; fails to find gold, 300; provides employ-ment, 300-1; greatness of, 302

Parnell, Delia Tudor Stewart, 178, 273 n.223, 301
Parnell, Emily, 167
Parnell, Fanny, 258
Parnell, Sir John, 261
Parnell, John Henry, 166-7
Parnell, Thomas, 166
'Parnell Commission', *see* Special Commission
'Parnell Manifesto', 23-7, 39, 213-4
Pearse, Patrick, 255
Phoenix Park, murders, 246; Parnell speech at, 245
Pigott, Richard, 10, 124, 273 n.240
Pinkerton, John, MP, 114
Pitt, E.W., 72
Plan of campaign, 120, 132-3, 251, 276, 287-90
Plunkett, David, 205
political economy, Parnell's opinion of, 292
Pope-Hennessy, Sir John, 68, 70, 166
Protestants, Irish, 114, 186 n.105, 260, 264-7

Quinn, J.P., 179-81

Radicals, 226, 292
Redmond, John E., MP, 10-11, 24, 30, 43, 47, 49, 50, 52, 100-1, 142, 144-5, 146, 151, 154, 156, 158 n.69, 169, 173, 187, 246, 265, 302
Redmond, William A., MP, 11, 155
Rendel, Stuart, 21, 107 n.49
Rhodes, Cecil, 291
Ribblesdale, Lord, 281
Robbins, Alfred, 15, 25, 41, 61, 72, 164-5, 181, 256
Ronayne, J.P., MP, 70
Rooney, William, 257
Roscommon Herald, 162
Rosebery, Earl of, 226, 269 n.84
Rotunda, Parnell speech at the, 61-4, 101, 238-9, 294
Russell, Sir Charles, QC, 203
Russell, Irish journalist, 180
Rylett, Rev. Harold, 167

Sadlier, John, MP, 208, 247
Salisbury, Marquess of, Prime Minister, 14-15, 75
Sarsfield, Patrick, 70, 206
Saturday Review, 73
Schnadhorst, Francis, 94
Sexton, Thomas, MP, 14, 19, 23, 28, 31, 38, 42-51, 53, 91-7, 103, 113, 142, 229
Shakespeare, quoted, 122, 139, 169
Shanks, Cllr. James, 119
Sheehan, Canon P.A., 169-70
Sheehy, David, MP, 53, 113, 166
Smith, F.E., MP, 302
Socialism, 298
South Africa, Parnell compares Connaught to, 291
Special Commission, 12, 46, 203, 214, 244, 249, 273 n.223
Spencer, Earl, 19, 137 n.61
Spectator, 72, 87, 181, 235, 245, 266, 276
Stanhope, Philip, MP, 30, 48
Stansfeld, Sir James, MP, 48-9
Stead, W.T., 17, 47, 72-3, 75, 93, 261
Stephens, James, 248, 250, 252-3
Steyning, marriage of Parnell and Katherine O'Shea at, 126, 133
'Stop Thief' series of leading articles in *National Press*, 121-4, 235, 300
Stuart, Prof. James, MP, 30, 48, 95
Sullivan, A.M. (snr.), MP, 235, 236-7
Sullivan, A.M. (jnr., later Serjeant), 88
Sullivan, Denis Baylor, 88
Sullivan, Donal, MP, 13, 14, 15, 236-7
Sullivan, T.D., MP, 13, 103, 200 n.22, 235, 236-7

'*Suppressed*' *United Ireland*, 64, 105 n.26
Tanner, Dr. Charles Kearns Deane, MP, 66-7, 70, 81, 199, 231
Thornley, David, 302
Times, The, 12, 69, 93, 95, 112, 116, 188
Tone, Theobald Wolfe, 255, 265
Tralee, 278; Parnell speech at, 87, 253, 264
Tully, Jasper, MP, 162
Tuohy, J.M., 15, 18, 37, 51-2, 58 n.3
Tynan, Katharine, 62, 169, 182

Ulster, 114, 260, 265, 267, 281-2
Unionists, Irish, 177, 265-7, 281-2
United Ireland, Parnell forcibly repossesses, 64, 66, 72-3, 111, 131, 132, 161, 169, 196, 209, 252, 259, 265

Walsh, William, Archbishop of Dublin, 55-7, 83, 99, 127, 262
Webb, Alfred, MP, 15
Wellington, Duke of, winter quarters of at Torres Vedres, referred to by Parnell, 63
Westport, Parnell speech at, 162-4, 212-3
Whistler, James Abbott MacNeill, 165
Wicklow, 290-2, 299-301
Wilde, Oscar, 78 n.58, 160, 269, 303 n.4
Wyse-Power, John, 249

Yeats, W.B., 1, 75, 182, 256-7
Young Ireland League, 256-7